CW00794135

Good
Enough
Endings

RELATIONAL PERSPECTIVES BOOK SERIES

Volume 44

RELATIONAL PERSPECTIVES BOOK SERIES

LEWIS ARON & ADRIENNE HARRIS

Series Editors

The Relational Perspectives Book Series (RPBS) publishes books that grow out of or contribute to the relational tradition in contemporary psychoanalysis. The term "relational psychoanalysis" was first used by Greenberg and Mitchell (1983) to bridge the traditions of interpersonal relations, as developed within interpersonal psychoanalysis and object relations, as developed within contemporary British theory. But, under the seminal work of the late Stephen Mitchell, the term "relational psychoanalysis" grew and began to accrue to itself many other influences and developments. Various tributaries—interpersonal psychoanalysis, object relations theory, self psychology, empirical infancy research, and elements of contemporary Freudian and Kleinian thought—flow into this tradition, which understands relational configurations between self and others, both real and fantasied, as the primary subject of psychoanalytic investigation.

We refer to the relational tradition, rather than to a relational school, to highlight that we are identifying a trend, a tendency within contemporary psychoanalysis, not a more formally organized or coherent school or system of beliefs. Our use of the term "relational" signifies a dimension of theory and practice that has become salient across the wide spectrum of contemporary psychoanalysis. Now under the editorial supervision of Lewis Aron and Adrienne Harris, the Relational Perspectives Book Series originated in 1990 under the editorial eye of the late Stephen A. Mitchell. Mitchell was the most prolific and influential of the originators of the relational tradition. He was committed to dialogue among psychoanalysts and he abhorred the authoritarianism that dictated adherence to a rigid set of beliefs or technical restrictions. He championed open discussion, comparative and integrative approaches, and he promoted new voices across the generations.

Included in the Relational Perspectives Book Series are authors and works that come from within the relational tradition, extend and develop the tradition, as well as works that critique relational approaches or compare and contrast them with alternative points of view. The series includes our most distinguished senior psychoanalysts along with younger contributors who bring fresh vision.

RELATIONAL PERSPECTIVES BOOK SERIES

LEWIS ARON & ADRIENNE HARRIS
Series Editors

RELATIONAL PERSPECTIVES BOOK SERIES

LEWIS ARON & ADRIENNE HARRIS
Series Editors

Good Enough Endings

Breaks, Interruptions, and Terminations
from Contemporary Relational Perspectives

Edited by Jill Salberg

Routledge
Taylor & Francis Group
New York   London

Routledge
Taylor & Francis Group
270 Madison Avenue
New York, NY 10016

Routledge
Taylor & Francis Group
27 Church Road
Hove, East Sussex BN3 2FA

© 2010 by Taylor and Francis Group, LLC
Routledge is an imprint of Taylor & Francis Group, an Informa business

Printed in the United States of America on acid-free paper
10 9 8 7 6 5 4 3 2 1

International Standard Book Number: 978-0-415-99452-1 (Hardback) 978-0-415-99453-8 (Paperback)

For permission to photocopy or use material electronically from this work, please access www.copyright.com (http://www.copyright.com/) or contact the Copyright Clearance Center, Inc. (CCC), 222 Rosewood Drive, Danvers, MA 01923, 978-750-8400. CCC is a not-for-profit organization that provides licenses and registration for a variety of users. For organizations that have been granted a photocopy license by the CCC, a separate system of payment has been arranged.

Trademark Notice: Product or corporate names may be trademarks or registered trademarks, and are used only for identification and explanation without intent to infringe.

Library of Congress Cataloging-in-Publication Data

Good enough endings : breaks, interruptions, and terminations from a
  contemporary relational perspective / edited by Jill Salberg.
    p. cm. -- (Relational perspectives ; v. 44)
  Includes bibliographical references and index.
  ISBN 978-0-415-99452-1 (hbk.) -- ISBN 978-0-415-99453-8 (pbk.) -- ISBN
  978-0-203-88825-4 (e-book)
  1. Psychotherapist and patient. 2. Psychoanalysis. I. Salberg, Jill.

RC480.8.G664 2010
616.89'17--dc22   2009036087

Visit the Taylor & Francis Web site at
http://www.taylorandfrancis.com

and the Routledge Web site at
http://www.routledgementalhealth.com

Contents

Acknowledgments

First and foremost I am grateful to my authors. When I first approached people—a few of them only through e-mail correspondence—their response was quite positive to being part of this collection of papers. I am deeply appreciative that they felt they could and did trust me with their work. Some others I reached out to were acquaintances and friends who welcomed, as did I, the collaborative interchange we engaged in around my and their ideas surrounding the complexity of ending treatment.

I want to thank Lew Aron and Adrienne Harris, coeditors for the Relational Perspectives Book Series, for their support, encouragement, and guidance through this project. I had mentioned to Aron my interest in and early writing of a piece on termination. Not only was Aron enthusiastic but he helped me create a vision when he suggested that I finish the article so that I could turn my attention to editing a book on the topic, one sorely missing in the field. He has continued to be a generous friend, a smart editor, and a deeply enthusiastic presence and advocate. Additionally, I want to express my great appreciation to my assistant editor at Taylor & Francis, Kristopher Spring. He too has been steadfast on the course, gentle in his reminders, and wonderfully thoughtful and insightful around important decisions.

I am fortunate to have a community of close friends and colleagues who have been a great reservoir of intellectual and emotional support and enthusiasm. They include Bill Allured, whose photographic acumen enhanced my cover photo, in addition to what he provided in collegiality and friendship; Fran Anderson, who was of great help "coaching" me through the growing pains of learning to be an editor; and my other dear friends who have sustained me during the growth of my ideas, many months of writing and struggling to clarify points, either in dialogue or in response to my many drafts for this book: Sue Grand, Melinda Gellman, Dodi Goldman, Linda Jacobs, Bruce Reis, Dan Shaw, and Nina Thomas.

It "takes a small village" of companions to travel the road of writing and I have been fortunate to have been part of a wonderful writing group. I am grateful to Annabella Bushra, Anita Herron, Liz Goren, Linda Luz-Alterman, Therese Ragen, Melanie Suchet, and Alexandra Woods. To our writing teacher and my friend Carole Maso, I will always be in her debt for opening me to this world of language and writing.

I feel so fortunate to have been mentored by Stephen Mitchell and Phillip Bromberg at crucial points when they seemed to offer exactly what I needed to further my thinking and growing as an analyst. I am thankful for the opportunities provided to present my early work to candidates at: the New York University Postdoctoral Program in Psychotherapy and Psychoanalysis and the Stephen A. Mitchell Center for Relational Psychoanalysis. I also want to thank my patients who have worked with me and trusted me and, in many ways, have been my greatest teachers.

I want to thank my parents for their belief in me, and my children, Jordan and Adam, who share in my joy and pride in this accomplishment. Last, I thank my husband Michael who has always been enormously supportive, believing in my ability and vision often before I did, and for his ongoing encouragement and love.

Thanks to *Psychoanalytic Dialogues* for permission to reprint material from my article "Leaning into Termination" (2009), which now forms parts of sections in Chapters 1 and 7.

Contributors

Anthony Bass, Ph.D., is on the faculty and a supervising analyst at the New York University (NYU) Postdoctoral Program in Psychotherapy and Psychoanalysis. He is the president of the Steven A. Mitchell Center for Relational Studies, a founding director of the International Association for Relational Psychoanalysis and Psychotherapy, and joint editor-in-chief for *Psychoanalytic Dialogues.*

Martin Bergmann, Ph.D., teaches a course on the history of psychoanalysis at the NYU Postdoctoral Program in Psychotherapy and Psychoanalysis. He is the author of numerous books, including *The Evolution of Psychoanalytic Technique* (Basic Books, 1976), *Generations of the Holocaust* (Basic Books, 1982), *The Anatomy of Loving* (Columbia University Press, 1987), *In the Shadow of Moloch* (Columbia University Press, 1992), *The Hartmann Era in Psychoanalysis* (Other Press, 2000), and (with his son Michael Bergmann) *What Silent Love Has Writ: A Psychoanalytic Exploration of Shakespeare's Sonnets* (Separate Star, 2007). He is also the editor of *Understanding Dissidence and Controversy in the History of Psychoanalysis* (Other Press, 2004), which received the Gradiva Award. In 1997, Dr. Bergmann received the Sigourney Award for outstanding contributions to psychoanalysis. In 1998, he received the Distinguished Psychoanalytic Educator Award from the International Federation for Psychoanalytic Education.

Jeanne Wolff Bernstein, Ph.D., is past president of the Psychoanalytic Institute of Northern California and is a supervising and personal analyst on its faculty. She serves on the editorial boards of *Psychoanalytic Dialogues, Studies in Gender and Sexuality,* and *Contemporary Psychoanalysis.* Dr. Wolff Bernstein has published articles on psychoanalysis and the arts and on the different schools of thought in psychoanalysis, particularly on the work of Jacques Lacan. The 2008 Fulbright Scholar at the Freud Museum in Vienna, Austria, she is in private practice in Berkeley, California.

Ronald Britton, M.D., is well known internationally as a psychoanalytic writer, teacher, and clinician. His books include *The Oedipus Complex Today* (Karnac, 1990), *Belief and Imagination* (Routledge, 1998), and *Sex, Death and the Superego* (Karnac, 2003). In addition to his clinical papers, he has written on the relationship of psychoanalysis to literature, philosophy, and religion. Dr. Britton is a former chair of the Department for Children and Parents, Tavistock Clinic, president of the British Psycho-Analytical Society, and vice president of the International Psychoanalytical Association.

Steven Cooper, Ph.D., is a training and supervising analyst at the Boston Psychoanalytic Society and Institute, a supervising analyst and on the faculty at the Massachusetts Institute for Psychoanalysis, and Clinical Associate Professor of Psychology at Harvard Medical School. A joint editor-in-chief of *Psychoanalytic Dialogues*, Dr. Cooper is the author of *Objects of Hope: Exploring Possibility and Limit in Psychoanalysis* (Analytic Press, 2000). He has a private practice in Cambridge, Massachusetts.

Jody Messler Davies, Ph.D., is editor-in-chief Emeritus, and current associate editor of *Psychoanalytic Dialogues: A Journal of Relational Perspectives*. She is on faculty, a supervisor, and former cochair of the Relational Track of the NYU Postdoctoral Program in Psychotherapy and Psychoanalysis; founding vice president of the International Association for Relational Psychoanalysis and Psychotherapy; and founding member of the Stephen A. Mitchell Center for Relational Psychoanalysis. Dr. Messler Davies is on the editorial boards of *Gender and Sexuality* and *Psychoanalytic Perspectives*, and is also on the faculty and a supervisor at the National Institute for the Psychotherapies, The Massachusetts Institute for Psychoanalysis, and The Institute of Contemporary Psychoanalysis, Los Angeles. She is coauthor (with Mary Gail Frawley-O'Dea) of *Treating the Adult Survivor of Childhood Sexual Abuse: A Psychoanalytic Perspective* (Basic Books, 1994) and is currently working on a new book, *Transformations of Desire and Despair: Clinical Implications of the Theoretical Shift to a Relational Perspective*. Dr. Messler Davies has written on the topics of trauma, dissociation, multiplicity of self-organization and termination, as well as a series of papers on sexual and erotic aspects of the transference/countertransference processes.

Stefanie Solow Glennon, Ph.D., is a supervising analyst at the NYU Postdoctoral Program in Psychotherapy and Psychoanalysis, a supervising analyst at the Institute for Contemporary Psychotherapy, and on the faculty at the Stephen Mitchell Center. On the editorial board of Psychoanalytic Dialogues, Dr. Solow Glennon has written in the areas of mourning, immediate experience, obesity, and artistic expression.

Dodi Goldman, Ph.D., is a training and supervising analyst and on the faculty of the William Alanson White Institute. He is the author of *In Search of the Real: The Origins and Originality of D.W. Winnicott* (Jason Aronson, 1993) and serves on the International Advisory Board of the Israel Winnicott Center. Dr. Goldman has a private practice in Manhattan and Great Neck, New York.

Sue Grand, Ph.D., is on the faculty and is a supervisor at the NYU Post doctoral Program in Psychotherapy and Psychoanalysis, and on the faculty at the Psychoanalytic Institute of Northern California. Dr. Grand is an associate editor of *Psychoanalytic Dialogues* and the author of *The Reproduction of Evil: A Clinical and Cultural Perspective* (Analytic Press, 2000) and *The Hero in the Mirror: From Fear to Fortitude* (Routledge, 2010).

Jeremy Holmes, M.D., FRCPsych, is a psychoanalytic psychotherapist in private practice in North Devon and visiting professor of psychotherapy at the University of Exeter, United Kingdom. Dr. Holmes's recent books include *The Search for the Secure Base* (Routledge, 2001) and *Textbook of Psychotherapy* (coedited with G. Gabbard and J. Beck, Oxford University Press, 2005). His latest book is *Exploring In Security: Towards an Attachment-Informed Psychoanalytic Psychotherapy* (Routledge, 2009).

Lynne Layton, Ph.D., is assistant clinical professor of psychology at Harvard Medical School and is in private practice in Brookline, Massachusetts. She has taught courses on women and popular culture and on culture and psychoanalysis for Harvard's Committee on Degrees in Women's Studies and Committee on Degrees in Social Studies, and she currently teaches at the Massachusetts Institute for Psychoanalysis. Dr. Layton is the author of *Who's That Girl? Who's That Boy? Clinical Practice Meets Postmodern Gender Theory* (Analytic Press, 2004), which won the Association of Women in Psychology's Distinguished Publication Award; coeditor of *Bringing the Plague: Toward a Postmodern Psychoanalysis* (Other Press, 2002); and coeditor of *Psychoanalysis, Class and Politics: Encounters in the Clinical Setting* (Routledge, 2006). She is editor of *Psychoanalysis, Culture, and Society* and associate editor of *Studies in Gender and Sexuality*.

Bruce Reis, Ph.D., is on the faculty of the NYU Postdoctoral Program in Psychotherapy and Psychoanalysis and the Stephen A. Mitchell Center for Relational Psychoanalysis. He is on the editorial boards of the *International Journal of Psychoanalysis*, the *International Journal of Self-Psychology*, and *Studies in Gender and Sexuality*. Dr. Reis is a frequent writer on the topic of intersubjectivity and phenomenology in clinical psychoanalysis. He is the coeditor (with Robert Grossmark) of *Heterosexual Masculinities: Contemporary Perspectives from Psychoanalytic Gender Theory* (Routledge, 2009).

Jill Salberg, Ph.D. (editor), is adjunct clinical associate professor at the NYU Postdoctoral Program in Psychotherapy and Psychoanalysis, where she teaches and supervises and is a member of the faculty at the Stephen A. Mitchell Center for Relational Psychoanalysis. She is also on the faculty of the National Institute for the Psychotherapies and is a training supervisor at the Institute for Contemporary Psychotherapy. Dr. Salberg's articles on Freud, gender, termination, and Judaism and psychoanalysis have been published in *Psychoanalytic Dialogues* and *Studies in Gender and Sexuality*; and she has chapters in *The Jewish World of Sigmund Freud* and *Answering a Question with a Question: Judaism and Contemporary Psychoanalysis*. She is a member of the Women's Mental Health Consortium at Weill Medical College and is in private practice in Manhattan.

Sandra Silverman, LCSW, is a supervisor and faculty member at the Institute for Contemporary Psychotherapy and the Psychoanalytic Psychotherapy Study Center. She is in private practice in New York City.

Neil J. Skolnick, Ph.D., is former cochair of the relational track at the NYU Postdoctoral Program in Psychotherapy and Psychoanalysis, where he is also a supervisor and faculty member. He is on the board of directors and faculty at the National Institute of the Psychotherapies (NIP) and its two affiliated psychoanalytic training programs: The Institute for the Psychoanalytic Study of the Self (IPSS) and the National Training Program (NTP), as well as the Westchester Center for the Study of Psychoanalysis and Psychoanalytic Psychotherapy (WCSPP). Dr. Skolnick has been active in promoting regional contemporary psychoanalytic training programs throughout the country, including in Kansas City, Minneapolis, and Sacramento. He has coedited two books, *Relational Perspectives in Psychoanalysis* (Analytic Press, 1992) and *Fairbairn, Then and Now* (Analytic Press, 1998). Dr. Skolnick maintains a practice in psychoanalysis in New York City.

Introduction

Jill Salberg

Never can say goodbye . . . tell me why, is it so, so very hard to go?
Don't want to let you go, never can say goodbye, no, no, no.

The Jackson Five, "Never Can Say Goodbye"

How do we come to say goodbye? We offer patients a deeply felt connection, which can stir and fulfill longings for recognition, and a relatedness that may be more fulfilling than other relationships. It is within this satisfying relatedness we hope for a transformative experience. Why would a patient want to relinquish, give up this rich attachment, and end gratifying work? Why ever leave? From the other side, how do we as therapists or analysts know when enough work has been done? Additionally, if the work is deeply satisfying and we become attached, why ever stop?

My own engagement with the topic of termination began a number of years ago when I presented a case (Salberg, 2009; Chapter 7) to candidates at an analytic institute. The particular treatment was one in which I made the decision to terminate the treatment. Despite considering the case of my patient Ellen to be a "failed treatment," I felt it was a good case for candidates because it was clinically interesting in a messy, difficult sort of way and seemed to be the kind of case candidates might relate to. I was right but surprised to learn that they also felt it was far from a treatment failure; some even felt that it was a success. It took some time for me to process the idea and to see that the lens they were using was not the same lens I had used. It forced me to start calling into question my own idealizations of treatment goals and to reconsider what an ending might look like.

Additionally, it was useful for me to discover that, despite my own shift from a one-person psychology based in object relations theory to a two-person relational approach, this change had not included rethinking the way in which I might consider the ending of treatment. My personal shift occurred in the mid- to late 1980s while in analytic training at the New York University Postdoctoral Program. At that time, this shift felt revolutionary. However, in the current contemporary scene, these categories seem to be in greater dialogue with each other and often it is neither a one-person nor a two-person approach but it is both and in which ways they inform a more encompassing picture.

I turned to the literature as a way to investigate what had been written about termination and to find my bearings. I came upon an outstanding article by Martin Bergmann (1997; Chapter 2) in which he incisively determines that the field has been negligent in developing a true paradigm for termination. I found his proposal simultaneously reassuring and disturbing. Further reading confirmed much of what Bergmann had assessed, and I also learned that over the years, both before and after Bergmann wrote his article, others had remarked on the slim writings on the topic. I became quite curious as to how it happened that theorizing about termination was a kind of lacuna in which development of thought had seemingly stopped evolving.

Interestingly, while I had been collecting the papers for this book, *Psychoanalytic Inquiry* had been on a somewhat similar course, publishing a special issue "Loving and Leaving: A Reappraisal of Analytic Termination."* (In 1982, *Psychoanalytic Inquiry* published a special issue on termination, hence "reappraisal" in the above title, which I will discuss later in this chapter.) Far from coincidence, the conterminous publications reveal an obvious need for review and revision of our concepts surrounding the end of treatment. The proposition of the editors of *Psychoanalytic Inquiry* is that the paradigm shifts within psychoanalysis from objectivism to constructivism, and from a more intrapsychic conception of mind to what they refer to as "relational field theory," warrant a new examination of termination. They also note that the research findings from neuroscience, infant–mother, and attachment research are important for consideration as well. Although I am in complete agreement with their premises and goals, I see the shifts in the field as having more layers.

My own training as a psychologist occurred during the 1970s and was greatly influenced by the prevailing conception of Freudian psychoanalysis as expanded by Anna Freud, Heinz Hartman's ego psychology, and the work of Margaret Mahler. American psychoanalysis had been greatly influenced by the influx of Freudian analysts emigrating from post–World War II Europe, and their view, as well as Hartmann's theory of autonomous ego functioning, was that the goal of treatment was to implement intrapsychic structural change. Effectively, this meant a stronger, more autonomous ego. A readiness to end treatment would mean an emergence from dependency to independence without the need of the analyst. Self-analysis became the end goal that still sounds right, but how to achieve it remains a troubling question. Aron (as interviewed by Safran, 2009) views the emphasis on autonomy as a direct result of how treatment, largely dominated by male

---

* 29(2), 2009; issue editors: James L. Fosshage and Sandra G. Hershberg.

medical psychoanalysts, reified a cultural value that split analysis, manliness, and autonomy from psychotherapy and feminine relational values (see also Benjamin, 1998; Hoffman, 1998). Mitchell and Harris (2004) considered certain features of American culture and history that might have helped create an American psychological sensibility. They touch on certain themes that I would consider iconographic of psychoanalysis in the United States. Among these are pragmatism, freedom, and manifest destiny.

With this in mind, I can see Margaret Mahler's work as having a uniquely American interpretation of Freud. Mahler's (1967, 1975) theoretical conceptualization of the processes of separation-individuation and what later, jointly with Fred Pine and Anni Bergman, became known as the "psychological birth of the infant," was a vision that sees development as not only linear in design but that privileges individual autonomy, believing it to be the end goal of psychological development. The infant was understood to be born into a symbiotic early relationship with the mother who, in the best of circumstances, supported stages of emancipation from this symbiotic union. Not unlike other ideas of the 1970s, such as self-actualization, the fully grown self was autonomous and freed from dependency. Such a view valorizes the needs of the individual whose pinnacle of development is complete autonomy, over the interrelatedness of self with other or self-in-community. Layton (Chapter 11) believes this to be embedded within Western culture. Mahler's belief that the child's development inevitably leads to full individuation is an outgrowth of this sensibility, this pride in a kind of "separation as accomplishment." Aron (1996) believes that the shift in psychoanalysis toward a relational approach can be seen also as an outgrowth of the effects of feminism. Specifically, he writes, "Papers emphasizing attachment as a central aspect of clinical psychoanalysis and relatedness and empathy as just as important as independence and autonomy have similarly been influenced at least indirectly by the feminist critique of the idealization of independence and the isolated self of our culture" (pp. 20–21).

I do not want to sound as if Mahler had such a wrong-headed idea; given the prevailing conceptual framework of a one-person psychology, her theory expanded ideas on early child development. I was enthralled with her work, as were my graduate school cohorts. She captured many of the childhood, adolescent, and even adulthood conflicts that we all felt vulnerable to. When I entered my own analysis, I believed I would be learning how to fully separate and individuate from my family of origin and complete what had felt, heretofore, to be an incomplete process. Staying attached had not felt like a welcomed option, because it felt shameful in its link to dependency issues.

To my mind, the relational paradigm shift that Fosshage and Hershberg referred to would then also include conceptions of intersubjectivity, mutuality, and the treatment as cocreated by the dyad. Many of these relational ideas resulted from and were integrated with the mounting evidence from infant–mother and attachment research that show the multiple ways the infant and caregiver are mutually affecting and regulating each other from birth. This is not only at odds with Mahler's theory of separation and individuation but also with the idea that individual autonomy would need to include complete independence from others. Thus, it seemed decidedly necessary to me that the termination literature would equally need some revisions to reflect this kind of clinical research evidence.

It was while reading Davies' (2005; Chapter 6) article on her own conceptualization of ending treatment with her patient using relational concepts such as multiplicity that I began to reformulate my work with Ellen (see Salberg, 2009; Chapter 7) as a relational termination. As it unfolded and I met with Ellen later on, I realized that I had "enacted" an ending with her. I became more convinced that there were new ways to explore how we understand and can conceptualize the ending of treatment. Although the early work of relational writers had been exploring and reformulating theory and technique, the emphasis had been on what happens during the treatment. Ironically, the end was overlooked, as if no end was in sight or sadly, that the end might take care of itself. Many of the concepts that relational authors have written about in general can apply equally to and be useful as constructs regarding termination.

I believe that terminations can be understood as cocreated enactments of complex unconscious processes between patient and analyst and will expand upon that more fully within my chapter. However, if we believe that certain experiences need to be lived firsthand in the analysis, and that enactments carry deeply felt, sometimes dissociated experience, then it follows that enactments around termination will occur. Bromberg (2006) absolutely believes that not only is termination not such a "benign" phase, but it often will draw us into yet another round of enactments crucial to ending. He states that "in this final stage of treatment, a relational context of new shared meaning could be created (or more accurately, cocreated) from what was being enacted around the termination itself" (p. 19).

Additionally, what has become coined as the "relational tradition" (Mitchell & Aron, 1999) has typically drawn upon a diversity of topics, including but not limited to intersubjectivity theory, object relations, interpersonal relations, self-psychology, constructivism, and attachment theory. Many of these topics have not been part of the termination literature. In particular, I felt that it was a major void to be conceptualizing the ending of treatment without including what we now understand about attachment from all the years of infant–mother research and attachment theory writings. Fundamentally the analytic dyad forms an attachment system, and we need to think inclusively about our endings in the context of our attachments and often differing attachment styles.

In deciding which authors to include in this volume, I used a model loosely based on Stephen Mitchell's ideas that there is a landscape in psychoanalysis. His was of multiple points of view dialoguing with each other. I combined that concept with what Spezzano (1995, 1997) conceptualized as the American middle school. He conceived of an evolving group, echoing but not the same as the middle school of the British Psychoanalytic Society. For the British Society, the middle space was between Klein and Freud, but in America, Spezzano (1995) conceives of it as follows:

> Between the various relational theories (object relational, interpersonal, self psychological, trauma-abuse), on the one hand, and the various classical ego analytic theories on the other. This "middle" integrates British theory (both object relational and neo-Kleinian) with American interpersonal psychoanalysis (the Sullivanian or William Alanson White tradition) as well as with contemporary psychoanalytic theories of affect (Stein, 1991) and motivation (Greenberg, 1991). (p. 23)

In 1997, Spezzano added to this the topics of intersubjectivity and unconscious communication.

In many ways, this book represents my attempt to house a middle school approach. I compiled what I consider to be a group of the most original writers and important papers representing a broad spectrum of points of view. Some of these writers come close to a middle school approach; some do not, but have been included because of my sense of how papers and ideas, when read together, can illuminate each other. What was also interesting to me was seeing how writers from different positions struggled with the problematic nature of ending treatment. Some of these papers feel surprisingly to be in dialogue with each other, although not explicitly.

Part I, "Termination: Theories and Positions," is the most broadly inclusive in the book. I started the section with a historical overview (Salberg, Chapter 1). Many of the papers and books on this topic provide a selective review of the literature. I felt it was lacking and therefore important to give a sense of the trajectory of theoretical work on termination. My own preference is to see how history informs the context for a generation of analysts who then train and influence the next generation. This is a decidedly intergenerational transmission approach to history but one that I hope will prepare the reader to appreciate more fully the papers that follow. Martin Bergmann (Chapter 2) represents a contemporary and deeply thoughtful Freudian view. He delineates what needs to be internalized—what needs to become self-analysis—before ending can occur. Ronald Britton (Chapter 3) exemplifies an evolution of British Kleinian thinking that includes an excellent synthesis of Bion and Steiner. Britton believes that it is not so much a cessation of symptomatology that we look for to indicate a readiness to end but rather an ability to regain internal stability—a flexibility of the personality to rebound from internal upsets along with a sense of hope. Jeanne Wolff Bernstein (Chapter 4), writing from a Lacanian perspective with great clarity and richness, illustrates Lacan's project to expand upon Freud's seminal idea on termination: no cure is completed unless the death drive is apprehended behind any symptom formation. Building upon Freud's recommendation that any analysis must reach beyond the bedrock of castration, Lacan suggests that the subject must cross the plane of identification in order to apprehend the fantasm that he or she constructed in order to respond to the fundamental question of what the Other wants from me. Jeremy Holmes (Chapter 5) provides an important background in Bowlby's attachment model and integrates modern attachment theories into psychotherapy and psychoanalytic theories and practices. He reminds us to be mindful of the attachment style of the patient and the therapist as we coconstruct the treatment and we begin to conceptualize how to terminate. I included a seminal paper by Jody Messler Davies (Chapter 6), who was one of the first relational writers to cogently and thoroughly address termination. Davies has often written movingly of her work with patients, and this paper, in particular, demonstrates how her use of her own work on multiplicity and dissociative self-states informs her thinking on termination.

Part II, "On the Clinical Frontier," includes work of a group of relational writers who, through their clinical work, have continued to conceptualize what a relational theory of termination would feel and look like. The authors in this section approach clinical endings with interesting sensibilities and ways of engaging themselves, their patients, and theory. In Chapter 7, I trace my own evolving theoretical development across three terminations and determine that ending is a rupture of a profound attachment. Consequently, it is primed for dissociated enacted experiences. I look at how time, in its complexity, can be perceived differently under the sway of these experiences and track this through multiple endings across three treatments. Sue Grand (Chapter 8) questions the very nature of the analytic enterprise—that in forming an analytic bond we are inevitably heading toward rupture and grief. She explores this using her work with a patient who engaged in an *analysis interruptus* by continually starting and stopping the work. Steven Cooper (Chapter 9) finds that ending, including the intrinsic ambiguity over timing, presents an opportunity for examining previously underappreciated aspects of the transference–countertransference relationship, including the analyst's "countertransference of indeterminacy." In presenting close process material with his patient, Cooper argues that what may have historically been considered regression during the ending process is sometimes better understood as the analytic pair's unconsciously motivated attempt to examine these points of enactment. Sandra Silverman (Chapter 10) writes movingly about how our work with certain patients around ending reveals how permeable the wall may be between our lives and our patients' lives. She considers loss, survival, and "going-on-being" as they impact termination. Lynne Layton (Chapter 11), while walking us through two terminations, suggests that our literature's tendency to equate termination with reaching a certain level of maturity betrays a devaluation of dependency. She finds what she calls "maternal resistance" in our literature, ourselves, and our patients, and argues that if *this* resistance remains unanalyzed, we may not know what we have lost at the end of an analysis.

Part III, "Musings on the Multiple Meanings of Ending," offers writings from a more meditative perspective on ending and loss while raising the dilemmas involved in relational treatments. Bruce Reis (Chapter 12) sees an analogue between Winnicott's idea of the fate of the transitional object, not internalized as much as relegated to limbo, and what continues on after ending treatment. He weaves Freud's early idea of *nachträglichkeit* and Laplanches's translation of the term as an "afterwardness" with contemporary research and thinking on memory to create a new conceptualization of the finality and continuity of treatment. Neil Skolnick (Chapter 13) proposes that relational psychoanalytic theory is better suited for a flexible definition of when termination actually occurs. Using his own experience as an analyst, Skolnick describes how once we transcend a mourning model of termination, it becomes feasible to examine the process in a nonlinear temporal and mutual fashion. Dodi Goldman (Chapter 14) argues that it makes a difference whether psychoanalysis is thought of as a treatment or as an experience. By considering psychoanalytic views of pain and suffering, aloneness, the transformative Other, illusion, attachment, and clinging, Goldman explores how analysts and patients collaborate, clash, or shift over time as they negotiate a consensual language for knowing when "enough is enough." Stefanie Solow Glennon (Chapter 15) raises the question of the impact on termination of the "relational turn" in psychoanalysis: As analysts have become less remote and anonymous, might this lead to interminable treatments? When discussing a particular patient who she believes is ready to end but who states, "Why would I *choose* to say goodbye to you?", Glennon questions the literature and includes an afterword written by her patient. The section concludes with Anthony Bass (Chapter 16) who explores the idea that in analyses guided by contemporary principles of intersubjectivity and constructivism, terminations are ambiguous and cocreated, rather than definitive. From this perspective, there is always more analytic work to be done; endings often make way for new beginnings and a new phase of work, as patient and analyst take their work as far as they can before finding their way to a unique ending. It is this broad, diverse multiplicity of voices and points of view that I have found enriching and enlivening within the field of relational theory and psychoanalysis.

Last, I would like to offer some history regarding this book's title. I had been working hard to understand my treatment of a patient, which I had terminated in the 1990s, and as part of that internal processing I had been writing about and presenting the case for a few years. In the article that eventually came out of that process (Salberg, 2009), I had struggled with what I felt had been a subtle but nonetheless present idealized conception in the field of what a fully realized analysis might look like. Perhaps this had been part of the dilemma I had in ending my own first analysis, which I have also written about (Salberg, 2009). I wrote, "If we 'lean' into termination, can we surrender our wish for an idealized ending? Can we see more clearly that it is quite a complicated dilemma, staying or going, for both the patient and for the analyst?" (p. 709). My belief that there is no complete or ideal ending to any analysis led me to imagine what might be, in Winnicott's vernacular, a "good-enough" ending.

I am not the first to imagine this. Hoffman (1998) called the concluding chapter in his book *Ritual and Spontaneity in the Psychoanalytic Process*, "Constructing Good-Enough Endings in Psychoanalysis." Hoffman argues well that endings take many forms, none perfect and most certainly not always under one's control. Termination for Hoffman would then include more broadly all endings, even the end of life. More recently Gabbard (2009), whose paper is entitled "What Is a 'Good Enough' Termination?" persuasively argues that we need multiple scenarios for terminating treatment, not a one size fits all approach. As is frequently done in jazz music, I am "riffing" on the melody of others, adding my own variation on the chords, sometimes in harmony, sometimes discordant but "good-enough" all the same.

Termination has always been a problematic word that we have inherited from a poorly translated version of Freud's original work on ending analysis. Many analysts would prefer any word other than termination, a term that suggests being fired, exterminated, or gotten rid of. Many of us have learned that endings become an interruption rather than a completion. Some patients return to either continue the work or even commence a new piece of work, which then is moving toward yet another ending. As I indicated in the title of this book, my sense of "good-enough endings" would include these breaks and interruptions, as they form the kind of treatment a particular patient may need and consequently shapes with their therapist or analyst. I would no longer consider when a patient returns for more work that it is an indication that the prior work be considered incomplete. Additionally, in rethinking how we conceptualize ending treatment, we may in fact be redefining what a good-enough treatment is.

This book is not meant to be a final word on ending—rather it is a way to enter, a place to reflect on ideas and last, a guide toward continuing the work and continue thinking. What follows in Chapter 1 is an overview of where the field and literature on termination started and the evolution of its concepts and ideas. Although several relational writers, whom I have included in my historical overview, have written on termination, there has not yet been developed a body of relational literature that would constitute relational theory on this subject. This has felt like a vacuum that this book hopes to fill. Like all good analyses though, you have to understand where you have been, to figure out where you want to go.

REFERENCES

Aron, L. (1996). *A meeting of minds: Mutuality in psychoanalysis*. Hillsdale, NJ: Analytic Press.

Benjamin, J. (1998). *Shadow of the other: Intersubjectivity and gender in psychoanalysis*. London: Routledge.

Bergmann, M. (1997). Termination: The Achilles heel of psychoanalytic technique. *Psychoanalytic Psychology, 14*, 163–174.

Britton, R. (2005, November). There is no end of the line: Terminating the interminable. Paper presented at Institute for Psychoanalytic Training and Research. Conference—When Do We Terminate: The Concept of Termination Revisited, New York.

Bromberg, P. (2006). *Awakening the dreamer: Clinical journeys*. Mahwah, NJ and London: Analytic Press.

Davies, J. M. (2005). Transformations of desire and despair: Reflections on the termination process. *Psychoanalytic Dialogues, 15*(6), 779–805.

Fosshage, J. L., & Hershberg, S. G. (2009). Loving and leaving: A reappraisal of analytic termination. *Psychoanalytic Inquiry, 29*(2).

Gabbard, G. O. (2009). What is a "good enough" termination? *Journal of the American Psychoanalytic Association, 57*(3), 575–594.

Hoffman, I. Z. (1998). *Ritual and spontaneity in the psychoanalytic process: A dialectical–constructivist view*. Hillsdale, NJ and London: Analytic Press.

Mahler, M. (1967). On human symbiosis and the vicissitudes of individuation. *Journal of the American Psychoanalytic Association, 15*, 740–763.

Mahler, M., Pine, F., & Bergman, A. (1975). *The psychological birth of the human infant*. New York: Basic Books.

Mitchell, S. A., & Aron, L. (Eds.). (1999). *Relational psychoanalysis: The emergence of a tradition*. Hillsdale, NJ: Analytic Press.

Mitchell, S. A., & Harris, A. (2004). What's American about American psychoanalysis? *Psychoanalytic Dialogues, 14*, 165–191.

Safran, J. D. (2009). Interview with Lewis Aron. *Psychoanalytic Psychology, 26*, 99–116.

Salberg, J. (2009). Leaning into termination. *Psychoanalytic Dialogues, 19*(6), 703–722.

Spezzano, C. (1995). "Classical" versus "contemporary" theory: The differences that matter clinically. *Contemporary Psychoanalysis, 31*, 20–46.

Spezzano, C. (1997). The emergence of an American Middle School of Psychoanalysis: Commentary of Karen Rosica's paper. *Psychoanalytic Dialogues, 7*, 603–618.

Part 1

Termination: Theories and positions

Chapter 1

Historical overview*

Jill Salberg

Although Freud (1912) had written some early papers on technique, the question of termination was first raised in a monograph, *The Development of Psychoanalysis*, by Ferenczi and Rank (1924). They proposed that when a full transference neurosis had developed in the patient, the analyst then, "sets a definite period of time completing the last part of the treatment" (p. 13). Rank's (1924) book, *The Trauma of Birth*, instigated a heated debate about the shortening of treatment. Rank and Ferenczi had experimented with setting a time limit and had found that this stirred up separation anxiety and maternal transference. For Rank, separation carried the meaning of disconnection from mother as well as the final separation of death, and so the time limit of therapy evoked maternal separation anxiety and existential death anxieties, both aspects of Rank's new theories. These ideas stirred up a huge controversy that lasted for a few years and partially ended with the departure of Rank, both from Freud's inner circle and eventually to America.

I want to draw attention to the fact that Rank and Ferenczi had noted certain problems within analytic treatment, which they were trying to creatively think about. The idea that treatment needed some push, some added pressure for the patient to work through the transference neurosis led to their formulating the setting of an end date. This idea has persisted throughout the history of psychoanalysis and has continued to gain and lose favor. Dupont (1994), in discussing the letters between Freud and Ferenczi during the time of the Rank controversy, noted: "The crisis centered around the same problems that periodically arose between the two men: technical attempts to shorten analysis (fixation of a termination date, active technique, and so forth); pathogenic effect of phantasy vs. trauma; verbal remembering vs. re-experiencing through repetition" (p. 312). These are the same issues we continue to struggle with today, some of which will be taken up in this book.

---

* Parts of this chapter originally appeared in *Psychoanalytic Dialogues*, 19(6), 2009, pp. 704–722.

Despite Freud having also used the setting of a time limit with the Wolf Man, he was not in favor of this device, fearing that instead of speeding up the work, the reverse would occur with an increase in resistance by the patient to the psychoanalytic work. No doubt, setting the termination date, especially an early one, would catalyze a great many reactions from patients including creating a kind of crisis in the treatment. Perhaps Rank believed that this was a recreation of the original crisis, the birth trauma, so it easily fit in with the theories he was developing—theories that Freud would come to feel were too far a departure from his own formulations of psychoanalysis. Unfortunately, the controversy around Rank's ideas became a problem for Ferenczi who wished to remain theoretically loyal to Freud and thereafter began to distance himself from Rank.

The earliest paper solely on termination was written by Ferenczi (1927) and was partly his attempt to differentiate himself from his earlier work with Rank. Interestingly, the paper reflects Ferenczi's now arguing against the shortening of treatments and his emphasizing working for as long as the patient wanted to continue. It is a paper filled with idealism along with high standards for the analyst. He believed that the analyst "must know and be in control of even the most recondite weaknesses of his own character and this is impossible without a fully completed analysis" (p. 84). What standard of a "fully completed analysis" could Ferenczi have been thinking of? Clearly it was not his analysis with Freud, an analysis that had been three brief, interrupted sets of meetings that totaled 7 to 8 weeks. Further, Ferenczi felt that Freud, by not continuing the analysis, abandoned the process too soon, before a negative transference could be elaborated and worked through (see Aron & Harris, 1993). In fact, later in his paper he says, "The proper ending of an analysis is when neither the physician nor the patient puts an end to it, but when it dies of exhaustion…A truly cured patient frees himself from analysis slowly but surely; so long as he wishes to come to analysis, he should continue to do so" (p. 85). (Bass, in Chapter 14, reflects further on Ferenczi's contribution.) For Ferenczi, termination involved a gradual and spontaneous mourning of childhood longings, something he had not been able to fully do with Freud. One can only imagine that Ferenczi might have been chiding Freud.

Freud (1937) articulated his own views on ending analysis quite late in his life in "Analysis Terminable and Interminable." We cannot know why Freud did not include a paper on termination earlier when he wrote his original papers on technique, although I imagine he did not yet think that termination might prove to be troublesome. The technique papers had been written while Freud still ascribed to the topographic model of mind. Making the unconscious conscious was still the goal, along with symptom relief, so it is very likely that once the symptoms were gone, ending was considered to be a *fait accompli*, something easily done. With the shift to the structural model, Freud was moving from a strict emphasis on the unconscious nature of the drives to the relationship between the agencies of the mind: id, ego, and superego. This would come to include a shift from id analysis to an emphasis on the ego, its mechanisms of defense, and analyzing fully the transference neurosis. The goal for Freud, remember, was where id was, now ego should be.

It is important to have this historical context in mind when reading Freud on termination because of what may have been on his agenda. Leupold-Löwenthal (1987), in discussing Freud's paper, believes that, "After Anna Freud's *The Ego and the Mechanisms of Defense* (1936) and Heinz Hartmann's Vienna lectures on ego theory (1939), ego psychology had increasingly become a central aspect of the theory of psychoanalytic technique" (p. 52). Further, he believes that the 1936 International Psychoanalytical Association (IPA) Congress in Marienbad, Czech Republic, on "The Theory of Therapeutic Results" was upsetting to Freud, and his paper on termination may very well be a critical and perhaps "last word" on that meeting. By the time of his termination paper, Freud is elderly, worn out by his long fight against a cancer that had returned once again, along with his ongoing battles to keep psychoanalysis thriving as he envisioned it, while watching "the gathering storms" of his world inexorably moving toward war. Freud wrote,

> The discussion of the technical problem of how to accelerate the slow progress of an analysis leads us to another, more deeply interesting question: Is there such a thing as a natural end to an analysis—is there any possibility at all of bringing an analysis to such an end? (p. 219)

It is not surprising then that his tone is somewhat skeptical and at times pessimistic about the results of psychoanalysis, concerned whether it can safeguard against a return of symptoms or even from new symptoms cropping up. Analyses had been increasing in length, something he now had to accept and reckon with. He notes and distinguishes between the miseries of Europe with the prosperity of America. Freud suggests that short-term therapy is a wrong-minded adaptation to the fast pace of American life. Additionally, Rank had settled in America and was practicing what Freud feared was a diluted and not true form of psychoanalysis. Later in his paper, Freud cites Ferenczi's paper on termination and remarked, "The paper as a whole, however, seems to me to be in the nature of a warning not to aim at shortening analysis but at deepening it" (p. 247). Freud is agreeing with and warmly recalling Ferenczi, who, although 17 years younger than Freud, had predeceased him 4 years prior to this paper's publication.

This paper then becomes a last word in the long conversation Freud had engaged in with numerous colleagues. (For a fuller elucidation of views on Freud's paper, see the collection of papers in the International

Psychoanalytic Association Educational Monograph no. 1, *On Freud's Analysis Terminable and Interminable*, edited by Joseph Sandler.) He refuted Rank's time-limited approach, and one of the cases Freud discusses is of a discontented analysand, already an analyst in the field (see Freud, 1937, p. 221n, where Strachey states that Jones believes he is discussing Ferenczi). After ending his analysis, this man became a teacher in the field who ends up berating his analyst for not having "finished the analysis," something Ferenczi rebuked Freud for. Sounding disheartened, Freud comes to the conclusion that even a successful analysis is *not* a prophylactic against future illness, perhaps suggesting some awareness of the limitations of his technique.

Reich (1950) was the first analyst to notice and comment on the paucity of psychoanalytic thinking and writing on this topic. What I hope to show is how the topic is both picked up and then dropped at different times throughout the literature. Returning to Ferenczi's and Freud's papers that, although written late in their lives and careers, feel very much in dialogue with each other (see Bergmann, 1997; Reich, 1950). Freud's tone was much more pessimistic than Ferenczi, but he raised three possible points of view regarding termination: the skeptical, the optimistic, and the ambitious. Freud (1927), who reminded us that our ideals were often illusions and that the road to reality was lined with disappointments, held the skeptical and, I might add, somewhat ambivalent view. The optimistic stance, held by Ferenczi, reveals his belief in the possibility of a fully curative analysis, exposing his longing for a deeper, more fully elaborated analysis with Freud. This very well may have been Ferenczi's ambition toward which his experiments with "active" technique and mutual analysis were directed (see *The Clinical Diary of Sándor Ferenczi*, edited by J. DuPont). His experimental work provoked condemnation from Freud who felt that Ferenczi was departing from the techniques of psychoanalysis as Freud had conceived of them.* What has become known as the "relational turn" hinged in many ways on the rediscovery and consideration of these alterations in technique.

While attempting to hold these two disparate points of view, Reich (1950) raised another concern: "In nearly all cases which I have analyzed there remained a wish to be loved by the analyst, to keep in contact with him, to build up a friendship" (p. 181). This is interesting given that up until

---

A footnote from Ferenczi's letter to Freud (#1236, August 29, 1932): "When I visited the Professor...I told him of my latest technical ideas....The Professor listened to my exposition with increasing impatience and finally warned me that I was treading on dangerous ground and was departing fundamentally from the traditional customs and techniques of psychoanalysis. Such yielding to the patient's longings and desires—no matter how genuine—would increase his dependence on the analyst. Such dependence can only be destroyed by the emotional withdrawal of the analyst....This warning ended the interview. I held out my hand in affectionate adieu. The Professor turned his back on me and walked out of the room" (p. 443).

the time of her writing, the early analysts were often each other's patients, colleagues, and confidantes. Although she goes on to suggest that this is a derivative of early longings from the original objects, the parents, I understand this also to be a hint of what is often going on between patient and analyst in the room. To my mind, there is a unique, special, and deep bond that develops between the analytic dyad, particular to that pair that in many ways feels the way deep friendship *can* feel and interpretation cannot quite dissipate, nor perhaps should it (see Salberg, Glennon, and Layton, Chapters 7, 15, and 11, this volume).

Freud (1937) acknowledged that many of the cases he was treating (as opposed to the early days of psychoanalysis) were "training analyses," a relatively new concept for the first generation of analysts and not a requirement as it is today. Returning to another part of his paper, Freud, no longer skeptical or ambivalent, wrote, "There was no question of shortening the treatment; the purpose was radically to exhaust the possibilities of illness in them and to bring about a deep-going alteration of their personality" (p. 224). Here is ambition laid bare—we as analyst/patient need a radical transformation of ourselves in order to effectively cure our patients. Is there any way to hear this but as a kind of grandiosity entwined with idealization? What would such an alteration of oneself look like, and does this then become an impossible standard for an already impossible profession?

I believe the ambitious point of view, one that was held simultaneously by both Freud and Ferenczi, reveals the ongoing problematic relationship that the field has inherited regarding termination. There is an unspoken but nonetheless prevalent idealization of what a fully complete analysis might look like. Certainly the bar is set high for analysts with Freud suggesting that analysts should routinely return every 5 years to undergo a further analysis.* How are we to hear and understand this? As Freud approaches his death, he wants to wrap up his life's passion and work and in so doing had to wrestle with his own loss of idealism and omnipotence. Unfortunately, there were no easy endings in sight. A more accurate translation of the title of Freud's paper would be "Analysis Finite and Infinite." Freud becomes aware of what continues, even beyond analysis when he obsesses over symptoms returning, or when he returns to the questions of what needs to be accomplished during an analysis, the bedrock he refers to when he speaks of castration fear, penis envy of women, and resistance against submission in men. (Bernstein will address this in Chapter 4, offering a Lacanian point of view and answer to Freud's concerns.) His use of the term *bedrock* suggests his favored metaphor of archeology implying

---

* Fenichel had written and circulated "A Review of Freud's 'Analysis Terminable and Interminable,'" which was later translated from the German and published in the *International Journal of Psycho-Analysis* in 1974. In this review, Fenichel critiques Freud's view on the training analysis and states that the "training analysis should be especially thorough and—if necessary—also especially long" (p. 115).

a place to dig down to where one can then build up. What if treatment is really the opposite? What if it is more about expansion? Then, what would be needed is a growing curiosity toward one's affective states and a greater capacity for deep engagement in one's life and relationships. Berry (1987) wrote what feels more in line with my own sensibility, "The idea of an analysis that never comes to an end may be momentarily reassuring, but can it be sustained? ... The unconscious can never be exhausted and thought never ends" (pp. 99–100). Given Berry's point, it is inevitable that the internal work would continue posttreatment (see Reis, Chapter 12, this volume).

Freud died when the world, as he knew it, was thrust for the second time into the violent chaos of World War. Many of the first-generation analysts had already fled Europe, mostly for England and America, with some going to South America and Palestine. The psychoanalytic world had endured multiple and compounding losses. Freud had died—a loss whose impact would be nearly impossible to comprehend. Concurrent with Freud's death was the personal dislocation of so many analysts fleeing war-torn Europe and the dangers of the Holocaust that were no longer a threat but a reality. The devastation to families, homes, countries and the world as they knew it was incalculable.

The war ended and the British Psycho-Analytic Society held, in 1949, what I believe was the first symposium on the topic of termination, entitled "Criteria for the Termination of an Analysis."* It is not surprising that loss, mourning, and endings began to preoccupy this generation of analysts; in fact, it would take years, generations even, to fully process those losses and integrate them into our understanding of how things end. I want to touch on a few of the ideas raised at this meeting and in the journal compilation.

The papers ranged from discussing actual technique of terminating, the formulation of termination criteria, to some experiential case material. Marion Milner (1950) argued that as analysts, we have effectively bypassed true termination, having become analysts ourselves and therefore living out our identifications with our analysts. This statement reveals an often unacknowledged truth, and one that has not been often discussed or integrated into our termination literature. Milner then presented a brief case in which despite a persistent and painful unremitting symptom, the patient terminated her five times a week, 2-year analysis with Milner. She arranged, as part of the termination process, to see the patient at five different times over the course of some months. Milner tells us, "This ending was not something which happened as a logical result of the patient's being considered cured; in fact, the ending preceded the cure by many months, for it was not until the analysis had actually stopped that the symptom began to move at all" (p. 191). It was during those posttreatment sessions when Milner believed the working through of analytic work took place, essentially as posttermination consolidation that was aided by contact with the analyst

---

* This was later published in 1950 in the *International Journal of Psycho-Analysis*, 31.

(see Bass in Chapter 16 and Silverman in Chapter 10, for reworked endings and posttermination work).

Hoffer (1950), while being keenly aware of what the presenting intra-psychic issues may have been for any patient, believed that the criteria for termination should dovetail with the technical aspects of how to work on these intrapsychic issues. He suggested that transference work is the fulcrum whereby a remembered experience is revived within the transference neurosis. Criteria would then be seen as the reduction of the patient's need to repeat the past in the present, and eliminating or lessening the repetition compulsion. This would happen as part of the patient's identification with the analyst and development of the patient's own capacity for self-analysis. Rickman (1950) further outlines criteria for termination believing they all hinge on "irreversibility" or the full integration of all psychic gains and no regression. Again we hear extremely high standards and I am left wondering who of us reaches that pinnacle?

Balint (1950), who was analyzed by, trained with Ferenczi, and carried within his own work the seeds of Ferenczi's ideas, wrote that although we may have some excellent criteria to determine when it is time to terminate, the criteria are quite "perfectionistic." Rather, Balint turns to what ending feels like experientially:

> It is a deeply moving experience; the general atmosphere is of taking leave for ever of something very dear, very precious—with all the corresponding grief and mourning—but this sincere and deeply felt grief is mitigated by the feeling of security, originating from the newly-won possibilities for real happiness. Usually the patient leaves after the last session happy but with tears in his eyes—I think I may admit—the analyst is in a very similar mood. (p. 197)

Balint captures the poignancy in ending for both the patient and the analyst. (Many chapters in this book capture this as well, for example, Davies in Chapter 6, Cooper in Chapter 8, and Holmes in Chapter 5.)

Melanie Klein, writing in 1950 and later in 1957, compared termination to a nursing and weaning experience in which mourning, associated with depressive position anxieties and loss, is the crucial experience to be tolerated. Klein is staking a claim for her theoretical expansion of Freud's ideas when she locates criteria for termination within the realm of overcoming persecutory anxieties and tolerating depressive concerns over one's own destructive impact. She stated,

> Failure in working through the depressive position is inextricably linked with a predominance of defences which entail a stifling of emotions and of phantasy life and hinder insight. If during an analysis we succeed in reducing persecutory and depressive anxieties and, accordingly,

in diminishing manic defences, one of the results will be an increase in *strength* as well as in *depth of the ego.* (pp. 79–80)

She also tempers this position by pointing out the limitations of the psychoanalytic method. She further stated, "When the loss represented by the end of the analysis has occurred, the patient still has to carry out by himself part of the work of mourning. This explains the fact that often after the termination of an analysis further progress is achieved" (p. 80). Although similar in tone to Freud's ideas regarding loss, mourning, and the internalization of the object, I want to highlight that Klein's notion suggests the limitations of what transpires during an analysis. She is specifically stating that some meaningful work continues to occur posttermination. (Britton, in Chapter 3, will present a contemporary Kleinian view.)

An interesting and perhaps overlooked paper by Edith Buxbaum (1950) was published within the same journal, although not given at the British Psycho-Analytic meetings of 1949.* Buxbaum was born in Vienna and received a Ph.D. from the University of Vienna. She trained with Anna Freud and was one of a group of "lay analysts" whom Freud approved. She fled the Nazis and Vienna in 1938 and came to New York where she was an analyst for 10 years before she moved to Seattle and helped to build the Seattle Psychoanalytic Institute. A main reason for Buxbaum's departure from New York had to do with the controversy regarding lay analysis. Earlier in 1911, A. A. Brill had established the New York Psychoanalytic Society and made sure that only medical doctors could train there. Despite theoretically being completely in line with Freud, Brill vigorously defied him over who could be allowed to practice. Richards (1999), in discussing Brill's rift with Freud over the lay analysis question, referred to Brill[†] as establishing a "politics of exclusion." Buxbaum was excluded from New York Psychoanalytic and left for Seattle where she would continue working as a psychoanalyst.

Her paper on termination has a sensibility to it that reads as if written today, not 60 years ago. After reviewing some of the current points of view on termination (Freud, Ferenczi, Lorand, Reich, Alexander), she turns to discussing cases and how termination decisions, whether holding strictly to a date or being flexible, need to be determined on a case-by-case basis. In one particular case, the patient had agreed to end treatment around Buxbaum's summer vacation on the condition that she could return for some sessions afterward. Buxbaum noted:

---

[*] Buxbaum read this paper at the Joint Meeting of the Psycho-Analytical Societies of Los Angeles and San Francisco, October 1949.

[†] Brill had been instrumental in getting New York State to establish a law giving physicians exclusive primacy to practice as psychoanalysts and lay analysts, called "nonmedical analysts," were only allowed to practice as "Psycho-Analytical Educators."

What seemed to be important in the process of ending this analysis was that the patient made the decision and set the time, being able to return to me when she wanted…Ending the analysis was perhaps the most important part of the analysis in this case. The patient was allowed to wean herself on a self-demand system, one might say, instead of being exposed to a repetition of the trauma of rejection. (p. 187)

See Grand (Chapter 9) for her patient's conception of ending, as well as Goldman (Chapter 15).

Another patient, whose painful memories from childhood surrounding her mother's remarriage and birth of a younger brother, evidenced and seemed to become enacted around terminating. After much work on this had occurred, Buxbaum wrote,

The patient turned to me in a different way, telling me that she knew many of her feelings were transference feelings, that some of these would probably remain to some degree but that she felt that aside from them there were some real feelings which had nothing to do with the analysis. My response to that was that I thought that was so and that analysts had feelings for their patients too. We parted on that note of mutual acceptance. (p. 188)

Further, Buxbaum encourages analysts to speak with patients on a reality level, helping the patient toward the end of the work to establish a real relationship:

We do in general credit patients with a great deal of unconscious understanding of the analyst's personality, which goes side by side with transference feelings. It seems to me in keeping with the analytic process, through which unconscious material becomes conscious, that such unconscious understanding of the analyst should become conscious too, even though a residue of transference may remain. (pp. 187–188)

Buxbaum's point of view moves away from the traditional perspective that maintained the analyst as the arbiter and one to decide the ending of treatment. Her affectively responsive approach to her patients seems consonant with a less hierarchical stance and a movement toward a more mutual dyadic relationship, without the analyst fearing indulging or seducing the patient.

Within the American literature, many of the papers written on termination have agreed with a checklist of criteria as a means of evaluating readiness to terminate. Symptom removal was deemed an unreliable indicator and one that could occur as part of the proverbial "flight into health." The lifting of repression and as a consequence infantile amnesia along with transference analysis had long been Freud's criterion, but with the influence of Hartmann (1939) and ego psychology, additional criteria now included lessening of defensive structure, enlarging of ego functioning, ameliorating a harsh superego, and thorough analyzing of the transference and coming to a realistic appraisal of the analyst (for excellent reviews of this literature, see Bergmann, 1997; Blum, 1989; Firestein, 1974, 1982; Novick, 1982). Glover (1955) was the first to propose an actual "termination phase" to the treatment. He believed that this phase was crucial in bringing the patient from a regressive experience in the analysis, to fully analyzing the transference, and thus having the patient come to see the analyst as a non-transference object in order to complete the work. Long analyses were also beginning to be frowned upon along with the idea of some patients having character problems not amenable to psychoanalysis—the "analyzability" issue. Ticho (1972) raised the topic of differentiation between treatment goals (the goals of the analyst) and life goals (the goals of the patient), indicating they may not always be the same.

In reviewing this literature, I am impressed by the legacy of Brill's establishment of American psychoanalytic policies and politics and what I would call a "medicalization" of Freud's work. By attempting to establish and protect psychoanalysis, Brill fiercely believed—and battled Freud whose own view opposed Brill—that its rightful place was as a medical specialty of psychiatry. Effectively, what this would and did accomplish was to organize theories of pathology into disease classifications, which could then be "treated," and only by psychiatrists, with the new therapeutic technique. The next logical step would include conceptions of therapeutic action in terms of "cure." If ending treatment is considered possible once the patient has been cured, then strict criteria as to what constitutes treatment and when that treatment is no longer necessary needs to be established and set by the physician. Brill wanted psychoanalysis to have the same status and authority as the medical profession.

Loewald (1962), in writing about internalization and termination, agreed with Klein that mourning is the central problem and task of termination. (Schafer, 2002, and Britton, 2006, also agree with the Kleinian view of termination as a mourning process.) Expanding on Freud's (1915) object relations formulation in "Mourning and Melancholia," loss, for Loewald, is structure building, growth producing, and therefore necessary. Loewald (1962) stated,

> Mourning involves not only the gradual, piecemeal relinquishment of the lost object, but also the internalization, the appropriation of aspects of this object—or rather, of aspects of the relationship between the ego and the lost object which are "set up in the ego" and become a relationship within the ego system. (p. 493)

In 1988, Loewald wrote further about termination and questioned whether we can analyze termination at all:

There remains the irreducible fact that precisely this form of experiencing and understanding itself is about to end, is itself about to become part of the historical past....During therapy, we say, everything is grist for the mill; but what if the mill itself is to be dismantled? (p. 156)

Given this, in Loewald's mind, termination is both problematic and yet a necessary part of the analytic process. Most analysts today would agree that loss is one of the many themes embedded within the complexity of how termination is dealt with.

Writing from within the interpersonal tradition, Levenson (1976) strikes a different chord in terms of ending. He likens terminating treatment to the work of artists, such as poets or painters suggesting that it is an "aesthetic" decision more than hard and fast criteria. He wrote,

There are some therapists who would agree with Valéry when he said of a poem, that it is never finished, it is only abandoned. There are others who take the opposite view: that every artist should have someone standing by with a mallet to hit him over the head when his painting is finished. In other words, therapy can be conceived of as having a definite end which should not be overextended; or, as having no end at all. (p. 338)

In 1982 *Psychoanalytic Inquiry* published a special issue on termination and included the following authors: Novick, Rangell, Siegel, Viorst, Limentani, Dewald, Gillman, and Firestein. As far as I can tell, this is the first invited collection of papers for publication on this topic, and it reflects a genuine effort to systematically attempt to conceptualize termination. Novick, who has written extensively on termination, explores and delineates seven major issues:

1. Types of termination: mutually agreed upon, forced or unilateral. Within this category he also looks at when the termination is timely or premature.
2. Preconditions for the terminal phase (drawing upon Glover and others in agreeing this is an important phase of treatment).
3. Criteria for beginning a terminal phase.
4. Technical considerations regarding start of the terminal phase.
5. Actual terminal phase.
6. Goals of the treatment.
7. The postanalytic phase.

His work is thoughtful and thorough and raised important questions that today are being considered in a different light. Specifically, who knows when it is time to end? Novick believed that the terminal phase would be known by the analyst's intuition and then he or she would start raising it with the patient. Although I very much appreciate the sensibility of intuition as an analytic tool and the move away from a strict medically informed set of criteria (although Novick uses that as well) to apprehend the dawn of the end of the work, the unquestioning belief in the authority of the analyst is the bedrock beneath this. Otherwise, why would the analyst intuit this any sooner or better than the patient, especially if the patient is approaching ending the work? Would we not hope that the patient may actually be as good a judge at this point as the analyst?

Also in this issue, Limentani, in reviewing his own notes on years of work with patients, describes a number of cases where unexpected termination had a profound impact, often untoward, on the patient and the work. Writing in a self-revealing and contemplative manner, Limentani reveals how trust is the core tie and issue with patients, and unanticipated disruptions erode and sometimes destroy basic trust. Additionally, three authors present small research findings: Gillman, Firestein, and Viorst. Firestein (1978), whose earlier work of interviewing eight analysands posttreatment, along with interviewing the analyst and faculty supervisor of each case, gave us great insight into the complexity of the termination process. In this issue, he again interviews 12 senior analysts. He focuses on the analyst's styles, techniques, and theoretical understandings of termination and ends with a strong appeal that more emphasis be placed on teaching termination in institutes and training programs, something that today is still at issue.

Many of the articles on termination in this issue of *Psychoanalytic Inquiry* still reflect an authoritative stance. I have contrasted this authoritative stance with articles that portray a less dogmatic position toward ending treatment as seen in the writings of Balint, Bergmann, Buxbaum, Milner, and Loewald, to name a few. The following is taken from another article in the issue by Viorst (1982):

> A patient is nearing the end of a lengthy analysis. The fantasy is that his analyst, who has a pair of tickets to an Isaac Stern concert, offers him one of the tickets as a gift. At the concert hall he sits beside the recipient of the analyst's other ticket, who turns out to be none other than the analyst's lovely, and unmarried, daughter. They talk, they start to date each other, they fall in love, and soon they are happily married—living, of course, not too far from daddy-analyst. A typical patient's fantasy? Not quite. The fantasy belongs not to the patient but to the analyst. At the end of an hour one day, the analyst found himself caught up in this pleasant reverie which, he explains, "both took care of my fatherliness and met the needs of my patient to hold onto me," (p. 399)

In her article, which was a write-up of her research on analyst's responses to termination, Viorst interviewed 20 analysts at great length. Her findings suggest and reinforce how difficult termination is for analysts. She reveals how difficult it is for analysts to anticipate their own countertransference reactions and yet how deeply felt and reparative working on these reactions can be for the analyst. One analyst, quoted,

> Says that termination is requiring him to work through, at a deeper level, his anger and disappointment regarding his own father. It will also, of course, require him to relinquish his gratifying good-son role, the loss of which, he now recognizes, "made me not eager to push termination forward." (p. 409)

Many of the analysts she quotes are learning a great deal about what had been, in Bollas's terms, "the unthought known." Viorst sees in some ways termination as the great equalizer, both participants have to give up unrealistic goals and grieve multiple losses. She ended the paper summing up:

> It is this integrative aspect of the analyst's response to loss that I found particular interest in my research. In several of the interview's the analysts—often to their own surprise—traced how they had used a patient's termination phase to resolve some piece of their own unfinished business: to work through the oedipal denigration of father, to relinquish the wish to undo mother's castration, to deal with guilt without resorting to self-betraying acts of reparation, to convert certain magical strivings into a useful and gratifying sublimation and in the one case to comfort and tame self-destructive narcissism. (Viorst, 1982, p. 417)

Despite the illuminating nature of this small research project, Viorst's finding does not get integrated into theoretical approaches to termination, but remains an interesting sidebar. What does seem to percolate throughout this issue of *Psychoanalytic Inquiry* are the effects of termination on the analyst. This is new terrain and suggests how complex the analyst's participation may be. It is interesting to note this, given the issue date of this journal (1982) and to remember that Greenberg and Mitchell's *Object Relations in Psychoanalytic Theory* was published the following year (1983). Change was in the air.

In 1993 at the Annual Spring Meeting of Division 39, a panel was given entitled "Go the Distance: Thoughts on Termination."* From this panel, Bergmann (1997) stands out, along with the earlier work of Blum (1989), as one of the few people willing to criticize the field for not having developed a

---

* The panel's papers were later compiled, along with other invited writers, for a special section on termination, with guest editors Lane and Hyman, in *Psychoanalytic Psychology*, 1997.

paradigm for termination. (Bergmann's paper continues to be an important work and for that reason has been reprinted and included as Chapter 2 in this book.) Bergmann believes this deficit is a direct result of the shadow of Freud: "Had we idealized Freud less, we would have realized earlier that psychoanalytic technique lacks anything like a 'royal road' toward termination" (p. 163). In a later paper, Bergmann (2005) elucidates further that a necessary criterion for termination rests on the analysand's ability to replace the analyst with an internal capacity for self-analysis. In this way, Bergmann believes that we, as analysts, need to help the patient develop the necessary ego strength to enable this kind of internalization.

Jack Novick also was on the Division 39 panel and continued his further consideration of the topic of termination still within a traditional framework (1988, 1997, 2006). As part of the later journal compilation, Novick (1997) raised a new angle from which to view the problems of termination. He suggested that our own reactions as the therapist/analyst to the concept of termination, what he refers to as the "resistances of analysts," have prevented us from both formulating a theory of termination and teaching it. He argues that this approach has made termination an "inconceivable" idea, which he traces back to Freud. The early forced terminations by Freud with analysands who later became analysts have instilled a kind of transgenerational transmission of traumatic endings embedded within the field. Novick maps an interesting history:

> As we know, Freud used the method of forcing a termination in the case of the Wolf Man....He had abruptly ended Helene Deutsch's analysis to make room for the Wolf Man's return to treatment in 1919. She in turn ended Margaret Mahler's analysis by proclaiming that Mahler was unanalyzable and summarily dismissed her. Ruth Mack Brunswick was known as a gifted clinician, a favorite of Freud's, and he sent the Wolf Man to her in 1926 for further treatment. But, as suggested by Rosenbaum (1987), Freud forced the ending of her analysis in the same way as he had ended the analysis of Deutsch and the Wolf Man. That is the way Ruth Brunswick ended the analysis of Muriel Gardiner, an important figure in the history of psychoanalysis, one of the last of the prewar generation of analytic students....The other great teacher who had an enormous influence on American psychoanalysis was Heinz Hartmann, and suffice to note that he was analyzed by Freud between 1934 and 1936. The generation of analysts influenced by Loewenstein, Hartmann, Deutsch, Mahler, Brunswick, Sachs and other European émigrés included Arlow and his colleague Charles Brenner, who together were responsible for the creation of mainstream American psychoanalysis. Brenner, in his book *Psychoanalytic Technique* (1976), stated that it is the analyst's responsibility to present the decision to

terminate to the patient, whether or not the patient has reached the same conclusion at the same time. (pp. 148–149)

He further believes that "we" analysts effectively bypass true termination by the fact that, like it or not, we see and interact with our former analysts and patients within our institutes and at professional gatherings. (Milner also suggested this as early as 1950.)

Novick, in my view, struck an important chord by both looking back to the early foreparents of psychoanalysis and then tracing the legacy of traumatic terminations across generations in our work and into our theories. What we bypass in the field is the necessary process of true mourning and loss, for both analyst and patient, inevitably limiting our conceptions of termination. This I would consider as the realm of the subjectivity of the analyst, which must be part of the mix when working with patients.

RELATIONAL AND CONTEMPORARY CONCEPTIONS

A relational perspective conceives of the analytic relationship as being mutual while asymmetrical and cocreated by the analytic dyad. Ending the treatment would then be an outgrowth of the mutual and differing experiences of a particular dyad. For the early relational writers, termination of the treatment was not in the forefront but was considered a natural outgrowth of theoretical and technical considerations. Stephen Mitchell (1993), in *Hope and Dread in Psychoanalysis,* believed that the ending of an analysis was unnatural but nonetheless necessary. Mitchell maintained that "Ending is necessary, if the analytic work is not to become a static alternative to a fully lived life" (p. 229). What Mitchell is reminding us to remain cognizant of is that ending the analysis is a benefit and a tool at our disposal. It is within ending that some of the necessary integrative work of analysis occurs, and only then can someone fully incorporate and put to use the gains they have made within the analysis. Further, in his book *Influence and Autonomy in Psychoanalysis*, Stephen Mitchell (1997; as well as Aron, 1996, Renik, 1993, and others) agreeing with Racker (1968), who believed that the patient's and analyst's dynamics inevitably interact, wrote, "If analytic work is deeply engaged, the patient always gets under the analyst's skin" (pp. 5–6). It follows that this would be part and parcel of the difficulties in ending the work. Mitchell (1993) also believed that "this subtle dialectical process [is] central to all analyses—the capacity to hear, hold, and play with an interpretation, neither surrendering to it as powerful magic nor rejecting it as dangerous poison—not as a criterion of analyzability but as a criterion of readiness to terminate" (p. 83).

In *Ritual and Spontaneity in the Psychoanalytic Process: A Dialectical-Constructivist View*, Hoffman (1998) sees ending within a developmental context. He wrote, "It's a matter of reaching a point where it seems desirable to end, to absorb the pain of real loss, in order to get that much better, in order to take what is mutually understood to be that further developmental step" (p. 257). He also argues the importance of the existential aspect of our own mortality as it relates to the sense of time and endings within the treatment relationship. He believes that avoidance of termination issues is a kind of grandiose maneuver to avoid the issue of death—the analyst's or the patient's. Ultimately Hoffman believes, as evidenced in his chapter on termination entitled "Constructing Good-Enough Endings in Psychoanalysis," that we cocreate with our patients the treatment and ending that fits the work (1998, chapter 10).

Although writing within a contemporary Freudian perspective, Orgel (2000) speaks of ending in a very intersubjective way. He wrote, "I want to focus on termination as the mutual decision of two people to leave an extraordinary day-to-day relationship" (p. 720). Later he stated, "I believe that insofar as an individual is capable of becoming significantly attached to another, and insofar as an analyst can bear to allow the attachment to deepen by appropriate, timely, nonbrutal, nonauthoritarian jargon-free interpretations of transference and resistance, no analytic pair ever gives up the relationship easily" (p. 724). We can hear the influence of relational ideas concerning the mutuality of the relationship as well as the impact of attachment research findings on the lived experience of this analyst. Orgel clearly knows that ending is complicated for the patient and for the analyst. He also believes that Freud never spoke about the mutual loss involved in ending because of Freud's inherent belief in the hierarchical nature of the treatment relationship. Relational theory, as influenced by postmodern ideas, questions the authority of the analyst and attempts to undo the hierarchy inherent in Freud's theories.

Davies (2005; Chapter 6, this volume) has written that termination can be viewed as an iteration of the concept of multiplicity; it is not one good-bye but numerous ones from each of the multiple self-states of both the patient and the analyst. She believes that the complex intersubjective matrix of loving and hating feelings, of vulnerabilities and anxieties, as well as the analyst's and the patient's defensive positions reemerge during this phase, along with the transformations that the analytic work has fostered. Therefore, the termination phase becomes that much more difficult for both participants to traverse, perhaps explaining why many analyses become either inextricably long or end by a forced situation, such as relocation due to work or new life situations such as, marriage, divorce, or death.

Although not writing from directly within a relational framework, Schlesinger (2005) adds complexity to the issue of termination. He offers the idea that a linear model does not do justice to the series of beginnings and mini-endings that occur across the work. He notes that patients can experience working through important material as a kind of ending with a sense of loss while also realizing that they are once again starting some new area, or investigating new material in their life. He proposes, in lieu of a linear model, a helix model that betters fits the cyclical nature of the work.

Bonovitz (2007) considers termination as a complex, messy enterprise. He believes that many of the concerns that get activated around termination are related to anxieties over one's own mortality (we can hear the influence of Hoffman's ideas in this regard) and also over a transference-laden parricide, the killing off of one's analyst/parent. In discussing the termination of a female patient, Bonovitz is attentive to and tells us of his own complicated participation while cocreating a particular ending. He slowly comes to realize that the patient "needs," as part of her analytic work, to leave him, something she had not been able to do with her own parents. (See Salberg, Chapter 7, this volume, for a discussion on helping patients to take leave of us.)

I believe it is vitally important to integrate attachment theory and research into our ideas regarding the ending of treatment. Some of this has begun to be addressed in a recent issue of *Psychoanalytic Inquiry* (2009). Specifically Craige (2002, 2009), in her research work on the posttermination phase of treatment, found that the mourning processes lasted between 6 and 12 months in most cases and that this was highly correlated with strong and positive attachment experience to the analyst/therapist. She believes that the greater sense of loss is indicative of this positive valued experience and suggests altering our ending technique as follows. She recommends that there be a mutual expression of the meaningfulness of the relationship and the ensuing loss. She supports this idea referencing the two-person psychology relational literature and the attachment findings. She further recommends that the analyst be available posttermination for phone or in-person follow-up sessions. I agree with her findings and recommendations as possible alterations as they fit the dyad. Some patients want and need to check in from time to time, some prefer not to.

Frank (2009) takes issue with the classical idea of a permanent separation as the landscape of termination. Frank and I are in agreement in viewing Craige's recommendations as valuable but rigid, or as Frank suggests, "prescriptive." He counsels: "When we approach analytic endings flexibly on a case-by-case basis, termination potentially becomes an opportunity to develop a unique ending that has the most appropriate meaning for the members of the analytic pair" (p. 151). What Frank posits is a fully relational, mutual, and cocreative process that translates into singularly distinctive endings with options.

A further indication of how timely reexamining termination has become is a recent article by Gabbard (2009). He tries to dismantle the analytic myth of a perfect analysis or termination, believing instead that we continue throughout our lives with internal struggles, such as depressive position issues. He further feels that it is accurate for the field to lack a paradigm for termination and that what we need are multiple scenarios for what would then be considered, in the vernacular of Winnicott, "good enough" endings. I am in agreement with much of this but feel that Gabbard, in discussing both one-person and two-person approaches to treatment, still seems to land on the side of the patient as the one struggling with termination. I can see his attempt to include the countertransference of the analyst, but then he does not want to "implicate" the analyst. In this way the patient carries the enactment potential: "The characteristic enactments of unconscious internal object relations continue to occur, but the patient who is in analysis begins to observe these relational patterns as they develop" (p. 586).

I would argue that in fact "we analysts," despite having once been "patients," have not necessarily gained immunization to such struggles—only experience. It is my contention that the ending of treatment is a struggle for analysts, as well as patients, and one that we do not necessarily have a high-ground perspective on. Many of us carry inner voices from our training—be they training analysts, supervisors, or mentors—whispering how much more work there is yet to be done. We also have our own attachments to our patients: the ones we feel we helped, or the ones we feel we still need to help, or even the ones we feel help us to be better versions of ourselves. Without a fuller exploration of the subjectivity of the analyst, the view and elucidation of how one terminates a treatment remains unidimensional, focused exclusively on the patient. Additionally, each patient creates a unique bond in treatment, as does each analyst. The ending of the treatment will need to be shaped by the distinctive fingerprint of the treatment. In this way, Gabbard (2009) is quite right asserting the need for a kind of multiplicity of endings. This would then match the multiplicity of selves that Davies (2005) has suggested need to come on stage to say good-bye at the end of treatment. Additionally, there are all sorts of issues involved in contemplating ending: attachment, gender, dependency, financial concerns, longings for authenticity, strivings for power, along with reparative hopes and destructive wishes. I believe an appreciation of this complexity is necessary and needs to be reflected in our theoretical writings. In this way, our clinical work informs and alters our theories, expanding the ways we reflect upon and then enter any current clinical moment.

REFERENCES

Aron, L., & Harris, A. (1993). *The legacy of Sándor Ferenczi*. Hillsdale, NJ: Analytic Press.

Aron, L. (1996). *A meeting of minds: Mutuality in psychoanalysis*. Hillsdale, NJ: Analytic Press.

Balint, M. (1950). On the termination of analysis. *The International Journal of Psycho-Analysis, 31*, 196–199.

Bergmann, M. (1997). Termination: The Achilles heel of psychoanalytic technique. *Psychoanalytic Psychology, 14,* 163–174.

Bergmann, M. (2005). Termination and reanalysis. In E. Person, A. N. Cooper, & G. Gabbard (Eds.), *Textbook of psychoanalysis* (pp. 241–253). Washington, DC: American Psychiatric Publishing.

Berry, N. (1987). The end of the analysis (D. Macey, Trans.). In J. Klauber, *Illusion and spontaneity in psychoanalysis* (pp. 99–130). London: Free Association Books.

Blum, H. P. (1989). The concept of termination and the evolution of psychoanalytic thought. *Journal of the American Psychoanalytic Association, 37,* 275–295.

Bonovitz, C. (2007). Termination never ends: The inevitable incompleteness of psychoanalysis. *Contemporary Psychoanalysis, 43,* 229–246.

Britton, R. (2005). There is no end of the line: Terminating the interminable. Paper presented at The Institute for Psychoanalytic Training and Research Conference—When Do We Terminate: The Concept of Termination Revisited, November 2005, New York.

Bromberg, P. (2006). *Awakening the dreamer: Clinical journeys.* Mahwah, NJ: Analytic Press.

Craige, H. (2002). Mourning analysis: The post-termination phase. *Journal of the American Psychoanalytic Association, 50,* 507–550.

Craige, H. (2009). Terminating without fatality. *Psychoanalytic Inquiry, 29,* 101–116.

Davies, J. M. (2005). Transformations of desire and despair: Reflections on the termination process. *Psychoanalytic Dialogues, 15*(6), 779–805.

Dupont, J. (1994). Freud's analysis of Ferenczi as revealed by their correspondence. *International Journal of Psychoanalysis, 75,* 301–320.

Falzeder, E., Brabant, E., & Giampieri-Deutsch, P. (2000). *The Correspondence of Sigmund Freud and Sándor Ferenczi* (Vol. 3), *1920–1933* (P. T. Hoffer, Trans.). Cambridge, MA: Belknap Press of Harvard University Press.

Fenichel, O. (1974). A review of Freud's "Analysis Terminable and Interminable." *International Journal of Psycho-Analysis, 1,* 109–116.

Ferenczi, S. (1927). The problem of termination of the analysis. In M. Balint (Ed.) & E. Mosbacher (Trans.), *Final contributions to the problems and methods of psycho-analysis* (pp. 77–86). London: Hogarth, 1955.

Ferenczi, S. (1988). *The clinical diary of Sándor Ferenczi* (J. Dupont, Ed.). Cambridge, MA: Harvard University Press.

Ferenczi, S., & Rank, O. (1925). *The development of psychoanalysis.* New York and Washington, DC: Nervous and Mental Disease Monograph Series (No. 40).

Firestein, S. (1974). Termination of psychoanalysis of adults: A review of the literature. *Journal of the American Psychoanalytic Association, 22,* 873–894.

Firestein, S. (1978). *Termination in psychoanalysis.* New York: International Universities Press.

Firestein, S. (1982). Termination of psychoanalysis: Theoretical, clinical and pedagogic considerations. *Psychoanalytic Inquiry, 2,* 473–497.

Frank, K. (2009). Ending with options. *Psychoanalytic Inquiry, 29,* 136–156.

Freud, S. (1915). Mourning and melancholia. In J. Strachey (Ed. & Trans.), *The standard edition of the complete psychological works of Sigmund Freud* (Vol. 14, pp. 243–258). London: Hogarth.

Freud, S. (1927) *The future of an illusion*. In J. Strachey (Ed. & Trans.), *The standard edition of the complete psychological works of Sigmund Freud* (Vol. 21, pp. 1–56). London: Hogarth.

Freud, S. (1937). Analysis terminable and interminable. In J. Strachey (Ed. & Trans.), *The standard edition of the complete psychological works of Sigmund Freud* (Vol. 23, pp. 211–253). London: Hogarth.

Gabbard, G. O. (2009). What is a "good enough" termination? *Journal of the American Psychoanalytic Association, 57*(3), 575–594.

Glover, E. (1955). *The technique of psycho-analysis*. New York: International Universities Press.

Greenberg, J. R., & Mitchell, S. A. (1983). *Object relations in psychoanalytic theory.* Cambridge, MA: Harvard University Press.

Hartmann, H. (1939) Psychoanalysis and the concept of health. In *International Journal of Psycho-Analysis, 20*, 308–321, and reprinted in H. Hartmann, *Essays on ego psychology* (pp. 3–18). New York: International Universities Press, 1964.

Hoffer, W. (1950). Three psychological criteria for the termination of treatment. *International Journal of Psycho-Analysis, 31*, 194–195.

Hoffman, I. Z. (1998). *Ritual and spontaneity in the psychoanalytic process: A dialectical-constructivist view.* Hillsdale, NJ: Analytic Press.

Klein, M. (1950). On the criteria for the termination of a psycho-analysis. *International Journal of Psycho-Analysis, 31*, 78–80.

Klein, M. (1957). Envy and gratitude. In *The Writings of Melanie Klein* (Vol. III): *Envy and gratitude and other works* (pp. 247–263). London: Hogarth, 1975.

Leupold-Löwenthal, H. (1987). Notes on Sigmund Freud's "Analysis Terminable and Interminable." In J. Sandler (Ed.), *On Freud's "Analysis Terminable and Interminable."* International Psychoanalytical Association Educational Monographs (No. 1).

Levenson, E. (1976). The aesthetics of termination. *Contemporary Psychoanalysis, 12*, 338–341.

Limentani, A. (1982). On the "unexpected" termination of psychoanalytic therapy. *Psychoanalytic Inquiry, 2*, 419–440.

Loewald, H. W. (1962). Internalization, separation, mourning and the superego. *Psychoanalytic Quarterly, 31*, 483–504.

Loewald, H. W. (1988). Termination analyzable and unanalyzable. *The Psychoanalytic Study of the Child, 43*, 155–166.

Milner, M. (1950). A note on the ending of an analysis. *International Journal of Psycho-Analysis, 31*, 191–193.

Mitchell, S. A. (1993). *Hope and dread in psychoanalysis*. New York: Basic Books.

Mitchell, S. A. (1997). *Influence and autonomy in psychoanalysis*. Hillsdale, NJ: Analytic Press.

Novick, J. (1982). Termination: Themes and issues. *Psychoanalytic Inquiry, 2*, 329–365.

Novick, J. (1988). The timing of termination. *International Review of Psycho-Analysis, 14*, 307–318.

Novick, J. (1997). Termination conceivable and inconceivable. *Psychoanalytic Psychology, 14*(2), 145–162.

Novick, J., & Novick, K. K. (2006). *Good goodbyes: Knowing how to end in psychotherapy and psychoanalysis*. New York: Jason Aronson.

Orgel, S. (2000). Letting go: Some thoughts about termination. *Journal of the American Psychoanalytic Association*, 48, 719–738.

Racker, H. (1968). *Transference and countertransference*. New York: International Universities Press.

Rank, O. (1924). *The trauma of birth*. London: Kegan Paul, 1929

Reich, A. (1950). On the termination of analysis. *International Journal of Psycho-Analysis*, 31, 179–183.

Renik, O. (1993). Analytic interaction: Conceptualizing technique in light of the analyst's irreducible subjectivity. *Psychoanalytic Quarterly*, 65, 495–517.

Richards, A. (1999). A. A. Brill and the politics of exclusion. *Journal of the American Psychoanalytic Association*, 47, 9–28.

Rickman, J. (1950). On the criteria for the termination of an analysis. *International Journal of Psycho-Analysis*, 31, 200–201.

Schlesinger, H. (2005). *Endings and beginnings: On terminating psychotherapy and psychoanalysis*. Hillsdale, NJ: Analytic Press.

Spezzano, C. (1995). "Classical" versus "contemporary theory: The differences that matter clinically. *Contemporary Psychoanalysis*, 31, 20–46.

Spezzano, C. (1997). The emergence of an American Middle School of psychoanalysis: Commentary of Karen Rosica's paper. *Psychoanalytic Dialogues*, 7, 603–618.

Ticho, E. (1972). Termination of psychoanalysis: Treatment goals, life goals. *Psychoanalytic Quarterly*, 41, 315–333.

Viorst, J. (1982). Experiences of loss at the end of analysis: The analyst's response to termination. *Psychoanalytic Inquiry*, 2, 399–418.

Chapter 2

Termination

The Achilles heel of psychoanalytic technique*

Martin Bergmann

The psychoanalytic literature dealing with termination is reviewed in support of the central idea of the author that psychoanalysis, and particularly the literature on technique, has so far failed to offer a paradigm for termination. As a result, psychoanalytic practitioners are left without guidelines as to how to bring the psychoanalytic process to an end. In the second part, the reasons and conditions that are responsible for the clinical fact that many analyses are not self-terminating are discussed. Two main reasons are given: Most wishes to terminate are reaction-formation against deeper dependency needs. In the course of psychoanalysis, these are eliminated as resistance, allowing repressed dependency needs to surface. Genuine wishes for independence are difficult to foster. For many analysands, transference love is the best love relationship that life has offered. Understandably, they are reluctant to give it up. In other analyses, the psychoanalyst has inadvertently entered into an equilibrium in the analysand's life. This too makes termination difficult. In real life, only death and hostility bring a libidinal relationship to an end. The kind of termination psychoanalysis demands is without precedent.

A HISTORICAL SURVEY AND STATEMENT OF THE PROBLEM

In retrospect, we should have been more surprised than we were that Freud's papers on technique never included one on termination. Had we idealized Freud less, we would have realized earlier that psychoanalytic technique lacks anything like a "royal road" toward termination. In the early days of psychoanalysis, there were only two kinds of terminations. Either the analysand interrupted the course of the analysis on his or her own—an act usually

---

* This chapter originally appeared in *Psychoanalytic Psychology, 14*, 1997, pp. 163–174. (Reprinted with permission.)

attributed to the analysand's resistance, or the analyst at some unspecified date informed the analysand that the analysis was finished or coming to an end. How many analysands never finish their analysis, we do not know, but we do know that Dorothy Burlingham's (1989) analysis with Sigmund Freud continued for many years, daily, until close to Freud's death.

Hurn (1971) and Blum (1989) concluded that psychoanalysis lacks a paradigm for termination. Blum (1989) found:

> During Freud's lifetime there was an opening and middle phase of clinical analysis. There was no description of a concluding or terminating phase in an otherwise open-ended, timeless analytic process.... Termination had not been taught or supervised in analytic training. Prior to 1950 it had been assumed that anyone who could conduct analysis properly could terminate it correctly. A terminated case was not required for institute graduation, nor for certification in the American Psychoanalytic Association. (pp. 275, 283)

The first psychoanalysts to address difficulties in termination were Ferenczi and Rank (1924). In keeping with Freud's (1914) idea that during psychoanalysis the infantile neurosis is transformed into a transference neurosis, they advocated that the analyst should set the termination date the moment this transformation occurs. They believed that only then could a repetition of clinging to the early object be avoided. The termination date must be set this early if fixation on the mother is not to give way to transference fixation. They advocated that analysis must end before it can become a vehicle for the repetition-compulsion.

Ferenczi (1927/1955) published the first psychoanalytic article devoted to the process of termination:

> • The proper ending of an analysis is when neither the physician nor the patient put an end to it, but when it dies of exhaustion .... A truly cured patient frees himself from analysis slowly but surely; so long as he wishes to come to analysis he should continue to do so....The patient finally becomes convinced that he is continuing analysis only because he is treating it as a new but still a fantasy source of gratification, which in terms of reality yields him nothing. (p. 85)

He emphasized that neurotics will relapse into illness after termination as long as reality and fantasy are not rigidly separated.

In subsequent psychoanalytic literature, it was Ferenczi rather than Rank who was always quoted when the desire to return to the womb was considered an important unconscious wish, as one can see today in the writings of Bela Grunberger (1971/1979) and Janine Chasseguet-Smirgel (1986). The type of ending that Ferenczi advocated was revived by Goldberg and

Marcus (1985) and called "natural termination." After the publication of Ferenczi's diary (1988), it is easy to see that Ferenczi's view of termination was already influenced by his feeling of disappointment in his analysis with Freud.

Arlow (1991) believes that Freud's (1937) "Analysis Terminable and Interminable" is a contribution to technique. Rather, it is an argument against Ferenczi's reproach that Freud failed to bring his analysis to a satisfactory conclusion, and a philosophical statement expressing Freud's belief in the death instinct and other forces limit analyzability. Freud regarded penis envy in women and passivity in men as a "rock bottom" that is immune to psychoanalytic change. In discussing the Wolf Man, Freud noted, "It was a case of treatment inhibiting itself. It was in danger of failing as a result of its partial success" (p. 217). Premature terminations happen because the good is the enemy of the better.

In 1937, ego psychology had only recently begun. It is striking to see how much weight Freud assigned to the abnormal ego that treats recovery as a danger. He maintained that psychoanalysis achieved its best results when the ego of the patient has not been significantly deformed by the neurotic illness. Mistakenly he thought that this is the case in traumatic neurosis (1937, p. 220).

In the optimistic phase prior to "Analysis Terminable and Interminable," psychoanalysts were preoccupied with what psychoanalysis should achieve rather than what it can achieve. Nunberg (1932/1955) devoted the last page of his book to the changes that should be brought about through analysis. Termination results when (a) what was hitherto unconscious becomes conscious; (b) the representations of the instinct enter consciousness more easily and consequently the id is under less tension; (c) the ego that does not have to spend energy on defenses becomes stronger; (d) fantastic thinking subject to primary process is replaced by realistic thinking subject to secondary process; (e) the ego is enriched through assimilation of repressed material; and (f) the severity of the superego is mitigated tolerating the repressed. It is not difficult to see that these were idealized statements rather than empirical observations.

In keeping with his paper, "The Synthetic Functions of the Ego" (1930), Nunberg stressed that the ego brings the striving of the id into accord with the demands of the superego. In this view, the strengthening of the ego brings peace where intrapsychic conflict had reigned. The unification of Germany and Italy, still fresh in memory, served as a model for this thinking.

Glover (1955) devoted two chapters to the terminal phase. There he observed that "the opportunities of watching a classical analysis coming to a classical termination are much less frequent than is generally supposed" (p. 140). The reason such terminations are rare is that many analytic cases never go beyond transference manifestations, and unless a transference neurosis takes hold, a classical termination was thought by Glover to be impossible. The great majority of analyses end for external reasons, when a symptomatic improvement occurs, or when the patient defeats the analyst in an oedipal struggle expressed in a premature termination.

In the same volume, Glover published the results of an extensive questionnaire submitted to members of the British Psychoanalytic Society. The majority admitted that their criteria were intuitive. In 1968, a similar oral survey of senior analysts in the United States was presented at the annual meeting of the American Psychoanalytic Association in Boston (Firestein, 1969). The results were fascinating in their diversity.

A somber attitude is found in Waelder's (1960) elementary book on psychoanalysis. He stated:

> If the scientific goal of psychoanalysis is the complete understanding of a person's psychic life, normal and pathological and a complete reconstruction of the development of the personality, no analysis is ever complete. From a therapeutic point of view, when the pathological structures have been understood both dynamically and genetically, if all has been worked through and the psychopathology has disappeared or become controllable, therapeutic termination has been achieved. In actual practice this is not always possible. Psychoanalysis should therefore be terminated when one has reached the point of diminishing returns. (pp. 242–243)

This echoes Freud's statement (1937, p. 219) that analysis should terminate when it reaches a stage where no further change could be expected.

In his monograph *The Theory of Psychoanalytic Technique*, Karl Menninger (1958) devoted the end of a chapter to "the termination of the contract, the separation of the two parties," where he expressed surprise at the vast difference of opinion about the average length of an analysis. He designates as tragic, or even farcical, analyses that last over 10 years. In Menninger's view, termination begins when a change of direction has taken place from regression to progression. A series of insights combine to usher in the termination phase. The analysand realizes that in many respects, he has never grown up and will always be unsatisfied when he compares himself to certain memories and fantasies. The love he sought from the analyst he is now ready to seek elsewhere. He recognizes that the analysis did not fulfill his wishes but did what was needed for him to reach a better understanding of himself:

> I have gotten what I paid for; I can do for myself. I can assume a mature role in preference to one of expectant pleading; I can substitute hoping for despairing, enjoying for expecting, giving for taking. I can endure foregoing what must be foregone and accept and enjoy without guilt such pleasures as are accessible to me. (p. 159)

A review of the literature on termination in psychoanalysis (Firestein, 1978) shows, if read critically, that there is disagreement about the "when" as well as the "how." Most papers discuss what analysis should achieve rather than what it does achieve. Warnings to psychoanalysts abound in this literature. We should beware of "symptomatic cure," "flight into health," and "transference cure."

In the first international congress after World War II, an important symposium on termination took place. I have observed that most psychoanalytic schools are initially far more certain of the result they can obtain than they are later in their development. The symposium showed that by that time, ideas of termination were cast in terms of the different schools that had come into existence. Melanie Klein (1950) emphasized that the analyst is introjected into the analysand as a persecutory as well as idealized object. The split between the two must diminish if a reliable termination is to be reached. Only then can good objects as distinguished from idealized objects be securely established. This view advocates a permanent resolution of the conflict that can withstand the test of time.

Although psychoanalytic ego psychology stressed the significance of attaining secondary ego autonomy and the enlargement of the conflict-free sphere of the ego, Hartmann (1939) lowered the sights by noting that "a healthy person must have the capacity to suffer anxiety and to be depressed" (p. 6). Aarons (1965), following in Hartmann's footsteps, suggested that "the analysand's ego functions must attain a position of maximum secondary autonomy." Similarly, Zetzel (1965) stated that "the analyst as an object for continued object ego identification must be retained within the area of autonomous ego functions" (p. 50).

Under the influence of Arlow and Brenner (1964), the entire vocabulary of the Hartmann era, with its emphasis on secondary autonomy and conflict-free spheres, was pushed aside. The aim of analysis shifted to bring about a change from pathological compromise formation to a relatively healthy one.

Brenner (1976) asked when an analysis should be terminated, or how much one should expect to alter a patient's psychic conflict for the better (p. 173). He answered that it is a question of balancing pros and cons, for symptoms often disappear as do characterological problems, "but psychic conflict that results from instinctual wishes never disappears" (p. 176).

I interpret Brenner's remark to mean that the beneficial results of psychoanalysis cannot be looked upon as a permanent achievement. What has in fact been achieved is a balance of forces that hold true for certain conditions but can be overturned in less favorable ones. Brenner's view mirrors the circumstances of our outer world, for we now believe less in the permanence of any social order.

Within the Brennerian orbit, termination is arbitrary, but the statement that psychic conflict never disappears, although true, must be modified in practical terms. The conflict ceases to be significant when (a) it is no longer expressed in symptoms or character traits; (b) misuse of reality as an arena for the expression of intrapsychic conflict has come to an end; or (c) anxiety and depressive affects no longer dominate the intrapsychic picture. This can happen only when the ego, in Nunberg's (1930) earlier formulation, is strong enough to dominate the other intrapsychic agencies. Under Brenner's (1976) influence, we have to recognize that health is not the peaceful state of Pax Romana, but the result of a new ego dictatorship over other components of the personality. The power of basic fantasies over a person has been broken, but they still exist and may at some future date rebel against the ego.

Arlow's (1969) growing emphasis on the significance of unconscious fantasy function, and the view that unconscious fantasies are hierarchically organized like different editions of a book around a small number of infantile wishes, also influenced thinking on termination. Abend (1988) urged a greater emphasis on specific fantasies that arise when the termination phase is considered. He suggested that as long as the wish to terminate is fueled by unconscious fantasies, the termination is bound to be premature. He noted, however, that these termination fantasies do not always emerge with sufficient clarity, leaving a residue of primary process fantasies associated with termination.

How can termination best be achieved? Fleming and Benedek (1966), in keeping with the ethos prevalent in the 1960s, emphasized mutual agreement rather than the psychoanalyst setting an arbitrary date. They felt setting a date in advance activated the mourning process, which is the very essence of the termination work. Their views were influential and echoed in subsequent literature.

Most analyses terminate at the end of the analytic year or when the analysand embarks upon a new life goal such as a new job, marriage, or the birth of a child. However, such termination has been criticized as being based on an outer rather than an inner state. Loewald (1962), like Fleming and Benedek, stressed that the replacement of the real analyst by an internalized one can only be achieved through a process of mourning. What needs emphasis is that, without the support and presence of the analyst, mourning may turn into depression or hostility toward the analyst after termination.

A decisive new step in the real world tends to eliminate the mourning process. Because so many analysands cannot terminate, Kubie (1968) suggested that the work of termination be undertaken by a new analyst. To bring psychoanalysis closer to life, many analysts have resorted to a termination based on weaning. Stone (1961) suggested that, in certain cases at least, the process of weaning be emulated by the gradual reduction of hours.

In an article written in 1969, I suggested that impending termination is often communicated by a dream. In such situations, dreams are reported because the patient can communicate only in code. It is an indication of inner conflict (p. 363). Following the primary process, a dream can express both a wish to leave and a fear of loss. This was emphasized by Bond, Franco, and Richards (1992). They devoted a chapter in their book to "indicators of pretermination as revealed in dreams" and another to "the good termination dream."

In summary, there are several reasons the termination date should be set in advance. The first is to wait out the elation often associated with termination and allow the mourning process to be worked through. The second is a growing belief that there are specific primary process fantasies associated with termination that require time to emerge. These fantasies have a tendency to remain repressed until the analysand is convinced he or she really is terminating. A third function of the termination process is to assist the ego in accepting the reality principle and relinquishing hopes for a glorious termination that is beyond the capacity of the ego (Orens, 1955).

I am fully aware that no historical survey can be free from the bias of the summarizer. My aim in citing the literature was to confirm that psychoanalysis never developed the technique of termination to the same level as transference analysis or analysis of defenses. If my argument is convincing, then my title "The Achilles Heel" is justified.

WHY PSYCHOANALYSIS NEED NOT BE A SELF-TERMINATING PROCESS

Psychoanalysis is the only significant human relationship that terminates abruptly. In real life, we encounter three types of termination of human relationships: geographical separation, transformation of a friendly or love relationship into a hostile one, and death. The analysand, however, is supposed to bring about separation under conditions of love and gratitude. All life experience runs against such a termination. To be sure, the child separates from the parent, but this separation occurs in stages and is never complete. Psychoanalysis makes demands on internalization that are not asked for in any other human relationship.

By analyzing defenses, the analytic process eliminates the neurotic wishes to terminate; the analysis exposes fear of reliance on the analyst, a host of paranoid fears, and finally works through the fear of many analysands that they will be forsaken. When this stage of security and trust is reached, a passive regression within the analysis becomes possible. We can then hope for a new beginning with a genuine nondefensive separation process. In practical terms, it is easier to terminate an analysis if the possibility of a newer love relationship or a reordering of an older love relationship is realistically possible. When this is not the case, termination is more difficult, as there is less for the analysand to gain.

There are analysands for whom transference love, in spite of its lack of physical intimacy, is the best love relationship they ever had because of the potentialities for fantasy and idealization. When at some point the analyst feels no new insights are forthcoming and pressures the analysand to terminate, the analysis may terminate but the analysand quickly seeks a new analyst so the state of transference love can continue.

I indicated (Bergmann, 1987) that the selection of a love object depends on two different capacities. There is the capacity to combine the refinding of an old love object with the capacity to hope that the new love object will heal the wounds the old one inflicted. It is also dependent on the ego's capacity to tolerate a compromise formation where the selected object is good enough, even though it falls short of all one's wishes. When neither the first nor the second condition is attainable, transference love will be preferred to love in real life.

Under such conditions, there is great pressure on the analysand to start a new analysis. Given that analysts today are divided into warring schools, the analysand is likely to find a sympathetic analyst of a different school who will agree that the limitations of his previous analysis were due to the previous analyst's school. New hope is kindled, and a new beginning will be made that may or may not result in a better termination.

In a previous publication (Bergmann, 1988), I observed that Annie Reich (1958) was the first to recognize that transference may not always be resolvable. This is particularly true when the analyst represents "the first really reliable object relationship in the patient's life" (p. 236). I emphasized that in many cases, the state of transference love may not successfully translate into a capacity to love in real life. Because the analyst makes fewer demands on the analysand than persons in real life and asks for less reciprocity, many people can develop transference love but are incapable of translating it into real life. I (Bergmann, 1988) further noted:

> Every analysand enters analysis with some combination of primary process fantasies of what the analysis will accomplish and realistic secondary process realizable hopes. As the transference deepens and transference neurosis gains in strength, the primary processes become increasingly important. However, the decision to terminate, if it is not faulty or premature, is by its very nature a secondary process decision. (p. 149)

We learned from Freud (1905, p. 222) that all findings are refindings. To the extent to which the analyst has become "a primary love object," the analysand, upon termination, may look to refind a love object modeled after the analyst. Such transfer may or may not be appropriate from the point of view of the ego, for example, when an analyzed woman finds a much older person because the analyst was old. Dewald (1982) stressed that successful termination requires the process of mourning on the part of the analysand as well as the analyst. A too-early refinding of a new object often results if the analysand is trying to avoid the mourning process. Novick (1982) deepened our understanding of the termination process when he stated: "It is not the analyst as a real or transference object who is relinquished and mourned, but a part of the self, often the infantile self which is guiltily discarded." Loewald (1988) also stressed mourning as the key to termination. But he added the important observation that in some cases, the transference neurosis comes into full bloom under the pressure of the vacillation to terminate or not to terminate. For at that moment, the past becomes acutely alive. It is during this period of threatening termination that passive homosexual wishes may emerge for the first time. Thus, the prolonged analysis that never reaches the termination phase shields the analysand from many painful feelings and deepening insights.

If we move from a one-person psychology to a two-person psychology, as Balint (1969/1979) suggested, we will note that both analysts and analysands must contend with two opposing forces. The first is the struggle against a utopian solution, the high expectation that both have about what psychoanalysis ought to achieve rather than what it realistically can achieve. The other and opposite danger is of a premature loss of faith, as succumbing to a depression or a sense of defeat before the repetition-compulsion. Both patient and analyst may be in danger of bowing prematurely before the power of the repetition-compulsion or of the superego of the analysand that does not permit progression beyond a certain point. Often, this point is reached when the analysand senses that his or her capacity for enjoying life or success have gone past what the analyst has achieved. An analysand may terminate the analysis out of fear of an oedipal victory. Cases of such clinical stalemates are frequently discussed in supervision and clinical seminars. New insights into a case gained by the therapist often bring about a new hope of curability.

We should differentiate between preconditions for psychoanalysis and preconditions for termination of analysis. Many analysands develop the capacity for free association, are capable of expressing and utilizing transference interpretations, and do well in analyzing their dreams. Yet they are unable to terminate because the preconditions for termination are very different from those for analyzability. Unfortunately, we cannot judge ahead of time whether a given analysand will develop the capacity to replace the analyst by self-analysis and continue his or her inner development after termination. Our theory assumes that the analyst is a fantasy object, and when the power of fantasy recedes, real objects offering mutuality and real gratification will be sought, but this is not always true in all situations.

I wish to emphasize one further aspect of the problem that has not, to my knowledge, been discussed in the literature on termination. Most patients seek psychotherapy or psychoanalysis when a preexisting equilibrium in their lives has ended for outer or inner reasons. The disequilibrium has evoked feelings of anxiety or depression, and analytic help is sought because the patient alone cannot find a new balance. It happens quite frequently that the analysis helps establish an equilibrium.

For example, an analysand enters analysis because of unbearable marital conflict or because of conflict between the marriage and extramarital relationships. The analysis establishes a new equilibrium, and instead of extramarital relationships, the analysand now finds that he or she can tolerate the marriage, provided the complaints about the marital partner and some of the love feelings frustrated in the marriage can be directed toward the analyst. The analyst as the other love object is more acceptable and safer than an extramarital love object. When this situation is not understood, or even if it is understood and subject to psychoanalysis, it may still happen that the restoration of a new equilibrium without the analyst's participation is beyond the capacity of analyst and patient to achieve. This can result in a prolonged analysis or, if the analysis is terminated, the preexisting analytic equilibrium demands refinding. Because human perfection is never obtained, the analysand will seek the lost equilibrium by a new analysis.

In the hopeful cases, it is the new ego, as Nunberg (1930) has foreseen, that brings about termination in its quest for a richer life after termination. But we may not always be able to effect this. The ego's capacity to bring about termination is a new and highly complex ego function that must be implanted, nurtured, and supported by the analyst throughout the duration of the analysis. Freud (1937) recognized many of the forces that limited the power of psychoanalysis. To these we must add another: the inability of many to acquire the necessary ego strength for termination. If we do not succeed in fostering this capacity, we face the danger of the sorcerer's apprentice, who can cast the spell but does not know how to bring the magic he has evoked to an end.

Particularly difficult, but also deeply moving, are the former analysands who return to us when they are confronted with terminal illness. Now the aim is no longer cure, but to die in close relationship with a person who did not disappoint the analysand. Such returns, which incidentally occur more frequently when the analyst grows older, represent the final battle between libido and aggression. As the life force begins to ebb, these returning analysands have convinced me with particular force that the analyst remains the libidinal object often of last resort.

In spite of the large literature on termination, no paradigm of termination has been made part of the professional equipment of the psychoanalytic practitioner. In this absence, the psychoanalyst is under the pressure of his superego to terminate treatment, often prematurely, to escape the inner accusation that he exploits the analysand for libidinal or financial purposes. At the same time, he is under the opposite pressure, based on the idealization of psychoanalysis, that more would have been achieved had he or she been more experienced or knowledgeable. Though there are general signs that the analysand has entered the termination phase, the termination moment is still a matter of art rather than science. Some analysts and analysands are better at guessing when the optimal point has been reached than others. Premature terminations and unproductively prolonged analyses cannot, at the present time at least, be avoided.

REFERENCES

Aarons, Z. (1965). On analytic goals and criteria for termination. *Bulletin of the Philadelphia Association for Psychoanalysis, 15*, 97–109.

Abend, S. M. (1988). Unconscious fantasies and issues of termination. In H. Blum, Y. Kramer, A. K. Richards, and A. D. Richards (Eds.), *Unconscious fantasy, myth and reality: Essays in honor of Jacob A. Arlow, MD* (pp. 149–165). Madison, CT: International Universities Press.

Arlow, J. A., & Brenner, C. (1964). *Psychoanalytic change and the structural theory.* New York: International Universities Press.

Arlow, J. A. (1969). Unconscious fantasy and disturbances of conscious experience. *Psychoanalytic Quarterly, 38*, 1–27.

Arlow, J. A. (1991). Perspective on Freud's "Analysis terminable and interminable" after 50 years. In J. Sandler (Ed.), *On Freud's "Analysis terminable and interminable"* (pp. 73–88). New Haven, CT: Yale University Press.

Balint, M. (1979). *The basic fault.* New York: Brunner/Mazel. (Original work published 1969)

Bergmann, M. S. (1966). The intrapsychic and communicative aspects of the dream: Their role in psycho-analysis and psychotherapy. *International Journal of Psycho-Analysis, 47*, 356–363.

Bergmann, M. S. (1987). *The anatomy of loving.* New York: Columbia University Press.

Bergmann, M. S. (1988). On the fate of the intrapsychic image of the psychoanalyst after termination of the analysis. *Psychoanalytic Study of the Child, 43*, 137–153.

Blum, H. P. (1989). The concept of termination and the evolution of psychoanalytic thought. *Journal of the American Psychoanalytic Association, 37*, 275–295.

Bond, A., Franco, D., & Richards, A. (1992). *Dream portrait: A study of nineteen sequential dreams as indicators of pretermination.* Madison, CT: International Universities Press.

Brenner, C. (1976). *Psychoanalytic technique and psychic conflict.* New York: International Universities Press.

Burlingham, M. J. (1989). *The last Tiffany: A biography of Dorothy Tiffany Burlingham.* New York: Atheneum.

Chasseguet-Smirgel, J. (1986). *Sexuality and mind: The role of the father and the mother in the psyche.* New York: New York University Press.

Dewald, P. A. (1982). The clinical importance of the termination phase. *Psychoanalytic Inquiry, 2*, 441–461.

Ferenczi, S. (1955). The problem of termination of the analysis. In *Final contributions to the problems and methods of psycho-analysis* (pp. 77–86). London: Hogarth. (Original work published 1927)

Ferenczi, S. (1988). *The clinical diary of Sándor Ferenczi* (J. Dupont, Ed.). Cambridge, MA: Harvard University Press. (Original work published 1985)

Ferenczi, S., & Rank, O. (1924). *The development of psychoanalysis.* New York: Nervous and Mental Disease Publishing.

Firestein, S. K. (1969). Problems of termination in the analysis of adults. *Journal of the American Psychoanalytic Association, 17*, 222–237.

Firestein, S. (1978). *Termination in psychoanalysis.* New York: International Universities Press.

Fleming, J., & Benedek, T. (1966). *Psychoanalytic supervision.* New York: Grune & Stratton.

Freud, S. (1905). *Three essays on the theory of sexuality.* In J. Strachey (Ed. & Trans.), *The standard edition of the complete psychological works of Sigmund Freud* (Vol. 7, pp. 135–245). London: Hogarth.

Freud, S. (1914). *On narcissism: An introduction.* In J. Strachey (Ed. & Trans.), *The standard edition of the complete psychological works of Sigmund Freud* (Vol. 14, pp. 73–102). London: Hogarth.

Freud, S. (1937). Analysis, terminable and interminable. In J. Strachey (Ed. & Trans.), *The standard edition of the complete psychological works of Sigmund Freud* (Vol. 23, pp. 209–254). London: Hogarth.

Glover, E. (1955). *The technique of psychoanalysis.* New York: International Universities Press.

Goldberg, A., & Marcus, D. (1985). "Natural termination": Some comments on ending analysis without setting a date. *Psychoanalytic Quarterly, 54*, 46–65.

Grunberger, B. (1979). *Narcissism.* New York: International Universities Press. (Original work published 1971)

Hartmann, H. (1939). Psychoanalysis and the concept of health. In *Essays on ego psychology* (pp. 3–18). New York: International Universities Press.

Hurn, H. T. (1971). Toward a paradigm of the terminal phase: The current status of the terminal phase. *Journal of the American Psychoanalytic Association, 19*, 332–348.

Klein, M. (1950). On the criteria for termination of a psychoanalysis. In *Envy and gratitude and other works* (pp. 43–47). New York: Delacorte.

Kubie, L. S. (1968). Unsolved problems in the resolution of the transference. *Psychoanalytic Quarterly, 37*, 331–352.

Loewald, H. W. (1962). Internalization, separation, mourning, and the superego. *Psychoanalytic Quarterly, 31*, 483–504.

Loewald, H. W. (1988). Termination analyzable and unanalyzable. *Psychoanalytic Study of the Child, 43*, 155–166.

Menninger, K. A. (1958). *Theory of psychoanalytic technique.* New York: Basic Books.

Novick, J. (1982). Termination: Themes and Issues. *Psychoanalytic Inquiry, 2*, 329–365.

Nunberg, H. (1930). The synthetic functions of the ego. In *Practice and theory of psychoanalysis* (pp. 120–136). New York: International Universities Press.

Nunberg, H. (1955). *Principles of psychoanalysis.* New York: International Universities Press. (Original work published 1932)

Orens, M. (1955). Setting a termination date: An impetus to analysis. *Journal of the American Psychoanalytic Association*, *3*, 661–665.

Reich, A. (1958). A special variations on technique. In *Psychoanalytic contributions* (pp. 236–249). New York: International Universities Press.

Stone, L. (1961). *The psychoanalytic situation: An examination of its development and essential nature*. New York: International Universities Press.

Waelder, R. (1960). *Basic theory of psychoanalysis*. New York: International Universities Press.

Zetzel, E. R. (1965). The theory of therapy in relation to a developmental model of the psychic apparatus. *International Journal of Psycho-Analysis*, *46*, 39–52.

Chapter 3

There is no end of the line

Terminating the interminable

Ronald Britton

"There is no end of the line" in analysis—only the final stopping place at which the analyst gets off. The analytic process does not end for the patient when the sessions end, and the concern of both analyst and patient is that the further journey can be accomplished by the patient without the analyst. I will later in this paper liken this to the transition that takes place in Bunyan's *The Pilgrim's Progress* (1907) when he loses his companion Faithful, the personification of Faith, and survives only by finding a replacement Hopeful. He is the personification of hope who has been made into Hopeful by observing the adventures and vicissitudes of the Pilgrim and Faithful.

However, I will first review the issues of termination in Freud and Klein and then, using some clinical material of my own, try to look at the necessary conversion of circular analytic movement into linear development for the ending of analysis. I turn first to Freud's paper "Analysis Terminable and Interminable" (1937) and then Melanie Klein's paper "On the Criteria for the Termination of a Psycho-Analysis" (1950).

Freud's paper, written 3 years before his death, has a distinctly valedictory quality. Uncharacteristically for Freud, it is not very well organized and it is a mixture of review, restatement, and revision. As ever, realism and truthfulness are given pride of place, which is the strength of the paper, but it seems as if he was haunted by some feelings of failure and preoccupied with the limitations of analysis rather than its successes. He wrote, "It looks as if analysis were the third of those impossible professions in which one can be sure beforehand of achieving unsatisfying results. The other two, which have been known much longer, are education and government" (p. 248).

I think there are two particular analytic ghosts that haunt the paper: the analysis of Ferenczi and that of Freud's daughter, Anna. The last section is almost like a postscript to a letter to Ferenczi written after his death. Ferenczi, according to Jones (1937, p. 221), featured in Freud's paper anonymously as the patient described as "The man who had been analyzed [apparently successfully, who] became antagonistic [years later] to the analyst and reproached him for having failed to give him a complete analysis," because sufficient "attention was not given to the possibility of a negative transference" (pp. 221–222). Freud defended himself by suggesting that "it was not currently active in the patient himself at the time" (p. 222).

Also included in Freud's reflections on past cases in this paper is that of the Wolf Man, who reentered analysis with Freud and subsequently with Ruth Mack Brunswick. Reading her subsequent account of her impressive later analysis, I am struck by the unanalyzed negative transference to Freud that surfaced in the subsequent analysis. This is not to claim that we know better, but we can profit from others' mistakes as well as our own. If we are able to see these things, it is because of what Freud taught us. It must often be the case that great innovators cannot so easily incorporate the implications of their own new theories into their already existing technique as those who follow them. I will later in this paper say something the same of Melanie Klein, who having described projective identification did not really incorporate its technical ramifications and implications into her analytic work.

By the time Freud wrote "Analysis Terminable and Interminable" in 1937, his elucidation of the superego and the enormous significance of internalization in mourning had given rise to a surge in psychoanalytic understanding, but neither have much part in this discussion of the factors determining success in analysis. He reminds his readers that he has adopted a model in which a destructive instinct coexists with a life instinct, so that internal conflict remains inevitable, but he does not really apply it in this paper. Freud sounds discouraged and isolated from colleagues on the subject of the death instinct and turns to the Ancient Greek philosopher Empedocles for moral support. He writes, "I am well aware that the dualistic theory according to which an instinct of death or destruction or aggression claims equal rights as a partner with Eros as manifested in the libido, has found little sympathy and has not really been accepted even among psychoanalysts" (p. 244). It does not play much part in his discussion of termination or the relation between ego and the internal forces it needs to tame, or any part in the discussion of the alteration of the ego and its relation to the id. However, another sentence captures his profound sense of the eternal struggle of the human condition.

"One feels inclined to doubt sometimes," Freud (1937) wrote, "whether the dragons of primeval days are really extinct" (p. 229). "Every normal person" he wrote, "in fact is only normal on the average. His ego approximates to that of the psychotic in some part or other and to a greater or lesser extent" (p. 235). Anyone familiar with Bion would recognize that sentence as anticipating his ideas about the psychotic and nonpsychotic parts of the personality.

I think this notion that the archaic remains latent in us all was a motif that persisted in Freud's writing from quite early stages. For example, in his "Thoughts for the Times on War and Death" (1915), even before he formally adopted the concept of the destructive instinct, he wrote,

[Our] loved ones are on the one hand an inner possession, components of our own ego; but on the other hand they are partly strangers, even enemies. With the exception of only a very few situations, there adheres to the tenderest and most intimate of our love-relations a small portion of hostility which can excite an unconscious death wish. (p. 298)

He concluded this passage with these comments: "...our unconscious is just as inaccessible to the idea of our own death, just as murderously inclined towards strangers, just as divided (that is ambivalent) towards those we love, as was primeval man" (p. 299).

His comment in his termination paper that "one feels inclined to doubt sometimes whether the dragons of primeval days are really extinct" has an echo in one of Melanie Klein's (1958) last papers, when she surprised some of her followers by harking back to her own early ideas on archaic objects suggesting that they continued to exist outside the superego in some untamed, unmodified form:

Even under (such) favourable conditions, terrifying figures in the deep layers of the unconscious make themselves felt when internal or external pressure is extreme. People who are on the whole stable—and that means that they have firmly established their good object and therefore are closely identified with it—can overcome this intrusion of the deeper unconscious into their ego and regain their stability. In neurotic, and still more in psychotic individuals, the struggle against such dangers threatening from the deeper layers of the unconscious is to some extent constant and part of their instability or their illness. (pp. 242–243)

Her phrase, "people who are on the whole stable," who can overcome this intrusion and regain their stability, sounds like a prescription for a desirable outcome of an analysis. I would emphasize that her word is *regain* not *retain* their stability. Is this perhaps the criterion for readiness to conclude an analysis, not freedom from nightmares or incursions of daytime panics but the capacity to recover from them? She tells us that this stability depends on having "firmly established their good object" and being "closely identified with it." This is a condensed statement that requires a great deal of unpacking to be appreciated even by those familiar with Klein's metapsychology. It is at the heart of her psychoanalytic thinking about termination of analysis.

She wrote a paper on the subject of termination in 1950 when entering the last decade of her own life, and it, like Freud's, has a valedictory quality. In it, she immediately makes reference to her paper "On Weaning" which she wrote much earlier in 1936, a year after she first introduced the concept of the "depressive position." In the weaning paper, she emphasized the internalization of good experience as creating self-confidence and self-regard as well as providing a buttress against bad internal objects and bad feelings. She wrote,

> The child mentally takes into himself—introjects—the outside world.... First he introjects the good and bad breasts, but gradually it is the whole mother again conceived as a good and bad mother which he takes into himself. Along with this the father and the other people in the child's surroundings are taken in as well, ...if the child succeeds in establishing within himself a kind and helpful mother, this internalized mother will prove a most beneficial influence throughout his whole life.... I do not mean that the internalized good parents will consciously be felt as such...but rather as something within the personality having the nature of kindness and wisdom; this leads to confidence and trust in oneself and helps to combat and overcome the feelings of fear of having bad figures within one and of being governed by one's own uncontrollable hatred; and furthermore, this leads to trust in people in the outside world beyond the family circle. (p. 295)

This paper (Klein, 1936) on weaning was written more or less at the same time that she introduced her concept of the infantile depressive position in her paper "A contribution to the psychogenesis of manic-depressive states" (1935); she further developed her ideas in "Mourning and its relation to manic-depressive states" (1940). Donald Winnicott thought this was her most important contribution and that it was as indispensable to psychoanalysis as Freud's concept of the Oedipus complex (1962).

Joan Riviere (1936), armed with Klein's new concept of the depressive position, enlarged on Freud's suggestion that unconscious guilt caused the negative therapeutic reaction which she coupled with the "recalcitrant" narcissistic cases described by Abraham (1919). She linked narcissistic character with the manic defense and emphasized that patients prone to negative therapeutic reactions, which included those suffering from incipient melancholia, anticipated that catastrophe would follow from the development of insight. Riviere began in this paper another line of thought that has developed since and become a central Kleinian and post-Kleinian thinking. She wrote of a "general system of defence," not single defenses but an organization of interdependent, perpetuated defenses; the manic defense was the prototype she described. Since then we have met descriptions of such systems as narcissistic organizations (Rosenfeld, 1971), defensive organizations (O'Shaughnessy, 1981), and pathological organizations (Steiner, 1987).

Klein's work on the paranoid-schizoid position, including the description of projective identification, came later than the depressive position and led her to concentrate on how difficulties in the paranoid-schizoid position would handicap the individual in his or her approach to the depressive position. Since then, Bion's (1962) concept of the container and the contained has added to our understanding of what is involved in the movement from paranoid-schizoid to depressive. It brought to the fore in Kleinian thinking the indispensable role of the mother's capacities for maternal reverie in the encounter with the infant, and how this is mirrored in the analyst's countertransference experience. It also drew attention to another therapeutic benefit of analysis provided by the analyst's hoped-for capacity to contain and articulate the nameless, projected experience of the patient.

Like the Oedipus complex, the depressive position eventually became regarded as the gateway to integrated development rather than a pathological entity. But it is not the end of the story. The integration of the depressive position has to be relinquished in order to move on, whether in analysis or in life, and a period of unintegration has to be tolerated with its associated anxieties before new knowledge or experience can be integrated. This is never more true than at the end of an analysis. If this is not possible, something is clung to—something certain or someone regarded as unchangeable. This raises the threat of interminability.

I think it is best to regard "interminability" as a psychopathological feature of the personality and not simply a prolongation of analysis. We need not wait to discover years down the line that an analysis is interminable. It can become evident much sooner, that the transference–countertransference situation has been incorporated into the pathological organization of the patient in such a way that being in analysis becomes a condition of the patient's stability. The sooner the nature of this pathological organization can be detected and analyzed the better, but it is by no means easy to do this or even possible for some time. This is because the pathological organization may be, as in the case I am about to discuss, not an obviously fixed, unchanging position but a repetitive cycle that conceals its static nature. In order for such analysis to be satisfactorily terminated, the cycle needs to become linear, the path of the analysis to be into the unknown future and not a regression into a familiar cyclical sequence.

A CLINICAL ILLUSTRATION

Every case has its own characteristics, but I want to illustrate my approach by giving a brief description of the analysis of a depressed patient which lasted 9 years. This analysis ended some time ago and I am able, therefore, to say something about the aftermath. There has been no further depression; her professional life has continued to develop and her personal life has been substantially better. She described herself later as sadder and wiser.

Mrs. D was a 40-year-old, divorced, professional academic who came from a part of the United Kingdom where political differences caused tension and violence. This prompted her to leave her family home for London to pursue her postgraduate academic career. She was an only child. Her parents were united by their political beliefs, and she, who did not share them, hated their prejudices. Her reason for seeking analysis was for depression; she also felt blocked in her work and unable to write.

She had a previous analysis but thought it was not helping and she became desperate. She only felt able to leave it if she knew she could have analysis with someone else almost immediately. Later, she was to tell me that she thought her previous analyst, a woman, was afraid of her and that the male analyst she then consulted but rejected before seeing me was not going to be strong enough. When I first saw her I thought she was profoundly depressed and possibly suicidal. There was a pervasive grimness about her and no sign of the lively person with a sense of humor that I was later to get to know. I soon realized that she was unusually honest but socially disadvantaged because she was incapable of ordinary hypocrisy. She was given to strong direct feelings of both love and hate and had quite marked masochistic tendencies.

The recurrent cycle in the analysis that I want to talk about had three phases. The first was characterized by aspiration and ambition, accompanied by feelings of hopelessness and inferiority; the second phase was of actual analytic progress that was accompanied by rivalrous feelings; the third phase was dominated by internal threats of death.

In the first, the phase of aspiration and inferiority, I was idealized as her analyst. This was of small comfort to her, as my imaginatively enhanced achievements set her a standard by which she judged herself to be a failure. Her idealization of me took the form of believing, erroneously, that whatever I did was a result of "effortless superiority," hence any struggle or effort on her part was a sign of failure. In this stable but stifling system, I appeared to be the external representative of her ego-ideal by which her superego, modeled on her mother, measured her and by which standard she was to be forever a failure. It was as if she believed that if she was perfect she could be loved, by her superego but not otherwise.

Her quick grasp of my interpretations and her ability to further her own analysis by her own capacity for insight was clear to me, but not to her. In retrospect I can see that in this phase, the internal agreement, between her negative self-opinion and the adverse judgment of her superego, gave her a sense of internal coherence and safety at the expense of self-denigration and marked pessimism.

I came to think that this was based on her fantasy that if she was perfect she would be a manifestation of her mother's ego ideal, an incarnation of her mother's abandoned psychic ambitions. In fact, her mother was a chronic psychic invalid incapable of effort who only valued effortless achievement, whereas one of my patient's virtues was her capacity to struggle, as a consequence of which she was successful. The more she did this, therefore, the more she differentiated herself from her mother, and the more she differentiated herself from her mother, the more she believed she was at risk of attack. In this phase, Mrs. D was chronically, mildly, depressed, but stable.

The second phase was one in which there was a mitigation of self-depreciation, an enhanced ability to work, and instead of a masochistic acceptance of inferiority, the stirrings of ambition and rivalrous feelings in the transference. Whenever I said something that had not already occurred to her, that led to the wish "if only I had thought of that." There was an immediate longing to be able to do that, to be like that. This was rapidly followed by feelings of hatred toward me and a wish that I should suffer some misfortune. This, in turn, led to pain and remorse. Working through this phase led to painful progress for both of us before there was eventually a lightening of mood and a spurt of spirit, more positive transference feelings, and open expressions of gratitude. This would then lead to phase three.

This phase can be described as a negative therapeutic reaction. It came with greatest force at a point in the analysis when progress had enabled her to finally achieve the academic position to which she had long aspired. There was a sequence of attacks, each following a similar pattern. The first component was a psychosomatic reaction that then served as the basis for doubt about the efficacy or usefulness of her analysis. We were both failures and our analytic baby was stillborn. Analysis of this would lead to remission of the psychosomatic symptoms, only for it to be followed by a hypochondriacal conviction that she was suffering from a fatal illness. One such sequence will give the flavor of the transactions. Mrs. D began writing and she found herself, to her surprise, inundated with ideas and a feeling of pleasurable anticipation instead of her usual dread or stultification. The feeling of excitement gave way to an episode of paroxysmal tachycardia that frightened her and put a stop to the writing. Fortunately, it rapidly responded to physical treatment from a cardiologist and the writing resumed and continued to flourish, but my patient did not. She became convinced that she was suffering from a fatal illness. At first it was leukemia, then cancer of the bowel, and eventually cancer of the breast. This developed into a more general fear of death that she now described as somehow extraneous, like fate. "It feels like a terrible irony," she said, "just when I get what I have wanted all these years, I will die. I feel cursed, as if someone had put a curse on me." At other times when we reached this point it would be expressed as "just when I have profited from my analysis and might enjoy life is it not ironic that I will die."

Eventual recovery from this belief system would lead us back once more to what I have called phase one, that is of aspiration, hopelessness, and inferiority. I was restored as an idealized figure and she as hopelessly inferior. It would be easy to see this as progress particularly if one accepted the projection of superiority that was offered, but it was a regression.

The breakdown of this pathological three-part cycle when it came did not lead us to tranquil waters but to a deepening of despair, a more disturbed transference and countertransference experience, and a great deal more uncertainty for both of us. The change came when the internal death threats of the third phase were seen by both of us to be infiltrated by her own projected death wish. The strength of the internal death threats diminished the more her own desire for death was acknowledged. Her basic *wish* to die became quite conscious and was linked to disappointment and disillusion. Why, she would say, should she endure this analysis that stimulated so much and provided so little, just so I could satisfy my curiosity and demonstrate my abilities? It was not going to make any difference to her but just reveal more aspects of herself she could not stand.

Her state of mind at this point could be described in Milton's (1975) words: "Save what is in destroying, all other joy/To me is lost" (*Paradise Lost*, IX, 478–479). Why, she asked, should she live as she did with her wretched personality, born to live an unhappy life, born, not because she chose to exist, but because she was conceived out of some casual, thoughtless, sexual pleasure of her parents? They, she claimed, had forced life on her and then became the objects of her continual concern as inadequate parents, who nevertheless were a continuous source of worry, so that now she could not commit suicide for fear of the effect of it on them.

As we disentangled her own wish for death from the internal death threats, she seriously contemplated giving up analysis because she was assailed by envious feelings and felt very guilty for hating me; she could no longer bear attacking me and enduring the remorse that followed. But giving up her analysis meant giving up all her ambitions as she believed she needed it. Her suicidal wishes became stronger, and then she cursed me for making it impossible to kill herself, as she felt unable to inflict her death on me; I therefore kept her alive against her wishes.

She was now, as Klein and Riviere described, in the depressive position: persecuted by depressive anxiety for her loved and hated objects that she believed she could never repair. Reparation was a concept Klein developed from witnessing the efforts of her children's patients to repair the toys whose damaged state greatly troubled them after they had inflicted it. The adult counterpart is in the realm of ideas, where our critical attacks lead to damaged perceptions of our objects and our adult reparation takes the form of forgiveness. A historically defective object cannot be restored, but an internal object relationship can be repaired.

Nevertheless, analysis of the various death threats and death wishes, repeatedly disentangling what belonged to her and what was a property of her internal object, began to change things. The overall effect was that the internal object, which could only be described initially as a murderous superego, lost its moral power within the patient's internal world. It could no longer be described as having the role and power of a legitimate tyrant but became something felt by my patient as an alien presence; it was no longer a ruthless but legitimate monarch but something more like organized crime. The threatening voice, when evident, no longer had the oracular power of the superego, experienced as fate or righteous punishment. This I have described as the emancipation of the ego and I see it not so much as taming the superego as dethroning a usurping ego-destructive object.

As this process of disentangling took place, Mrs. D's analysis was flooded with memories of her mother. As a child she was beaten by her mother, whom she recalled threatening to kill her. From the outset it seems her relationship with her mother was troubled. As a baby she was passionately attached to her mother's breasts and was weaned late and with great difficulty. In contrast to this, she carried for life an image of her mother's eyes staring at her and her mother's voice screaming at her in hatred. Her analysis was filled with live and painful recollections of her mother from time to time, which appeared to be part of a process of recategorization of good and bad memories, and a reshaping of the internal relationship. The gradual displacement of the hostile internal object from its position as superego and the diminution of her actual mother's power to demoralize her moved in parallel.

If we think of analysis as having a beginning, a middle, and an end, this was the middle. There was no longer a sense of crisis. The weekend interruptions and the analytic breaks were less hard for the patient. Each week started out with anxiety and ended with good-humored reflection. The initiation of the idea of ending some day was really made in the form Freud describes in "Negation" (1925). In other words, the patient opened the subject by saying that the analysis could never end. The problem was from that moment on the table.

This led us to the idea of naming a day sometime in the future, and this existed as an unspecified date for some time before finally it was decided a year ahead.

Mourning in anticipation of the ending begins in earnest in the terminal phase and continues after the ending for some time. It meant in Mrs. D's case contemplating my death at some future date probably while she was still alive, a radical change from her earlier position in which she repeatedly scripted her own death.

TERMINAL PHASE

Melanie Klein emphasized that the announcement of termination mobilizes all the persecutory and depressive anxieties, and that repeatedly working through to the depressive position is what is needed. All that is true, but I think something else happens and that we have to go beyond the depressive position. When I came on the analytic scene in the 1970s, there was a line of thinking among some Kleinians that saw arriving at the depressive position as the end of the road, in much the same way genital maturity had been idealized in Anna Freudian circles.

However, post-Kleinian theory, led by Bion, implies that the depressive position is no final resting place: that leaving the security of that coherence for a new round of fragmented persecuting uncertainties is necessary for development. I attempted to produce a model that makes this distinction. It is based on a modification of Bion's formula and makes use of John Steiner's (1987) concept of pathological organizations. My model describes the movement through each position in turn as part of a continuous, life-long, cyclical development and limits the word *regression* to describe a retreat to a pathological organization.

I described in addition to the familiar predepressive position *Ps* a postde-pressive position that I call *Ps(n + 1)*. Whereas the familiar *Ps* is characterized by the fears that accompany integration, *Ps(n + 1)*, the postdepressive posi-tion, is characterized by fears of disintegration. Though in *Ps(n + 1)* certain valuable functions associated with the depressive position are temporarily lost, I do not regard it as regression but as developmental (Britton, 1998).

I think *Ps(n + 1)* is appropriate to the terminal stage of analysis. The future is uncertain, the life events to be experienced are not yet known, and how the analysis will be seen retrospectively cannot be predetermined. For Mrs. D, uncertainty about her own development and how her relationship with me would turn out divested of its idealization provoked anxiety: first, a fear of nothing making sense; and second, of nothing having value. This would tempt her into a regressive return to her self-abasement and mas-ochistic surrender; repeated emergence from those states of mind, however, seemed to give her confidence and greater optimism about the future.

At the end of an analysis, the country to be traversed by the patient alone is as yet unmapped; what the analysis might provide is a compass and a map reference of the starting point. What enables us to move on with con-fidence without certainty? Is there an invisible accompanying figure once the analyst has gone?

In order to think about this, I return to *The Pilgrim's Progress*, John Bunyan's fictional dream of the way to salvation, in effect a theological account of recovery from melancholia. Christian, the pilgrim self, after emerging from the slough of despond, gains an indispensable companion, Faithful. However, when they reach Vanity Fair, a township based on shopping, sex, public relations, and corruption, Faithful and Christian are arrested for doubting the goods sold in Vanity Fair and for saying they only want the truth. Faithful is found guilty of heresy and disturbing the peace. The chief prosecutor is Mr. Envy and the jury is Mr. Blind Man, Mr. No-Good, Mr. Malice, Mr. Love-Lust, Mr. Live-Loose, Mr. Heady, Mr. High-Mind, Mr. Enmity, Mr. Lyar, Mr. Cruelty, Mr. Hare-Light, and Mr. Implacable. Faithful is found guilty and executed by scourging, buffeting, lancing, stoning, and finally burning.

However, Christian is able to continue his pilgrimage because he gains a new companion, Hopeful, who was made so (that is, full of hope) by beholding Christian and Faithful, their suffering, their words, and their behavior: "Thus, one died to bear testimony to the truth and another rises out of his ashes, to be a companion to Christian in his pilgrimage" (p. 99). Together they face and eventually escape from the Giant Despair who imprisons them in Doubting Castle. It is in Doubting Castle that Christian says "For my part I know not whether it is best to live thus, or to die out of hand. My soul chooseth strangling rather than life, and the Grave is more easy for me than this Dungeon" (pp. 115–116). Hopeful rescues Christian from his suicidal wishes first by pointing out that it would be murder upon his body and soul, and then by reminding him of how he had successfully endured and bravely faced the dangers of his earlier journey, the one accompanied by Faithful. Christian, following this, suddenly remembers he has a Key in his bosom called promise that will open any door, and so they escaped from Doubting Castle and the Giant Despair.

Hopeful seems to me to be a personification of what Klein meant by internalized good parents, as she wrote, "not something felt as such but as something within the personality having the nature of kindness and wisdom that leads to confidence and trust in oneself" (pp. 115–116). In theological terms, the Holy Spirit rather than the incarnate Christ. Hopeful, according to Bunyan, is made out of observation of the original pair's (Christian and Faithful's) adventures, suffering, fidelity, and fortitude. Taking Bunyan's model, it would seem that the postanalytic patient would face the unknown future with a live, internal, hopeful presence that was born within the analysis, from the observation and registration of that earlier journey in the company of the now-departed analyst. It seems to me like the transformation of faith in the analyst into a hope that a similar use of the mind will enable future recoveries to be made from as yet unknown pitfalls, a hope based on the observation, experience, and recollection of the journey made with the analyst through its many vicissitudes. The Pilgrim finds himself a prisoner of Giant Despair in Doubting Castle, where he almost succumbs to the Giant's suggestion that he kill himself, but Hopeful reminds him:

> What hardship, terror and amazement he has already gone through and art thou nothing but fear?... Remember how thou played with the man at Vanity Fair and wast neither afraid of the Chain, nor cage, nor yet of bloody death: wherefore let us bear up with patience as best we can. (p. 117)

In our parlance, afflicted with difficulties, incarcerated in doubt, and deafened by the voice of the giant despair, the patient-pilgrim is rescued from suicide by the voice of hope that reminds him of similar situations in his analysis when he had Faithful as his companion. In Bion's words, hopefulness, the only companion of our postanalytic days, is based on learning from experience. The analysis provides this experience if it is observed, noted, and recollected. It is not terminable while hope resides only in the body of the analyst, nor is it going to be successful in as yet unknown difficulties if it provides only a psychoanalytic bible.

REFERENCES

Abraham, K. (1919). A particular form of neurotic resistance against the psycho-analytic method. In D. Bryan, & A. Strachey (Eds.), *Selected Papers of Karl Abraham*. London: Hogarth, 1973.

Bion, W. R. (1962). *Learning from experience*. London: Karnac, 1984.

Britton, R. (1998). *Belief and imagination: Explorations in psychoanalysis*. London: Routledge.

Bunyan, J. (1907). *The Pilgrim's Progress*. London: Dent.

Freud, S. (1915). Thoughts for the times on war and death. In J. Strachey (Ed. & Trans.), *The standard edition of the complete psychological works of Sigmund Freud* (Vol. 14, pp. 275–288). London: Hogarth.

Freud, S. (1937). Analysis terminable and interminable. In J. Strachey (Ed. & Trans.), *The standard edition of the complete psychological works of Sigmund Freud* (Vol. 23, pp. 211–253). London: Hogarth.

Klein, M. (1935). A contribution to the psychogenesis of manic-depressive states. In R. Money-Kyrle (Ed.), *The writings of Melanie Klein* (Vol. 1, pp. 290–305). London: Hogarth, 1975.

Klein, M. (1936). Weaning. In R. Money-Kyrle (Ed.), *The writings of Melanie Klein* (Vol. 1, pp. 290–305). London: Hogarth, 1975.

Klein, M. (1940). Mourning and its relation to manic-depressive states. In R. Money-Kyrle, B. Joseph, E. O'Shaughnessy, & H. Segal (Eds.), *Guilt and Reparation* (Vol. 3, pp. 236–246). London: Hogarth, 1975.

Klein, M. (1950). On the criteria for the termination of a psycho-analysis. In R. Money-Kyrle (Ed.), *The writings of Melanie Klein* (Vol. 11, pp. 78–80). London: Hogarth, 1975.

Klein, M. (1958). On the development of mental functioning. In R. Money-Kyrle, B. Joseph, E. O'Shaughnessy, & H. Segal (Eds.), *The writings of Melanie Klein* (Vol. 3, pp. 236–246). London: Hogarth, 1975.

Milton, J. (1975). *Paradise lost*. New York: W. W. Norton.

O'Shaughnessy, E. (1981). A clinical study of a defensive organization. *International Journal of Psycho-Analysis, 2*, 359–369.

Riviere, J. (1936). A contribution to the analysis of the negative therapeutic reaction. *International Journal of Psycho-Analysis, 17*, 304.

Rosenfeld, H. (1964). An investigation into the need of neurotic and psychotic patients to act out during analysis. In *Psychotic States: A Psycho-Analytical Approach* (pp. 200–216). New York: International Universities Press, 1965.

Steiner, J. (1987). The interplay between pathological organizations and the paranoid-schizoid and depressive positions. *International Journal of Psycho-analysis, 68*, 69–80.

Winnicott, D. W. (1962). A personal view of the Kleinian contribution. In *The maturational process and the facilitating environment* (pp. 171–179). London: Hogarth, 1972.

Chapter 4

Beyond the bedrock

Jeanne Wolff Bernstein

Freud's last words on the status and efficacy of psychoanalysis in his 1937 seminal paper "Analysis Terminable and Interminable" still ring true today and raise profound questions with which we continue to struggle. Near the end of his life, Freud was deeply troubled by the turn psychoanalysis had taken among some of its practitioners. On one hand, there were those analysts who—like many patients—complained that psychoanalysis was a "time-consuming business," and advocated for ways to shorten the duration of analysis. Prominent among those appealing for a shorter "cure" was Otto Rank, who had immigrated to the United States and had suggested that if the primal trauma of the act of birth could be dealt with in a short "subsequent" analysis, "the whole neurosis would be got rid of" (1937, p. 216). Freud did not feel very friendly about suggestions of abbreviating the thorough work of analysis and reasoned that although Rank's argument was "bold and ingenious," it was nonetheless the product of its time, "conceived under the stress of the contrast between the postwar misery of Europe and the 'prosperity' of America, and designed to adapt to the tempo of analytic therapy to the haste of American life" (p. 216).

Closer to home, Freud was also concerned about the path that other colleagues had taken, whom he rather carefully (and ruefully) identifies as "optimists." They were primarily interested in the question of technique, and less so in the pursuit of the metapsychological questions that were stirring at the heart of psychoanalysis. In his paper "Analysis Finite and Infinite" (1991), Leupold-Loewenthal illuminated the highly political stance Freud takes in what was then a hotly contested discussion between those ego psychologists who were primarily interested in "the alteration of the ego" in contrast to a minority of psychoanalysts who were recognizing the supremacy of the life and death drives and the difficulties they tend to cause in the conception of a cure. Leupold-Loewenthal underscores the political stance Freud took without directly naming names when he wrote in 1937, "In this field [the alteration of the ego], the interest of analysts seems to me to be quite wrongly directed. Instead of an enquiry into how a cure by analysis comes about (a matter which I think has been sufficiently elucidated) the question should be asked of what are the obstacles that stand in the way of such a cure" (p. 221).

After Freud's publication of *The Ego and the Id* (1923), the study of the ego had become quite the trendy subject to pursue, and many analysts became primarily, if not exclusively, interested in how the ego could be cured in the process of an analysis. The International Psychoanalytical Association (IPA) congress in Marienbad, Czech Republic, in 1936 proved to be a showcase for these burgeoning, optimistic ego-psychologists who under the leadership of Ernest Jones put together a symposium that was to document the therapeutic results of psychoanalysis. Ranging from Edward Bibring's "A General Theory of Therapy" to Otto Fenichel's "The Efficacy of Psychoanalytic Therapy," to James Strachey's "The Theory of Therapeutic Results in Psychoanalysis," this prominent group of analysts was eager to show how the removal of symptoms through a removal of repression could yield long-lasting therapeutic results. Freud, however, was dismayed by this hopeful attitude expressed at the Marienbad congress, and as Leupold-Loewenthal (1991) wrote, "surely was opposing any theoretically based optimism, optimism not borne out by his clinical work. His attitude thus ran counter to the trend of the Marienbad symposium. His paper is in fact an indirect criticism of the matters on which analysts' interest were centered in 1936–1937" (p. 61).

Freud had recognized for some time that the death drive was the powerful force behind the symptom and had realized that the simple lifting of repression, as he had thought to be the case in the beginning of his psychoanalytic discoveries, was not enough to envision a cure. Drawing from his own clinical experience, Freud had understood that the workings of the death drive would eventually cause havoc in any analytic treatment. Since 1920, Freud had already described the various forms of a negative therapeutic reaction—unconscious guilt, masochism, need for punishment—which could stall the progress of any analytic treatment. However, it had become quite clear to Freud, near the end of his life, that many of his fellow analysts had ignored his misgivings and had instead focused their attention upon the ego and its capacity to adapt itself to the demands of the internal and external world. The analysts who were interested in showing the efficacy of analytic treatment at the Marienbad congress in 1936, were those who gravely doubted Freud's theory of the death drive, considering it to be a temporary aberration of his thinking.

Thus, a closer reading of Freud's "Analysis Terminable and Interminable" reveals a hard-fought debate about the death drive and about the question whether analysis is capable to reach beyond the bedrock of castration in order to catch the workings of the death drive. Because Freud considered psychoanalysis to be the only treatment for neurosis, he nonetheless did not feel pressured to consider it to be a foolproof therapeutic technique; he never promised a happy end, and he was troubled to see his followers attempting to pledge one in response to the pressures of the time. Not much has changed since Freud's times. Psychoanalysts feel nowadays similarly bombarded by health insurance companies and other sweet-talking therapies to promise quick results to impossible disorders, and like in the late 1930s, many modern-day analysts are still swayed today to promise a quicker cure to the maladies of the day. In 1937, Freud wrote, "Of the three factors which we have recognized as being decisive for the success or otherwise of analytic treatment —the influence of traumas, the constitutional strength of the drives and alterations of the ego—what concerns us here is only the second, the strength of the instincts" (p. 224). Yet this second factor, the constitutional strength of the drives, began to be overlooked, and until today figures rarely in a discussion of analytic treatment. Even though the alteration of the ego may no longer be such a central point of focus, the influence of external traumas has almost completely overshadowed all other concerns. Under the large rubric of object relations, the first factor mentioned by Freud has come into full prominence and has nearly erased the other two factors of the drives and the alteration of the ego. How we interpret traumas, how we live with traumas, and how we are influenced by the traumas of our previous generations has filled the psychoanalytic landscape with the analytic tool almost shifting completely to an analysis of the transference/countertransference relationship within which past and present traumas repeat themselves.

Given this present-day context, Freud might have felt today as left alone by his psychoanalytic adherents as he did back in the late 1930s, and may have also only found solace and understanding in the Greek philosopher, Empedocles, who shared his thinking about the mysterious workings of Eros and Thanatos. In 1937, Freud wrote:

> The philosopher taught that two principles governed events in the life of the universe and in the life of the mind, and that those principles were everlastingly at war with each other. He called them...[love] and...[strife]. Of these two powers—which he conceived of being at bottom "natural forces operating like instincts, and by no means intelligences with a conscious purpose—the one strives to agglomerate the primal particles of the four elements into a single unity, while, the other, on the contrary, seeks to undo all these fusions and to separate the primal particles of the elements from one another.... The two fundamental principles of Empedocles...are both in function and name, the same as our two primal instincts, Eros and destructiveness, the first of which endeavors to combine what exists into ever greater unities, while the second endeavors to dissolve those combinations and to destroy the structures to which they have given rise. (p. 246)

Freud became convinced that any analysis could only have a chance at success if the analyst "uncovered what lay behind the id," and set an end to the "constant swing backward and forwards like a pendulum between a piece of id-analysis and a piece of ego-analysis" (p. 238).

Jacques Lacan was one of the few analysts who understood the somber tone of Freud's paper and who took heed of Freud's warning that psychoanalysis would sell out, were it not to concern itself with the powerful forces of the life and death drives. Instead of interpreting Freud's warning as a sign of his growing pessimism about his life, Lacan comprehended very early what was at stake in Freud's late thinking. As a young and nearly unknown French analyst, Lacan presented what was to become his famous paper on the "mirror stage" at the same Marienbad congress where Loewenstein, Bibring, Hartmann, and Fenichel, among others, praised the work of the ego and discussed the importance of the therapeutic action. In this early paper, Lacan identified the ego as an illusion, as a part of the psychic apparatus that was the narcissistic source of illusions and delusions and therefore did not need to be fortified and supported as his Austrian and British colleagues advocated. Moreover, Lacan was beginning to lay the ground for his work upon the fantasm, the basic fantasmatic structure through which every subject organizes his desire in relation to his drives vis-à-vis the Other. Thus, the subject relates to the external world through this fundamental fantasm which is to be uncovered throughout the work of an analysis and traversed at the end of it.

Lacan's concept of the fantasm is an indication of the degree to which he took Freud's advice to heart that the death drive could only be reached if one moved beyond the bedrock of castration. In contrast to the ego psychologists and object relationists, who spoke of internal objects and internal object relations that were modeled on external relations and distorted by powerful unconscious fantasies, Lacan developed the concept of the *objet a*, which is the object of the drive. Unlike an internal object, the *objet a* cannot be found in a relationship but can only be apprehended in a conjugation. What does that mean? What Lacan suggests is that every subject defines itself or conjugates itself in relation to the Other in either an active, passive, or self-reflexive form; either it is the one who tortures the other, or is the one who wants to be tortured by the other, or is the one who tortures himself or herself. Lacan refers here indirectly to Freud's 1915 paper "Instincts and Their Vicissitudes," where Freud describes the active, passive, and self-reflexive positions the drive takes in order to guarantee itself satisfaction. In the obsessional neurosis, for instance, Freud wrote that

> There is a turning round upon the subject's self without an attitude of passivity towards another person: the change has only got as far as stage (b). The desire to torture has turned into self-torture and

self-punishment, not into masochism. The active voice is changed, not into the passive, but into the reflexive middle voice. (p. 128)

This fundamental, organizing fantasm is difficult to apprehend and is deeply unconscious to the desiring subject. In order to free oneself from the gripping power of this drive object—which typically compels the subject to be ensconced in a deep, repetitive structure—the subject has to pass through the plane of identification to discover what has constituted him or her at the very core of his or her being. In the case of an obsessional neurosis, for instance, the symptom of self-punishment, anchored in the cross-currents of the drives, constitutes a distorted representation of the fantasm with which the subject protects himself or herself from the ravages of the drives, while at the same time ensuring himself or herself a constant source of pleasure through the constructed fantasm. These essential passive/active/self-reflexive scenarios encapsulate the tension between the life and death drive and shape the desiring subject in his or her symptom formation.

Psychoanalysis has to find ways of using interpretation to go beyond speech in order to reach the real—the register of nonrepresentability—to address the core of the symptom. Lacan insisted that no analysis could be complete unless one had worked "on the fantasm" and understood the close tie that exists between the symptom and the "fantasm." Freud's (1905) *Three Essays on the Theory of Sexuality* plays a prominent role in Lacan's understanding of the symptom and the "Lust" (i.e., the *jouissance*) that is so intrinsically embedded in any symptom formation. In the first essay of his three essays, Freud suggests that the sexual drive is not an instinct but a drive whose reality is rather aberrant and not to be located in either the instinctual or natural realm. Using the oral drive as a general model of illustrating how a drive operates, Freud explains how a particular pleasure unfolds in the infant independent and autonomous of the pleasure of nourishment. Using thumb sucking (*lutschen*) as a model, Freud shows that sucking reveals an independent source of pleasure which derives from nourishment and then detaches itself. "Thumb sucking," he writes, "appears already in early infancy and may continue into maturity, or even persists all through life. It consists in the rhythmic repetition of a sucking contact by the mouth (or lips). There is no question of the purpose of this procedure being the taking of nourishment" (pp. 179–180). However, Freud recognizes very quickly that the purpose of nourishment is delayed, and that something else installs itself in the activity of sucking, namely, the sexual pleasure that goes along with the intake of nourishment. This idea of delay constitutes, as Toboul (2006) wrote:

A memorable moment in the history of psychoanalysis since this is the first proof of infantile sexuality. The sexual distinguishes itself from a special satisfaction, different from the satisfaction of nourishment.

It even supposes a delay of the nourishment activity and produces an autonomy of a new source of pleasure. (p. 3)

In a footnote added in 1919, the same year Freud wrote "The Uncanny" and "A Child Is Being Beaten," Freud quoted a Dr. Galant, who had published an essay on "*Das Lutscherli*," which describes the confession of a grown-up girl who never gave up the pleasures of sucking and describes its advantages over kissing in the following words:

It is impossible to describe what a lovely feeling goes through your whole body when you suck; you are right away from this world. You are absolutely satisfied, and happy beyond desire. It is a wonderful feeling; you long for nothing but peace-uninterrupted peace. It is just unspeakably lovely: you feel no pain and no sorrow, and ah! you are carried into another world. (p. 181)

This sense of "another world" (*entrückt in eine andere Welt*), of a "happiness beyond desire," of "absolute peace," a world without words, constitutes the universe of the death drive, of *jouissance* which fixates the subject in his or her attainment of pleasure. This world lies beyond the bedrock of castration that is to be touched by the analyst through words. How does one reach a realm so constitutional to the subject that lies beyond words and is "happy beyond desire"? Freud provides the answer, but, I believe, left it to Lacan to work out its clinical implications. After Freud firmly establishes that the need for nourishment is clearly detached from the need of sexual satisfaction, he also argues in the same paper that there exists no necessary relationship between the object and the drive. "It has been brought to our attention," Freud (1905) wrote,

That we have been in the habit of regarding the connection between the sexual instinct and the sexual object as more intimate than it in fact is. Experience of the cases that are considered abnormal has shown us that in them the sexual instinct and the sexual object are merely soldered together [*verlötet*].... It seems probable that the sexual instinct is in the first instance independent of its object; nor is its origin likely to be due to its object's attractions. (pp. 147–148)

In this key phrase, Freud underscores that there is no direct relationship between the object and the drive, but that in the realm between object and aim, a fantasm installs itself around which the infant attempts to answer the question of what the Other wants from him. Like Freud, Lacan insists on the concept on fixation and argues that the *objet a* is fixated to something partial, and it is the fantasm that arrives at articulating in some fashion how the drive engages the object, which in turn functions as the real motor of the unconscious. The aim of the drive is to obtain satisfaction but not so much through the object but through the fantasm attached to the object. Hence, the subject is intensely fixated upon his or her fantasm—perverse, abject, or depressing and humiliating as it may be just so as not to lose the fundamental source of his or her unconscious pleasure/*jouissance* attached to the object of the drive.

Reparative therapeutic work gratifies the death drive and thus interferes with the work of analysis because it responds to demands that are endless and never essentially gratifiable. The Lacanian analytic position is one of not giving into demands, but instead of opening oneself up toward the *objet a*, the object of the drive which creates desire, and not to back away from it with rationalizations, explanations, and empathic understanding. Most often the demand of the *objet a* is to want to be the phallus, or to have the phallus, or to make oneself to be the phallus of the Other, all of which are positions that are considered to be of illusionary nature. Two modern-day constructions of such an idealizing demand are either to want to be the phallic woman or to be the noncastrated man for the Other, unconscious demands that lay beyond the bedrock of castration. Freud ends "Analysis Terminable and Interminable" with the observation that two corresponding themes "come into especial prominence and give the analyst an unusual amount of trouble.... The two corresponding themes are in the female, an envy for the penis—a positive striving to possess a male genital—and, in the male, a struggle against his passive or feminine attitude to another male" (p. 250). Freud was convinced that "the repudiation of femininity" lay beyond the rock of castration and propelled the most ferocious defenses in an analytic treatment. Much of Lacan's thinking about femininity is informed by Freud's late conclusion that the *Ablehnung der Weiblichkeit* is at the core of every neurosis. Lacan takes it further and argues that this *Ablehnung* is not a simple repudiation but a foreclosure that leaves a hole or gap in the unconscious. Although the little girl recognizes that the mother does not have it all, she devalues (*entwertet*) the mother and with it her own femininity. The little boy, on the other hand, overcompensates the mother's lack with his hypermasculine protest and defends against a passive attitude toward his father. Rather than revalorizing the mother's value/feminine sex as Ernest Jones or Karen Horney proposed, or suggesting scenarios of maternal or infantile devouring or annihilation fantasies as Klein did, Lacan insists on the importance of the early maternal castration. He argues that any foreclosure of early maternal castration prohibits the subject from psychically separating from the mother. If a woman or man cannot accept maternal castration, he or she remains stuck through his or her symptoms of disavowing his or her own femininity. Freud's explanations that negative therapeutic reactions are evoked by unconscious guilt, or by a need to be punished, or by a masochistic stance that does not allow the analysand to get better, we have to conclude, following Lacan thinking, that all such symptoms are reflections of a deep resistance to acknowledge the mother as lacking.

The central question thus becomes the castration of the Other, not so much the castration of oneself, but the deep recognition that the M/other is castrated. Once the subject acknowledges the maternal castration and recognizes that the mother is not all, he or she can ask who he or she is for this incomplete mother. What does the subject have to be to fill up the maternal lack? Only when the subject can acknowledge this lack, can he or she begin to ask these fundamental questions to which he or she responds with fantasmatic scenarios that become represented in a distorted version of the subject's symptom. However, if the subject cannot bear to recognize the maternal castration, he or she is caught in an endless and highly resistant cycle where the girl/woman denies castration and insists that she has a penis after all, or the man engages in a hypervirile performance to deny his castration. In *The Ego and the Id* (1923), Freud remarks in a footnote that he came across a case of a young married woman "whose story showed that, after noticing the lack of a penis in herself, she had supposed it to be absent not in all women, but only in those whom she regarded as inferior, and had still supposed that her mother possessed one" (p. 31). If the young girl/woman denies castration, she is bound to be fixated in a permanent idealization of the mother/father which in turn feeds upon her repudiation of femininity. Only the castrated woman who acknowledges castration is not unconsciously abhorred by feminity. In the end, or at the end of an analysis, the subject detaches himself or herself from the construction of the fantasm he or she has constructed of the Other, and how she has responded to the castration of the Other. Once the plane of identification—formed in response to the castration of the Other—is traversed, the subject is liberated to his or her own desire. Lacan (1981) said as much when he wrote,

> The schema that I leave you, as a guide both to experience and to reading, shows you that the transference operates in the direction of bringing demand back to identification. It is in as much as the desire of the analyst, which remains an x, tends in a direction that is the exact opposite of identification, that the crossing (*franchissement*) of the plane of identification is possible, through the mediation of the separation of the subject in experience. The experience of the subject is thus brought back to the plane at which, from the reality of the unconscious, the drive may be made present. (p. 274)

In the end, the desire of the analyst is crucial for an understanding of the analytic frame within which the subject can eventually "gain distance from the fantasm" and be freed from the captivating power of the drive. As I mentioned earlier, it is absolutely essential during the analysis to speak about the fundamental fantasm because it is through the fantasm that the subject constructs his or her access to reality. What is it that the Other wants from me, what is that the mother desires from me that I can fulfill? The response to this fundamental question is always a fantasmatic one, structuring the subject's later response to the external world. For this precise reason, it is important that the analyst occupy a place in the analysis of absolute difference, of absolute otherness so as not to encourage further imaginary identifications that only lead to repetitions of past events, relationships, and forgotten acts. Throughout his work, Lacan emphasized that the analyst take up the position of the "dummy," the one who in the game of bridge makes absence present. Although the analysand invests the analyst with a great deal of knowledge and projects upon him or her the idea that he or she is the "subject who is supposed to know," the analyst knows nothing, and it is this nothingness that is the greatest gift he or she can give to the analysand. Akin to Lacan's definition that "love is giving something you don't have to somebody you don't know," the analyst's greatest gift is to give his or her nothingness, which in turn elicits the analysand's speech. In "The Direction of the Treatment and the Principles of Its Power" (1958/1977), Lacan argued, "Thus the analyst is he who supports the demand, not as has been said, to frustrate the subject, but in order to allow the signifiers in which his frustration is bound up to reappear" (p. 255). The Lacanian analyst is not to stand in the place of an empathic, commanding ideal with whom the analysand is to identify, but instead, he or she is to stand in the place of the *objet a*, which is the object of the drive that causes desire. In other words, the analyst stands in the place of the *objet a*, the unspeakable, that which waits to be expressed because as Lacan explains in "On the Possible Treatment of Psychosis" (1956/1977), "In the place where the unspeakable object is rejected in the real, a word makes itself heard" (p. 183). The analyst's desire is passionately restricted to desire itself, it is not a desire for knowledge or cure, but for the analysand's desire to discover his or her own unconscious desire, disentangled from the desire of the Other. As Katrien Libbrecht (1999) wrote: "Lacan claimed that the analyst must be possessed by a desire which is 'stronger' than the desires involved in the imaginary seductions" (p. 81), one that supersedes the idealizations and degradations into which the analysand typically attempts to ensconce the analyst. "The subject," Lacan (1977) wrote, "begins the analysis by speaking about himself without speaking to you, or by speaking to you without speaking about himself. When he can speak to you about himself, the analysis will be over" (p. 373n1).

Lacan thought of the end of analysis as a *passe* as opposed to an *impasse*, where the subject "speaks well" in accordance to his or her own ethics and with a knowledge that was born from his or her unconscious. The aim of analysis is to get out of the problematic posed by the repudiation of femininity and to find through "the pass" a new psychic reality, a new way of life other than the one that is locked up and closed in by a repudiation of femininity, as Freud had outlined it in "Analysis Terminable and Interminable." For the subject to speak in his or her own language at the end of an analysis, he or she must have crossed the plane of identification, passed through the fantasm, and abandoned the illusions that held him or her stuck in a symptomatic position. Instead of being lived by the symptom, the subject learns how to live with the symptom. Or, as Gueguen (1999) wrote,

> Analysis begins with a response of the real caught in the initial symptom from which the subject suffers and which pushes him to form a complaint addressed to the Other. It ends with another response of the real, accompanied by a consent of the subject, with what we call the final identification with the symptom. (p. 1)

Neither identifications nor ideals of love are sustainable at the end of an analysis. What emerges and remains instead, is a trusted knowledge of our own unconscious, or at least knowledge of how it functions. Knowledge gained through analysis is not a scientific knowledge, but a knowledge that surprises, that sees and hears connections in novel ways, that risks letting itself be surprised, and that simply rings true. At the end of his teaching, Lacan thought that the last risk that remained for the subject at the end of analysis was to fall in love with his or her unconscious and thereby ignore the distance to speech. In response to this last "risk," Lacan accentuated once again the difference between language and *lalangue* the way *lalangue* plays through slips of the tongue, puns, and jokes the unconscious into language. The *equivoke* in the use of language, best typified in the double meaning of the word or the pun, remains the most concise way of forming an analytic intervention, and constitutes at the same time, the best protection against the formation of new symptoms. The *passe* allows the subject to witness at the end of an analysis how a new knowledge was born that was not perceived by the subject before entering analysis, and that now informs and surprises him or her at every step of his way.

REFERENCES

Freud, S. (1905). Three essays on the theory of sexuality. In J. Strachey (Ed. & Trans.), The standard edition of the complete psychological works of Sigmund Freud (Vol. 7, pp. 125–248). London: Hogarth.
Freud, S. (1915). Instincts and their vicissitudes. In J. Strachey (Ed. & Trans.), *The standard edition of the complete psychological works of Sigmund Freud* (Vol. 14, pp. 105–216). London: Hogarth.

Freud. S. (1923). The ego and the id. In J. Strachey (Ed. & Trans.), *The standard edition of the complete works of Sigmund Freud* (Vol. 19, pp. 3–68) London: Hogarth.

Freud, S. (1937). Analysis terminable and interminable. In J. Strachey (Ed. & Trans.), The standard edition of the complete psychological works of Sigmund Freud (Vol. 23, pp. 209–254). London: Hogarth.

Gueguen, P. G. (1999, September). The pass between knowledge and belief. Paper presented at the ACF-VLB Study Day on "Responsibility and Psychoanalysis," Nantes, France.

Lacan, J. (1977). Ecrits. New York: W. W. Norton.

Lacan, J. (1981). *The four fundamental concepts of psycho-analysis.* New York: W.W. Norton Press.

Leupold-Loewenthal, H. (1991). Analysis finite and infinite. In J. Sandler (Ed.), *On Freud's "Analysis Terminable and Interminable"* (pp. 56–75). New Haven, CT: Yale University Press.

Libbrecht, K. (1999). The original sin of psychoanalysis. In D. Nobus (Ed.), Key concepts of Lacanian psychoanalysis (pp. 75–100). New York: Other Press.

Toboul, B. (2006). The object in Freud and Lacan. Unpublished paper.

Chapter 5

Termination in psychoanalytic psychotherapy

An attachment perspective*

Jeremy Holmes

A good starting point for discussing termination is "Analysis Terminable and Interminable" (Freud, 1937), written 2 years before the author's death at the age of 82. But as Pedder (1988) points out, the English title could more accurately have been translated as "Analysis Finite or Infinite." The very different linguistic harmonics of that road not taken might have steered therapists away from the abortive or guillotine-like implications of termination, and the irritable connotation of interminability, suggesting instead themes of separation, death, a timeless unconscious, and the infinity of irreversible loss.

The questions surrounding termination are fairly simple, even if the answers are less so. *When* should one end—is it up to the analyst, the patient, or when an agreed fixed term is up? *How* should one end—abruptly, or with a gradual winding down of frequency of sessions? Are follow-up and "top-ups" allowable? *Why* should one end—what is the theoretical justification for an ending, how does one know that the job is done, and how does a decision to end emerge? *In what way* can one discern if an ending is good enough (analogous to a "good death" in the hospice literature), premature (as in the Dora case; Freud, 1907), or overdue (as with the Wolf Man; Freud, 1918)?

Although the questions, theoretical and practical, surrounding termination are clear, answers are less certain. Novick (1997) convincingly argues that, with honorable exceptions (e.g., Balint, 1968), "neither Freud nor his followers paid much attention to termination as a phase of treatment" and that "for almost 75 years psychoanalysts have been unable to conceive of the idea of a terminal phase" (p. 145).

Three possible reasons for this dearth seem relevant. First, ending therapy, as with embarking on one, is a real event, an enactment going beyond the bounds of transference and the imagination. The departing patient is not just deconstructing a transference, she or he is disengaging

---

* Portions of this chapter also appear in J. Holmes, *Exploring in Security: Toward an Attachment-Informed Psychoanalytic Psychotherapy*. London: Routledge, 2009.

from a fellow human being with whom many hours of close proximity and intimate affect-laden conversation have been passed (cf. Rycroft, 1985). Psychoanalysis struggles to theorize the real relationship—while this is home base for attachment theory (see Holmes, 2009). Psychoanalysis struggles to theorize the "real relationship." Attachment theory assumes that the therapist and the therapeutic setting provide a real secure base, whose function is to enable the client then playfully to explore the unreality, yet validity, of his or her transferential and other imaginings.

Second, a confounding issue for psychoanalysts is that they never fully undergo the process of disengagement that awaits the average analysand. The analyst perforce retains his or her fundamental belief in the potency and importance of psychoanalysis; is likely to have continuing contact with the analytic world, including his or her own analyst, through his or her professional society; and not infrequently undergoes second or even third analyses. If ending analysis is an analogue of leaving home, an analyst continues to retain a foothold in the parental mansion.

Third, the question of termination overlaps, sometimes in confusing ways, with the issue of the aims and objectives of analytic therapy and what a good outcome might be. Removal of symptoms, diminished splitting and greater integration of the personality, strengthening of the ego, overcoming of ambivalence toward the breast, genital primacy, formed the mantra of the early literature. More recently, as character disorder rather than neurosis have come to form the bulk of analytic practice, and subtle research methods for studying outcome have become available, earlier idealized views of analytic outcome have been tempered with reality. A more nuanced view of what can and cannot be achieved in analysis is beginning to emerge, in which the prime aim of therapy is to equip patients with new interpersonal and intrapsychic skills, and to help push psychic equilibrium in a more positive direction. The analyst needs to know when "enough is enough" and to guard against imposing his or her own narcissistic wishes, or colluding with those of the client, for a perfect outcome.

The bulk of this chapter is an attempt to use an attachment perspective to develop a more comprehensive theorization of termination. There follows a resonantly brief consideration of time-limited dynamic therapies, concluding with some broader psychoanalytically inspired reflections on loss, absence, and ending.

ENDING AND ATTACHMENT

I discuss the contribution of attachment to thinking about termination under four headings: theorizing loss in relation to secure and insecure attachments; termination as coconstruction; disillusion and dissolution of the secure base; and mentalizing as a core psychotherapeutic construct and its relation to endings.

Theorizing Separation and Loss

Bowlby (1988) saw the mutative potential of psychotherapy as arising out of a therapist–client relationship which assumes some of the characteristics of a secure base. A patient is a person in distress; distress triggers attachment behavior—other concerns are shelved and a secure base is sought. When no such attachment figure is available, or seen to be available in the patient's outside world, a professional who can alleviate distress through proximity, intensity, and sensitivity is required. This is the attachment formulation of the real relationship, the therapeutic alliance.

This reality provides the figured base against which transferential distortions, misguided expectations, unconscious wishes, and impulses, can be observed and made meaningful. Therapists' consistency, regularity, and responsiveness have the potential to alleviate distress and activate clients' capacity to explore their feelings and their relationships, including those with the therapist. The client's contribution to impediments with that process is the transference, the therapist's countertransference in the classical sense.

Setting up a therapeutic relationship is an inescapable "enactment" on the part of therapist and client: an action that is real, observable, performed rather than merely imagined, fantasized about, or desired. The latter come into play as the *meaning* of actions and their psychological reverberations become grist for exploration, but a vital precondition is the alleviation of attachment insecurity.

But if the reality of establishing an attachment relationship is central, so too is its ending. For Bowlby (1973), separation was the flipside of attachment: The purpose of attachment behaviors, on the part of both careseeker and caregiver, is to mitigate loss. Crying, proximity seeking, responsiveness, and soothing all work to ensure that an individual, when vulnerable—whether through physical immaturity, illness, or trauma—gains and maintains access to protection and succor.

When separation is irreversible (that is, at an ending), Bowlby and his followers such as Parkes (2006) identified the now familiar constellation of reactions and feelings: denial, angry protest, searching, despair, and recovery leading to the establishment of new attachments. Subsequent research on grief and mourning—both normal and pathological (Shaver & Fraley, 2008)—have in a number of ways fleshed out, and to some extent modified, Bowlby's original formulations on separation and loss.

First, a key issue in reactions to separations is not so much the physical presence, but the continuing *availability* when needed of the attachment figure (Klass, Silverman, & Nickman, 1996). As physical proximity, especially in older children, becomes less salient, what matters is knowing that a helper will be there when called upon. This sense of availability can transcend the total separation implicit in a death and make grieving bearable. Sources of comfort helping with bereavement include thinking what the lost loved one would have done in a given situation; conferring with photographs or letters; imagining or even hallucinatorily hearing the dead one's voice; and Proustian remembrance of good times past.

Second, as might be expected, attachment styles have a significant bearing on reactions to loss. There are two main patterns of pathological mourning: denial and chronic depression of mood on the one hand; and inconsolable preoccupation with the lost loved one on the other (Parkes, 2006). These map well onto the two principal patterns/styles of insecure attachment: deactivation of separation of protest, and hyperactivation and inconsolability (Mikulincer & Shaver, 2008). In the former, there is denial that the absence of the lost one matters, while physiological and psychological exploration reveal otherwise. In the other, there is a doomed and unassuagable effort to recover the lost loved one.

Third, Bowlby's somewhat pessimistic perspective on reactions to loss have been modified in light of the findings that under favorable conditions mourning can be negotiated successfully, and that persistent despair is relatively uncommon. The "transactional model of attachment" (Sroufe, 2005) suggests a dynamic interplay between attachment style and current relationships that accounts for variable outcomes in loss. A supportive context—whether this be through family, friends, belief system, social group, church, or therapist—eases the passage from grief to recovery; their absence adds to the burden of loss.

Finally, contemporary views on bereavement (Klass et al., 1996) emphasize the role of postloss continuing bonds, as already implied. Bowlby was critical of the idea of maturation as a process of increasing distancing from the primary object, in which an atomized autonomy replaced adherence and dependency. He conceptualized instead a move from immature to mature dependency. In relation to bereavement, his view was that "the resolution of grief is not to sever bonds but to establish a *changed bond* with the dead person" (1980, p. 399).

We can now apply these ideas and findings to therapy termination as a bereavement analogue. Separation and loss are intrinsic to the process of psychotherapy, which is punctuated by repeated separations, mostly planned and expectable, but also by occasional traumatic interruptions. The former include the end of each analytic hour, weekend, and holiday breaks; the latter therapist and client illness, and enactments on the part of therapist or client such as changing or forgetting sessions, double booking, muddles over times, turning up on the wrong day, and the like. All of these are potential grist to the mentalizing mill.

Ending therapy is a real loss; a significant segment of the client's life is no longer there. A secure space and time where distressing events and feelings can be digested is now empty. A person who focuses her attention and sensitivity on one's inner world is now absent. One is on one's own with one's story, feelings, and life history. But, like every aspect of psychotherapy, an ending is "polysemic" (Tuckett et al., 2008). Depending on mood and perspective, the meaning of an ending can be a death, a bereavement, a completion, a liberation, a funeral (with or without a tearfully convivial wake), or a joyful moment of maturation and leaving home.

Ending brings gain as well as loss: the time and money invested in therapy is now available for other projects; the client no longer feels so dependent; autonomy and maturity are reinforced; and he or she feels more psychologically robust, more able to provide security for others, and less in need of it oneself. Just as the bereaved are sometimes said to have earned their widow- or widowerhood, the discharged therapy client likewise may feel he or she has earned his or her liberation from the obligations, mysteries, and miseries of therapy, while still mourning its now-absent comforts and gifts. One way of seeing the point at which ending begins to enter the therapeutic frame is when for the client the balance sheet of benefit and investment shifts away from the former toward the latter, the effort beginning to outweigh the gains.

These attachment-informed perspectives have a number of clinical implications. First, therapists should bear in mind the client's predominant attachment style. Deactivating clients may well appear to take an ending in their stride, apparently seeing it as inevitable, natural, and appropriate, presenting themselves as eager to move onto the challenges of real life, now that their symptoms have diminished and they feel stronger. Regret, doubt, anger, and disappointment may be conspicuous by their absence, gratitude superficial and conventional rather than deep-rooted. The therapist will direct the client's attention to what is missing as manifest in dreams, failed appointments, seeking other forms of treatment, or in manic cheerfulness, fulsome gratitude, or pollyannerishness papering over grief-sprung cracks in the personality.

Clinical folklore holds that as the end of therapy approaches, the client's symptoms, even if alleviated during the course of therapy, may reappear. This is perhaps particularly likely for hyperactivating clients who may overestimate the negative impact of ending. The therapist may be tempted into a premature proffering of extensions or suggesting an alternative therapist or therapy (such as a group), in ways that are driven by countertransference-induced guilt rather than clinical need. Such posttherapy arrangements may well be appropriate but should not be allowed to divert therapeutic focus from first working through the ending.

Second, the client's social context should be taken into account when deciding on either offering time-limited therapy, or finding an appropriate moment to conclude open-ended treatment. Time-limited therapy is much more likely to succeed when the client has a good social and emotional network to which he or she can return once therapy is over. For more disturbed clients in long-term therapy, if treatment has not managed to facilitate the capacity to generate outside attachments, posttherapy relapse is likely. In partial contradiction of the point made above, therefore, such clients may need further therapeutic arrangements such as group therapy or key worker support, and the reality of this needs to be discussed as a period of intensive individual analytic therapy draws to its conclusion.

Third, the therapist needs to consider the meaning of availability and continuing bonds as conditions for secure attachment, the latter being a key outcome goal for therapy. This may well already have arisen during the course of therapy in relation to separations. One client, who had experienced traumatic separation from both parents at the age of 8 when he was in hospital for a year with tuberculous osteomyelitis, asked at the start of once-weekly therapy: "Can I e-mail you between sessions if there are things that crop up during the week?" My rather rigid response was to say "On the whole I would prefer that we contain issues within the sessions, and that e-mail is used for practical things like changes of time." It was only after some months of therapy that he felt safe enough to reveal how put down, rejected, and angry he had felt by my response, and to be able to explore how this had evoked echoes of his childhood feelings of emptiness and terror when cut off from his parents when in hospital.

The same client was keen that we should have a follow-up session 6 months after our 1-year period of therapy came to an end. For him, such an actualizing manifestation of availability seemed needed, and it would have been churlish to refuse. Other clients are able to tolerate complete separation from therapy, continuing to draw on its benefits through when needed, imagining what their therapist might have said, or having fully internalized the mentalizing function that (see below) is the essence of the developmental help offered by analytic therapy. Attenuated therapy (winding down from intensive work to fortnightly or monthly sessions for a while) or offering an occasional limited series of sessions if a crisis arises in the client's life are other examples of helping the client to maintain a live sense of an available attachment figure.

Responses to ending can be theorized, bringing together the Bowlbian perspective with Kleinian ideas of working through loss (Klein, 1940). Klein's starting point is Freud's paper "Mourning and Melancholia" (1917), which is usually seen as the germ from which the field of object relations grew. Freud describes the ego as a "precipitate of abandoned cathexes"—in other words, the developmental process involves internalizing what were previously external relationships with significant Others. For this to happen, the bereavement process has, at each stage of development, to run its course. This means, especially from a Kleinian viewpoint, coming to terms with ambivalent feelings toward an object on which one is dependent—and therefore which has the potential to abandon one. *Odi et amo*; love and hate inextricably coexist, and it is only once ambivalence is transcended that full "reinstatement of the lost object" in the ego is possible. Only when that mature state is reached is gratitude possible.

Therapists, especially when working in a time-limited way, need to be aware of how this inevitable ambivalence will color reactions to ending. I suspect that my client who asked for a follow-up wanted to be reassured that his hatred of me and my relative unavailability would not have killed me off in his absence. This is not, as I see it, an argument against various forms of attenuated ending, but more a reminder that the meaning of such arrangements must always be thought about and discussed in therapy—in other words, mentalized.

Termination as coconstruction

The relational approach takes it as axiomatic that the clinician's as well as the client's states of mind need to be taken into account if clinical phenomena are to be fully explored and understood. At first glance, this viewpoint seems to equate to object relations theory (ORT), which moved beyond Freud's original intrapsychic account to an interpsychic one in which the therapist's emotional responses to the client were, via projective identification, included in the therapeutic mix. But here the clinician's own projects and personality remain in the background; his or her main role is as a reflexive receptacle for the client's projections. Relational and attachment approaches go two steps further. First, by reviving Freud's (see Bollas, 2009) throwaway remark that analysis at its best involves the direct communication of one unconscious (the patient's) with another (the analyst's), the role of the analyst's implicit character and belief system is acknowledged. Second, and flowing from this, comes the idea of the "analytic third" (Benjamin, 2004; Ogden, 1987), the unique relational structure of any given therapy, built from the differing contributions of clinician and client, but directly derivable from neither.

From this, the clinically obvious point it follows is that any given client will have a different therapeutic experience with different therapists, and that a given therapist will establish very different therapeutic relationships with different clients. It should also be noted however, in contradiction of an absolutist relational viewpoint, that difficult clients tend to do badly by whomever they are treated, and that excellent clinicians tend to make most of their clients better (Beutler et al., 2004); in the latter case, it may be the very flexibility and capacity to accept differing "analytic thirds" that contribute to these "supertherapist" successes.

Attachment research has contributed some empirical data in support of these general considerations. Dozier, Stovall, and Albus (2008) measured clinicians' as well as their clients' attachment styles, looking specifically at the interactions between them. They employed two binary classifications for clinician and client: secure/insecure and deactivating/hyperactivating (using the earlier terminology avoidant/ambivalent), and then related these to process analysis.

Their findings suggested that therapeutic process differed markedly for secure and insecure clinicians. The latter tended to reinforce and amplify their clients' patterns of insecurity; the former tended to "redress the balance," pushing against the client's insecure attachment strategies. Thus, with deactivating clients who tend to play down feelings, drop out early, and miss sessions, insecure clinicians failed to chase up such clients, cut sessions short, and went along with superficial reassurances from their clients that they were feeling better. Secure clinicians questioned all these, pushing for buried feelings. Conversely with hyperactivating clients, insecure clinicians tended to become embroiled in escalating demands for more and more help, while secure clinicians were better able to maintain boundaries and offer a secure therapeutic frame.

It should be noted that the clinicians in this study were not trained psychotherapists but mental health workers with different professional backgrounds: social work, nursing, psychology, and so on. Nevertheless, there is no reason to suppose that similar considerations do not apply to psychoanalytic therapies. Based on the Dozier et al. findings, therefore, the "too early/too late" dilemma in psychotherapy can be understood in terms of the fit between patient and therapist (Holmes, 2001). With an avoidant/deactivating patient and an analyst whose attachment style leads him or her to overemphasize interpretations and intellectual formulation, the ending might be too early. Conversely, with a hyperactivating client and an analyst with a tendency to rely excessively on support and affective resonance, the therapy might become protracted and the ending too late.

The moral is a mentalizing one (see below): "Clinician, know thyself." Therapists need to be aware of and allow for their own attachment styles if they are to offer mutative rather than quasi-collusive treatments. Each analyst will have his or her unique termination style, evoked to some extent by any given patient, but also manifesting his or her own attachment history and predilections. The lineaments of an ending need to be thought about as coconstructed. The task is not so much to get it right, as to use the ending as a powerful exemplar from which the client can learn about the ways his or her unconscious shapes the way he or she handles, and has handled, loss and separation. In facilitating this, the therapist must abstract his or her own attachment style from the therapeutic equation in order to see the client's for what it is.

Dissolution or disillusion

Why should the ending of a therapy matter? After all, the ending of other professional relationships—a builder whose job is finally done, a banking or legal relationship concluded—is usually a relief. By contrast, the therapist and therapeutic relationship are invested (cathected) in a way that makes them affectively salient. The therapist has become an attachment figure, a person with the properties of a secure base, the loss of whom evokes the attachment constellation of pain, protest, despair, and recovery already described.

The question of how an attachment relationship, as opposed to other connections such as friendship, colleagueship, and professionalism, is established is not entirely clear. Bowlby (1956, quoted in Cassidy, 2008) put it well: "To complain because a child does not welcome being comforted by a kind but strange woman is as foolish as to complain that a young man deeply in love is not enthusiastic about some other good looking girl" (p. 12). An attachment relationship is one that permeates or "penetrates" (Hinde, 1979) every aspect of a person's life in ways that mark it off from others. The more that this is true for a therapeutic relationship, the greater is the significance of its ending.

In classical psychoanalysis, negotiating the oedipal situation entails renouncing the breast, coming to accept the inevitable discrepancy between wish and reality. In the neo-Kleinian model of Oedipus, the child who can tolerate parental intercourse and his or her own ambivalent feelings is liberated: able to think for himself or herself, and to identify with, or turn toward, the father and through him the outer world, as he or she moves away from maternal dependency (Britton, Feldman, & O'Shaughnessy, 1989).

Winnicott's (1971) transitional space model introduces a third term between the nirvana-like world of unbridled need and wish, and the harsh, brutish, brevity of reality. In transitional space, wish and reality overlap so that the baby's hallucinatory illusion of the breast is matched by the mother's *actual* provision of it. This real, albeit short-lived, blissful fit becomes the basis for later play, creativity, and hope. In the Winnicott model, there are also repeated failures of fit—a mother is, can, and should only be "good enough." There is a necessary disillusionment with the breast if the child is to move toward independence and new attachments, and to avoid the narcissism that finds intolerable the inevitable discrepancy between wish and reality.

Resistance to termination can be seen as impediments to these developmental processes. The therapist and therapy are invested with indispensability, an illusory and anachronistic carryover of infantile needs and wishes into the present. The therapist fails to meet the client's overweening need and so cannot be relinquished. Or the therapist provides only the maternal half of the parental imago, and so cannot point the client toward independence. Hatred and need are so stark that they cannot be brought together into the depressive position. Failure (in the sense of "good-enoughness") is only bearable if balanced by a sufficient bank of success. As Novick (1988) put it:

Seldom mentioned in the literature is the necessity for disillusionment in order to begin the process of giving up and mourning the omnipotent mother–child dyad. To a certain extent, the analyst must be experienced as a failure for the patient to respond fully to the treatment as a success. (p. 362)

An attachment relationship is one in which needs are actually met by the Other—to a greater (in secure attachment) or lesser (insecure attachment) extent. It seems likely that an effective therapist offers analogous responsiveness, sensitivity, and attunement to that of the security-producing caregiver. There will be occasional "moments of meeting" (Stern, 2004), where the therapist's understanding matches the client's affective state in ways that parallel the advent of the breast at the moment of its hallucination.

But as well as being there for the patient, the therapist is also, albeit in a regular and predictable way, *not* there. It is possible that it is precisely the nature of this absence that marks out someone with secure base properties from, to use Bowlby's phrases, a "kind but strange" or some "other good-looking" person. During separations, a secure base figure holds the careseeker in mind, and stays in the mind of the careseeker. A client similarly has the right to expect his or her therapist to hold him or her in mind between sessions, and to refer back to things said and felt in previous sessions. As the salience of therapy becomes established, the sessions and the person of the therapist enter the patient's stream of consciousness and unconsciousness (dreams of the therapist, slips about the therapist's name, intrusions of therapeutic vocabulary into the client's idiolect, etc.).

Weekly therapy patients often report in the early stages of therapy: "what we were discussing last week stayed in my mind for a couple of days afterwards and then seemed to fade." The frequency of sessions could almost be dictated by the time it takes for these memories to fade; the shorter the time, the more frequently sessions are needed. This affective object constancy, I suggest, is the basis for the salience of the therapeutic relationship, and what perforce attenuates when therapy comes to an end.

The psychoanalytic frame is ideally suited for the investigation of these issues. By apparently offering nothing other than predictability availability and responsiveness, the analyst enables the wish/reality discrepancies to be explored; every ending and break is a rupture in which absence can make the heart grow fonder—or more enraged; termination becomes a mini-mourning in which separation solidifies into irreversible loss.

Reich (1950) made a very clear comparison of the ending of analysis with mourning from a patient who came to her for a second training analysis, several years after the first analysis with another analyst. His description of his reaction to the termination of his first analysis was quite revealing:

I felt as if I was suddenly left alone in the world. It was like the feeling that I had after the death of my mother.... I tried with effort to find somebody to love, something to be interested in. For months I longed for the analyst and wished to tell him about whatever happened to me. Then slowly, without noticing how it happened, I forgot about him. About two years later, I happened, to meet him at a party and thought he was just a nice elderly gentleman and in no way interesting. (p. 182)

Seen this way, transference becomes more than merely a repetition of past relationships. It is an investment of the therapist with properties of a secure base that reflect not just the wish, say, for an ever-available attuned primary object, but also the real responsiveness of a fellow human. The ending of a relationship, including a therapeutic one, entails real dissolution as well as disillusionment, and real gratitude for the (albeit professional, and professionally rewarded) love and attention the analyst provided.

The work of mourning is no more and no less than the dissolution of this investment. The conscious awareness of someone who was once everything begins to fade into the background; eventually all that is left is a scar that, like a healed physical wound, imposes its restrictions, great or small. A lost parent, partner, or worst of all a child, inhabits the psyche forever; but as the pain of loss gradually lessens, new investments become possible. When this process is incomplete, there may be an inconsolable effort to replace like with like, eternally in search of what is irretrievably lost, so condemned to everlasting disappointment. Only when this transference is dissolved are new beginnings possible.

In psychotherapy, coming to terms with loss starts with the establishment of a professional relationship; moves into the all-important transferential investment reactivating past attachments and losses; and ends with acceptance of separation, loss, and the fading of the transference.

When I retired from my full-time practice as a psychiatrist, I decided, among the other *rites-de-passage* of separation from a job I had undertaken for 30 years or so, to have a leaving tea party for my patients. I took the list of all my clinic patients and sent each of them an invitation.

These were not, strictly speaking, psychotherapy patients, but, rather, people with severe mental illnesses whom I had gotten to know quite intimately over the years. We had, together, gone through the vicissitudes of psychiatric practice: Most had been in-patients, some involuntarily so, incarcerated at the stroke of my pen. I had prescribed medication for them, written letters about them, helped them to find accommodation, and had seen them regularly in my supportive clinic (typically for half an hour or so every 8 weeks), so that I knew a lot about their lives (as well, no doubt, as much not known). They too had gotten used to me as their psychiatrist, tolerating me, more or less, my good and bad points.

As the day of the party drew near, I became more and more anxious. Would anyone turn up? Would my guests have anything to say to each other, or would the whole thing be conducted in a funereal silence? I wanted to give my patients a good-bye present. The time was near Easter, so a chocolate egg seemed suitable. I had, a la Winnicott, originally thought of a teddy bear (i.e., prototypical transitional object) for everyone, but the cost was prohibitive, so I settled for a post card *depicting* a teddy bear. On the back I wrote a note of gratitude—without his patients how empty a health worker's life would be. (Thanks to the UK National Health Service, we are paid so that our patients can be seen "free at the point of need").*

As the party transpired, my fears were confounded. The turnout was good, and the atmosphere was sociable and festive. Music played, food was scoffed, jokes were told, and even one or two games were played. (I had prepared a box of chocolates wrapped up in "pass the parcel" as an ice-breaker.) I enjoyed myself and so, it seemed, did everyone else. The event was indistinguishable from the outside from any tea party with a group of people who knew each other quite well—there is a subculture of psychiatric patients which means that one way or another they help and interact with each, possibly far more than professionals give them credit for.

The whole event reminded me of a scene from the film version of that painful (for a psychiatrist) masterpiece *One Flew Over the Cuckoo's Nest* in which the inmates on the mental hospital escape for a day and, led by the Jack Nicholson character, hire a boat for a trip on the river. Just as they are setting out they are challenged by the boat owner: "Who the hell are you, escaped nuts or something?" There is a terrible moment when the viewer thinks all will be revealed and they will miss their pleasure trip, but in a moment of inspiration Nicholson introduces each one as distinguished professors. As the camera pans across the familiar faces, the inmates are miraculously transformed from the emiserated inhabitants of an impoverished and degraded mental hospital world into the distinguished faces of freedom and respectability. Oddness becomes lovable eccentricity and genius. Context and expectation are all.

So, too, at the party my patients appeared utterly normal and behaved accordingly. What is more, they treated me as though I was one of them: kissing, hugging, gossiping, teasing, enquiring as they might with a friend or colleague.

As I reflected on this moving event afterward, I realized the reason I had decided that a party was needed both for me and my patients in order to

---

* As an aside, the teddy bear postcard was something of a joke to myself. I once attended a debate between the proponents of psychoanalysis, and those who advocated cognitive analytic therapy which uses written communications and instructions to patients (Ryle, 1990). Although cognitive therapy can be useful, I had argued that giving very disturbed patients written communications was comparable to offering a hungry crying baby a piece of paper with the word "milk" written on it and expecting that to assuage the distress.

help with the "dissolution of the transference" (Sarra, personal communication, 2003). My patients needed to disinvest me with the power of good and evil, and to see me for what I was—a person like them, nearing the end of his working life, frail, flawed, slightly lost without his role and his job, wanting to say good-bye. I needed to be diminished, made vulnerable and ordinary in their eyes, so that they could begin to move on and to invest my successor with the transference that I had carried for all the years we had been working together. Reciprocally, I needed to forget their patient-hood and dependency (theirs on me; mine on them), their vulnerability, and to see them, like everyone else, as equals, with their strengths and frailties.

All this was sad, and somehow humbling, but also reassuring. Attachment and separation, investment and disinvestment are part of the flux of life, two poles whose psychomagnetic field we inhabit, orienting ourselves endlessly between the affective demands of fantasy, and triangulation of reality.

Mentalizing termination

Mentalizing is metaratiocination, thinking about thinking. It starts from the Kantian perspective that absolute truth is ungraspable, and that reality is always filtered through a mind (Allen & Fonagy, 2006). However, the combination of two minds looking at the same phenomenon means that, via triangulation (that is, two perspectives, the patient's and therapist's, on the same fixed entity), reality can be more or less approximated (Cavell, 2006).

This chapter has been informed by two perhaps paradoxical principles. First, a perfect ending is both impossible and undesirable. There will always be themes and issues left unexplored in any given therapy. Interviewing analytic patients 5 years posttermination showed that although most were much better, the presenting conflicts and themes had not gone away, but had merely become less dominant and overwhelming (Bachrach, Galatzer-Levy, Skonikoff, & Waldron, 1991). Although the evidence suggests that for clients with complex disorders longer therapies have better outcomes, there will always be for one reason or another—money, time, geography—a point when therapy perforce comes to an end. Improvement in therapy takes the form of a negative logarithmic curve (Orlinsky, Grawe, & Parks, 2004) which means that the "law of diminishing returns" operates, and that it takes more and more time to produce a smaller and smaller benefit. The search for perfection, on the part of either patient or therapist is, as already mentioned, a narcissistic delusion that needs to be examined, mentalized, and discussed, rather than acted on, by inaction in relation to ending.

The second implicit point is that an ending cannot be other than an enactment. A decision is made: We will end on such and such a day, after so many sessions, with this or that follow-up arrangements, or none. Because the aim of therapy is to replace action with thought, ending is in this sense always countertherapeutic. But neverending therapy is ultimately equally unhelpful. The resolution of this paradox lies in the concept of mental-izing. If the main therapeutic leverage in psychoanalytic therapies is that they instill the capacity to think about thinking, and therefore better to know oneself and others, and self–other interactions, then it is not so much ending as such that matters, as the capacity to *think* about termination, the feelings it engenders, and its meaning, antecedents, and sequelae.

Here is an example illustrating these points. John, in his early forties, was in once-weekly psychoanalytic psychotherapy. His presenting wish was a vaguely expressed desire to "gather my strengths." He had a varied life course, including living in a Tibetan monastery for a while in his twenties, but had settled down, working part-time as a teacher, and devoting himself to his family of three children. He saw his wife, a lawyer, as more of a "high-flyer" than himself, as was his father, a headmaster of a large secondary school.

Sent to a high-pressure academic boarding school at age 8, he felt under-valued by and estranged from both his parents, typified, he said, by finding a letter home he had written from school signed with both his first and sec-ond name, Jon Smith, as though he could not otherwise be certain that his mother (whom he perceived as wrapped up in his baby sister) would know from who it came.

About a year into therapy, he began his session by saying how much better he was now feeling, less compelled to control his wife and children, more ready to lead his own life rather than seek out "wise men" (including, by implication, his therapist) who he had thought were in possession of the answers he was looking for.

Despite this apparent vote of confidence, I sensed there was an implicit attack in this announcement and that he was somehow angry with, or dis-appointed in, me. While mulling this over, I noticed that a potted plant on my window sill looked neglected and half-dead for want of watering, thinking to myself that "I must do something about that before my next patient comes."

I said "I wonder if you are trying out in your mind the idea of leaving therapy." He said "yes," hurriedly adding "not immediately of course."

I asked when the thought had first arisen. "I think it was when I was in your toilet after my last session," he replied, "it seemed so neglected, so full of cobwebs. It reminded me of my Dad, with his stellar career—yet he neglected all the other parts of his life."

"You included?" I asked. "I can hear a story of disillusionment, or disap-pointment here."

"No I don't feel disappointed, sad perhaps. I realize I've made my own choices; what matters to me is my wife and family, the everyday things of life. I feel happy to live by my own lights now, not following an impossible dream of my Dad's."

"And you seem to be feeling that the so-called 'wise men,' including me, are an illusion, they neglect what really matters to you; the answers lie within yourself," I suggested, adding, "I have to confess that I was thinking about that plant over there; it looks, like you, as if it could have done with some tender loving care."

"Well, I suppose I do feel angry with you for not transforming me into the perfect person I thought I wanted to be, but also grateful at the same time for the attention and validation you have offered me," he said.

As he left he said jokingly, "I don't need to go to the toilet today!"

I replied in kind: "But it's *pristine*, all the cobwebs have been cleared away!" We both laughed; the session seemed to end with a good feeling on both sides.

John was deciding to end therapy, prematurely perhaps, but perhaps in a more creative and balanced way than the little boy who had to remind himself of his father's name when writing home. He now knows who he is, and is not. He is more autonomous. He can turn to his high-flying wife with his own manhood more firmly established, less needing to be control-ling, or to borrow an idealized masculine identity from his wise men. His feeling of having being "unwatered" as a child is confirmed, via triangula-tion, with my sense of having neglected my plants. He can see his feelings for what they are—real but not necessarily appropriate to the context he finds himself in. The rupture of the dirty toilet, perhaps a receptacle for his shitty feelings of rage at neglect and lack of care as a child, became a vali-dating moment, moving him from immature dependency (the wise men, the high-flying wife) to mature dependency (leading his own life, caring for his family). By acknowledging that the toilet *was* dirty, while at the same time exploring what a dirty toilet might represent in his inner world, transfer-ence and reality were beginning to be differentiated. This example of rup-ture repaired gave him a sense of validatory empowerment and enabled him to decide to leave therapy at a moment that, on balance, felt right to him.

BRIEF DYNAMIC THERAPY: FOREGROUNDING TERMINATION

The rationale informing brief dynamic therapies (e.g., Gustafson, 1986) begins and starts with termination: "in my beginning is my end" (Eliot, 1986). A time limit is implicit from the first moment of therapy. The thera-pist will count down, usually starting each session by announcing "this is our seventh session" or "we've another three sessions to go" or something similar. The termination hangs above the therapy from the start—conspic-uous either by its absence (patient pretending it does not exist, sometimes collusively with the therapist); or by its inhibitory presence ("what's the point of going into all this, I'm only going to be seeing you for another six times"); but always grist to the mentalizing mill (e.g., "I wonder if the fact that you know you are going to lose me means that you cannot fully make use of me, rather as you never really let your weekends-only Dad know how angry you were with him for leaving your Mum").

Different varieties of brief dynamic therapy handle the ending in different ways. Balint (1968), who realized that for psychoanalytic psychotherapy to reach out from the ivory couches of Hampstead to the masses, it must perforce abbreviate itself, and who had himself suffered major discontinuities in his life (leaving Budapest for the United Kingdom to escape the Nazis, the premature death of his first wife), suggested that at the end of therapy the patient should feel both very much better *and* very much worse, and that what mattered was that this could be acknowledged (i.e., mentalized). Mann's (1973) 12-session, take-it-or-leave-it approach is justified as an analogue of the existential irreversibility of death. If the pain of loss can be experienced, it can be transcended; follow-ups and interminable therapies are simply attempts to evade the reality of irreversible separation. Ryle's (1990) Cognitive Analytic Therapy (CAT), already mentioned, offers, after the prescribed 16 sessions come to an end, a tangible good-bye letter, a memento that can mitigate absence and trigger the activation of an internalized good object that effective therapy can instate. Intensive short-term dynamic psychotherapy has a developing evidence-base (Malan & Della Selva, 2006) and is unabashedly time limited, but pays less attention to termination than other short-term therapies. Its emphasis is on trauma resolution through direct emotional confrontation of avoided feelings—fear, rage, pain, and yearning. This approach is perhaps theoretically closest to Freud's (1937) formulations, and picks up on his observation that perhaps only traumatic cases are capable of full resolution.

CONCLUSION

Yalom (2008) makes a convincing case that death anxiety, a fundamental existential issue, tends to be avoided by patients and therapists. Addressing the full implications of termination brings one face-to-face with the transience of life, the distorting impact of trauma on development, the limitations of therapy, and the inevitability of suffering. Schopenhauer (1984), the supreme yet unbowed pessimist, introduced to Western philosophy the Buddhist precept that suffering is where we start from, and that embracing suffering is the first step toward transcending it.

Intrinsic to this is the distinction in Schoperhauerian philosophy between the "world as will," and "world as idea," the former corresponding roughly with Freud's notion of the unconscious, the latter with the conscious mind. The Will, like the unconscious, is infinite and timeless, driven by intrinsic energetic forces that predate human existence and will continue once human life has passed from the universe. The world as idea is the familiar world of experience, in which time's winged arrow is always felt at one's back—in Marvell's "had we but world enough and time" view a good way for a man to persuade a woman to yield to her libido before the death instinct once more holds sway. A balanced combination of acceptance of suffering and *carpe diem*, living in the present moment, are the antidotes to the despair that might seem to be the inevitable consequence of "full catastrophe living" (Kabat-Zinn, 1990).

Against this synchronic/diachronic dichotomy of time, one can set the biologically informed attachment view of a life cycle with its nodal points. These include in the upswing: conception, birth, weaning, walking, talking, school entry, friendship, adolescence, sexual experimentation, leaving home, finding a sexual partner, occupation, procreation, and parenthood. Then follow from the zenith the beginning of the slow pathway to involution: children leaving home, declining powers spiritual and temporal, the mitigating pleasures of grandparenthood, diminishing responsibilities, returning freedom to play, and looking back on life's troughs and peaks. Each of these, especially if interrupted or perverted by trauma, will play themselves out in their positive and negative aspects, in the metaphor of the therapeutic relationship (Waddell, 1998). The task of the therapist is to tune into the pulse of this underlying biological trajectory and to bring them into consciousness so that the patient can better understand where he or she is on life's journey.

To conclude, illustrate this, and as an antidote to Schopenhauerian gloom, consider the stage and screen hit *Mamma Mia!* adapted from the 1968 film *Buona Vista, Mrs Campbell*. The success of the piece depends largely on its sing-along use of music from ABBA, a palindromic Swedish 1970s two-couple pop group, now disbanded, each man–woman partner now separated.

The setting is a Greek Island. Sophie, a teenage girl, brought up by a single parent, Donna, who runs a hotel that has seen better times, is about to get married. Her fiancée, Sky, is a reluctant bridegroom and feels they would be better off exploring the world (and perhaps each other) before deciding on marriage. Sophie does not know who her father is; her mother's diary suggests three possible candidates. Unbeknownst to Donna, Sophie invites all three to the wedding. Who is the real father? Sophie assumes that she will be able instantly to select the right one when she meets them, but to her dismay she discovers the pre-DNA truism that no one can be absolutely sure who their father is, and that they are all possibilities. Who is to give her away? In her confusion she asks each one of them. The wedding ceremony begins. The naïvely presiding Greek orthodox priest invites the father to give the bride away. All three rise to assume the honor. Sophie graciously accepts their blessing, is happy to waive the DNA test and accept all three as her fathers, but suddenly announces that she is not ready for marriage and that the wedding is off. At this crisis point, one of the three fathers, Sam, steps into the breach: "Why waste a good wedding?" he says, and proposes to the love of his life, Donna. She accepts. Sophie and Sky are delighted and relieved and announce that they will embark on a round-the-world trip, and the movie ends happily with Greek feasting and dancing.

The attachment implication is that one can only leave home if there is a secure base to return to. Now her mother has a man, Sophie can now look after herself rather than play the role of the parentified child looking after her mother (a common pattern in children with disorganized attachment styles). With a secure base now in place and available when needed, she is free to explore the world.

The psychoanalytic implication is that once an internalized good "combined parent" is instated, one is liberated to explore one's own emotional and sexual life. Renunciation of oedipal longings to possess the parent, attendant feelings of sadness and envy overcome, is a necessary developmental step toward psychosexual maturity. Finding a good internal combined ("primal scene") parent, accepting and transcending one's envy and feelings of exclusion, and desire to control and possess the primary object, and embracing the independence and freedom of movement (literal and metaphorical) that implies, are the parallel psychoanalytic conditions for termination. Successful termination of therapy implies the establishment of a more-or-less secure attachment dynamic, with internal feelings of security matched by external relationships, including, if need be, a continuing relationship with a therapist.

In both perspectives, coming to terms with loss is a central theme. Sophie can leave home and move onto new attachments (from Donna to Sky) secure in the knowledge that Donna, herself at last firmly attached to Sam, will be available to her when needed. Donna is securely instated in Sophie's inner world. Sophie no longer needs to push Donna's neediness away, thereby evading her own vulnerability, or cling adhesively to Sky in ways that inhibit her exploration. Her inner world is intact, not threatened by her own aggression, and not needing a rigid external scaffold to support it. The listener, bathed in nostalgia, is reassured that despite the vicissitudes of life—the passing of time, loss, separation (including the dissolution of ABBA as a group and of its members as couples), failure (the marriage that never happened, Donna's single parenthood, Sam's divorce)—through the healing power of music continuity and reparation are possible.

Similar principles apply, all being well, to the therapeutic powers of psychotherapy—including its termination.

REFERENCES

Allen, J., & Fonagy, P. (Eds.). (2006). *Handbook of mentalization-based treatment.* Chichester: Wiley.

Bachrach, H., Galatzer-Levy, R., Skonikoff, A., & Waldron, S. (1991). On the efficacy of psychoanalysis. *Journal of the American Psychoanalytic Association, 39,* 871–911.

Balint, M. (1968). *The basic fault*. London: Tavistock.

Benjamin, J. (2004). Beyond doer and done to: An intersubjective view of thirdness. *Psychoanalytic Quarterly, 73*, 5–46.

Beutler, L., Malik, M., Alimohamed, S., et al. (2004). Therapist variables. In M. Lambert (Ed.), *Handbook of psychotherapy and behavior change* (pp. 227–306). Chichester: Wiley.

Bollas, C. (2009). *The infinite question*. London: Routledge.

Bowlby, J. (1973). *Separation*. London. Penguin.

Bowlby, J. (1980). *Loss*. London: Penguin.

Bowlby, J. (1988). *A secure base*. London: Routledge.

Britton, R., Feldman, M., & O'Shaughnessy, E. (1989). *The Oedipus complex today*. London: Karnac.

Cassidy, J. (2008). The nature of the child's ties. In J. Cassidy & P. Shaver (Eds.), *Handbook of attachment: Theory, research, and clinical applications* (pp. 3–20). New York: Guildford.

Cavell, M. (2006). *Becoming a subject*. Oxford: Oxford University Press.

Dozier, M., Stovall, K., & Albus, K. (2008). Attachment and psychopathology in adulthood. In J. Cassidy & P. Shaver (Eds.), *Handbook of attachment: Theory, research, and clinical applications* (pp. 497–519). New York: Guilford.

Eliot, T. S. (1986). *Collected poems*. London: Faber & Faber.

Freud, S. (1905). Fragment of an analysis of a case of hysteria. In J. Strachey (Ed. & Trans.), *The standard edition of the complete psychological works of Sigmund Freud* (Vol. 7, pp. 3–226). London: Hogarth.

Freud, S. (1917). Mourning and melancholia. In J. Strachey (Ed. & Trans.), *The standard edition of the complete works of Sigmund Freud* (Vol. 14, pp. 243–258) London: Hogarth.

Freud, S. (1918). From the history of an infantile neurosis. In J. Strachey (Ed. & Trans.), *The standard edition of the complete psychological works of Sigmund Freud* (Vol. 17, pp.). London: Hogarth.

Freud, S. (1937). Analysis terminable and interminable. In J. Strachey (Ed. & Trans.), *The standard edition of the complete psychological works of Sigmund Freud* (Vol. 23, pp. 211–253). London: Hogarth.

Gustafson, J. (1986). *The complex secret of brief psychotherapy*. New York: Norton.

Hinde, R. (1979). *Towards understanding relationships*. London: Academic Press.

Holmes, J. (1997). *Attachment, intimacy, autonomy*. New York: Jason Aronson.

Holmes, J. (2001). *The search for the secure base: Attachment theory and psychotherapy*. London: Routledge.

Holmes, J. (2009). *Exploring in security: Towards an attachment-informed psychoanalytic psychotherapy*. London: Routledge.

Kabat-Zinn, J. (1990). *Full catastrophe living*. New York: Delta.

Klass, D., Silverman, P., & Nickman, S. (Eds.). (1996). *Continuing bonds: New understandings of grief*. Washington, DC: Taylor & Francis.

Klein, M. (1940). Mourning and its relation to manic depressive states. In *The writings of Melanie Klein (Vol. 1): Love, guilt, and reparation* (pp. 262–289). London: Hogarth.

Malan, D., & Della Selva, P. (2006). *Lives transformed: A revolutionary method of dynamic psychotherapy*. London: Karnac.

Mann, J. (1973). *Time-limited psychotherapy*. Cambridge, MA: Harvard University Press.

Mikulincer, M., & Shaver, P. (2008). Adult attachment and affect regulation. In J. Cassidy & P. Shaver (Eds.) *Handbook of attachment: Theory, research, and clinical applications* (pp. 503–531). New York: Guilford.

Novick, J. (1988). The timing of termination. *International Journal of Psycho-Analysis, 15*, 307–318.

Novick, J. (1997). Termination conceivable and inconceivable. *Psychoanalytic Psychology, 14*, 145–162.

Ogden, T. (1987). *The matrix of the mind*. Northvale, NJ: Aronson.

Orlinsky, D., Grawe, K., & Parks, B. (2004). Process and outcome in psychotherapy. In M. Lambert (Ed.), *Handbook of psychotherapy and behavior change* (pp. 227–306). Chichester: Wiley.

Parkes, C. (2006). *Love and loss: The roots of grief and its complications*. Washington, DC: Taylor & Francis.

Pedder, J. (1988). Termination reconsidered. *International Journal of Psycho-Analysis, 69*, 495–505.

Reich, A. (1950). On the termination of analysis. *International Journal of Psycho-Analysis, 31*, 179–183.

Rycroft, C. (1985). *Psychoanalysis and beyond*. London: Chatto.

Ryle, A. (1990). *Cognitive analytic therapy*. Chichester: Wiley.

Schopenhauer, A. (1984). *Essays and aphorisms*. London: Penguin.

Shaver, P., & Fraley, R. (2008). Attachment, loss and grief. In J. Cassidy & P. Shaver (Eds.), *Handbook of attachment: Theory, research, and clinical applications* (pp. 48–77). New York: Guilford.

Sroufe, L. (2005). Attachment and development: A prospective, longitudinal study from birth to adulthood. *Attachment and Human Development, 7*, 349–367.

Stern, D. (2004). *The present moment in psychotherapy and everyday life*. New York: Norton.

Tuckett, D., Basile, R., Birkstead-Breen, D. et al. (2008). *Psychoanalysis comparable and incomparable*. London: Routledge.

Waddell, M. (1998). *Inside lives*. London: Karnac.

Winnicott, D. W. (1971). *Playing and reality*. London: Routledge.

Yalom, I. (2008). *Staring at the sun*. London: Piatku.

Chapter 6

Transformations of desire and despair

Reflections on the termination process from a relational perspective*

Jody Messler Davies

Termination: What a flat and one-dimensional word to capture such a rich, multidimensional, and deeply difficult process. Termination is the moment at which patient and analyst sit together, poised, holding the disparate threads of a tapestry of meaning they have woven during the course of the treatment. This tapestry tells the story of how one life has engaged another life and how, in so doing, it has explicated its own unique synergy of historical moments, intense affect states, internal systems of meaning construction, and object relatedness. In many cases, the tapestry depicts a rather bold and epic narrative, the heroic story of a journey undertaken by two brave souls: A journey in which battles have been fought, some lost, some won; evil demons and wild beasts have been met and hopefully subdued; love affairs have been imagined, played out, and transformed; and moments of remarkable intimacy and vulnerability hereafter bind the souls of our two courageous travelers. This tapestry, the work of an intensive psychoanalysis, is living testament to what systems theorist Gregory Bateson (1973) described by saying, "It takes two...to know one." (In essence, he was describing the wisdom that life is a hazardous journey, and, to survive intact and with self-awareness, we must travel together.) We know, as analysts who sit holding the threads of this fabric, that there comes a time when we must somehow finish our tapestry, cutting the threads loose and binding the colors and textures and patterns together in a way that somehow manages to hold them all, preventing the escape of any errant thread that can unravel the whole and destroy what patient and analyst have worked so hard to create.

It has always been of interest to me that Freud had little to say about the termination of a psychoanalysis. He never wrote a technical paper on the subject, and there are very few technical suggestions sprinkled throughout his other papers, even "Analysis Terminable and Interminable." Ferenczi, always an abundant source of rich and creative (if controversial) technical

* This chapter originally appeared in *Psychoanalytic Dialogues*, 15(1), 2005, pp. 779–805. (Reprinted with permission.)

clinical advice, did write a paper on termination that he presented to the tenth International Psychoanalytic Congress in 1927. In this paper, he stated simply, "The proper ending of an analysis is when neither the physician nor the patient puts an end to it, but when it dies of exhaustion, so to speak" (p. 85). Written from his particular historical context in the development of psychoanalytic thought, Ferenczi's advice is predicated on the belief that because transference love is a fantasy, resolution of the transference will obviate the need for and dependency upon the treatment. It was not until 1955 that Edward Glover identified a "termination phase" of the psychoanalytic treatment and offered some technical recommendations for its handling. Even so, writing on the subject remained sparse until the early 1970s, three quarters of the way through the 100-year history of our field, a remarkable thing if you think about it.

During this time, a fair body of literature on termination emerged, but my review of the literature suggests that these recommendations rest upon a fairly classical notion of mind and of the psychoanalytic process: resolution of a linear and oedipally organized transference neurosis; a relatively one-sided exploration of the patient's experiences of loss, death, abandonment, and grief; and an emphasis on the patient's identification with what has been called the "analyzing function" of the analyst in preparation for the postanalytic phase. The emphasis is clearly on the patient's history on how the loss of the analysis and the analyst trigger the reemergence of earlier trauma and unresolved grief. In essence, the mourning process at termination involves the analyst as a "stand-in" of sorts, a representative in part for all of the unmourned, ungrieved, unresolved abandonments and separations suffered by the patient.

I would not want to disagree with these aspects of the termination process. I believe them to be important and essential aspects of what must transpire in the ending of an analysis. However, I do believe that a more contemporary rendering of mind and a more intersubjectively conceived treatment demands that we go beyond these considerations, asking ourselves how our evolving understanding of the therapeutic action of psychoanalysis requires that we rethink and elaborate that which becomes necessary during the termination process, given the particular model of mind we hold and the particular elaborations of psychoanalytic technique we employ. Writing from a contemporary Freudian perspective, Martin Bergmann (1997) put forth the view that psychoanalytic writing on technique has failed to provide a useful paradigm for the termination process. Bergmann went on to explore the idea that most patients have little impetus to terminate, given that their counterdependency needs have been successfully analyzed during their treatments. For many patients, Bergmann suggested, the analytic relationship is the best love relationship they have ever experienced. From a more interpersonal perspective, Edgar Levenson (1978) suggested that termination is more a matter of aesthetics than of technique, comparing the analyst's sense of when to end a treatment with the painter's decision to acknowledge that his work of art is complete. For Levenson, every termination, much like any analytic dream, has within it the totality of the analysis and of the analyst–patient relationship and is therefore uniquely organized and experienced by each analytic dyad. Irwin Hoffman (1998), speaking about the termination process from a relational perspective, wrote,

> Although we cannot change any moment as it was experienced, we can make choices that affect the meaning to us of any particular moment as we think of it in retrospect. Death puts an end to any chance to revise the meaning of our experience by reinterpreting earlier experiences in light of later ones. (pp. 245–246)

Hoffman goes on to point out that death is not the equivalent of termination, although this distinction can sometimes be obscured in the traditional termination literature. Termination does, however, put an end to the analytic relationship as the analytic couple has come to know and experience it and involves the transformation of this relationship into something quite different from what it has ever been before. The particular quality, the way we choose to negotiate the narcissistic vulnerabilities of the termination process, may forever color how we remember the entirety of the experience.

From this sampling, one senses that regardless of psychoanalytic orientation—Freudian, interpersonal, or relational—contemporary psychoanalysts have come to understand that the waning therapeutic reliance on a "blank screen" analyst poses new problems for the termination process. In this particular regard, Stephen Mitchell (1997) wrote,

> We all have a deep, intuitive sense of the importance of the lasting internal presence of and identifications with one's analyst(s) that is difficult to reconcile with the myth of the generic analyst and the perfectionistic ideal of a "complete analysis." This presence derives not just from the analysts' interpretations or their professional or work ethic or their supportive understanding, but to their subjective way of being, a sense of what they are like, their feel for life. We come to know only the version of the analyst that comes alive through his role in the analytic process. Yet, that version is deeply personal. (p. 27)

And Anthony Bass (2001), in a vision most closely akin to my own—because it stresses not only the patient's experience of loss and identification, but the analyst's own experience as well—wrote,

> I find that the word *termination*, with its dictionary denotations of "confinement," "finality," "bringing something to a stop so that it extends

no further," fails to capture crucial dimensions of those moments when, at the end of the day, endings and beginnings merge, forming a unity.... Most often, life goes on for analyst and analysand alike, though when the partnership has fulfilled its potential, neither is the same for having met the other in the way they did, and the trajectory of both lives will not be quite the same for the encounter. (p. 700)

This paper represents my own attempt to understand the process of termination given the dissociation-based model of mind and therapeutic function about which I have written in many earlier papers (e.g., Davies, 1996, 1998a, 1999). Toward this end, I ask you to imagine that the threads of a psychoanalytic tapestry, particularly a relationally designed one, are the self-states of patient and analyst, the developmentally organized systems of identifications and counteridentifications, concordant and complementary (in Racker's, 1968, conceptualization) that have engaged, disengaged, fought, loved, struggled, and survived to tell their story, a story of the patients' unique internal self-organizations, the meanings created by these organizations, and the varieties of engagement with significant others that have the potential to emerge and solidify from within them. The termination process, seen from such a vantage point, is not, then, just a long good-bye. Termination so conceived involves a multitude of good-byes—many, many good-byes—between the self-states of patient and analyst, good-byes that emanate from a multitude of developmental epochs and from different centers of developmental trauma, conflict, and meaning making. From my own perspective, each good-bye deserves its own attention; each one is different; each one holds the potential not only for growth, emergence, and liberation, but also for grief, despair, and narcissistic collapse. Termination is not a unitary and linear process, but one that is contradictory and complex, containing many, often irreconcilable, experiences of the same separation and ending. Each good-bye between analyst and patient holds the potential to define the entire experience of the analysis and to determine how that experience is remembered and held over time.

As with any intensely intimate relationship, if the ending is marked by emotional honesty, respect for the feelings of the other, and a gentleness that speaks to the vulnerability of the moment, the relationship can be jointly grieved and may yet be remembered with warmth and a preponderance of loving feeling that supports the narcissistic injury imposed by the loss and separation. Where emotional dishonesty or the projective disavowal of unacceptable self-states or affect states, by either participant, comes to define the emotional landscape, narcissistic outrage may come to supplant the mourning process, and resentment and contempt may forever cloud even the most positive and loving memories of the analytic process.

Within the multiplicity of psychoanalytic "endings" involved in the termination of any given analytic treatment, we find not only self-other organizations and engagements from different developmental epochs of the patients' and analysts' lives, but also self-other organizations that emanate from different points along the path of analytic change and transformation. These are the "emergent" self-states, organizations of self that have grown out of the analysis, which have grown up in relation to the analyst as a "healthier" object who has struggled along with the patient to find new resolutions to old, developmentally determined identificatory conflict. Such new and emergent self-states are particularly vulnerable to the challenges of termination and must withstand its assault. We might say that one of the signals that the patient is ready to consider entering a termination phase is that these emergent self-states appear firmly established and resilient enough to survive the loss of the analyst and the potential revitalized reemergence of bad objects and sadistic introjects that might once again rise up against those healthier emergent self-states, particularly at this moment of vulnerability, in the analyst's absence, to challenge newly emergent meanings. How the emergent self–other organizations of patient and analyst experience, understand, and survive the termination process creates further cocreated new experience and contains the potential to strengthen new structures and enhances the transformation of old meaning schemas.

But I think it is safe to say that the termination phase of treatment gives rise to particular difficulties for the relational analyst and calls into question, perhaps more than any other phase of the treatment, some of the specific challenges and dangers that may be unique to working within a relational framework. I have written on earlier occasions (Davies, 1998c, 1999; see also Hoffman, 1998) that whereas the neutrality and abstinence of the classical psychoanalyst might leave certain patients untouched and unchanged by the process, the significant emotional engagement and participation of the relational analyst could, in the end, leave particular patients extremely vulnerable to an experience of having been seduced and then abandoned. "Why should I care about you?" asks the vulnerable patient. "Who are you that you should matter to me?" "Why should I let myself care about you— love you—when in the end this treatment has to end?" We might well ask ourselves, "Why indeed?"

Jay Greenberg (2001) suggested that relational analysts have substituted "a new relationship with the analyst"—and the kind of transference gratification, even love, that this implies—for the deeper insights and intense affective experience he views as more endemic to a classical position. Although I agree with Greenberg that relational analysts often write about the "new analytic object relationship," I believe that his interpretation of this phrase represents an imprecise and unfortunately reductive description of what we relational analysts are actually going about in our psychoanalytic work. It seems to me that the relationships we construct with our patients are actually templates—beloved templates perhaps, but templates nonetheless. For what we offer patients, within a relational psychoanalysis, is the opportunity to explore how their unique internal organizations of self–other experience tend to envision and construct relationships with significant others: how early implicit relational systems somehow organize and control not just the past, but also the present and the future. We can only imagine what we have known. Our analytic intent is not simply to provide patients with new experiences, but to give them the tools, knowledge, insight, and self-awareness to enable them to construct for themselves, in our absence and when we are gone, new relationships from within emergent self-states, new relationships that do not conform to the old, stereotypically neurotic and frustrating patterns of their past.

However, to do this we must actually engage with them *in* a relationship, not a superficial provision of emotional supplies that occurs only in the here and now of interpersonal relationship, but a deeply felt, emotionally intense, mutually constructed experience of their own unique systems of self–other organizations and identificatory and counteridentificatory conflicts existing between self-organizations out of which they construct their contemporary relational world visions. We involve ourselves in their internal worlds, we immerse ourselves deeply; according to Stephen Mitchell (1986) we dance the patient's dance. We try to feel their rhythms in our bodies and our bones and our minds and our hearts, how the patient does it, how the patient feels it, what the patient thinks about it, and with whom the patient chooses to do it all. We take for granted that along the way our own self-states, our own identifications and counteridentifications, will involve us in a deeply felt personal way, as they engage in unconscious enactments that draw us more deeply, into the unconscious dimensions of the patients' experiences and our own.

For relational analysts and patients, it is the mutual struggle out of these emotional imbroglios, the journey from enactment to acknowledgment, to interpretation, and ultimately to self-reflection, that eventually creates analytic insight and change. And although the process for patient and analyst is surely asymmetrical, we understand that the struggle out of enactment to self-reflection proceeds for both of them as the multiple self-states of the patient engage with the multiple self-states of the analyst in patterns of engagement unique to their particular dyadic process. Patient and analyst alike will question each other and their own internal object worlds. How do I construct my relationships? Why do I construct them this way? What does this have to do with my own history of past relationships? What significant identifications are problematic for me in choosing significant others? Do I want to keep going the way I have been going? And ultimately, "how do I do it differently?"

But here we understand that "doing it differently" is not simply a matter of instruction, interpretation, and evolving cognitive insights, although these are all contributing factors. Changing the implicit memory systems that unconsciously influence our unconscious object-related choices must, also, we now know, involve a deeply felt, affectively powerful enacted experience of something new and different emerging out of the old, self-destructive repetitions. We must repeat, unlearn, and relearn, like changing a tennis serve or an intricately choreographed dance step. We must practice it—we cannot accomplish the change by merely thinking it; we must do it again and again and again, falling into old patterns and reminding our bodies, "This is the old way...this is the new way...this is why it is hard to do it the new way...but remember, body, you must do it the new way." Perhaps this is what we have always meant by "working through."

The conundrum, of course, is that to engage so mutually and so intensely, over such a long expanse of time, involves both participants in the psycho-analytic process in a profoundly mutual, deeply felt, and deeply loving (at times, hating) relationship. Termination, seen from this light, stands as one of the very few moments in life when we actively choose to permanently end such a mutually loving relationship. "Why should I let myself love you?" asks the vulnerable patient, "if ultimately this relationship has to end?" Why indeed? Such questions become particularly bittersweet and poignant when we consider how the termination process exposes the multiple self-states of patient and analyst alike to potentially humiliating experiences of feeling unloved, passed over, outgrown, and dispensed with. Even when our adult selves are ready to move on, prepared for new adventures—adventures that can be consummated, lived out, and fulfilled—there are younger, more vulnerable, less narcissistically evolved states who hold on and hold back, that are confused, injured, and abandoned. "Why are you doing this?" "What have I done wrong?" "Why don't you love me anymore?" "Did you ever *really* love me in the first place?" "Please don't leave me." "Can I ever let myself love or trust again?" I daresay that such infantile states exist for patient and analyst alike. And although there may be some differential in how readily they are evoked and under what conditions (please note the often infantile reactions of analysts who believe that a patient is terminating "prematurely"), they are at no point in treatment so much in danger of lending their particular world vision to the entire psychoanalytic endeavor as they are during the narcissistic vulnerabilities of the termination phase.

How then do we conclude a psychoanalysis, given the multiplicity of endings that must occur and the range of developmental epochs from within which they must be negotiated? How do we conclude without the experience of seduction and abandonment infusing and toxifying the entire endeavor, forever coloring the analysis with representations of analytic violation, betrayal, and abandonment? In recent years (Davies, 1998b, 2003), I have written a good deal about the developmental shift between oedipal and postoedipal forms of relatedness, and about the ways in which infantile, oedipal love and transference love hold in common the potential for a highly romanticized, deeply bewitching, all-consuming and utterly impossible love—a love of mythic, epic proportion, a love designed to be healing and compensatory on the one hand, but a love that must also be relinquished and transformed in order for the child or patient to move on to more realizable forms of romantic engagement. (For additional perspectives on the postoedipal phase, see Bassin, 1997; Cooper, 2000; Loewald, 1977.) I have suggested that it is, most often, during the termination phase of a treatment that patient and analyst struggle to de-idealize and transform this experience of mutual perfection—accepting each other's imperfections, vulnerabilities, and flaws, renouncing both the adored other and the adored self, holding potential disappointments in the other and in the self, and yet holding these disappointments with the knowledge and wisdom that imperfection is inevitable and paradoxically enriches and deepens that which we are capable of feeling for another. If one accepts these ideas, as well as my basic premise (Davies, 1998b, 2003) that children must (contrary to classical theory) both win and lose their oedipal struggles, then how do we allow for our patients' symbolic victories in this arena without seducing, overstimulating, and essentially retraumatizing them? And how do we suggest that our need for each other may be at an end and conclude a psychoanalysis without evoking the narcissistic collapse of the patient into another, perhaps more destructive, retraumatization defined by the experience of being devalued, dismissed, and discarded by an adored other?

There is, then, a direct parallel between the termination phase of an analysis and the movement from oedipal to postoedipal forms of relatedness. Both involve the slow undoing and renunciation of an illusory love, illusory not in the sense of being artificial or fake, but illusory rather in both its imagined perfection and the sense that it is ultimately unrealizable in the external world. One of my favorite poets, Emmanuel Ghent (1992), wrote,

> So often it happens that the route to truth is through the intensity of illusion. Is not analysis a veritable playpen for transference and countertransference, and what are these if not vehicles for finding truth by knocking on the walls of illusion? Are not dreams the quintessential illusions, fictions? Are not most art forms—lines on a flat plane or ambiguous words in blank verse or people playing roles on stage—are not these all built on illusion? And do not all these lead us, through illusion, to encounter a level of truth and reality that is otherwise inaccessible? (p. 139)

Both oedipal love and transference love are necessary. They are foundational. They can both burn hot and deep. But ultimately both represent loves that cannot be lived out and consummated in real time and space without the profound traumatization or retraumatization of the child or the patient. They must be relinquished and mourned. To my way of thinking, it is within the space defined by these two potential forms of retraumatization—the place between triumph and failure, the space between adoration and scorn—that the essential and life-affirming process of termination must occur. For termination, so configured, becomes not just a psychic space in which to reprocess and grieve unmourned losses, but also a space in which we attempt to learn how to sustain desire for that which we cannot possess, how to tolerate disappointment even in our most heartfelt pursuits without converting this disappointment into scorn and ultimately retaliatory preoccupations. The paradox of termination, then, involves sustaining disappointment in our deepest places while at the same time sustaining as well our love for those who inflict these same wounds. Such a capacity comes, I believe, from the dawning mutual recognition that it is only such disappointment in oedipal or transference love that allows the patient to move on to a love that is less illusory and less unrealizable, one that is ultimately more nourishing and consummated. It involves recognition, as well, that intimate love can only be sustained in the shadow of disappointment, and that to sustain such intimate attachment the patient must be capable of sustaining desire as the idealized perfections of early infatuation give way to a love that is more accepting of mutual, interpenetrating vulnerabilities (Davies, 2003). Both patient and analyst must come to accept, perhaps to "surrender" (Ghent, 1990) to the idea that in walking this very, very fine line between desire and despair, the analyst not only disappoints the patient, but also frees her to move on in life to a love that can be realized and consummated in the fullest sense.

The termination of a relational psychoanalysis involves, then, for me, three significant dimensions that may distinguish such a process from the final stages of a more classically rendered treatment. First, it involves a process of multiple endings and multiple good-byes, each of which occurs between a significant self-state of the patient and a significant self-state of the analyst. These good-byes evoke different developmental eras, different affective colorations and intensities, different cognitive schemas, and different transference–countertransference reenactments and potentials. Second, such a termination involves a mutual letting-go process, a letting go that—like one's oedipal relationships—involves loss and necessary mourning on both sides of the process; a letting go that involves the slow, nontraumatic transformation of mutually idealizing yet impossible experiences of compensatory perfection and love into an acceptance of vulnerability, mutual interpenetrability, and the capacity to experience loss or defeat without a renunciation of hope and a full engagement with the promises of the future. Such a process involves acknowledging the analyst's penetrability as well as the patient's—how the analyst has been touched and permanently changed by her work with any given patient, and it involves creating a space for the analyst's mourning process to proceed along with (although perhaps not symmetrical to) the patient's.

The third dimension of this model subsumes the first two and holds firmly to the conviction that implicit memory systems—what has been termed *procedural relational knowing*—can only be changed by actual, felt, enacted experience that is rehearsed and practiced over significant periods of time and in the presence of significant others. I firmly believe, therefore, that the termination of the analytic relationship, the final consolidation and internalization of all that has been achieved during the course of the treatment, must occur in the ultimate relational negotiations between patient and analyst that both repeat old relational experiences, and then unlearn and relearn newer ways of transforming these unsatisfying patterns. In the final days, the insights that have been gained from a thorough reworking of the past, of significant past object relationship and conflict, must be brought to bear within the analytic dyad, serving as a deeply unsatisfying counterpoint to the transformations that are struggling for breath and life in the final days of the work together, and are somehow captured by and reflected in the way in which the potential narcissistic injury is transformed (see Davies, 2003).

Let me share with you some moments that are drawn from the termination process with my patient Karen. I do not attempt to be thorough in my rendering of this process, and I do not attempt to provide you with a detailed portrayal of how these three issues manifested in this analytic treatment, or how they came to be resolved between us. I do, however, attempt to provide a tableau of sorts that might serve to evoke these dimensions of termination and give us a reference point for later discussion. Some of you may remember Karen. A long clinical paper on Karen's treatment (Davies, 2003) attempted to capture the enormously difficult process of engaging with Karen's almost relentless malignant projections, and how she and I struggled to survive these projections, to understand their functions, and to soften—over time and with much effort—their toxic effects on our relationship. Much of this effort involved my being able to recognize, hold, and sustain Karen's destructive and reparative engagements and self-states, and my allowing Karen to see the complexity of my own motivations, destructive and reparative, as well as the self-states in which those forces resided. It was only in seeing me own and attempt to metabolize my own destructiveness and shame that Karen could overcome enough of the blinding shame she felt regarding her own malignant envy and rage, to halt the process of projective evacuation, and to begin bridging the split into complementarity that made feeling loved and feeling sane, at the same time, irreconcilable experiences for much of Karen's life.

I invite you now to once again join Karen and me. We are, at this point, 8 years further along into Karen's analysis. The selves now set before you would probably, on the surface, be unrecognizable to those of you who suffered with me through some of the more difficult phases of my work with Karen in the earlier paper. Gone is the sullen deadness of Karen's gaze.

The enormous down jacket in which she swathed her despair and hopeless-ness has been replaced by an attractive and stylish outfit more revealing of her body, eyes that hold energy and hope, and plans that communicate belief in a future that will hold emotional nourishment, even love. In the 8 years that have transpired, Karen finished her B.A. and earned a master's degree in special education. She survived some pretty rocky and mutually destructive relationships with enough of herself intact to meet, date, and fall in love with Brian. Lest you believe that I am telling you some kind of psychoanalytic fairy tale of untold therapeutic success in the land of the impossible, let me assure you that Karen can still be extremely difficult. She is moody, often petulant; she is narcissistically vulnerable and prone to feeling victimized and shamed with relatively little external provocation. I know that Karen will always be intense, and I suspect that she will often be challenging and provocative in intimate relationships. But Karen has come to know her selves. She understands and recognizes her own self-states. She has a sense of the developmental crises around which they have emerged. She knows them, recognizes them, understands how old each is, how each thinks and reacts, and to which of her significant objects each belongs. She knows what kind of reaction each self-state is most likely to stimulate in others. Most important, perhaps, she knows how to take care of each of them, and she knows to whom she can turn for help if her attempts at self-nurturance falter.

Karen knows also that I care about her deeply. She knows that I am proud of the newer selves that have emerged in our work together and in the courage and hope she is bringing to bear on her future. But she knows as well that I have come to understand and care deeply for the more angry, rageful, and envy-filled self-states that marked much of our analytic work together. And although she recognizes the pain and suffering evoked in oth-ers by those selves, she has also come to appreciate the adaptive, survival functions they served for her, the ways in which the present she loves might not have been possible without these defensive hatreds of the past. Karen knows that I appreciate this as well and that I am grateful to her more hateful selves, for even though they have forced upon me moments of pain-ful self-awareness (awareness of personal self-states that I might choose to ignore or forget), they have also protected Karen. They have made it pos-sible for her to survive her childhood and they have brought her into the analysis, into the work with me, and into my life.

There is more work that Karen and I might do to solidify the gains she has made in her treatment. But Brian has just been accepted to graduate school in California, and they have decided that Karen will go with him. They will move in together. They are planning to marry.

Karen will look for her first teaching job in special education on the West Coast. Karen and I choose to believe in her future, and we begin the difficult process of ending her analysis and transforming our relationship into something that will never again be quite the same.

During the course of this work, Karen and I move fluidly among self-states and object relationships that have defined the transference–countertransference process during particular phases of her analysis. We learn to recognize, both of us with some surprise, the reemergence at this time of self–other experience that we believed had been worked through and transformed. I learn from my work with Karen that self-states are rarely laid to rest, that their transformation in the course of analytic work is relative and fluid, their reemergence in interpersonal construction and experience always a potential in the context of particularly vulnerable experience.

I begin to recognize in my work with Karen at this time the illusive appearance and disappearance of a part of her I have known: the Karen of that earlier paper—the Karen who is relentless, demanding, unsatisfied, at times inconsolable; the Karen it is hard to love, hard to tolerate, hard (at times) not to hate. She is not present in the way she once was, but she darts in and out of our work together, a tease, a provocateur, a felt presence. Her appearance surprises both of us. Karen embodies her unwillingly and ambivalently. I accept her reappearance but welcome her back with deep reservations of my own. In these moments with me, she is sullen and despondent. How could I be letting her go? she asks. Maybe she should be with me and not Brian. Perhaps she should stay behind for a year or two and do more analytic work. Perhaps I am actually relieved to see her leave, secretly eager for her to go. Perhaps I do not really care about her as I have claimed. Perhaps it has all been a lie, a therapeutic strategy, a manipulation. "Perhaps I have been an idiot," cries Karen, ultimately, "to ever believe you could care about me, to be sucked in and now spit out by you. How could I ever have believed you really cared, why in the world did I let myself become so vulnerable?" Why, indeed?

Such questions reverberate in transference–countertransference processes representing a host of different developmentally meaningful dyadic pairings. Will the termination of Karen's analysis be remembered and recorded as a hostile abandonment, a premature casting out to a cold and uninviting world? Or will the letting go represent the ultimate loving gesture, the relinquishment of the analyst's narcissistic needs to hang on to the patient's idealized oedipal love in order to free the patient for a genuinely intimate and mutually interpenetrating postoedipal love? One must presume that the working-through process will resound on multiple levels, evoking reminiscences and dyadic relational processes from a host of developmental crises.

Part of our conventional psychoanalytic wisdom holds that symptoms will tend to reappear around termination. Part of what I am suggesting today is that not only symptoms reappear at termination, but also the self–other paradigms and organizations from which those particular symptoms arise and within which they have taken hold. We come to a point where Karen's sullen and despondent self-state takes up a protracted residence. It is not quite as it was before, because she and I both realize who we are dealing with: We know this self, we know her reactions, we know her triggers, and we know what she stimulates in both of us. We each know that she and our more toxic reactions to her represent parts of us—not all of us, just parts. She is like a rather unwelcome relative who—knowing we do not particularly enjoy her—has come for a visit, nonetheless determined to impose herself upon us. Why has she come, Karen and I wonder? What might she want? I take note, at this particular time, that this self-state of Karen's seems younger, more frightened, more vulnerable than she did in past appearances. She wonders out loud, "What will become of me?" She brings me dreams that seem to reflect her own impending death. She seems sad and tiny, as if the life is draining out of her. I find myself associating to the movie *E.T.*, to the creature who lay dying because the present environment could not support his life form. I think at that moment of the highly significant extraterrestrial dream that Karen brought me 8 years ago, at a particularly significant moment in her treatment (see Davies, 2003, for a transcript of this dream). I begin to listen to her self-state differently, more literally; I take the dissociation in the transference more concretely and allow myself to suspend reality long enough and deeply enough to believe that I am witnessing and speaking with a different Karen. In terms I have used elsewhere (Davies, 1996, 1998a), I am experiencing a therapeutic dissociation, but this time in the countertransference.

The next time Karen asks me, "Why is she here, why has she come?" I feel more ready to respond.

"I think she is angry with me, Karen, because I am so busy saying good-bye to you that I have forgotten about her, forgotten to say good-bye to her as well. She feels that I am eager to see her go because I have been too caught up with you, too involved with the exciting changes and things that are happening to you to recognize how frightened she is that we are abandoning her. I think I can understand how she feels. I think she is right, that we may have inadvertently abandoned her to survive this time in our relationship all alone."

Karen faces me quietly, pensively; her face reflects surprise, confusion. Something inside her is attempting to reorganize, to take in what I am saying, to evaluate its emotional salience. One can almost sense a movement back and forth across time, our time together—hers and mine, this history of our multiple transference–countertransference engagements—and across Karen's own personal history (the death of her father, her mother's illusive psychotic abandonments). They are all present in these few moments when Karen sits silently staring at me. We are not back in the past and we are not now in the present, but we are in both, and we are also all of the moments and selves that we have been with each other in between.

"She is afraid she is going to die without you," mumbles Karen, as if she is unprepared for the words that tumble from her. I suspect that she has not thought them before; they emerge in the moment. The meaning to be made lies unformulated between us (Stern, 1983). "Brian doesn't know her. Only you and I know her. Brian can't know her, he can know about her, but he can't know her. She is too old. She is too young. She is too far away and long ago to make sense to him, or to me when I am with him. No one has ever liked her or cared about her but you, Jody. She's so scared."

"I think she has come to say goodbye, Karen," I say, "to be a part of our saying goodbye to each other. I think she needs to know that I care about her deeply and that I will miss her, despite how difficult she can be, and that I will hold her inside me so that she won't vanish into thin air. I think somehow she has figured out that if I keep her alive, then she can go on being, that she doesn't have to die, even if you and Brian are occupied elsewhere."

"But she only lives between us, Jody. And if there is no us, then she will vanish and die and I will never find a way to be whole."

"There will always be an us, Karen," I tell her. "The analysis will end, but you and I will go on being, inside of each other. That will not end."

"Can she call you sometimes?" Karen asks.

"Of course she can," I respond. "You know that you can pick up the phone and call when and if you need or want to, but I think she needs to know that, too. She needs to know that she can call me—that if she finds herself feeling that she is disappearing, dying, fading, she can call me to make sure she still exists, at least inside of me. She can call to find out how she is doing."

"What if you die, Jody? What if something happens to you?" Karen asks.

I think here of the sudden and premature death of Karen's father when she was 9 years old. And I am moved by Karen's courage and boldness in approaching an aspect of this termination—the possibility of my death—that I had not brought up with her (see Hoffman, 2006). "I can't promise not to die, Karen," I respond. "You are the last person I would ever make such a promise to. But if I die, when I die, you will still have me inside of you. I will hold her inside of me so that she may live on, and you will hold me inside of you so that she and I can live on together no matter what happens to each of us on the outside."

Karen is quiet for several minutes. "I am okay," she tells me. "But she is crying so hard inside me. She wants you to know that. And she wants you to know how much she would love to be sitting on your lap, crying while you hold her. But she knows she is too big for that."

"You are too big for that, perhaps," I respond, "but she isn't, and I so wish that I could do that for her. I can imagine it so readily. I can hold that image in mind along with you, so that maybe in the particular space that you and she and I share, she will actually feel some of that experience of being held."

When I look up at her, Karen has her eyes closed tightly. She is curled up in the chair, arms wrapped around her knees, crying very quietly, rocking almost imperceptibly. "Shh," she signals me, "shh." So, rather than speaking, I close my eyes as well and return to my enjoyment of the internal image that Karen and I had been sharing.

Amid the profound intimacy of this mutual grieving process comes a crisis, unexpected and unbidden, which threatens to destroy or at least to challenge the mutual love that Karen and I are attempting to preserve and transform in the ways I have described. This crisis is one example of the kind of disappointment that will challenge the imagined perfection of what we have created together and lead either to the internalization of a good, but not idealized, object experience (see Skolnick, 2006), or a challenge that will threaten to destroy that good object experience altogether. Three months prior to our agreed upon termination date, Karen raises with me the question of whether or not I might consider traveling to California to attend her wedding. I cannot say that I am shocked, for I have been aware of a disappointment that I will not be present to see Karen married—a subtle, almost preconscious disappointment that she and Brian have chosen to have their wedding in California. I should mention, in this regard, that I have attended weddings and other profoundly important events in the lives of certain patients with whom I have had a very long and deep connection. It has not happened often, but it has occurred at times over the course of my career. In all cases, I have attended only the more official aspect of the event—that is, the wedding ceremony but not the reception, the graduation but not the party. Indeed, I had been at Karen's graduate school commencement. So, when Karen began speaking of her wedding to Brian, I entertained fantasies that this could well be another of those situations in which I might be present to witness and share in her joy, representing for her as I witnessed the event all of the emergent, "new object" self–other organizations that could only live and breathe in the intersubjective space created by our relationship with each other.

Karen's father was dead; her psychotically depressed mother was enraged at the imagined abandonment symbolized by Karen's marriage and deeply envious of Karen's joy in the love she had found. In observing her wedding ceremony, I could represent the postoedipal parent freeing her child of the destructive, envy-filled dyadic enmeshment, of the parasitic, cavernous, and unrelenting need that marked her preoedipal relationship with mother. I might represent the absent father, "giving away the bride" to another man who could satisfy her in ways that I could not. In short, I might represent and hold firmly the space Karen and I had created, in which joy, love, and hope for the future could at least momentarily hold off envy, despair, and even death.

So, when Karen informed me that she intended to hold her wedding in California, I initially felt surprise, along with a host of as yet unformulated, somewhat darker emotions that I would understand and embrace more fully over time—smaller voices, younger voices, voices I could easily choose to disregard—even dissociate—but voices whose message pressed to be heard. "How could she do this?" "Doesn't she want me at her wedding?" "Doesn't she *need* me at her wedding?" There were even darker, smaller voice: "Doesn't she love me?" "How could she toss me aside at a moment like this?" And the smallest, darkest voices of all said, "The hell with her, who needs her anyway? If she wants to go, let her go." Why had I let myself love her? Why, indeed?

Our psychoanalytic tradition makes it too easy, I believe, to pathologize such musings on the part of the analyst—unresolved separation issues, overinvestment in the patient, overinvestment in the treatment, neurotic or characterologically pathological countertransference. We dehumanize ourselves in this process of psychoanalytic self-cleansing, depriving ourselves of the developmentally embedded voices that speak to us from earlier and more troubled times in our own lives, voices that will teach us (if carefully listened to) to listen to our patients more carefully, voices that will teach us to understand things, irrational things, that our more rational and mature selves have chosen to "outgrow." If we, as clinicians, accept our younger selves as never quite outgrown, but instead as reduced in psychic potency and influence, we bring a compassion to our understanding of patients that challenges their own more self-hating and self-abusing self-states. We allow patients to identify with us not only in our healthiest and most mature states of mind, but also in our willingness and enhanced capacity to listen to—without disowning—our more troublesome inner voices, to integrate rather than to disown the irrational, narcissistically injured (even sadistic) undertones in ourselves. We teach them to survive the shame that can potentiate and perpetuate self-evacuation, and to draw back within the self the organizations of mind and experience that toxify their present-day relationships and world-visions when projected rather than held and metabolized. It is only by drawing these self-organizations back into the self that we, analyst and patient, are able to replace enactment with self-reflection.

Ultimately, in the case being described, it was only by acknowledging that parts of me felt hurt, narcissistically injured, and excluded by Karen's decision to hold her wedding in California, that I could assure that those self-states would not insidiously gain control of the psychoanalytic process and permanently darken our termination process. By acknowledging them and listening to them, I become capable of arguing with them, disputing their logic, and replacing their world vision with one that is wiser, more mature, more recognizing of the needs of the other, and more willing to tolerate frustration and personal disappointment. Here the letting go of Karen and my own fantasies about her moving on without me required an adjustment on my part not unlike the kind of process, which I have described, that the oedipal parent must go through in order to free her child to move from an oedipal love organized around idealized parental figures to a post-oedipal love that can be lived and consummated in real time.

I had to acknowledge that there was a strong, healthy, sizable aspect of Karen who knew that it was time for us to end our psychoanalytic relationship; a part of her who recognized that if she were to marry, to move, to begin a life with Brian, our relationship—hers and mine—must be reduced from the primacy it had once held and assume a less salient, more behind-the-scenes, organizing function in the preconsciousness of her day-to-day existence. I was forced to acknowledge that choosing to hold her wedding in California was Karen's way of beginning our ending. And a strong, sizable, healthy aspect of me was going to have to accept her wisdom and silence my own younger, more vulnerable, and aggrieved self-states. I also recognized that this negotiation would not be easy. There were aspects of Karen who clearly remained unaware that marrying in California was her choice, that it was a decision—a decision that was at least in part designed to create a boundary between our world and her new life. And unaware she was on that particular day, when she looked at me, filled with an abundance of eagerness, enthusiasm, and hope (all of the emotions for which she and I had fought so long and so hard), and asked, "You will come to the wedding, won't you, Jody? I mean, I know it's a long way, but you wouldn't miss it, you couldn't miss it, could you?"

It was one of those moments one never forgets as an analyst. Eleven years of four-times-a-week psychoanalytic work—good, hard, effective work— were being dangled ever so provocatively, and yet unknowingly, just within snapping distance of the omnivorous jaws of the composite bad object monster. Staring into those hopeful, joy-filled eyes, recognizing the enormous emotional risk that Karen was undertaking in extending her invitation, remembering as well the deadened gaze, the joyless hopeless soup that had marked so much of our work together, and drawing those two faces into rapid juxtaposition, I wondered simultaneously how I could not go. And yet how could I go? It was an extraordinary moment for a psychoanalyst, and yet a completely mundane one as well. We have all faced such moments, probably more times than we care to remember. It is patently clear, in these moments, that much of how the psychoanalytic relationship will be recorded and remembered will be constructed between us in the moments and days and weeks that follow.

Before any words could shape themselves, Karen read and ascribed meaning to my hesitation. "Never mind," she said. "I can see that you don't want to come. I'm sorry that I asked, sorry that I presumed so much. It was stupid and childish of me. I don't know what made me think..." Her voice trailed off. Bitterness, humiliation, and grief struggled for primacy in the complex battle for control inside of her. A paroxysm of tears followed. We sat silently, Karen crying externally, I crying internally. There are no magic words or magical interpretations that safeguard us or the treatment in such moments. We trust in the strength of what has already been cre- ated. I will spare you the expletives that followed any attempt on my part to empathize with the pain I was creating for Karen with my decision. And yet I felt that I must take some responsibility for the pain she was feeling. I felt that I must also reassure Karen that her wanting me at her wedding was neither childish nor stupid. She met these comments with her usual acerbic, "Doesn't much matter what it is or isn't; you're not coming. That's all that matters." By the end of this session, Karen was wondering what the point was in discovering and reconnecting with all of the younger selves inside of her if the result was only to have them be crushed and rejected all over again. As she exited the session, I could hear her muttering to herself: Why had she let herself trust me, who was I that she imagined I could help her, why had she trusted me? Why, indeed, I wondered along with her on this particular afternoon.

But Karen, because she was Karen and not someone else, came back the next day and the day after that, and the day after the day after that. The very same tenacity that had, in the past, driven me to distracted states of therapeutic despair now clung for dear life in a desperate search for thera- peutic purpose and redemption. I tried, gingerly, to suggest to Karen that her choice to hold her wedding in California might have meaning; that its meaning might suggest that a part of her recognized her need to move on, to move our relationship gently into the background, to be fully in the pres- ent and with Brian in a way that my presence could potentially disrupt. But Karen knew me so well. After 11 years of analysis, she knew not only her own multiple self-states as they spanned her developmental history, but she had a pretty good sense of some of mine as well. So she moved for the jugu- lar. "You're just pissed off, Jody. You get like that sometimes, you know. Your feelings are hurt that I'm getting married in California, that I didn't think more about you. And this is your way of getting back at me. We can talk all about these littler, younger Karens, but we both know there are lit- tler, younger Jodys as well. And I know them. I've seen them."

One can see, I hope, how such an interpretation, particularly when aimed against an aspect of the analyst's experience that has remained unreflected on, might give rise to a deepening enactment and mutually regressive trans- ference–countertransference impasse or stalemate. But having described such destructive reenactments in the work with Karen on prior occasions (see Davies, 2003), I would now like to look at what I would regard as a more optimal response. In doing so, I trust the reader to understand that any given interaction could go either way and that any analysis will hold both optimal and not so optimal interactions and engagements.

Given that I had, on this particular occasion, thought at great length about my younger self-states and their reactions to this particular clini- cal choice, I felt able to meet Karen's accusations with far less shame than might have been stimulated for me otherwise. In fact, I found myself rather impressed and somewhat amused by her ability to offer such a complex and insightful interpretation of my character. I must admit that I was rather proud of Karen in that moment. I am sure that a smile crossed my lips as she offered her rather accurate, although incomplete, interpretation of my experience. And I nodded in agreement as she spoke. "You are right, Karen," I responded. "I did struggle with those feelings when I heard you were going to have your wedding in California. All the littler parts of me *were* angry and hurt and disappointed. And they did make kind of a fuss, and think unkind things, and contemplate unkind gestures of revenge." Here a slight smile, a counterpart to my slight smile, crossed Karen's lips. I continued, "But I'd like to think that those little ones of mine aren't running the show and calling the shots any more than your little ones are, at this time. You are forgetting that there is an older part of me as well, hopefully a little wiser and a little more temperate and a little more willing to think about what your needs and desires are at this very crucial juncture of your life. I've spoken to those younger ones of mine, the same way you've learned to speak with those younger ones of yours. I've explained to them why I think you need to do what you are doing. They don't like it very much, but I think they understand. It might have been nip and tuck in there for awhile, but I don't think this is their decision. I believe—of course, we both know I can't be sure—but I believe that this decision is *mine*. I know you don't like the decision, but I do really believe that I made it as your analyst, and not as an injured 6-year-old."

"How can you be so sure?" countered Karen.

"Well, I'm not sure," I responded. "But to the extent that I feel confident enough, it's because the decision is making me miserable. I don't think 6-year-olds make choices that make them miserable. I really want very much to be at your wedding you know. Most of me, about 90 percent, all but the very most grown-up parts of me, think that I am making a very bad decision. They don't like it at all, any more than you do. That's why I think it's the grown-up."

"Really? You really want to come?" asked Karen.

"Really, truly, I want to come." I responded.

"This being a grown-up thing sucks sometimes, it's very hard to bear," mumbled Karen, in the end.

"It's very hard to bear in this case, Karen, for both of us. And the problem is, I'd like to tell you that it gets much easier over time, and with practice, but it doesn't. "

It is hard to give a sense, in a written paper, of the ebb and flow of an issue like this, of how the disappointment, rejection, rage, and ultimate acceptance moved in and out of the clinical foreground over the months that followed. Such an issue is never resolved in one interaction, and I offer the interaction that I do as a kind of sampling—an example, brief and incomplete, of the way in which this kind of work would proceed from the center of my own clinical sensibility. If I had more time, I would provide other moments from the termination of Karen's analysis, moments which, when taken together, would provide more of that tapestry of which I spoke, more of the disappointment and narcissistic injury that must be juxtaposed and held against moments of such intense intimacy. I would hope to give a deeper flavor of the richness and nuance, the then and now, the you and me, the termination or graduation, the ending or commencement, the you-can-have-it/you-can't-have-it, the I-love-you-dearly-but-I-am-going-to-let-you-go-anyway quality of a fully rendered end to this remarkable and unique human relationship. But that is not possible. In the end, perhaps my sense of wanting more time or more space in this paper is an enactment of sorts. For any termination is marked by that experience, of wanting just a little more time to do a little more work on a few crucial and not entirely completed issues ("If we just had a few more sessions, a few more hours, a few more minutes...").

Likewise, no vignette can capture the entirety of an analytic process. I believe that no clinical moment communicates a singularly pivotal moment within an analytic treatment. That has not been my intent. Rather, the specificity of the clinical material presented attempts to capture a clinical sensibility, a sensibility that is exemplified in a moment, but that infuses every clinical moment and every clinical choice point we make in the infinite number of such moments comprising any given analysis. With gratitude to William Blake, I choose to believe that we can hold the world—our analytic world—in a grain of sand. We can find eternity, the patient's eternity, within the confines of a single hour. So I offer this fragment, this grain of Karen's analysis, as only a single moment of parting held against the backdrop of the ways in which Karen and I came together.

There are those of you who will be surprised that I chose not to attend Karen's wedding, and there will be those who will be shocked that I entertained the notion at all, even as a fantasy. My intent in writing this paper has not been to stress the rightness or wrongness of any one clinical choice, or even to recommend my own particular style of working through this decision within the treatment. In this particular moment, I seek to stress my belief that any psychoanalysis is an amalgam of moments. Some are deeply gratifying moments that rework earlier traumas, deprivations, and sadomasochistic interactions; these are moments that suggest a newer and healthier form of object relatedness and set in motion the relinquishment and mourning of what we call "bad object ties," allowing emergent self-states and new self–other interactions to be internalized in their stead. But other moments stress the limitations of the psychoanalytic process and of the analyst, the frustrations, deprivations, and peculiarly ungratifying forms of relatedness that are its own unique creation.

I have come to believe most strongly that it is neither the gratifications nor the frustrations that in the end create therapeutic change. It is rather in the space created between gratification and frustration, the space between desire and despair, that mourning and acceptance can give way to new beginnings and set in motion hopeful potentialities in which psychoanalysis can work its own best and most particular form of transformational magic. For this mourning to occur, we as analysts must come to terms with our limitations and struggles, and we must own them. In the end, we must let our patients go with the full knowledge that they are not separating from idealized, all-perfect, and all-knowing others, but from human beings, who like themselves are fragile and flawed; human beings who have, nonetheless, done their best, struggled, and stretched in order to create something in the work, something for the patient that is rich in beauty, potential, and pathos. I am reminded, in closing, of Emily Dickinson (1891):

> For each ecstatic instant,
> We must an anguish pay
> In keen and quivering ratio
> To the ecstasy. (p. 58)

Karen and I must both come to terms with the limits of what we can give to and get from each other. She must look to others for what I cannot provide, without devaluing out of disappointment that which I have been able to give. And I must let her go, let her seek from others what she and I cannot share. I must relinquish her idealization of me before she will be able to do so, and in so doing free her to go forth, holding the ability to survive disappointment in one hand and the capacity to sustain hope in the face of such disappointment in the other.

This presentation is a deeply personal act of mourning—mine for Karen. Karen is still in California. She has been there now for a good number of years. I hear from her regularly, but not frequently, letters and photos that depict a life fully lived and the passage of years. I sense that I am with her. And Karen is with me. In my work as an analyst, I have learned immeasurably from her treatment. But, more important, as a person I hold inside of me Karen's courage and tenacity, her relentless unwillingness to let go and succumb to despair. I sense her sometimes, even in my most difficult personal struggles, as an identification, a person, a relationship that lives on inside of me. I feel deeply fortunate that we shared a part of our lives with each other.

Termination, then? What an odd word for such a poignantly bittersweet moment, a moment of utter stillness in which past, present, and future hold sway simultaneously, a moment in which to take a deep and lasting breath before moving on.

REFERENCES

Bass, A. (2001). It takes one to know one: Or, whose unconscious is it anyway? *Psychoanalytic Dialogues, 11*, 683–703.

Bassin, D. (1997). Beyond the he and she: Postoedipal transcendence of gender polarities. *Journal of the American Psychoanalytic Association* (Special Supplement), *44*, 157–190.

Bateson, G. (1973). *Steps to an ecology of mind.* St. Albans, UK: Paladin Books.

Bergmann, M. S. (1997). Termination: The Achilles heel of psychoanalytic technique. *Psychoanalytic Psychology, 14*, 163–174.

Cooper, S. (2000). *Objects of hope: Exploring possibility and limit in psychoanalysis.* Hillsdale, NJ: Analytic Press.

Davies, J. M. (1996). Linking the "pre-analytic" with the postclassical: Integration, dissociation, and the multiplicity of unconscious process. *Contemporary Psychoanalysis, 32*, 553–575.

Davies, J. M. (1998a). Multiple perspectives on multiplicity. *Psychoanalytic Dialogues, 8*, 195–206.

Davies, J. M. (1998b). Between the disclosure and foreclosure of erotic transference–countertransference: Can psychoanalysis find a place for adult sexuality? *Psychoanalytic Dialogues, 8*, 747–766.

Davies, J. M. (1998c). Thoughts on the nature of desires: The ambiguous, the transitional, and the poetic: Reply to Commentaries. *Psychoanalytic Dialogues, 8*, 805–823.

Davies, J. M. (1999). Getting cold feet, defining "safe-enough" borders: Dissociation, integration and multiplicity in the analyst's experience of the transference–countertransference process. *Psychoanalytic Quarterly, 68*, 184–208.

Davies, J. M. (2003). Falling in love with love: Oedipal and postoedipal manifestations of idealization, mourning, and erotic masochism. *Psychoanalytic Dialogues, 13*, 1–28.

Dickinson, E. (1891). *The complete poems of Emily Dickinson* (T. Johnson, Ed.). Boston: Little, Brown & Co.

Ferenczi, S. (1927). The problem of termination of the analysis. In M. Balint (Ed.) & E. Mosbacher (Trans.), *Final contributions to the problems and methods of psycho-analysis* (pp. 77–86). London: Hogarth, 1955.

Ghent, E. (1990). Masochism, submission and surrender: Masochism as a perversion of surrender. *Contemporary Psychoanalysis, 26*, 108–135.

Ghent, E. (1992). Paradox and process. *Psychoanalytic Dialogues, 2*, 135–159.

Glover, E. (1955). *The technique of psychoanalysis.* New York: International Universities Press.

Greenberg, J. (2001). The analyst's participation: A new look. *Journal of the American Psychoanalytic Association, 49*, 359–381.

Hoffman, I. Z. (1998). *Ritual and spontaneity in the psychoanalytic process: A dialectical-constructivist view.* Hillsdale, NJ: Analytic Press.

Hoffman, I. Z. (2006). The myths of free association and the potentials of the analytic relationship. *International Journal of Psychoanalysis, 87*, 43–61.

Levenson, E. A. (1978). The aesthetics of termination. *Contemporary Psychoanalysis, 12*, 338–341.

Loewald, H. (1977). The waning of the Oedipus complex. In *Papers on psychoanaly-sis* (pp. 384–404). New Haven, CT: Yale University Press, 1980.

Mitchell, S. A. (1986). The wings of Icarus: Illusion and the problem of narcissism. *Contemporary Psychoanalysis, 22,* 107–132.

Mitchell, S. A. (1997). *Influence and autonomy in psychoanalysis.* Hillsdale, NJ: Analytic Press.

Racker, H. (1968). *Transference and countertransference.* New York: International Universities Press.

Skolnick, N. J. (2006). What's a good object to do? *Psychoanalytic Dialogues, 16,* 1–27.

Stern, D. B. (1983). Unformulated experience. *Contemporary Psychoanalysis, 19,* 71–99.

Part II

On the clinical frontier

Chapter 7

How we end

Taking leave*

Jill Salberg

It is never easy to say good-bye, to end a relationship, or to leave someone you care about and feel connected to. We start treatment with patients, each of us knowing that at some point this will come to an end. Despite this knowledge, both parties become engaged and, if things go well, deeply attached. What we ask of patients and of ourselves is not easy. The kind of attachment that is needed for the analytic work to be most effective is a thick, saturated kind of attachment with both known and yet to be discovered affective experience. By this I mean a form of loving connection whereby our mutual defenses start to ease away and the unconscious ways in which people engage each other begin to take the foreground. In such a holding type of transitional space, much work can occur. Without it, many ideas can be learned, but the potential for deeper affective experience may not emerge. How do we, patients and analysts, take leave of one another when we have developed such unprecedented closeness and richness of experience? Patients may fear ever replacing this closeness with others in their lives and so the loss feels too great. As analysts,[†] we too may resist losing the closeness to our patients but additionally we wonder, did we do enough, have things sufficiently changed for this person so that they can now carry on the work themselves? This is what Bergmann (1997) refers to as, "[replacing] the analyst by self-analysis and continue [ing] his/[her] inner development after termination" (p. 171). As a consequence, I believe ending treatment can create for many patients and for us a kind of crisis—the crisis of having to end and say good-bye. At that moment, we and the patient may wish for time to stand still, for things to not change while they are changing (Bromberg, 1998).

When the idea of ending treatment is raised, by the analyst or by the patient, the interesting thing that occurs is how time feels as though it

---

* Parts of this chapter originally appeared in Salberg, *J. Psychoanalytic Dialogues*, 19(6), 2009, 704–722.
† I will use the terms analyst and analysis throughout this chapter, but many of the ideas equally apply to therapists and patients in psychotherapy.

circles back on itself. You both remember whom you first became acquainted with while another version of who you have both become face each other. Time seems to collapse and expand simultaneously. Loewald (1972) understood one aspect of time in terms of its linking capacity, "We encounter time in psychic life primarily as a linking activity in which what we call past, present, and future are woven into a nexus" (p. 407). The expansive sense of time can be seen in the interaction of the multiple self-states of the patient and of the analyst. Like the visitations of the ghosts in Dickens' *A Christmas Carol*, selves from the past and present, and future selves still to be fully formulated, can be present and interacting in the room (Davies, 2005). Perhaps nowhere is this more pronounced than during termination, when we entertain and speculate about the future as that possibility which now has arrived. Further, Loewald (1962) understood that when there was too great a denial of loss surrounding ending, the sense of time could collapse. He wrote, "either we try to deny that the other person still exists or did exist, or we try to deny that we have to leave the beloved person and must venture out on our own. Either the past or the future is denied" (p. 485). We protect ourselves from impending loss; our minds collapse time.

I want to underscore the disorientation implied in Loewald's idea. To deny the past and/or the future is a form of dissociative thinking and creates an internal sense of an unmoored "liminal present." This unanchored experience is in opposition to what Winnicott termed our sense of "being in time" and can leave us feeling out of sync with time. Further, Winnicott understood that the devoted mother, the one who provides the good-enough nurturing environment for the child to develop a sense of going-on-being, is simultaneously allowing the child to develop without the stress of time. Ogden (2005) saw this as vital and wrote, "I view Winnicott's holding as an ontological concept that is primarily concerned with being and its relationship to time. Initially the mother safeguards the infant's continuity of being, in part by insulating him from the 'not-me' aspect of time" (p. 93).

I understand Winnicott's maternal sensibility as an aspect of what we provide as analysts in a similar sort of holding environment. But what happens when we are not always safeguarding timelessness? Consider the ways in which we, throughout the treatment, paradoxically limit and suspend time with patients. We give them set times for their appointments and limit the length of the hour, and despite all of that, we invite them into an ongoing dialogue, perhaps even an endless kind of conversation. Then at some point we say, time is up, the hour ends, and then further down the road we say that our talking has come to an end. This can be disorienting for many patients but something we all try to manage for them and ourselves. In ending treatment, we too are caught up in the disorientation because more is at stake for us.

In this chapter, I will be tracking my own evolving ideas regarding termination across three treatment endings—my own first analysis and my endings with two patients, while being mindful of the theme of time—its slippage, its presence, and then its passage. This journey reflects my own continual processing and reworking internally of overlapping endings. Although there is a last session, a final meeting between patient and analyst, I have found that the processing of the ending and consequently of the treatment itself often continues posttermination. Thus, time becomes quite subjective, endings become beginnings, and one treatment can illuminate another. Terminations are complex, affective transactions between both people that cannot be simplified or codified. These endings will directly reflect the specific analytic dyad and the relational dynamics at play during the treatment. Terminations are processes often primed for enactment for both the analyst and the patient. I discovered as much during an extended process of writing about ending with a patient who proposed "staying in therapy forever," a kind of interminability that ultimately led to my decision to terminate her treatment. (See, Salberg, 2009, for the extended case write-up). Even so, it was a case that continued to occupy a place in my ongoing thoughts and memory; it haunted me. It seems this was about mourning processes and the difficulties involved in termination. The story begins with ending my own analysis.

FIRST ENDINGS

After 13 years in analysis, I raised my desire to terminate to my analyst and was met with skepticism. Was I resisting further work? I listened to his concern and stayed 2 years longer, wondering whether there were things I had not gotten to. It was perplexing: I felt ready, but my analyst saw me as unfinished. Although I continued, this other feeling persisted—that I felt ready to try life on my own, with the tools I had acquired. And so, 2 years later, I raised again that I felt I wanted to end, and again heard disagreement. I did not believe I could open up this stalemate between us and chose to leave rather than engage in further exploration. I terminated a 15-year analysis in what felt like a less than satisfactory manner. I was saddened to leave, in this way, what had felt to have been a transformative experience. I later wondered, what had been unconsciously enacted and in play for both my analyst and myself?

My own experience has, not surprisingly, affected my work with patients around ending treatment, as you will see in my work with Ellen.* She was an attractive and deeply sad 32-year-old woman, single, unemployed, and living at home with her widowed mother. She came to see me telling me about the losses in her life: her father's death from a brain tumor and her

---

* This is an abridged version of case material that was originally published in Salberg, J., Leaning into Termination, *Psychoanalytic Dialogues* 19(6), 2009, 703–722.

older brother's long history of drug and alcohol abuse and early death at age 32. Ellen had retreated from life and her pain was palpable. She talked about her wishes and yet profound fears to move out of her mother's house into an apartment of her own. She fantasized about becoming a paraplegic, which captured her feeling of paralysis and deep wish to be taken care of. She feared that leaving her mother was tantamount to killing her. I felt sympathetic toward Ellen, who was caught in such a life and death loyalty battle. Her guilt was heroic, she was ready to sacrifice her life, and in fact she had sacrificed "real" living, being stuck in the past with no sense of hope about her own future.

Growing up, Ellen became the target of much of her troubled and acting-out brother's hostility and contempt. Whenever she walked past him he would spit at her. They shared a bathroom and he would spray urine all over the walls. She would feel disgust and then impotent rage because her parents seemed unable to effectively control him or help her. We talked about her feeling abused by him and overlooked by her parents. Her brother had always felt like a constant crisis, and since she was quiet, did well in school, and behaved well, she had felt completely forgotten about. Her brother, married with two children, had never worked steadily or been able to manage his life. He was in and out of drug and alcohol rehabs, never staying sober for long. Finally his wife had asked him to leave. Ellen recounted the following scene to me many times during our work. She had moved back home to help her mother with caring for her father during his terminal phase of battling cancer. Soon after the father died, her brother arrived at the family home with a paper bag of his things, hoping to move back in. Ellen answered the door only opening it a crack. He asked to come in, saying he needed a place to stay. Ellen flatly refused to let him enter, closing the door on him. Two years passed after Ellen refused to let him "come home" and he was found dead in a motel room in a neighboring state, probably from a drug overdose. She felt very guilty while also relieved over his death. He was dead and she believed she had killed him by wishing him dead all of her life, culminating in the act of closing the door.

In this punishing and pervasive way, Ellen kept her brother alive albeit as a fixed image that resisted any change, as if time stood still. In some way, this would haunt our work in terms of what use Ellen could make of me, my words, my feelings, my thoughts, and even my presence. If, as analysts, we are to be what, in Winnicottian terms might be considered "good-enough" objects, then our goal is to help our patients make use of us, to help them transform their sorrow into digestible, usable experiences. Within that enterprise, we facilitate seeing how they are trapped by the past, fearful of the future, and need help living within the parameters of today. Berry (1987) saw the analytic function as using time as a container: "The links the analyst makes through his interpretations connect moments that are far removed from one another in time, and they help time to become a container for the patient" (p. 121).

Ellen envied her brother, deeply wanting the attention and place he held in her family, but she was unable to see that he might have envied her as well. Neither one felt powerful. Envy can have that kind of hold on people when they are locked in age-old struggles and time stands still. Envy battles bleed into other arenas, and the present becomes a reflection of the past. Ellen and I became locked into our own kind of envy–power struggle where either you were the one filled with envy or you became the object of envy, and there was no place safe to stand. This was brought into focus by Ellen's anger when I moved my office and she saw the decorative style of painting I had done on my walls. I had somehow, unwittingly, done what she had secretly wanted to do but had been unable to accomplish in her apartment. I had not known about her desire for this particular wall treatment. While she had complained about being unable to fix up her apartment I had, without knowing it, invited envy fully into our relationship. My new office had upended her wish for a sense of superiority, leaving her holding the step down, powerless position. This was intolerable to Ellen and unsettling to me.

A recurring enactment had been set in motion—one, at that time, I had been unable to see. Ellen was often crying and feeling envious longing for what she perceived others had, and I was often feeling inadequate and ineffective as her analyst. In reliving her memories of her brother and family drama, I was to relive a version of my own familial envy. Neither of us felt effective or powerful, and we did not seem to have access to a way to transform the enacted memories into usable forms.

In the seventh year of treatment, Ellen had been raising the idea of ending, not in a deeply serious way—partly out of despair and partly as a threat. In one session, she said, "To acknowledge that this isn't working, my immediate conclusion is that I have to stop. I come and do my part but you're really supposed to be doing all the work, [tearily] you are to fix up my life." I was struck by the complex conflict Ellen was beginning to express that she and I had been in. Ellen could not allow anything I said to really affect her, thereby revealing me to be weak and helpless to help her. She could then remain in control and feel superior to me but at the cost of her own suffering. She tells me it both keeps her separately superior to me and also is a way of taking care of herself, a way of dealing with feelings of hurt or disappointment.

I was intrigued; this is something new, and I ask her to tell me more. She tells me how fearful she is of being disappointed if I cannot help her. Helping seems to entail full participation, and a deep power struggle becomes clearer. She says, "I don't know if you can help me. Something has to do with you taking over. I think I have resentment about your telling me what to do. Like my parents, they can't tell me what to do sometimes and not other times. It's not fair to come in and out of my life. I guess by acting incompetent and not knowing what to do its asking someone to come and take over. Maybe that's why I resent you. You want to come and tell me what to do sometimes, but then you say it's your life, you can do whatever you want to do. It doesn't change my life and it's not fair." I ask, "What would be fair?" She says, "You have to be there *all the time*. I have the image of your teaching me how to ride a bicycle and you disappear, disappear too soon."

Ellen wanted a kind of presence that she could control but that felt as if it came wholly from me. Ellen continued, "I guess if it was up to me I would stay in therapy forever, we'll grow old together. But I also feel I'm going to show you, you're so good, well here's the patient who seems alright but, I don't know why I have to do all the work? Can't I just show up?" This sounded promising in that Ellen was verbalizing the conflict I had felt so embroiled in with her. But I also felt her undertow. She deeply wanted to just "show up" and have it happen for her. She just as strongly needed to undo anything I said or did which might suggest that I did have something to give. I began to feel we were locked endlessly in the past, enacting and arguing with very little sense of things changing.

In the fall of what would become her ninth year in treatment I decided to suggest termination. Ellen was furious, feeling that I was "kicking her out." I said "I think I have said everything to you I can say. It is really up to you now if you want to make changes in your life or not. Sometimes the changes can be better seen or risks more easily taken when you are no longer in treatment. She was very angry, feeling it was akin to my pushing her off a bus, abandoning her and forcing her to leave before she reached her destination. I said, "I know you are angry about this idea. But I do feel that it's about doing things in your life now outside of here. I propose we spend the year working on this. If at the end of the year before we break for vacation we feel that something has shifted and there is something else to continue to work on, then we can reconsider. If not, then we will end." We spent that year in what felt like a stalemate, mostly with Ellen feeling justified in raging at me for "kicking her out of therapy." We ended that summer at the end of July.

A FEW YEARS LATER

I had written up this case and knew I would have to call Ellen for her permission to present our work together. That is what made her call to me feel so uncanny. She wanted to come in for a session, something had happened and she wanted to "check in." Ellen arrived and was somewhat nervous and chatty. She told me that something had happened at her apartment's co-op board meeting which had left her agitated and when she arrived back home she fell off a step ladder. She worried that she might be hurting herself out of a feeling of guilt. She was now the president of the co-op that she lived in, and that night she had helped the board reach a difficult decision for the building, refusing a request that the prior president had made. When I asked her what had left her agitated, she said, "It's just like when I locked my brother out of the house, didn't let him back home and I killed him." I asked, "Do you really still believe that you killed him?" She said she did.

Suddenly, I had a new picture of our work together and what had felt to me as my unilateral decision to terminate. I now realized in retrospect that the termination had been an enactment in two ways. First, just as she had closed the door on her brother, I had closed the door on Ellen. I believe that, unconsciously, I had understood that something had to be repeated, and relived for her to be able to metabolize and fully process her experience of her brother's death. Ellen and I reexperienced that moment when I fully insisted that she had to leave, and she had to accept those terms. However, unlike with her brother, this time no one died; rather both of us maintained the capacity to have independent lives. Only then could Ellen be freed from the shutting down of her life, a self-erected prison of memory and guilt. I too had become a prisoner, held captive by her and by my own memories. Additionally, I realized that my wish that my analyst had supported my ending treatment was revitalized and enacted in my insisting on Ellen's ending. Aron (2009) posits that "we mistakenly polarize memory and enactment, inner experience and outer behavior" (p. 14). I understand Aron to mean that enactments are a form of memory, and I would add that they are a form of working through. I am suggesting that my ending the treatment with Ellen, albeit an enactment, had been a kind of reparative activity around the original trauma of her brother's death.

When I could, I told Ellen that I had suddenly realized that my insistence to end our work created a reliving of what had occurred with her brother. "In some way I had to close the door on you and say, 'you can't come back,' but in a way in which no one died, no one was killed." I felt that Ellen understood what I was saying, and she then began telling me the ways in which her life had improved. We spent the rest of the session discussing what had been enacted between us. I ended the session by suggesting that she think about this and by inviting her to call to continue processing this with me. At the same time, I assured her that it would be alright not to call. I did not hear from Ellen, which felt like a good thing.

AFTER IT IS OVER: FROZENNESS

How do we really *know* when to say good-bye? Some patients come to see us and are wary of attaching, keeping us at arm's length, while others eagerly connect, sharing the intimate details of their lives. I have found that some patients haunt us during the work, while others haunt us after we end. Ellen did both for me. I now believe that she and I were engaged in a forestalled mourning process. Clearly, Ellen had real reasons to be in mourning and that is how she first came to me, but less clear were the ways that she and I would become entangled and enmeshed in parallel and intersecting mourning struggles, which had kept memory fixed. Separation issues, which here involved a sorrow for what never was, dotted Ellen's life and resonated with aspects of my own. Some of this I knew about and some I did not.

What I was less aware of was the impact of my unfinished and consequently undigested mourning process around ending my own analysis and how it would implicate me in my work. What obscured this was the fact that Ellen and I were in reversed positions; I had wanted to leave analysis and had wanted my analyst to support this—while she wanted to stay forever and wanted to be welcomed in doing so. Clearly our situation was primed for an enactment. I have come to believe many, if not all, terminations, are primed for enactment. The mutual processes of attaching and detaching, of growing close and then saying good-bye, elicit powerful feelings and equally powerful dissociative processes.

I can no longer think of my treatment and termination with Ellen without conjuring up the ending of my own first analysis. While working on this, I received in the mail two articles written by my former analyst with a brief note: "Dear Jill, I hope you and your family are very well. Enclosed reprints one old and one new. Best wishes." I was quite surprised, shocked even, to say the least, but I was equally puzzled. We had not seen or spoken in many years and I could not figure out the reason for this contact. Additionally, while brevity had been his long-standing style, this note felt positively cryptic. Why was he contacting me in this manner? As I saw the large manila envelope with his characteristic handwriting, which I simultaneously recognized and disbelieved, I thought to myself, has something happened? He is probably in his eighties, having retired from private practice a number of years ago. I felt a mixture of fear and curiosity. Why contact me *now*?

I wrote back to him: "I was surprised to receive your two papers without much of a note letting me know why the contact after so many years." I also filled him in on my life and my family and sent him two pieces of my own published work as well—one a memoir essay in which I felt he would recognize many of my family stories from our work together. I received back a letter in which he was noticeably conversational about life in retirement and he responded quite positively to the pieces I had sent him. But also, embedded in the letter, was a paragraph in which once again I could distinctly hear the voice of my former analyst, "I wish you would not be so harsh with yourself or with me and could ease up and enjoy more fully the present without marring it with grievances and disappointments of the past and being too critical. No one likes to be admonished or made to feel guilty."

I was stunned. I read this part over and over again. I had not been in treatment with him for 20 years and he *still* sounded as if he thought of me as his patient, and I *still* heard him as my analyst. Had I been admonishing? How was it, that in an instant I was back in time, back on the couch and filled with recrimination with his feeling the necessity to enlighten me? Did we both still hold each other in mind in some unchanged form from the time that we had ended?

I no longer believe in some idealized termination in which the trans-ference–countertransference relationship, now fully analyzed, loses its affective gravitational pull and the analytic dyad, diluted of its intensity, becomes normalized. This kind of interaction between my former analyst and myself has suggested to me that in some way we may remain for each other, as if, frozen in time, within memory. Despite long discussions prior to ending, I now can see that my terminating my analysis with him and his ending with me, in essence "our ending" had been incomplete on deeper levels. Our "frozenness" was a signifier of a loss not fully acknowledged and thereby incompletely mourned.

Before I say more about this, I want to turn to my most recent contact with Ellen that occurred a few months after I received my former analyst's letter. Although she had given me permission a long time ago to present our work, I knew I needed to speak with her again about the possibility of pub-lishing it. I called and explained this to her, suggesting that I would mail her the write-up and then we could meet to discuss it. When she came in and sat down, I could sense how anxious we were both feeling. She quickly said she was upset by the write-up and that it explained a great deal for her, for example, why she never thought to send me holiday cards. She was upset that I had not portrayed her in an attractive light and that I obviously had not liked her. She repeated this again and I responded by saying that I did like her and cared very much about her but that I had not liked what she had stirred up in me, how I had ended up feeling so stuck—that no matter what I tried I felt unhelpful and, worse, inadequate. It was hard to process all that I was feeling with Ellen. After our meeting, I remembered that I had liked her a great deal earlier in the treatment but that it had gotten lost in the struggles we had been continuously enacting with each other. I could see how the focus of my writing on those difficult feelings might have left her seeing only the most challenging and worst of my feelings.

Interestingly, she also did not remember, or fully believe, what I had writ-ten about her intense angry reaction to my new office and the way the walls had been painted. She remembered a dream, which she now spontaneously reported: "I dreamt that the walls in your new office were white and that you had brown bookcases. When I actually saw your office I felt relieved that it wasn't what I had dreamt." She then said, "I did wonder if we had been too close in age and that I had envied you, your life." I agreed that we were close in age and wondered as well if that had been a problem. I then suggested that my recollection of her reaction to my new office decor had brought her envy into the room and into our relationship while the dream she now reported kept envy at bay. She responded that she did not like me very much at times during our work.

I began to feel like I used to feel in sessions with her. Things felt slippery, moving quickly from what she felt was inside of me (you do not like me) to what was felt to be inside her (I do not like you). This rapidly shifting landscape, in which I never quite knew where I stood or what I was feeling, felt very familiar. I was amazed that we were back in the deadlock all over again. Was she right? Did I not like her? Did I paint her in a poor light to make my own case regarding ending her treatment? At the time we were ending, I had hoped I was doing what would be best for her and the treatment. Now I was no longer so sure.

The hour was almost over, and I raised with Ellen that if there were particular things she wanted me to change in the paper I would consider doing that, or if she wanted to write something herself I would consider including it. I also clearly stated that I would not publish this if she did not want me to. It felt important to me that this meeting be reparative, not injurious to her. She left saying she would think about it and get back to me.

During this waiting time, I thought how reminiscent it felt to be with Ellen and the uncanny parallels with what had simultaneously transpired with my former analyst. Once again, I wondered how is it that we are frozen, locked in our memories of each other? Frozenness has multiple aspects; it preserves something from the ravages of time while preventing anything from changing. However, in this kind of dormancy, some memories slumber while others are awake and active. Ellen and I reentered a part of our prior transference–countertransference struggle as if no time had passed, and I might add, as if we had not terminated our work. We were once again, as if time stood still, remembering each other by enacting our prior relational positions in the most intense and alive way. I also became aware that the way we were remembering each other at that moment also meant a forgetting, perhaps even a refusal, of our having ended our work. We were each keeping the relationship alive in a way that precluded knowing how we could be different with each other. Perhaps this is what often becomes protected when we "forget"; we prevent ourselves from recognizing a separation, a loss, and the necessary alteration that a full acknowledgment would mean.

At the end of 2 weeks, Ellen called and requested another session. She said she had realized after we met that she had not told me how much she felt I had helped her. She said, "I have so much to be grateful for, my mother is in her nineties and is in good health, I am also in good health." While she was telling me this, I remembered how many deaths had occurred in her family—good health was something not to be taken lightly. I also recalled our original ending, years before when she was so angry with me until the very end, feeling I was kicking her out. Afterward, she had written me a letter of gratitude for my caring and work with her. I thanked her for telling me this, feeling the wish to repair our ruptured ending and the role I had played in it. I said I wanted her to know that when I ended our work I had worried that I had failed her, and that I had not helped her enough to change jobs or in her desire for a long-term relationship. Perhaps that was part of my need to end the work, but I *had* really cared about her. She said she thought that we both had become too stuck on her changing jobs or meeting someone. She informed me that she is still with the same firm but working mostly on matters she is interested in.

Ellen then said she wanted to give me full permission to publish. I thanked her for this and for the opportunity to truly work something through with each other, to say good-bye in a new way, a more mutual way that freed us both from the old ways we had been stuck in. I believe that I had communicated to her my own wish to repair our ending. I reached out to her hoping she could meet me halfway. It was in between and during our second meeting that shifts had begun to occur internally for us both, and we were able to undertake a fuller explication of the difficulty we each had in ending the treatment. In this reliving of memory and action, a deeply reparative moment was allowed to occur and I believe we could now free each other to make greater use of the past. The protective inflexibility of memory had prevented both of us from knowing fully how we could be changed in the future by our past analytic relationship.

Quite a few months later I wrote back to my former analyst. In realizing that I had been keeping the termination of that analysis somewhat on ice, I had not let myself continue a certain process, which I now opened myself up to and entered. I realized that subtly in my response I had indeed scolded my analyst for the manner in which he contacted me. I was still harboring an injury over a kind of nonrecognition of my need to terminate. By coming to this awareness, I further realized that I also had withheld a deep gratitude for the work we had done together. I wrote to him explaining my complicated responses and telling him how much our work had given me and done for me. He wrote back saying how much he appreciated hearing my warm feelings about our work. I cried reading his letter, both glad that I had extended to him my deep gratitude, and truly feeling this loss because we had now fully ended.

ENDING ON HER TERMS

Many of these ideas were already part of my internal lexicon when it was time to terminate with my patient Shelley, someone I had worked with for close to 20 years. When Shelley first came to see me she had just turned 40 and was quite upset over being single and alone. Time had been kind to Shelley who did not look anything near her age, but she did not fully live in time either, believing she had plenty of time to meet a man and have children. She was strikingly beautiful and dressed in a decidedly sexual and fashionable style. She literally turned men's heads in the street and often easily met and dated men, but not very much would develop beyond this. It would take years for her to let me in as a person in her life and for me to feel connected to her. Before that, I came to inhabit her loneliness while working with her long before she could feel it herself. This loneliness had been some version of what Shelley had felt growing up in her family.

Shelley was the youngest of four, born ten years later than her next oldest sibling, and felt more isolated by dint of the years separating her from her older siblings, though no one in the family really seemed to feel any better connected. Shelley's mother had polio as a young girl, which left her legs badly weakened and necessitated leg braces and a cane for her to walk. Her father worked hard as an electrician and was chronically depressed. She often described him as if he were ghost-like, barely registering a presence because of his withdrawn, silent states. Shelley's earliest memory is of being in her crib, alone, with no one to pick her up. She spoke of feeling invisible in her family and of playing alone on the floor, never able to sit in her "crippled" mother's lap. This became a metaphor for us, first raising the question of whether she could feel welcomed into my lap. Much later, once she felt able to climb into that safe, warm spot with me, I wondered if she would ever leave to venture out into the world to attach, play, and partner with someone else.

Despite her longing for an intimate attachment, her relationships with friends and romantic relationships with men often seemed like ships passing in the night. Chemistry is what she stated she wanted with a man. True intimacy was a foreign land that had not yet been identified on her internal map. As far as I could tell, sex was the only idea of closeness that Shelley had. She simultaneously longed for and feared intimacy. Her template for closeness had been Saturday mornings with her father, her head on his chest as they watched cartoons together. Her father never spoke during this, and neither did Shelley. There were practically no other memories of being with her father except for her playing on the stoop outside the apartment building when he returned home from work. He would walk past her, without acknowledging her presence. She felt invisible at those times, a painfully vulnerable sense worsened by the shame it aroused and the nagging question, what was so wrong with her? These contrasting versions of being in relation with a significant person, of complete dependence and complete absence, haunted her relational world. What she feared most with a new man was his finding out how desperately needy she felt. To prevent this, she tried to project a "smooth as marble" exterior, no bumps or flaws, but also no way to enter. Her sense of a relationship was equally fashioned by her mother's compelling pleasure in reading romance magazines. Shelley felt this set the stage for her own fantasies of beautiful women awaiting the desire of a man. Not surprisingly and despite her considerable beauty and ability to easily attract men, her relationships quickly either drifted apart or left her more clinging and anxious. Shelley did not know what the "glue" was that kept people together and so when sensing a man's withdrawal she would feel confirmed in her worst fears—that her dependency drove him away.

For many years, I had the feeling of being an outsider, someone she dropped in to see and tell stories to but nothing more. Feeling oddly used and useless, I would wonder to Shelley what she thought I might feel about many of the things she told me. She found the question strange and had no clue how she would know what I might be thinking. Despite her striking outward appearance of sexual vivacity, she was quite deadened to any inner world. Although chemistry is what she claimed to want with men, taking action was how she responded to any hint of a feeling. I was struck by her lack of "reflective functioning," sensing that for Shelley action was always a relief. We spent many sessions working on my having an internal world filled with thoughts, feelings, hopes, desires, and reactions. I also imagined what she might be experiencing and filled with. I would suggest possible feeling states, painful emotions, which I believed made sense and that I could appreciate. This painstaking work with Shelley on what Fonagy and Target (1998) termed "mentalization and the self-reflective function" slowly allowed her to begin to feel more. I then began to hear about how humiliating it had felt to have a mother who was crippled, and her shame knowing she felt this way. At times she felt emotionally crippled like the mother and therefore unlovable. Additionally, her rage at her father slowly eroded the overidealized cartoon of closeness. She wept over his being gone and her not being able to even attempt talking with him, now that she had begun to learn how to speak to and with others.

Her mother's health deteriorated and she was now in a nursing home. The care was poor and so Shelley would often travel to her mother and spend the weekend caring for her. The roles became reversed as she bathed her mother, carefully rubbed moisturizer over her skin, and sometimes read the newspaper or a magazine to her. I was struck by Shelley's devotion and ability to be present as her mother's health worsened. After her mother died, there was a marked shift in Shelley. She had been grieving for so long that she now seemed finally released from the grip of both parents who had so little to give her. Soon after, she began to date more serious men which, ultimately, resulted in her living with a man for 2 years. We talked about how her mother's death left room for someone else in her life. Although it eventually did not work out with this man, Shelley now had the lived experience of commitment, the attempt to live a life with someone and to stay connected to him and to herself.

I had for some time thought ending might be nearly impossible. Despite the great deal of work we had done and the many improvements in her life, Shelley still felt to me to be very alone. Although she had a few close friends, there was no one special to her to spend time with or consider living with. She had often mentioned how much she wanted to get into a relationship while she was still in treatment so that I might help her work on it. Time continued to pass, as it does, and then Shelley brought up ending. I was surprised and unsure if she meant it. We talked about it, and she felt that I really had given her a great deal and that there was nothing new for us to work on. She did want to know that she could call me if she needed to; if she did become involved and wanted help with the relationship, she wanted to make sure that I would see her. This all felt very reasonable, perhaps too reasonable.

We set a date for our last session and then nothing much seemed to happen. Shelley would come into sessions without thoughts or feelings. When I would ask what she felt regarding our ending, without much affect in her voice she would say fine. As we got closer to our ending date Shelley went into a tailspin. Business was suddenly very bad and she was now in a crisis and could not imagine stopping our work. Shelley's business had always been variable, and I knew her deep anxiety when she believed the "bottom" had dropped out. Here is a place that time reenters: Back in historical time, her family struggled and was poor. For many years they lived in a walk-up building because it was cheaper, despite her mother's great difficulty walking stairs. Shelley's panic was partly related to memories of "hard times" of her family's struggles. Her perpetual high-alert system was to prevent history from repeating itself. But I felt that she was additionally recalling the internal poverty of her emotional environment and as a consequence the impoverishment of her own resources. This is what Winnicott refers to as the breakdown that has already happened or what Loewald might see as the past still too alive in the present. From this position, I felt it unreasonable to ask her to now face relinquishing her tie to me, one that had taken many years of difficult work for us to find our way. Her work had been in letting me care, believing that I would remain available to her so she could risk feeling what she had spent a lifetime trying to not know about.

This is the exact sort of crisis that termination can pose for many patients and for us. Past and present time begin to feel as if they are collapsing. I had already seen how holding a firm line with my other patient Ellen around a termination date had prevented both of us from fully accessing the dissociated feelings around that enactment. I was now of the mind to try something different and see if I could be and stay more flexible and curious about what was being enacted between Shelley and me. Therefore, I agreed to cancel the ending; Shelley calmed down and things in her life then seemed to improve.

We went through this scenario several times over the better part of a year before I fully realized that, despite real work crises, despite it not being talked about, both Shelley and I were enacting our reluctance to terminating our work. It took our enacting this several times for me to fully understand how overwhelming it was to her, and perhaps to me, and could not yet be known in thought and then put into language. These enactments held for her the dissociated feelings of the collapse of her internal world as well as her disbelief that she could calm herself down and function in her life. In response to our ending, she inhabited the helpless child self-state. My part of this enactment was a kind of complementary panic response feeling. I began to feel guilty that I was somehow pushing her into leaving—it had been a long treatment and somehow she could not leave. My "guiltiness" led me to believe, in the face of her panic, that I could not abandon her, necessitating my calling off our ending and rushing in to shore her up. I saw her more fragile self-state and believed that *that person* could not terminate. She would calm down and this other self-state would reemerge, this other Shelley who no longer felt desperation. As I began to better understand my own part of the enactment, I realized that in agreeing to set an end date, I now had, unwittingly, become a rejecting, bad object. Despite the request coming from Shelley, I began to realize that not all of her had wanted me to agree.

Often this deep ambivalence, stemming from the multiple self-states and the competing wishes those selves may have, dominates treatment endings (see Davies, 2005). I propose that this is an aspect of the destabilization during termination that analysts get caught up in as much as patients do. I have come to understand that we enter a sort of liminal state: a place in between the shank of the treatment when both of us are engaged in the work and that future place of posttermination. The analytic dyad is not there yet, so it cannot feel real. In some way it is both out of sync with time and beyond time. Perhaps we, both the analyst and the patient, panic because in not knowing what the future will be like, we fear that there is no future. It is then that retreating into a past and known self-state becomes compelling.

In my believing I was helping Shelley to end when and how she wanted to, I was nonetheless inexorably pulled into the drama of how hard it is to detach after years of working with someone whose attachment issues are linked to compromises and loyalty ties. It is hard to give up feeling needed in the ways in which we feel needed by our patients and to relinquish the pleasure we derive in reparative work. We ask a great deal of our patients and of ourselves in trusting this new kind of relationship. Further, when the end is reached, we must be ready to wave and say "so long." And so each time I agreed to a new termination date, I became for Shelley the mother who was too willing to let her go and who was not fully engaged with her. Each cancelled ending became a triumph for her child self-state who was finally no longer invisible and could impact her environment. In doing so, however, she was trapped in the past, a prisoner of time. I was able to start discussing this with Shelley and how such crises were what life is like now—in its ups and downs—and that I felt her panic had more to do with some terror over our ending. For me to begin these interpretative discussions, I had to be willing to accept that I would be disappointing one part of Shelley. I had to believe in a future that I could not know. I had to assure Shelley that she could continue "going-on-being" without me.

We were now able, after close to a year of end dates, cancellations, and renegotiations, to truly complete an ending process. Nonetheless, I do believe we needed that year and it was a critical part of *our* ending process, how Shelley and I needed to construct it and find our way. She was terrified of being alone, and I was frightened as well. Our enactments stirred up my own internalized history of being left alone too early, of becoming a parentified child and, as a consequence, precociously independent. I had not fully appreciated how much I felt the interior poverty of her object relational world which I then reacted to with worry that "she" was still alone in her life. Somehow, I felt she needed to have formed an intimate attachment, other than me, in order for her to be able to leave treatment. Although Shelley had grown a great deal, she still felt limited in her ability to truly feel another person's feelings. She could show more caring and interest in another person and could, after much discussion, understand another person's point of view, but it was not automatic, not yet in her bones. This was also an aspect of my countertransference of a worried maternal attachment. Termination pulls for these types of early, perhaps even primitive states in the analyst, and I needed to understand this so I could contain it for myself. In this regard, I grappled with whether I felt more work could help her and how long that would take. We had worked together for nearly 20 years, hardly a short amount of time. I certainly did not want to invoke the authoritative stance of my own analyst who, like many people in the field, had believed that "unfinished business" should be deemed indicative of and necessitating more work. I continued to wonder if I could trust Shelley to be a better judge here than I.

Despite my concerns about incompleteness, I decided we could do more work through the process of terminating, and that I needed also to support her desire to be on her own. We set a new end date 4 months away. This felt right to her, longer than her usual request of a month and shorter than my request of 6 months. I began to realize that it was most important for Shelley to be in control of this. Her entire childhood was colored not only by aloneness but also by her inability to have an impact on people. Shelley had to be the one in control of our ending, not without input from me, but not planned by me. My experience was one of encouraging her efficacy in decision making and in supporting her leave taking. (See Bonovitz, 2007, whose patient "needed" to be the one to leave as well.)

I have long felt the working-through process to be an abstraction without the experience-near quality of what it might look and feel like. Contemporary analysts of many persuasions now would agree that enactments are ubiquitous and are part of the analytic process. McLaughlin (2005) writes, "This, then, is how I see insight derived from analytic work being accomplished: from bits and pieces of experiential self-recognition gained, at times for both parties, in the immediacy of the actual relationship between the analytic pair, acquiring shape, meaning, and eventual articulation over analytic time" (p. 98). What I have come to see is that the working through, particularly when ending the treatment, contains and is comprised of enactments and dissociated self-states. It is important to understand that it is not regression that is occurring; rather, it is a deep resonant response to the possible rupture of the profound attachment between analyst and patient. We need to appreciate that this attachment is one we have been spending the entire treatment developing and understanding in terms of the patient's history and internalized relational world, as well as our own. Even with a great deal of time spent preparing for ending, it is nonetheless a rupture, an experience in many ways without precedence. Who ends a relationship that is close, nurturing, communicative, and is going well? Ending treatment for the analytic pair foreshadows an unknown future that can arouse not only past endings, ruptures, and losses, but a rupture that is occurring even as it is being considered and discussed as a possibility.

The tenor of this ending process was possible directly because of what I had gone through with Ellen years earlier. The ancient Greek philosopher Heraclitus, as well as Buddhists, have posited that you never step into the same river twice. I certainly felt I was changed by what I had lived through with Ellen. The meaning of the earlier enacted ending had only been accessible to me retrospectively, when Ellen came to see me and we were able to process it once again. This is the way in which time, not in its concrete linearity, but more in its linking capacity, is actively involved in our psychic lives. Now with Shelley, I was "linked" in my mind and in time with Ellen, our reworked endings and my own complicated ending of analysis along with the prior and current enactments with Shelley. We bring and live all of these versions of our enacted selves, creating a kind of rupturing moment that catches our attention. Within these moments with Shelley, multiple versions of each of us entered the scene and held the possibility for the creation of new links. Bergmann (2005), in writing about the difficulties in termination, states: "Psychic life is so constructed that nothing that once existed can cease to exist; our past is always with us" (p. 23). He is affirming the longevity of unconscious life which I believe makes us all vulnerable to its undertow while simultaneously allowing a kind of creative reworking all the time. Reis (2006), expanding upon Freud's concept of *nachträglichkeit,* writes, "Perhaps much of the most important work of an analysis is done after termination occurs, through a deferred action, an *après coup*, a *nachträglichkeit*" (p. 6). He reminds us that memories are always interacting with other memories, and current experiences interrelate with former memories and self-states so that posttermination work is in many ways a continuation of the work.

Shelley started grieving. She was amazed at what she was now able to feel, to imagine, and to recall. Her early years of being alone came back in a fully felt manner, and I could feel a shift in me, feeling more fully with her. She brought in the following dream:

> I walked into an empty room; people are in it, adults and family. There are big casement windows, the walls are white; it's a cold room. I came because I was friendly with one woman in the room. I saw this small girl crouched behind the couch. I leaned over to touch her cheek. It was me. She was feeling criticized, lonely and isolated with all her family members around her. I started to tell her that I loved her. There were these big antennas, steel structures. The family made fun of her because they felt she was crazy. I said I won't leave her.

Shelley knew this was an important dream and I agreed. The opening has the feeling of an actual memory, as if she was seeing and describing for me what her family's apartment looked like and felt like, all within the safety of our work. She said that she now understood what I had been saying about her being able to love the shameful, hurt, and unloved child inside of her. Shelley knew that the little girl in the dream was a part of her whom she had to take care of and love. This was very poignant for me and I became teary. She felt she could now do that, love that lonely child, and knew also that our ending did not mean abandonment. We had planned our final session a week after her 60th birthday. One of her cats, a particularly beloved one that she had been nurturing through cancer for over a year became sicker and died. Again we postponed terminating, with both of us realizing that this was a loss we needed to weather together.

As Shelley and I continued to talk about ending and what seemed to make it so difficult, I began to notice that the further away a termination date was set, the calmer Shelley seemed. The closer it became, the more upset or even panicky she became. However, my own internal states were a puzzle to me as her calmness made me quite anxious and her distress was perplexing. As I raised this with Shelley, she was able just then to share a latent fantasy that she had not spoken about with me. During the many years of our work, she maintained the idea/fantasy that, had we met outside the therapy relationship, we would have been friends. She imagined us having coffee, meeting for lunch, and so on. As we approached each set termination date, this fantasy began to feel impossible—we were not friends and could never be friends. Shelley further expressed the wish for us to become friends in the future, that friendship would be her "prize" for ending. This fantasy had to fade in the light of our actual ending. I now understood my feeling perplexed. I had not known of this fantasy, she had never spoken of it. In our ending, she would be relinquishing a wished for attachment while simultaneously giving up the very real attachment we had shared.

The nature of my termination with Ellen, years earlier, was not so much in the foreground of my mind, but clearly I had been deeply affected and changed by it. I was reluctant to exert that kind of "knowing" insistence over ending just because we had set a date. It felt more important to empower Shelley to choose to be able to walk away, for her to be the one to leave me. With this in mind, we set a new date for the summer. My only caveat was not to have it coincide with my summer vacation. I told her that we needed this to feel not like a summer break and unreal; there needed to be a time when she did not come to my office for her appointment but knew that I was there working. Again, it felt necessary for this to feel both real and to be her choice. We set a date and then soon after she requested an extra week, which I agreed to.

I also asked if she would write something about ending, explaining that I had been writing on this subject. I explained that I had been trying to create an ending with her that fit her needs and feelings. Shelley wrote the following:

> For me, I came to find out that termination is a process in of itself. I knew it was time for me to let go but it always seemed "not quite yet." Each time I came close to either setting an ending date or actually setting the date I would have a change of heart. Looking back I am not surprised that it has taken 2 years; in fact I am glad it did. It gave me the time to fully process moving on from a 20-year relationship. If I hadn't had the 2 years I would have missed out on knowing myself on an even deeper level. I remember when I first brought up leaving therapy; you thought 6 months might be a good amount of time to process leaving. I'm sure you remember that I thought 6 months was too long and not necessary. It turned out that I didn't have a clue as to what lay in store for me. I am grateful that you supported me in experiencing all my thoughts and feelings that came to the surface each time I got close to my cut-off dates. I remember what you once said to me when after 2 years of therapy I was impatient with myself for my lack of progress. You reminded me that I was dealing with 40 years worth of issues and that perhaps it was unrealistic for me to think I could deal with that in only 2 years. I can say for me the same holds true for the issues that arise when ending a 20-year experience, especially one that has been as beneficial as this.

I was deeply touched by what Shelley had written. She felt, at first, that the writing was something that had been imposed on her, and she was not going to do it. I had suggested it because, earlier in our work, when it had been hard for her to hold on to her feelings in between sessions, I had mentioned starting a journal. At that time, writing had made things more real for her, allowing her a felt continuity to her inner life. It was equally beneficial now; it gave Shelley a way to further reflect on this experience.

The second to last session arrived and Shelley walked in calm and relaxed and announced, "Today is our last session, I really don't need another session next week." Although I was surprised, nonetheless it felt right to me, Shelley was ending on her terms. At the end of the hour she asked if she could hug me good-bye. I said yes and found myself being not just hugged, but squeezed so tight that it hurt, and I spontaneously said "ow." Shelley let go of me and laughed saying she did not realize how strong she was.

POSTSCRIPT

During the time of this book and chapter's incubation, I had the following dream: "I dreamt that Stephen Mitchell had come back. I saw him and was showing him around NYU and thought to print out my paper on termination, the one that I was dedicating to him, to show to him. I tell others that he has come to visit." Stephen was a force in this field that many of us have been touched by and grateful for having had in our lives. He had been my teacher, supervisor, and mentor. For many he was a leader. His death was an unanticipated rupture for so many people—for his family an unimaginable loss—but for psychoanalysis and, in particular, relational psychoanalysis a great presence was now felt as an absence. His untimely death is yet another kind of forced termination in terms of supervisees, study group members, and patients. It has taken me many years to process how much he challenged me, inspired me, and instilled within me. It is in this way that Stephen has come back.

REFERENCES

Abraham, N., & Torok, M. (1972). Mourning or melancholia: Introjection versus incorporation. In N. Rand (Ed. & Trans.), *The shell and the kernel: Renewals of psychoanalysis* (Vol. 1, pp. 125–138). Chicago: University of Chicago Press.

Aron, L. (2009, June). Living memory: Discussion of paper by Avishai Margalit's "Nostalgia." Paper presented at the annual meeting of the International Association of Relational Psychotherapy and Psychoanalysis, Tel Aviv, Israel.

Bergmann, M. (1997). Termination: The Achilles heel of psychoanalytic technique. *Psychoanalytic Psychology, 14*, 163–174.

Bergmann, M. (2005). Termination and reanalysis. In E. Person, A. N. Cooper, & G. O. Gabbard (Eds.), *Textbook of Psychoanalysis* (pp. 241–253). Washington, DC: American Psychiatric Publishing House.

Berry, N. (1987). The end of the analysis. In J. Klauber (Ed.) & D. Macey (Trans.), *Illusion and spontaneity in psychoanalysis* (pp. 99–130). London: Free Association Books.

Bonovitz, C. (2007). Termination never ends: The inevitable incompleteness of psychoanalysis. *Contemporary Psychoanalysis, 43*, 229–246.

Bromberg, P. (1998). Staying the same while changing: Reflections on clinical judgment. *Psychoanalytic Dialogues, 8*, 225–236.

Bromberg, P. (2006). *Awakening the dreamer: Clinical journeys*. Mahwah, NJ: Analytic Press.

Davies, J. M. (2004). Whose bad objects are we anyway?: Repetition and our elusive love affair with evil. *Psychoanalytic Dialogues, 14*, 711–732.

Davies, J. M. (2005). Transformations of desire and despair: Reflections on the termination process. *Psychoanalytic Dialogues, 15*(6), 779–805.

Ferenczi, S. (1988). *The clinical diary of Sándor Ferenczi* (J. Dupont, Ed.). Cambridge, MA: Harvard University Press.

Fonagy, P., & Target, M. (1998). Mentalization and the changing aims of child psychoanalysis. *Psychoanalytic Dialogues, 8*(1), 87–114.

Freud, S. (1914). Remembering, repeating and working-through. In J. Strachey (Ed. & Trans.), *The standard edition of the complete psychological works of Sigmund Freud* (Vol. 12, pp. 145–156). London: Hogarth.

Freud, S. (1927). The future of an illusion. In J. Strachey (Ed. & Trans.), *The standard edition of the complete psychological works of Sigmund Freud* (Vol. 21, pp. 1–56). London: Hogarth.

Freud, S. (1937). Analysis terminable and interminable. In J. Strachey (Ed. & Trans.), *The standard edition of the complete psychological works of Sigmund Freud* (Vol. 23, pp. 211–253). London: Hogarth.

Loewald, H. W. (1962). Internalization, separation, mourning and the superego. *Psychoanalytic Quarterly, 31*, 483–504.

Loewald, H. W. (1972). The experience of time. *The Psychoanalytic Study of the Child, 27*, 401–410.

McLaughlin, J. T. (2005). *The healer's bent: Solitude and dialogue in the clinical encounter*. Hillsdale, NJ: Analytic Press.

Mitchell, S. A. (1993). *Hope and dread in psychoanalysis*. New York: Basic Books.

Novick, J. (1997). Termination conceivable and inconceivable. *Psychoanalytic Psychology, 14*(2), 145–162.

Ogden, T. (2005). *This art of psychoanalysis: Dreaming undreamt dreams and interrupted cries*. London: Routledge.

Reis, B. E. (2006). Time passes: Commentary on paper by Jody Messler Davies. *Psychoanalytic Dialogues, 16*(5), 599–602.

Salberg, J. (2009). Leaning into termination. *Psychoanalytic Dialogues, 19*(16), 703–722.

Chapter 8

Termination as necessary madness*

Sue Grand

David has been in treatment for about 5 years. For 3 years, there was an ordinary rhythm to his analysis. He was regular in his appointments, and in his payments. In the last 2 years, we are engaged in *analysis interruptus*—we meet, we stop meeting for several months, and then we meet again for a series of sessions. We are in our fourth cycle of this pattern. We stop, we resume, we stop. Each time, we talk about attachment and separation, about the limits, and the possibilities, of our relationship. He talks about extra-analytic contact, and postanalytic contact, and the peculiarities of the analytic situation. He came to psychoanalysis because he wanted to be able to love "full out." But in psychoanalysis, loss is imminent to love. Desire is awakened, and then, it is frustrated. Bonding is fulfilled, and then, it is severed. In all of its iterations, analytic love implicates grief. Every opening of the heart is shadowed by termination.

The celebration of intimacy, the imminence of loss: This is the paradoxical core of psychoanalysis. David has been confounded by this paradox since the beginning of his treatment. Analytic boundaries liberate and secure him. They free him to explore his feelings in the transference. What he feels is not pretty. But if he can do this with me, he might be able to love "full out." Wife, children, and friends, perhaps he could really be present with them. Perhaps he can really be present, inside himself. Moving through his world, David exudes warmth, humor, enthusiasm, and generosity. But his interior is remote. He can never fully feel others' affection for him, and he can never really give his full affection to others. For David, analysis is hope.

At the end of each session, that hope turns to despair. The hour is up: He feels that I am evicting him from my mind, and my heart. To David, this is a small death. It foreshadows a larger one. He anticipates a more permanent eviction: the end of his treatment. For several years, my clock seemed to regulate our bond. But it also awakened him from numbness. For much

---

* This chapter originally appeared in *Psychoanalytic Dialogues, 19*(6), 2009, pp. 725–735. (Reprinted with permission.)

of the session, he would try to be real. He would tell me about childhood, talk about his wife, and analyze dreams and erotic conflict. But he was just telling stories; he could not feel. Then weeping would erupt when his hour was over. His tears were attended by a visceral memory. I wanted to open this up. But all I could do was close it off. I made him leave while he was crying. I seemed cold and rigid. He felt greedy, and hurt, and deserted, and enraged. He hated my distraction and inattention. He was jealous of my "other children." He wanted empathy, limitless time, and exclusive attention. At the end of every session, I became the detested object of his dependence. Vulnerability was coextensive with abandonment and termination.

To me, these moments felt coercive, frustrating, *and* moving. He tried to steal time that was not his. He stonewalled my signals, and I had to push him out the door. His tears were a plea, an exploitation, and an accusation: "How can you leave me when I'm hurting? I thought you wanted me to feel!" He would deposit himself inside of me when I was already half-gone. He deposited himself inside of me *because* I was half-gone. By the next session, his injuries were buried. They disappeared into the interval between meetings; they reappeared again when he was leaving. We were never together when he was suffering, and we were never together in either his hate, or his need. I learned to function as his link, and his memory. At the beginning of our sessions, I would refer to our last ending. He recalled it, but he could not be *in it*, until the ending of the session. Then, he was in it again, and I was gone.

In that phase of his analysis, my empathic function could only be formulated as a retrospective. My concern always seemed to be belated: It referred to an experience that had already been missed. When he really needed my empathy, I would not give it. When my empathy was there, he could not receive it. All I could do was signify the link between vulnerability and leave-taking. In this way, the transference instantiated desertion. But that desertion was kept inside a resilient parental mind that could tolerate his hatred and reappear to contain him in the next session. I kept his tears inside me when he was gone. Gradually, his wound crept further and further into his hour. He wept when I was present. He felt his longing for dependence, and his dread of dependence, and the cold rage that was evoked by disappointment. He had an increased capacity for attachment, expressiveness, and object constancy. But every time his wound healed, it was ripped open by the prospect of termination. He was afraid to get well because *getting well* meant his final desertion, even though he knew he would decide when to stop.

In this treatment, ending is both necessary and impossible: It enlivens the dead baby inside of him, and it threatens to kill off the baby that has just been revived. For David, bonding is desolation, abjection, and falling to pieces. His infant self suffers from the schizoid problem described by Winnicott and Guntrip. David is endangered by contact, and he is endangered by the absence of contact. He comes alive with a howl; he assaults the object of his attachment. From early childhood on, he sealed himself away from others, and he sealed others away from himself. Now, he is aging. He has been a "prisoner of childhood" for over 70 years. Before he dies, he wants to know what it is like to feel alive.

And so, in the first 3 years of therapy, he went the distance. He wanted me to love him, beyond all others. He wanted to hurt me and soil me. He held me back from my next patient. If I took a minute to pee before his session, I could feel him smoldering. I could feel his desire for vengeance. In bad weather, I asked him to remove his boots in the waiting room. He was willful, he refused, he dripped snow and salt and mud on the rug in my office. He expressed his vengeance through the mess that he was making. He was afraid I would not love a nasty, messy baby. Whenever there was a bad storm, we knew we were in for a tussle. I would insist that he take off his boots. He thought I was fussy and rigid. But he was relieved that I did not give in. I wanted to know what it meant to him, to willfully soil my rug. This opened up visceral memories, and sadistic fantasies. On another occasion, he ignored his fee negotiation and sent me a reduced amount. In his next session, he made a pretense of innocence and waited to see what I would do. In his life, David seemed kind, and he kept his cruelty hidden. In analysis, these gestures were the merest surface of something that had always been secret. Sometimes, his coldness was stunning. It was redolent of that inhuman aggression that Guntrip (1971) linked to the schizoid problem. When people loved him for his warmth, David felt loved for a "false self." Hate and contempt neutralized his fear and dependence. But he was always lonely and hungry. When I inquired into his vengeance, he felt someone saw him at last.

Most of our work reckons with this dead infant self. But he is a sophisticated patient: He knows he is not my baby, and I am not his mother. He is a man of many parts, and he has multiple layers of conflict about getting close. Each of them is salient at one time, or another. Ultimately, he wants to know me, and to love me, as one real adult to another. Over the years, he draws closer to that ability. He feels more anxiety and less numbness and contempt. His relationships have been improving. And then, our sessions were interrupted by money trouble. He was not working, and his wife's job changed, and she was making less. I reduced his fee, but it was not enough, although he could never say what enough would be. If he was my *real* baby, he would not have to pay. But he is not my *real* baby, and so, he has to go. Money trouble demarcates reality. It is the occasion for mourning what I am not. It erects a limit that refers to the final limit of termination. He cannot afford treatment, but sometimes he needs it. So he stops, he returns, and he leaves again. He is reassured that he can always find me in my office.

It would be nice to think of this as a rapprochement phase of separation. But our contact does not feel like a secure but transient symbiosis; it does not feel like celebration, comfort, or refueling (Mahler, 1968). And it does not seem to have the joy, or the mastery, of Freud's *fort-da* game. We are certainly playing out something about disappearance and return. But we do not feel like we are playing. There is a lot of warmth when we meet. Still, something appears to be stuck. Every departure is a knot that we cannot seem to unravel. Termination is a recursive problem. It signifies autonomy, growing up, a capacity for ambivalent and imperfect love. But it also reignites his schizoid process. Bonding repeatedly turns into loss, and his infant self is returned to cold storage.

In our literature, there has been considerable discussion of *forced*, *delayed*, or *premature* termination. In this treatment, we seem to be inventing *serial* termination, and I wonder why we need to invent it. Whenever he goes, I do not know if, or when, he will come back. Each departure seems temporary. But one of these exits could lengthen into permanence. Perhaps, in a year or two, we will realize that this *was* our termination. For the two of us, time has always been problematic. It has been the referent for the fleeting nature of human contact. Perhaps our good-bye can only be formulated as a retrospective. Ours may be an unfulfilled parting. We may only recognize it in the future, as something that has passed, *without being shared*.

Or something may happen in his next series of sessions which will produce an alternate ending. At this writing, we are not meeting. Our past is unresolved, and our future is ambiguous. I am isolated from him, and yet, I am thinking about him. I am certain that he does not think I think about him when he is not present. As Bonovitz (2007) suggests, David might like to think that I have been affected by our encounter. It would mean a great deal to him if he thought that, as Bass (2001) put it, the "trajectory of both lives will not be quite the same for the encounter" (p. 700). But David cannot really imagine that he has left any imprint. He thinks that the longer he is gone, the more he will be forgotten.

To me, he is actually illuminated by his absence. In the passage of time, our relationship unfolds in my imagination. It accrues new dimensions. After I have been thinking about him for a while, he reappears, in real time. When we meet, neither of us knows what we are doing, or for how long. For both of us, attachment, mentalization, and separation are in a puzzling state of commentary and suspension. What does this say about this particular analysis, and what does it tell us about the analytic situation?

THE NECESSITY, AND THE PARADOX, OF ENDING

In my view, this enactment is particular to this dyad. But it also points to an impossible knot in our "impossible profession." Termination is not the final phase of an analysis. It hovers over every session, even if, as Slochower (2007) suggests, we construct a mutual illusion of timelessness in our work.

In psychoanalysis, the capacity to love has a privileged, and contradictory, status. Intimacy is a hard-won and complicated achievement. When that intimacy is established, we end it. As Davies notes, there is certain absurdity to this arrangement. Loss and separation are possibilities in every relationship. But where else do we embark on closeness, knowing that closeness *guarantees* loss? Where else do we work hard toward a goal, knowing that grief is an inevitable feature of success? This is the contradictory core of the analytic situation. Slochower (1998) put it succinctly: "the analytic relationship terminates just as it's 'getting good'" (p. 24). When the treatment is effective, the relationship is supposed to end. There is a taboo about having postanalytic relationships. In the dissolution of the transference, the relationship is supposed to dissolve. In these conditions, it is no surprise that the work proceeds slowly. It is a wonder that patients open themselves up at all.

Of course, there are worthy arguments for the analytic relationship ending. Most of these arguments are on behalf of the patient. But without endings, analysts would surely go mad from entropy and boredom. Just imagine if we spent decades with the same handful of patients—no one new coming, and no one leaving, and no hope for change or new stimulation. The same holds true for our patients—imagine that they stayed with their analyst, until their analyst died or retired. They might start to wish the analyst would hurry up and die. All of us have had stultifying experiences in which an analysis never seems to end. When patients and analysts hold onto each other for too long, vitality stalls, and the treatment can become its own pathogen. But most analytic dyads come to a moment of departure, in which analyst and patient go their separate ways. In many treatments, there is an organic letting go when the work seems to be done. In other treatments, there is a bumpy road to departure. In either case, there is much to be said for living through the experience of love and loss, relinquishing idealization, internalizing analytic function, discovering autonomy, reckoning with our existential condition, and turning one's gaze toward other relationships. In analysis, there are always boundaries, limits, and taboos. These vivify affect and desire; they illuminate intrapsychic and interpersonal process; and they should secure the patient from the personal needs of the analyst. Termination is the ultimate boundary in analysis. It is implied when the first session draws to its end.

For many reasons, termination is both necessary and inevitable. Still, there is something crazy about the way we think about our ending. If closeness guarantees loss in psychoanalysis, why do we pathologize the patient's fear of intimacy, instead of hailing it as a healthy defense? Which one of us is mad? Why have we constructed such a peculiar treatment paradigm in which we valorize intimacy and embed intimacy in loss? Why is the analytic ideal (Slochower, 2006) of termination unchanged, when we rarely live by our own rules?

As patients, many of us have continued contact with our analysts. As analysts, we hold onto to our patients for too long (Lionells, 2008). We have a professional heritage of forced terminations and delayed terminations (see Novick, 1997), and we constructed analytic institutes in which we never really lose our analyst. According to Levenson (1976), adolescents and young adults end their therapy when they reach "escape velocity" (p. 339). It seems to me that psychoanalysts rarely reach escape velocity—we may fight with our parents, but we tend to stay home with them. Nonetheless, we continue to espouse a neat phase of termination. We have begun to admit that we rarely achieve this, and we have an expanding literature that asks why we cannot do it (Bergmann, 1997; Novick, 1997). But we still expect our patients to navigate our contradictions. We fail to see their resistance to intimacy as iatrogenic. What does this say about our professional unconscious?

These questions become more possible in an era in which we are recognizing the prevalence of attachment disorders. According to Howell (2005), the most frequent underpinning of posttraumatic stress disorder (PTSD) is a disorganized or insecure attachment. Psychoanalysis originated as a quasi-medical treatment; its methodology was interpretation, and it excised mental illness. Symptoms were rooted in oedipal pathology. Until recently, we did not really know that we were treating trauma. As long as symptoms were linked to oedipal conflict, our treatment structure was an accurate mirror for our theory of psychopathology. To resolve illness, transference love had to be awakened, relinquished, and mourned. To love "out there," idealizing, incestuous love had to dissolve inside our office. Once the illness melted away, so did the relationship—even though it did not.

In contemporary psychoanalysis, we are less preoccupied with oedipal wishes, defenses, and gratifications. We are more concerned with the problems of trauma, attachment, fragmentation, and dissociation. In every theoretical orientation, we acknowledge the interactive relationship between patient and analyst. There is no sharp distinction between the real relationship and the transference. We study the totality of the dyad and have complex conversations with multiple self-systems. Now that we see the analytic dyad as a space of "asymmetrical mutual influence" (Aron, 1996), perhaps we can see the contradictions inherent in our own treatment structure. Perhaps we can admit to our own attachment problems. Maybe we can study the way we have written them into our law.

INTERPRETING TERMINATION AS A DREAM

In this spirit, I would like to propose something radical. I would like us to suspend, for a moment, all of our assumptions about treatment. The analytic situation was a brilliant invention. It is an idyll of experience that stands apart from all other human relationships. It has remarkable healing power. Without endings, this healing power would be compromised. Nonetheless, we can subject the analytic situation to a form of radical inquiry. We can examine our treatment structure the way we examine a patient's dream. When we analyze dreams, we honor the plasticity, and the inventiveness, of the unconscious. Because the mind can invent anything while it is asleep, we allow ourselves to ask *why* the mind has constructed this particular set of images, here, now. Let's try turning the same methodology on ourselves. Once, there was no psychoanalysis. The human mind invented analytic praxis—of all the shapes which treatment might have taken, *why* have we imagined *this particular analytic structure*?

As analysts, we believe that dreams are multiply determined. They are elaborations of history. They are communications about contemporary predicaments. They are compromise formations; they serve many masters and have progressive *and* defensive functions. To excavate their meaning, we suspend linearity and reason. We enter a hermeneutic labyrinth that has intrapsychic, interpersonal, and social features. Again and again, we begin our inquiry by asking *why* this, here, now. Each time we ask, we get another answer and open up another question. What would happen if we turned this lens on our treatment structure? What if we embraced our resistance to termination and asked what this resistance tells us about our professional history and our contemporary predicament? Perhaps we would reveal the *progressive* and the *defensive* functions of termination and illuminate its intrapsychic, interpersonal, and social functions.

To open such an inquiry, we must notice the obvious. In constructing psychoanalysis, we conceived an intimate pursuit with ruptured bonding at its core. We valorized a proper ending, we create training and institutes in which there is no ending, and we critique ourselves for failing to adhere to the law of termination. We instate our own taboos, and then, we break them. Then we reify our conventions, extrude our own subversion, and double-bind our patients. Why did we invent a practice that creates and ruptures bonds? Why must our own postanalytic attachments be illicit, and why do we forbid them to our nonanalytic children? We have begun to study our own contradictions, transgressions, and resistances. But the termination literature examines only the defensive function of these resistances and transgressions. It does not reveal the progressive function of transgression, and it never permits these transgressions to query our taboos. The termination literature is implicitly tilted toward making us better citizens who adhere to the law.

In my view, our resistance to termination is not just a defensive evasion of loss. It is a pathway toward knowledge, a new prescription for healing. In our early oedipal focus, I believe that we put our own schizoid problem into cold storage. Through our own enactments, we reveal that problem and try to repair that problem and allow it to enter our professional consciousness.

Oedipal theory was a brilliant formulation, and it continues to have curative resonance. But oedipal theory also provided excellent cover for a practice in which we invite, and undo, closeness. It revealed one form of conflict while enacting another. Now that we appreciate the existence of multiple self-states, we can retrieve our own dissociated self–other configurations— configurations infused with fragmentation, disordered attachment, and developmental arrest. If we look at the contradictions between what we say and what we do about termination, any good analyst would think we have a problem with intimacy. We seem to be expressing the longing for dependence, and the dread of dependence. Our law privileges autonomy, and actions create fusion.

When we act out like this, we are formulating a protest. We are pointing ourselves toward a new therapeutic. Like our patients, we have fissures in our capacity for intimacy and attachment. Like our patients, we cherish the hard-won adult relationship that emerges in psychotherapy. And like our patients, we inherited a worldview that devalues dependency and equates independence with maturity, mastery, and strength (see Layton, 2004). We have all been under attack by gendered splitting: only "girly-men," like Woody Allen, go on needing their psychoanalyst. Real patients are like Clint Eastwood: They grow up and get over it; they get going, and they know how to go it alone. No wonder we enjoy outing our patriarchal forebears who endorsed termination and then mucked it up. When Novick reveals the behavior of Freud and his followers, we love it. In private, our patriarchs were girly-men about separation, attachment, and loss. They were enmeshed and incestuous and needy and wounded; they were rejected and rejecting. Let's not trivialize our pleasure in this analytic gossip. In this pleasure, we find the whiff of social rebellion. As Layton (2004) notes, we have been made sick by this excessive valence on independence. This valence has contributed to the "need–fear" dilemma. It has made us counterphobic about our need for other. It has made us disdainful of the needy other. We drop bombs in our intimate relationships, and we drop bombs on the world stage. Perhaps psychoanalysts should reconsider healthy interdependence, even though we do not know exactly what that is or what it looks like at the end of analysis.

Given the cultural prevalence of attachment disorders, I think we need to revisit love, interdependency, and the nature of what Gerson called the "embedded self." As Sullivan (1953) once put it, "we are all much more simply human than otherwise" (p. 53). As analysts, we seem to want what most adult children seem to want: to grow up and individuate, and to be able to keep our "good enough" parents. As practitioners devoted to an intimate practice, we may actually want this much more than some of our own patients. If we look at the way we arrange our institutes, we certainly seem to want to go on loving our parents, somehow, until death intervenes. If Freud had not had extra-analytic, and postanalytic contact with his patients, he would not have had any colleagues, and there would have been no future for psychoanalysis. Our forebears may have been acting out their own attachment problems. But they also had a conflicted understanding that we *need* each other. What is curious, here, is the *denial* of that need, and the way we wrote that denial into our canon.

In this discussion, I am moving back and forth from the study of a particular psychoanalysis, and the study of psychoanalysis itself. Let us move back, for a moment, to the particularity of the analytic couple. Maturity, individuation, going-on-loving, and even death itself: These can take a multitude of forms in any given psychoanalysis. As Davies (2005) suggests in her paper on termination, they will take a multitude of forms within each psychoanalysis, because analyst and patient exist in multiple self–other configurations. Every analytic dyad will need to formulate complex and shifting positions about attachment, separation, and leave-taking. This can only happen if we listen to our resistances and transgressions and allow them to query the law of termination.

A recent issue of *Psychoanalytic Inquiry* was devoted to the nature of analytic love. In contemporary psychoanalysis, we have been increasingly open about what we are really doing, and what we are really feeling. We already admitted to hating our patient (Coltart, 1986; Grand, 2000, and so forth) and to desiring our patient (see Davies, 2005). Now, perhaps, we can turn to something that seems much more banal, even though it is not. What is love in the analytic relationship, and what do we do with it, when therapy is finished? If we can ask this question, we might understand what David and I are doing, as he comes and goes, without going.

ATTACHMENT AND SEPARATION: THE PERPETUITY OF ENACTMENT

With David, every break is framed as an interruption, and every interruption is precipitated by money trouble. He commits to a fee, and then discovers that he cannot (or will not) pay it. Fee reductions do not do it. He needs me to waive the fee, or slash the fee, even though he knows that he is not entitled. He cannot ever seem to *do* anything about his finances; he wants *me* to solve it, and he knows this is his problem. We both know that the fee is functioning like my clock. It is the litmus test of love, the perimeter of attachment. If I really care about him, I will not care about my fee. As an adult, he knows that I *do* care about him, *and* that I am also working and earning my living.

David never seems to have agency when it comes to leaving. He does not interrupt treatment because he *wants* to, but because he *has to*. He thinks he wants to stay. Once, he had an interesting solution: We could set up a *posttermination annuity*. He would pay a nominal fee *now*, while he was here. When he was finished, he would pay me in monthly installments. He would get to finish his therapy. And after he was gone, I would receive a modest income. To David, this was a fair proposal, in which everyone's needs would be covered. He seems innocent, and he really means it.

But to me, this is the latest move in a series of provocations. My coldness is always responsible for our separations. If I accepted the annuity, he could stay—but it never occurs to me to accept it. He is in his seventies, he does not work, he has no savings, and he is reliant on the modest income of his younger wife. Why would I labor now and hope for payment later? Why should I pay for his fiscal irresponsibility? If he dies, am I really going to hold his wife accountable for his debt? I want to talk about the unconscious meaning of his offer; he wants me to consider it. There is no getting around this one. I refuse and try to explain—but I avoid mentioning his age, or his death. I have disappointed him again, and once again, I seem to be pushing him out. Before he stops this time, we talk about the inventiveness of the annuity. From the beginning of our work, he has worried about our attachment. Is it reciprocal and authentic? Is it imaginary and one sided? Could we ever be two ordinary people, who like, and know, each other? Can we have some kind of relationship after therapy? If I would agree, would he really want it?

Ah, I said, but this annuity. You would be gone, I would not see you, but you could secure your place in my mind, over many years. And you could reverse your own predicament. I could be the needy baby, waiting for my feed, dependent. You could take your revenge, if you wanted. He gets it, we laugh; he feels childish, I feel like Scrooge. He cries, he says good-bye, and then, he leaves. And I am left thinking about my relation to money. Am I more attached to my fee than I am to David? If that is true, what does it mean about me, about us, about the culture in which we are embedded? And how does it refer to the culture of David's childhood? David was born to rich parents, just before the stock market crash of 1929. His parents had been elegant; they were the elite of Brooklyn, and they lived in opulence. They had an anglicized name and disdain for their poor Jewish relatives. Suddenly, they were bankrupt. Without wealth, they had, and were, nothing. They may have bonded to their infant prior to the crash. Afterward, they went dead, toward him and his brother, as well as to each other.

In his sessions, he relives the desolation that followed the crash. He would feel himself alone in his crib, in a dark room, with no one coming. As a toddler, he knows that he peed in bed, and that he smeared his shit on the walls. Session after session, he is in that crib. When he visualizes someone, it is a threatening presence. Dripping mud on my rug, he senses parental rage about cleaning up his mess. In another visualization, he crawls through empty rooms, searching for mother. When he finds her, she is kneeling and scrubbing; she will not turn to look at him. After the crash, all she does is hoard and clean. This imagery returns when I ask him to remove his boots in the waiting room.

Then later, they are in a cramped and dismal apartment. There is no privacy or escape from each other's bodies. There is one bathroom for four people. Someone is always peeing or pooping, and someone else is showering or dressing. Upper-class shame infuses this exposure. Genitals are always on display, but he has to pretend he is not seeing them. When he looks, he feels perverse. There is nothing warm in this intermingling of bodies. He does not feel anyone loves him or even that they see him. His father is bitter, caustic, and broken. His mother is lonely. By day, he saw no evidence of parental closeness. At night he heard the grunts of sexual intercourse. Arousal seemed cold, it was unwanted, and it seemed to hurt. Gradually, his mother turned to David for the affection she could not get from her husband. He wanted the embrace of a mother, but when she touched him, it was suffocating and repugnant. He remembers her seductiveness, as she undressed in front of him, in his parents' bedroom. He stared at her breasts, and his look felt prurient and incestuous. He could never find a comfortable mother, whom he could touch, or who could comfort him. In mid-childhood, he tried to choke his mother. In adolescence, he set fires, got in fights, and ran away from home. He was afraid of being wanted, and he was afraid of being left alone. He wanted a woman, he was smothered by women, and he thought he would hurt them with his angry desire.

In this family, money trouble foreclosed closeness, in every phase of development. Money glittered, it was elusive, and it eclipsed the human heart. It was the signifier for power and abjection, for craving and longing and loss. As a teenager, as a young man, and as an adult, it was the standard by which his mother measured him. He could make money, but he could never plan ahead, or conserve it. Of course, fees test our closeness. He keeps reenacting the crash and asking whether his analyst-parent can value something else about him or sustain a bond. But if I am too compliant about fees, I become the clinging mother, who needed him too much and wants to keep him for herself. If he goes, he loses his infant mother. If he stays, he is smothered. Termination is the perfect mirror for his need–fear dilemma.

In his prior treatment, David was engaged in another knot about money, boundaries, and termination. For 20 years, he had a warm and fatherly analyst, who filled the hole left by David's real father. Together, they focused on oedipal issues. They enacted attachment longings and never analyzed those longings or the need for some separation. In this treatment, David found himself as an artist, and he fell in love with his current wife. Something went very right, and very wrong, in this analysis. His first analyst seemed established, secure, and generous: He accepted David's paintings as payment, he went to his shows, and he rarely ended the sessions on time. Love was not soiled by materialism. Love was not ruptured by artificial boundaries. David's value was not defined by dollar signs. But the analyst's looseness had terrible consequences. After 15 years of treatment, David discovered that his analyst was sleeping with a female patient. He confronted his analyst, who admitted it, with some regret. Now, apparently, that was all over. For a few sessions, David howled with rage, betrayal, jealousy, and fear. Then, they told themselves that this episode was over. David stayed in analysis, and slowly, the treatment went stale. He would lie silently on the couch, with his silent analyst behind him. My patient became unable to speak, and the analyst's warmth became more remote. David was back in his crib and no one was coming. Eventually, his analyst retired, and when they said good-bye, it was forever.

David never told anyone about his analyst's transgression, until he entered treatment with me. In our work, he needed to explore his erotic transference; he was always frightened that I would violate our boundaries. All of this added extra layers of complication to David's need–fear dilemma: his wish for contact and his dread of contact. David's first analysis enacted attachment, it healed him, it aroused incestuous rage and anxiety, it betrayed him, it recreated his schizoid predicament, and then, it ended. Well, that did not work, and we cannot quite figure out what would. There are so many parts of him. All of them seem conflicted about staying and going. Some of them need flexible boundaries, and some of them need those boundaries to be rigid. And then, there is a grown-up David, who knows about the ultimate end that is coming. He is in his late seventies. He is earthy, funny, and enthusiastic. He has close friendships; he comes through for his friends. He is a thinker, and he likes to converse. We share political and social views. At the beginning of our sessions, we often have a good laugh. Despite his internal struggle, he is actually more present than most people whom I meet. And he knows that one day, he will die.

Over the time I have seen him, he has had prostate cancer and a heart attack. He will not always be here. I like him. An accident of fate brought us together as analyst and patient. As his therapist, I have seen the numbness with which he sealed his heart. I have watched him struggle, and open up. He got better, even though that meant that he might leave. Then, he had a heart attack. I went to see him in the hospital, and we talked about his heart. I asked him if he could really feel, and trust, the love of his friends and relatives. Without hesitation, he said yes. He knew his wife would not desert him, and he did not need to keep her at a distance, or punish her for her comings and goings. He was touched that I was there, and awkward in my presence. We both knew that my presence was a partial answer to his question. I was there as his analyst. But I was also there as a friend, as one human being to another, in a time of crisis. After that, I did not see him; he was on bed rest for 3 months. I called him once or twice to see how he was feeling.

Then, he came back to treatment and continued his cycle of coming and going. Each time, he would ask, who we might be to each other, if we ever finished. The infant inside of him will always want a mother. The dead baby inside of him is never fully healed. Now that infant has other objects, but his analysts have been his first parents. He may have finished analyzing the self who was in cold storage, but, as Annie Reich (1958) put it, analysis has been the "first really reliable object relationship in the patient's life" (p. 236). We do not know if the transference will ever resolve. Anyway, he is not finished with contact. And as a man facing death, it seems ridiculous to relinquish our "good enough" relationship, now that we have it. He imagines walks with casual and mutual conversation—about birds and gardens and the problems of local politics. He wants to get to know me, without the interference of our roles. I do not share his particular fantasy. Still, I think we might have found each other, as neighbors, in another setting. We attend the same community meetings and are active in the same local projects. A friendly acquaintanceship might have developed between us. As analyst and patient, this would certainly be complicated and, perhaps, inadvisable. It might deprive him of an analyst, in the future, should he need me. If I spent time with him outside the treatment setting, it might trigger his fear that I, too, would breach the sexual boundaries with my patient. I cannot imagine being uninhibited in his presence. The smallest contact would carry the weight of his greater need, and my greater knowledge. We have no answers. We are secured by our boundaries, but we are not persuaded by the law. In my practice, he disappears and reappears. His self states cohere, they unravel, they have objects, they become objectless, they are little, they are big, and they are growing old. They want to go on loving, until death parts us, for the last time.

REFERENCES

Aron, L. (1996). *A meeting of the minds: Mutuality in psychoanalysis*. Hillsdale, NJ: Analytic Press.

Balint, M. (1950). On the termination of analysis. *International Journal of Psycho-Analysis, 30*, 196–199.

Bass, A. (2001). It takes one to know one, or whose unconscious is it anyway? *Psychoanalytic Dialogues, 11*, 683–703.

Bergmann, M. (1997). Termination: The Achilles heel of psychoanalytic technique. *Psychoanalytic Psychology, 14*, 163–174.

Bonovitz, C. (2007). Termination never ends: The inevitable incompleteness of psychoanalysis. *Contemporary Psychoanalysis, 43*(2), 229–247.

Coltart, N. (1986). Thinking the unthinkable in psychoanalysis. In G. Kohon (Ed.), *The British School of Psychoanalysis: The independent tradition* (pp. 185–199). New Haven, CT: Yale University Press.

Davies, J. M. (2005). Transformations of desire and despair: Reflections on the termination process from a relational perspective. *Psychoanalytic Dialogues, 15*(6), 779–805.

Guntrip, H. (1971). *Psychoanalytic theory, therapy and the self*. New York: Basic Books.

Howell, E. (2005). *The dissociative mind*. Hillsdale, NJ: Analytic Press.

Layton, L. (2004). *Who's that girl? Who's that boy? Clinical practice meets postmodern gender theory*. Hillsdale, NJ: Analytic Press.

Levenson, E. A. (1976). The aesthetics of termination. *Contemporary Psychoanalysis*, *12*, 338–341.

Mahler, M. S. (1968). *On human symbiosis and the vicissitudes of individuation*. New York: Basic Books.

Novick, J. (1997). Termination conceivable and inconceivable. *Psychoanalytic Psychology*, *14*, 145–162.

Reich, A. (1958). A special variation in technique. In *Psychoanalytic contributions* (pp. 236–249). New York: International Universities Press.

Slochower, J. (1997/1998). Clinical Controversies: Ending an analytic relationship. *Psychologist-Psychoanalyst*, Winter 1997–1998, XVIII(4), 24–25.

Slochower, J. (1998). Clinical controversies: Ending an analysis. *Psychologist-Psychoanalyst*, 24–25.

Sullivan, H. S. (1953). *The interpersonal theory of psychiatry*. New York: Norton.

Viorst, J. (1982). Experiences of loss at the end of analysis: The analyst's response to termination. *Psychoanalytic Inquiry*, *2*, 399–418.

Chapter 9

The changing firmament
Familiar and unfamiliar forms of engagement during termination*

Steven Cooper

In analyses that have been ongoing concerns, initial discussions of termination often stimulate shifts in the patient's perspectives regarding the therapeutic work and the relationship between patient and analyst. The illusory, more open-ended canvas for expanding curiosity engendered by the analysis will soon be temporally framed, even if patient and analyst know that this ending can always be renegotiated at a later date. The patient's growth during analysis may also move from foreground to background as the patient's and analyst's limitations in promoting growth may move from background to foreground. In this paper, I am most interested in how the process of ending analytical work provides a context for exploring previously unworked-through and unexplored parts of interaction and experience.

Many analyses, including those that are highly productive, end at points at which the patient and analyst have run out of emotional and imaginative resources to take analysis to a further level of understanding. As Ferenczi (1927) put it: "The proper ending of an analysis is when neither the physician nor the patient puts an end to it, but when it dies of exhaustion" (p. 80). Some patients have been able to do enough productive work to place them in good stead in life and others return to us or someone else for more analysis at a later date. For still another group of analytic dyads, the decision to terminate seems to facilitate renewed levels of work and commitment to resolve forms of impasse. In any relationship there are multiple meanings when one person or both say that they are going to end the relationship. In the case of analysis, we hope that this is because the patient feels that he or she has been able to get what he or she wanted, or close enough to what he or she wanted. There are also relationships in which when one person says "let's stop," he or she is actually tendering an invitation not to stop but to try to be together in a different way: "Let's stop if we can't do something or understand something in a different way."

It is true that in some ways termination can be thought of as the beginning of an "infinite conversation" (Marshall, 2000) as the therapeutic

---

* This chapter originally appeared in *Psychoanalytic Dialogues*, 19(5), 2009, pp. 588–603.

relationship continues its dialogue through the individual's self-reflection. Yet I am also struck that the initial talks about ending a therapeutic process can often mark a clearer process of discussing the nature of the very finite conversation that has already been taking place. This realization of the limited nature of the conversation can be invigorating and can potentially expand the patient and analyst's field of vision. Regarding the latter type of endings, termination is a process by which analyst and patient resolve to try to get unstuck or move in different directions regarding a particular impasse, to try to grieve anew, and in a sense to push each other into both familiar but in some ways uncharted territory.

INTERPERSONAL ASPECTS OF REGRESSION OR REVISITING POINTS OF IMPASSE

The essence of termination as it is classically conceived is about how the loss of analysis and the analyst trigger the reemergence of earlier symptoms, trauma, and unresolved grief. Within this view, over the course of analytic work the patient has been able to resolve conflicts in a good enough way to suggest ending. In some sense, the analyst does not have an interpersonal connection, except as interpreter of the particular manifestations of transference expressed by the patient. The analyst is an auxiliary ego and superego, and in this sense, he functions as a kind of container for a new homeostasis composed of the patient's reconfigured symptoms (e.g., Loewald, 1960).

This view obviously does not emphasize how the dyad has worked with the patient's conflicts within the interactive context of analysis. Bollas (1989) put it well in saying that we as analysts "imagine" our patient's symptoms in a variety of ways over time. Symptoms within this view are seen both within an intrapsychic and dyadic/interactive context. In my view, this imagining includes how the analyst both thinks and feels about the patient's difficulties over time and also how we think about both the patient's and analyst's experience of how trauma, conflict, and particular affects are embedded in the interpersonal context of analytic work. My patient's flying phobia, for example, takes on different meanings for the patient over time as we realize that his unconscious fantasies involve the pilot being unreliable, like his preoccupied mother whom he has vowed to never trust again. I can experience his unconscious anxiety about trusting me despite his very conscious participation and his appreciation of me and what we do. Over time his symptoms will seem understandable, saddening, or exasperating to me as we look into this in both his external life and within the analysis. It is one thing to be a passenger *with* my patient, but another to be the pilot.

I recognize that sometimes a patient's struggles with painful affects, identity, and conflict may reappear during termination, and that some patients do indeed regress during termination, my attention is usually focused more on how self–other configurations related to conflict reappear and offer a new opportunity for examination. I am particularly interested in how the analyst is implicated in the patient's struggles by both patient and analyst. So I would suggest that some instances of what some might call regression or a kind of psychic slippage involve renewed risks for change, new presentations of unsolved problems that the patient is more willing to take on in the context of ending. In fact some clinical phenomena that look like regression are actually the exposure of unresolved conflicts within the patient and the dyad, more than actual retreat from previously consolidated gains.

I also wonder whether various versions of symptom regression in analytic work reflect a lack of sophistication about the idea that forms of impasse and stalemate are routine in every dyad and, thus, are likely to be revisited in termination. If we take it as a given that enactments are ubiquitous, then it makes sense that termination would stimulate new feelings and ideas about areas of enacted conflict and affect. I would take it even further and suggest that termination not only brings up an experience of losing the analyst but also of losing the particular forms of enactment/play to which the patient has become accustomed.

In a sense, I am suggesting that the patient and analyst are not only saying good-bye to each other as objects but they are also saying good-bye to an experience of the relationship, the dyad, the "being together." This includes aspects of affective resonance, empathy, limitation, and various forms of enactment. When people lose someone, they also lose an experience of self with that someone.

Regression in this context may relate to the patient's anticipation of what it will be like for him or her to not have his or her analyst, accommodations, adaptations, enactment, and all. The regression in a sense is related to an anticipated psychic future without these interpersonally enacted forms of conflict. Of course, the analyst need always consider the extent to which these feelings are also related to revived old object experience.

The notion of regression during termination has also been more strictly focused on the patient's behavior and experience as a sole player. This view fails to take into account the ways in which a psychoanalyst might "regress" in relation to the patient's changes during termination or, for that matter, to the loss of the patient. Klauber's (1977) examination of the analyst's regression in termination, dealing with particular patients who struggle with severe trauma related to object loss is an exception to this general statement.

THE COUNTERTRANSFERENCE OF INDETERMINACY AND TERMINATION

In my experience, there are those rewarding treatments when things have gone so well that patient and analyst "know" when it is time to stop. At least as often, however, there are the more raggedly textured endings familiar to most analysts, including stops and starts about determining when termination will begin.

Clarity about good work coming to an end is not only a fictive occurrence. However, to some extent, the literature on termination has fallen victim to the allure of linearity in the narrative of analysis, focusing on a story of progress up to a certain point to be followed by a degree of regression during the termination phase. It is my sense that some of the most successful analyses end with less regression and instead feature a revisiting of some of the same points of entanglement that accompanied analysis or that even fueled the initial decision to stop.

Rarely is termination clear except in circumstances when external factors come into play. The most frequently discussed reason for this lack of clarity is the reality that analyst and patient could potentially work on matters at hand for a very long, perhaps even an interminable amount of time (e.g., Bergmann, 1997; Freud, 1937; Levenson, 1976). A less frequently explored source for ambiguity about termination is the ubiquitous nature of enactment. If patient and analyst are always "in something or other," it can sometimes seem like they will not get out of that "something or other." The patient and analyst may also hold illusions about their ability to get out of this something or other as well.

Among the many versions of uncertainty and ambiguity that the analyst must hold, the ambiguity about when to end analysis is quite demanding. I call it the countertransference of indeterminacy, not to reify one more psychoanalytic concept, but to name it so that we can in some sense expect it. There are after all many forms of indeterminacy in analysis that the analyst struggles with (a few versions of the countertransference of indeterminacy), including the array of technical and theoretical choices about how to best help his patient. But the indeterminacy about how and when to end brings many issues to the fore regarding how ambitious patient and analyst should or want to be, whether they are giving up prematurely or whether they are avoiding in some way saying good-bye.

This indeterminacy about ending is complicated by the fact that many contemporary analysts see enactment as ubiquitous. Just as conflict is never fully resolved, nor does enactment of conflict ever take a time-out. The "unendingness" of psychoanalysis (another translation of Freud's word, *unendliche*) was, in a sense, Freud's (1937) realistic and sobering statement about the unending task of self-understanding. It was also his own way of noting the existential indeterminacy of self-knowledge. Contemporary psychoanalysts have more fully acknowledged their own participation in and experience of this indeterminacy as they know and are known by their patients.

Levenson (1976) has suggested that ending is often more a matter of aesthetics than technique, likening the decision to end to the painter who decides when the work of art is complete. I recently read that the head of

Pixar Films said, "Our films are never complete, they're only released." From the point of view of therapeutic accountability within a treatment situation, it can be disturbing to think about how vague and arbitrary these decisions may seem. Yet these statements also capture something that feels familiar to me about how murky the decision to stop can be both when the analysis has gone very well and also, when there are still points of difficulty that might be further resolved. When things have gone well, there is often the sense of pleasure about successful work, accomplishment for the patient and analyst, and a sense of connection. But this does not mean that the "when" takes on an easily discernable, concrete form, like the curtain drop for a play or the last out in a baseball game. When there is palpable and articulated uncertainty about whether the continued work will be helpful, often the ambiguity about the decision to stop feels rational and objective. Both Bass (2001; Chapter 16, this volume) and Davies (2005) articulated the denotations of finality associated with the word "termination" which fail to capture both the ways that endings and beginnings are less distinct as well as the enduring impact that both patient and analyst have had on each other.

Similarly, Levenson is probably implying that it may be more accurate to say that the very nature of termination is intrinsically ambiguous and that some analyses may toil under the notion that there will be more clarity at some point. Along these lines, many have noted that, ironically, a relational perspective is more objective because it conforms to the nature of what Merleau-Ponty (1964) meant when he said: "ambiguity is of the essence of human existence...thus there is in human existence a principle of indeterminacy...and this indeterminacy does not only stem from some imperfection in our knowledge." Perhaps Levenson is saying that termination at its best, for patient and analyst, has incorporated an understanding and acceptance of this indeterminacy.

I have found that issues of ending come in and out of focus for both patient and analyst throughout analytic work. When issues of ending come into central focus, they can be opportunities to work through a wide variety of forms of psychic conflict and accompanying elements of transference–countertransference engagement. Interestingly, analysts are often strikingly concrete about the ways that we listen to feelings and thoughts about termination. Sometimes we may have a tendency to be overly literal or concrete when a patient expresses a desire to stop, because we want to honor these desires and because, in truth, it is always the patient's decision about when to stop. At other times, we may be too reflexively drawn to thinking about mention of termination as a form of resistance. The analyst's personal anxieties about loss, concern for the patient, narcissistic anxiety about treatment failure, or economic issues may also contribute to a relative collapse in the analyst's reflective capacities about termination.

This raises the question of why we are sometimes less likely to think about the multiplicity of meanings suggested by mention of termination.

Even the words, "termination and interminable" are so different than more literal translations of Freud's words as "endingness and unendingness." Sometimes when I am surprised that a patient begins to speak of termination, I try to think about what we are not accomplishing or have not been able to accomplish that may be a source of unrest, sadness, or anger. In other words, the patient may be bringing up termination as a way of saying: "If I can't get more out of this or from you, I'd like to stop." Conversely, sometimes I try to think about what we are accomplishing that might be causing difficulty. For example, a patient might also be expressing something along the lines of: "I don't know if I can bear to talk about these feelings anymore."

One reason that we may be more concrete or literal about the meaning of termination than we are about other parts of analysis is because we have an ethical responsibility, as part of our accountability, to honor the decisions of our patients about when that process begins and ends. Psychoanalysis is a contractually arranged form of treatment. But I suspect that this is the easy explanation. I think it is likely that analysts truncate the process of analytic play—the consideration of multiple meanings—in relation to termination of analysis because of its connection to death. As Hoffman (1998) has suggested, death is always in the background of analytic work, but during termination it symbolically and affectively moves more into the foreground. Initial discussions of termination often open up how these experiences of ending and mortality are catalyzed.

TERMINATION AND THE PSYCHIC FUTURE

It is one thing to say that termination is not a temporally linear process, including as it does an intrinsically ambiguous indeterminacy about the nature of when and why we stop our work and whether or not we will resume at some point. It is another to say that regarding the patient's experience of time it is a particularly dense and "thick" (Tronik, 2003) period. The patient is coming to grips with a more explicit discussion and imagining of his psychic future. While every interpretation imagines a psychic future (e.g., Cooper, 1997; Loewald, 1960) for the patient, termination, in a sense, embodies this future. We are involved in helping patients to feel that future after analysis, including how the patient will hold the analyst in mind and how the patient imagines that the analyst will hold him in mind.

Density is also related to how termination includes many versions of good-bye involving multiple parts of both patient and analyst (e.g., Davies, 2005). Hopefully, some of the patient's identifications and counteridentifications have been expressed during analysis and are also familiar to the analyst during termination, though not always. It is also true that new parts of our patients sometimes emerge at this point. Seen in this light, part of termination is related to the ways in which both patient and analyst try once again to move from enactment to self-reflection in the context of far more explicit limitations of both time and possibility.

Once termination has been discussed, the landscape of the patient's psychic future has changed or, often, the beginning of this discussion marks how the patient is already imagining his psychic future. Part of the ways that the patient now considers his future involve not only that he will lose the analyst—lose his person and that person's insights about his struggles, affects, and conflict—but he will also lose the particular forms of analytic accommodation that have become a feature over the course of their work together. A few questions emerge in considering the implications of the loss of the interactive patterns that the patient and analyst have developed together. Will there be and are there other relationships that provide the same opportunities for engagement even in the form of acclimation to particularly demanding parts of being with this patient? In essence, how much have the particular forms of adaptation from the analyst to the patient and, of course, the patient to the analyst left room for the patient to experience himself or herself and the other in a way that feels alive and "real."

Often when things have gone well, the patient is aware that not everything is resolved and that this is part of the grief that the patient will experience and explore during termination. In such instances, if aspects of idealization are mourned as well as reality about limitation within both the patient and the analyst, then the psychic future is opened in a way that can be invigorating. However for patients who still feel a burr under the saddle as they leave analysis—something important that they have not been able to work out with their analyst—the psychic future can be dreadful, terrifying, or depressing. Even though it is hardly ideal to have an analyst who we feel is not able to help us understand or integrate some important matters, many patients are able to appreciate the ways in which the analyst has helped and struggles to help in new ways. Termination announces a farewell between two people, and ironically, it symbolizes the status of what has changed and not changed within the analytic work. This symbolization is ironic because even though the analytic change process actually continues after formal termination, the initiation of discussion about termination is often experienced as a kind of finality during parts of that process. In the best of circumstances it catalyzes new attempts to find the burr under the saddle and new modes of understanding.

Some patients who have been particularly resilient to stress and trauma and who are particularly gifted at eliciting in others a capacity to adapt to their fears may, I believe, have special difficulty with termination. For such patients, the psychic future represents an ambiguity about whether the conditions for relinquishing control established during analytic work will be in place in other new relationships and whether the equilibrium and safety of the analytic relationship will live on in more ambiguous circumstances. Termination poses both new opportunities and new challenges.

In particular, the analyst and such a patient may learn about ways in which the psychic future is unconsciously perceived as the past, linked to a time when the patient had little control. Thus, termination becomes a threat both to the patient's resilient adaptation growing up and to the growth that he or she has achieved doing analytic work. Termination challenges the patient's experience of the analyst's particular accommodations to the patient's resilient core, particularly when that resiliency has become organized around elements of unconsciously suspicious and controlling demands based on the other. In other words, termination can sometimes expose particular forms of interpersonal compromise involving impasse or avoidance on the part of the dyad.

ANDREW

I suppose it can be said about all of us that our adaptations are what allow us to be who we are and partly prevent us from becoming other than who we have been. Put another way, regarding both adaptation and defense, for better and worse, practice makes perfect. So, too, at an interpersonal level, in most if not all analyses, patients and analysts acclimate to each other's defensive styles even as we, as analysts, engage in probing and challenging our patient's inner lives, unconscious attachments, and identifications. We are able to engage our patients in analytic work to the extent that we have not aroused too much fear and too much repetition with old, traumatogenic objects. Yet, termination shifts the balance of old and new experience in ways that vary for different patients and different dyads.

Andrew's work with me during our initial talks about termination made particular aspects of transference–countertransference entanglement with each other more conspicuous.

I had been seeing Andrew for 4 years in analysis. He was now 37, married, and the father of two young girls. When I first met Andrew he was 25 and in medical school. We had worked together for 2 years while he completed school, and then he moved away for residency. When he returned to Boston to accept a more permanent job as a physician, he decided that he wanted to continue our work. Andrew is very smart and very sarcastic. He feels in some ways like a younger brother to me, and he felt that I reminded him of his 10-year-older brother in certain ways. Have you ever read the novel *A Heartbreaking Work of Staggering Genius* (Eggars, 2000)? It's the story of an older brother taking care of a younger sibling as a kind of substitute parent. Irreverent, funny, and pseudo-mature all come to mind when I think about Andrew. These are part of his substantial psychological strengths. On the other side was a deep level of suspicion and guardedness that made our work together sometimes feel constrained and filled with tension that I would not "get" him.

During our initial 2 years together, Andrew was primarily working on his devastatingly destructive relationship with his mother. Andrew's parents divorced when he was 6 years old. His mother was a very intelligent, very contemptuous woman who almost reflexively criticized everyone around her, especially Andrew and his 5-year-older sister. Andrew also had a brother 10 years older. His older sister was leveled by his mother and despite her attempts to revolt during adolescence, suffered enormous problems in self-esteem. Andrew's mother tried to eat her young. His older brother was spared by the mother, idealized and sexualized in some ways. This brother developed a kind of whimsical, boyish self, keeping a distant and somewhat dissociated relationship to the vicious parts of his mother.

Andrew had been partially protected from his mother by his older siblings, particularly his funny and idealized brother. Andrew developed a fierce, feisty self that was organized around insulating himself from his mother's constant jabs and putdowns about his interests and loves. Andrew felt that in particular, his innocence, such as his love of animals (two cats and a dog) was ridiculed. Andrew's father, like his 10-year-older brother, was boyish, a kind of Peter Pan–type figure who seemed to enjoy being with his youngest son but was not deeply involved with how he was getting along with his mother or his school life. Andrew experienced him as a kind of even older brother than his considerably older brother. Andrew's father, a scientist, liked to take him to science museums and fishing destinations which were exciting for Andrew. Still, he wanted to see his father everyday during his preteen years rather than only on weekends, and the time in between was painful. He longed to see his father.

At the end of our 4 years of analytic work, Andrew's life was in very good shape by his account. His career was quite rewarding and parenting was far more rewarding than he had ever expected. His colleagues in the medical school at which he taught were difficult in all kinds of ways common within academic departments, but he seemed to be thriving. In fact, he felt comfortable with his own voice and authority with his colleagues and students. His wife was sometimes not appreciative enough in his view, but he had perspective on their relationship, and they shared what he felt was a good life together with their two girls whom they adored. Indeed, it would seem that the only problem that was really conspicuous in Andrew's life was me—his relationship with me. He wanted to complete the analysis but it frightened him, not so much consciously in terms of what life would be like without analysis, but more that the termination process itself would be frightening. Andrew was concerned that it "wouldn't go well" and that he "wouldn't do it right."

During the analysis, Andrew's associative style was strikingly variable. For periods of the work, he seemed to speak with relative ease about his feelings about his early life, his children, relationships with others, including his wife, friends, and colleagues. He was curious and could collaborate relatively easily with me as we made connections, analyzed his conflicts, and helped him with many feelings of longstanding criticism from his mother. He enjoyed his dreams and we both found them helpful in understanding the different parts of Andrew's inner world. It seemed to me that Andrew was quite accepting of my input when he discussed his relationships with people other than me. Andrew received me, as it were when we were looking at the world outside the office.

However, when Andrew tried to speak about his relationship with me, it felt as though I was working with a different patient and that he was working with a different analyst. Sometimes Andrew seemed to fear criticism as he measured his words and thoughts, seeming to palpably calculate the safety provided him. At other times he feared criticism in a less directly observable, more inchoate way, and his discussion of termination began a lengthy phase of analysis in which he was having difficulty getting his session started despite his considerable verbal and intellectual facility. He would not know what to talk about—he spoke in quite awkward and contorted ways—and he kept having the feeling that I would see him as avoidant, which became a point of focus and pain.

Andrew directed a variety of types of sarcasm toward me when he was struggling. One type was tinged with anger, often anticipating a criticism or misunderstanding from me. At times he would also be a bit insulting about my interpretations, reducing them to even more simplistic offerings than had been my intention. We had concluded that such attacks were often preemptive strikes. While not easy for me, over the course of his analysis, I had learned to try to interpret these forms of sarcasm as protective for him and as involving elements of identification with his mother. Andrew found this interpretation quite helpful in his dealings with his wife and colleagues with whom he had been preemptively sarcastic as well.

Another form of sarcasm was borne of his pseudo-maturity in which he feigned a position of false knowing that concealed points of anxiety. Within this mode he was playful, knowing that I knew about the cover-up, and there were erotic components as well that we analyzed together. In this mode, he could wrap his father and brother around his finger, appealing to them to be strong and take care of him, but often with the sense that he would have to do something to seduce them rather than just receive their attention.

After 4 years of analytic work, Andrew was enormously appreciative. At some level he had felt safe and "understood" by me, which he said was incredibly gratifying. Although Andrew still feared my criticism, that fear had lessoned, to some extent, morphing into a set of feelings that we looked at in both go-rounds as partly related to his relationship with his mother. I asked myself repeatedly whether I was feeling critical of Andrew when he feared me being so; I never could recognize this feeling in myself. However,

I did have a fear of being disappointing to Andrew, essentially a fear of being criticized by him. I had never been very pleased with my progress in making use of these feelings in helping us work this out together.

I asked myself whether Andrew's difficulty starting sessions as he broached termination had some quality of regression. After all, Andrew had consciously grown to trust me a great deal, and we had worked with some of the most regressive parts of his maternal transference earlier in the analysis. So in one sense this seemed like a return to some of these painful affects. But it had another quality as well—a kind of return to unfinished matters between us, to knotty points of unresolved transference–countertransference engagement.

What had seemed unfinished to us both was the sense that he could not more fully surrender himself to anyone, always retaining aspects of his pseudo-mature, self-sufficient core. Had I in some way unconsciously developed the idea that something about this core part of Andrew's personality would never be relinquished through analysis? Were Andrew and I going to let him go with an unspoken sense of never really taking this on further?

Then there was the matter of how I had not ever felt very "resolved" about my own sense of inadequacy in regard to Andrew. Was my own insecurity in relation to him something that I had been unconsciously nihilistic about changing within myself? I thought of my heightened sense of self-consciousness about speaking and interpreting for fear that it would not be smart enough or new enough as an offering, partly as a response to Andrew's hypertrophied self-sufficiency. I had felt this early on in our work, but for long parts of analysis this had subsided as Andrew and I worked together in what seemed like productive ways. Andrew had scrutinized my words, often in playful ways, but nevertheless with some degree of edginess and hostility. We talked over the years about his various forms of identification with his mother at these times with me and with others—that he had a way of making the other feel scrutinized and evaluated. It sometimes inhibited me, and I tried to understand it internally as a reflection of some of the ways in which Andrew had felt inhibited with his mother and with me. This is not a common countertransference experience for me, but the origins for it within my own development were quite available to me throughout my work with Andrew. This awareness was of some help but was hardly a solution to the problem of my engagement with him. Interestingly, as Andrew began to talk about termination these feelings in me seemed to be heightened again.

So as Andrew began to discuss termination, he raised questions about whether he could feel more comfortable and safe with me. And I, too, understood that I wanted to feel more safe with Andrew. But Andrew's happiness in his outside life was leading him to want to complete our work. Andrew also wanted to feel more of a sense of resolution with me. At the particular point in our analytic work Andrew had determined that he was afraid of "abandonment more than criticism" which was for both of us a new real-ization. He did not really know what he meant by the word *abandonment*. Would I leave him, give up on him, pull the rug out from under him? With no particular external reason remaining to continue our work together, we both found this curious. Andrew said that he worried that working with me more might make him feel more strongly my absences than he had, saying that "you'll make me feel sort of abandoned—what if I get more connected to you than I am now and it gets cut off? I think that I'm afraid that if you get to know me more that you will feel it's bad to know me."

He asked me if he should stay. I said, "I think you're asking me if it will be good or bad for you and me to know you even more." He said, "I know that. Don't talk to me like that. You have to tell me what you think." I told him that it would be fine to go if that was what he wanted, though we had come so far that maybe we should try to figure this out better. This was the answer he was looking for. We both agreed that he wanted to stay but did not know if I wanted him to. This was a part of the fear of aban-donment that neither of us understood very well, particularly because we had worked together so long and I knew him in many ways. He said that he really did not understand what his goal was in staying except that he wanted to "end feeling good about what we'd done together." Neither of us knew what that meant.

It seemed relatively clear to both of us that this particular question about what I thought he should do involved an enactment in which he was asking me if I wanted him to stay. It seems in retrospect that it was a part of what he needed to feel from me in order to commit to completing his work with me.

So I offer a piece of process from one session and a summary of a lon-ger period of time to elaborate some of the various registers from which Andrew feared his own leaving me and, from his point of view, my leav-ing him. This particular session followed some sessions in which it was very difficult for Andrew to speak and to know what he wanted to talk about. He would playfully refer to his wishes to avoid something but it was unclear what he was avoiding.

A: Maybe I shouldn't continue. Maybe time to stop. I feel it that way. I would be willing to not see it that way. I feel drawn or pushed off ter-rain I'm on, trapped or pushed on to something I know I'm not com-fortable in.

I feel from you skepticism that the ways I have into feeling right now are a distraction from something else. It also sets you up. I know that you do think some of those things but maybe you're not thinking them when sometimes I think that you are. Then I act as you are making assessments about what's a distraction and what I'm not talking about which is fine. I mean in some ways I guess I'm seeking to know that you think that if you do. [*He's referring to the repeated difficulty he has been having in getting started in sessions.*] Then I get anxious and turn to you and want to know what you think and then I feel like it's going to be a disagreement.

s: Why's it going to be a disagreement?

A: I don't want to cast this as something you do. At these moments it feels like on the one hand I'm reacting to having a hard time talking, not knowing what to say and that you have an idea about what's going on. And that, something about how things play out when I have that particular anxiety, when you ask me about it I feel like we're not going to get anywhere.

  I think that maybe I feel afraid that you won't recognize or look at certain things with me because you think there's someplace else I should be looking. That maybe you think I'm avoiding something or speaking about the wrong area or thing. Then I can't get any help from you with looking inside, at where I am. In my mind, you telling me over and over again some account of, that stuff I am in is an avoidance of something else. Like it's not, frankly, of interest to you.

s: So the "me" in your thoughts at this point is imagining that I think you're not talking about something that I think that you should be talking about and that I won't accept or be curious about where you are now?

A: Then thinking all that entails a kind of moving off of that fraught, immediate present. [*He's referring to this inchoate moment when he cannot speak or does not know what he is feeling.*] Then I feel like I'm into another thing with you, now that there's a certain kind of avoidance of feeling with me and I don't know what to do.

  I feel like if I stop, feeling okay about myself, more than okay about myself that's the good outcome. Not the good outcome I was looking for. I'm really willing to listen, not try to close that down.

s: I think that sometimes when you begin the session with a sense of uncertainty about where you want to go, you become anxious and sarcastic about it. Then maybe I do something to make you feel that you actually are avoiding something, instead of figuring out what you actually are struggling to say.

A: Yes, and I don't know what I'm saying.

s: And so your sarcasm or anxiety about talking is made into something concrete by me in a way that isn't accurate and isn't accounting for what you're actually saying; and that maybe you and I don't know what you're saying and you feel I'm having a hard time helping you with that or being with you in that place of uncertainty about what you mean?

A: That's it, that I don't know what I'm saying and I want you to either know what I'm saying or not know and be with me there. In my mind, when I'm thinking about you listening to me so unable to start you're thinking these things about me avoiding things.

s: Yes. You know that the way this sometimes seems to me is that I'm being led into a particular kind of interaction, particularly when you're being sarcastic about what seems like your "avoidance" and then I believe you and then I disappoint you and you want to hold me accountable for it. You're saying that I'm not helping you to understand the sarcasm because I take it literally, not seeing that you don't know what you're feeling or wanting to say instead of "knowing" something about what you feel or want to say.

A: Yes. I'm saying that when I say things like "Do you know what I mean?" [*He reflexively says, "do you know what I mean," quite often, and it is extremely incongruous with how articulate he usually is.*] that maybe I'm not just asking you the many things that encompass what we've talked about (that you know, listening and caring about me).

s: You mean that when you say, "do you know what I mean?" you might be expressing a wish that *I* would ask the question about what you mean when maybe you aren't sure what you mean; so that you could sense more that I want to know what you mean.

A: Yes, that I wouldn't feel as I often do as though you think that I know what I mean when I ask you if you know what I mean and I want you to be with me in dislodging that and that instead I feel drawn into…well, sometimes you'll say, "why do you think I think that?" And I always feel when you ask me that, I sometimes want to say, "I don't know, I'm just saying something," and I feel drawn off of it as though you have a tendency—and it's not as though I don't know how it could happen—to think that I know what I mean or that I know what I'm saying. It's not where I am. [*Long pause.*]

And you sometimes think that I feel you're bumbling. My worry is not that you'll be bumbling but that you know how to do this with me and I don't know how to do it. That I'm failing. [*Very sad.*]

s: I do think that that's the familiar place you go to. You're telling me in very specific ways about a way that you wish I could listen to you or be with you and that I fail you sometimes in these ways but then you fall back to this—that it's a failing in you.

A: I could see that.

s: I think that you feel that I am missing you sometimes when you think that I think I know what you should be talking about. Sometimes I probably do think that you're avoiding something else and you read that from me. Sometimes I'm aware of *not* thinking that when you think that I am. I feel like your vulnerability about not knowing is scary and it shows up in not knowing what or how to speak—that you're showing it at these times and some of the time I'm not seeing it. And you get scared that I won't let myself be with you or don't know how to be with you when you don't know how to speak or how to begin. And that I won't let you know me not knowing.

A: Or maybe it worries me that you can't be with yourself not knowing so how can you be with me not knowing. Maybe that's what you said too.

S: I also think that when you feel so uncertain about these matters that maybe you also have feelings about wanting me to know what's on your mind without you telling me, especially if it feels so difficult to speak.

A. That makes sense to me.

Before exploring the bulk of this hour, it is perhaps most important to note what happened at the end of the session. Poignantly, Andrew has been able to explore a great deal about what he needs from me and his fears both about needing those things and about whether I will be able to participate with him in the way that he wants me to. By making the last statement that I made, in essence bringing up an additional level of wish and fear, I am once again focusing on something that he is avoiding. I was quite moved by his ability to tell me what he did in this hour, and it was striking to me that I did not convey more of this to him. By focusing on a whole other level of his wishes, I enact the very thing that he is complaining to me about—namely, that I keep thinking that there is something that he should be saying or exploring that he is not. This was an unconscious repetition of this pattern on my part and extremely interesting to me because I was so utterly moved by what Andrew was saying and in agreement with him—at least consciously.

As Andrew and I talked about these feelings, perceptions, fears, and wishes for many months, they played out in different versions of Andrew trying to find a way for me to be with him in his uncertainty. He wished for me to accompany him without feeling blamed and without feeling that I was isolating him in some position of power and authority about what he knew but was unwilling to discuss, and the like. We talked a great deal about how difficult this was for him and I tried to tell him as much as I could about my own experiences with him when he wanted to know about them.

It was difficult for Andrew as he got more into his feelings of my attributing intentionality to him (avoidance of something that he thought I thought he should be talking about) when he did not have words for feelings. He became more aware of feelings of helplessness about instances when he felt misunderstood by me. Eventually he was also able to experience his sadness both with me and, notably, his mother about his feeling that she was prone to attribute the worst kinds of intention to him.

Though this material was difficult and we were in a sort of crisis of self-sufficiency versus vulnerability, we were already starting to make some progress. Even though it is not conspicuous in the earlier vignette, Andrew still often seemed to be baiting me with a version of "I know more than you do about what I'm thinking and I don't want to talk about it." I was taken in by this for long periods of time, initially because it was fun and playful. He was being mischievous, and his baiting had a kind of eroticized quality to it as well. Even though a formulation of Andrew as having a kind of hypertrophied sense of self-sufficiency was well within my scope of vision, I could not really see the degree to which I was enacting this with him.

Andrew was in certain ways pretending to know. He was partly ashamed to not know what he needed. In a sense he was calling his own bluff by initiating the discussion of termination. This allowed him to communicate to me that I was not helping him work through ossified conflicts and identifications that he wanted to shed. I think that Andrew had, in a sense, used aspects of an older brother relationship/transference in which he could continue growing up as an adult, while basking in my regard. Yet Andrew did not really want to lose out on the opportunity to feel safe in a deeper way, perhaps not exclusively as a pseudo-mature little brother but instead allowing himself to be an innocent, playful little boy. In some way, the warmth of his brother's regard also overlapped with a certain kind of false, pseudo-maturity that comes with being a 7- or 8-year-old very bright, precocious little boy with his late-teenage brother and his friends.

Andrew was elaborating how he felt that I was mistuned to his anxiety about speaking (the presentation of a self-state of not knowing or not being able to speak), instead of being focused more on his critical, verbally deft, sarcastic, playful self. Andrew felt as though I did not know how to help him with the experience of not knowing what he wanted to talk about and that I focused on some defensive state of avoidance. I believe that he was trying to create a space that had not been allowed growing up—one in which Andrew did not necessarily know what he meant or how to express himself, or one in which he would speak to his dog as though the dog understood all of his words. When I thought about this particular hour later, I began considering about the degree to which I felt a sense of complementary countertransference, a sense of feeling that Andrew would often be disappointed or critical of me. Somehow we established an atmosphere infected by his mother in which no one could be right or be able to get it right. In this clinical moment that we are together, he can speak to me about this vulnerable self, but it is still "about" the self-state.

A few questions emerged for me about how we would proceed from here. During his moments of uncertainty about what to talk about, should I try more exclusively to help him identify his experience at those times? Would my attempts to focus more on his experience at these moments be felt as my own attempts to not let him know of my experience of being with him? To what extent have my interpretations of his identification with his mother moved him away from a more direct experience of whether these defensive postures are just protecting himself from me? What are the implications of trying to speak to Andrew more directly about how I experience him in the states when he "doesn't know" (perhaps states of more vulnerability) or his positions of sarcasm and self-protection? Will the experience of hearing more from me about what I am thinking and feeling have the potential for a new object experience or be experienced as an imposition of myself on him?

During this phase of analytic work, I felt as though we were getting into levels of suspicion and terror in Andrew that we had never explored together, paradoxically as we began trying to complete our work. We both began to realize that our decision to continue was born of a sense that we had done some very good work together, but that we had never been able to get as deeply into how unsafe it was for him to be a little boy with his mother, to in some way, yield his pseudo-mature (false) self. I tried to stay very close to Andrew's affects during this period of our work together. I tried (and with the help of a friend with whom I consulted) to question my own sense of defensiveness about his sarcasm to help him at these moments to see more about what was happening for him. When I felt baited into a sense that I knew something that he did not about what he should be talking about, I tried to see what he was feeling and noticing in himself and in me that would lead him to those conclusions. Since we so often analyzed this, if you will, "old object" transference, it seemed to me as important to try to talk to him more directly about how at some of these times I did not feel or recognize much about this business of knowing what he should talk about. I became responsive to his questions about my experiences of being with him when he was in a state of not knowing what to talk about. We felt awkward together, and he spoke for a long period of time about not believing that I was not critical of him. It seemed very productive, though there were no great revelations about what he was not talking about. What seemed crucial was Andrew's latitude to not know and to even be anxious about not knowing.

Regarding Andrew's sarcasm, I stopped thinking about and interpreting the ways that he might be making me feel as he had felt. I began simply asking him to tell me more about what was going on at these moments. I also was thinking about a prominent characteristic of my own father's intense intellectualism and my occasional sense of feeling scrutinized about my own intellect in comparison to his. It was difficult to feel my not knowing with Andrew without feeling criticized by him in a way that was quite similar to some of the ways that he had felt vulnerable with his mother. It was helpful to think about this.

The more that Andrew felt me being able to tolerate his uncertainty about what to talk about and even whether to continue his termination process, the more he began to focus on a sense of "fearing being lost" and what the future felt like in relation to me. Andrew was brought to many feelings about not "wanting to feel lost from me" and a "sense of not knowing if someone will find me." Leaving seemed to threaten everything for Andrew. Termination did not seem to involve his own leaving but, instead, being left.

He also began expressing many feelings about not trusting whether I could trust that he could do this analytic work. In this very productive moment, he also repeatedly wanted me to know that these questions "came from a place of optimism, not pessimism," what I would call, in keeping with Winnicott, a moment of hope.

In one session in which Andrew was expressing a fear of being lost from me when we said good-bye, he said that he was afraid of "feeling lost and not knowing if someone will find me. That old sense that somebody let me get lost. I don't want that to be my relationship to you." He was crying throughout this session. Andrew began to think about the Chet Baker film, *Let's Get Lost* (1988). He said that he wanted us to "get lost" together. I told Andrew that I thought that he wanted to allow himself to get lost *with* me, to not worry about whether I would find him, and for me to appreciate these wishes to be vulnerable. Andrew said, "I guess that's what the title means, that line between 'let's get lost but not too lost.' I guess I'd like us to be lost and that it would be fun for you and for me and I wouldn't feel like a failure." I spoke to him about how different I imagined it must feel to be lost alone instead of the possibility of feeling lost with me.

Of course, the idea of getting lost together is in many ways the essence of erotic experience. The erotic dimensions of Andrew's transferential experience had been far easier to explore throughout Andrew's analysis than the landscape he was more fully exploring here. The safer and closer Andrew felt to me, the more he began talking about how being lost together made him feel togetherness with me. I began to understand that, for Andrew, his sibling relationship and the sibling transference were both a source of nurturance and a form of interpersonal compromise formation that he was reluctant to abandon before he could more fully work out what remained for him without these compromises. To leave me, his older brother, and the good parts of his father made him feel abandoned. He would feel lost if we just said that "You're good now. Good to go. It's time for us to leave or you to leave." He wanted me to understand that he wanted to leave when he was ready to leave.

We were enacting elements of both his mother, who could not let him love his puppies innocently or be a curious little boy, and his brother, with whom he felt loved but had to pretend to know things that he did not know. It took me a long time to gain more purchase on my participation in enacting varying elements of a critical other or mother, my own identification with a child who felt criticized, a child who wanted to be an innocent (with his parents and older sibling), and a more mature child (with a brother who adored him but who expected him to be more grown up than he was).

Andrew and I grew a great deal together through this moving and difficult process.

For Andrew, as for many patients, termination and the future ideally represent a place to live as a self within a new, less traumatic context. But the psychic future, the end of analysis, became a threatening place for Andrew partly because it implied a loss of control. Termination challenged previously unassailable resilience as some important parts of his identifications and problematic relational patterns were still being repeated within the analytic dyad. In such circumstances, the end of analysis can be experienced as a temporal space outside the patient's control. The patient has no place to go with the adaptations that he or she has utilized and which have featured in analysis, leaving the patient without the good parts of the analyst and the analytic work and also without the opportunity to repeat enacted relational patterns (Cooper, 2008).

Termination for Andrew was equated with the feeling he recalled from early adolescence of having, through his own growth, given his father and brother license to dismiss him, to say, in effect, "You're good, you're on your own." This was why as he began his termination process he said, relating leaving me to feeling left by his father and brother, "I feel flummoxed by the future."

Naturally, termination is often discussed in terms that are more concretely related to the actual impeding loss of the analyst, and traditionally regression has been conceptualized as occurring in response to that loss. I have tried to suggest that termination also mobilizes an anticipation of the loss of the forms of enactment that have allowed the patient to grow during analysis, but that are not necessarily understood or resolved within the dyad. These enactments partially involve unconscious fantasies about the analyst and thus termination can pose a threat to the loss of these fantasies as well.

This loss of enacted patterns between patient and analyst is only part of what might be termed a loss of the dyad. It is of course difficult to differentiate clearly between the patient's deeply personal experiences of losing the analyst versus a sense of losing the dyad, but I think it is worth trying to consider both. In addition to enacted patterns that compose the patient's sense of the dyad are the many experiences of empathic resonance, intimacy, and limitation. There is a sense of losing the person of the analyst and, in terms of the loss of the dyad, "the way we were together."

Termination mobilizes the actual experienced discrepancy between habitually enacted relational patterns (interpersonal compromise formations if you will) and the needed, wished for, and unresolved parts of therapeutic work as the patient begins to feel the loss of analysis and the analyst. When termination comes up as a subject in these circumstances, it is often an acknowledgement of these forms of impasse and marks a moment in which analysis will either end in these less-than-optimal circumstances or become a kind of new beginning for the analytic pair.

Because to some extent these enactments are the stuff of all therapeutic work, termination provides another opportunity to revisit these enactments and to grieve the limitations of any analytic process.

REFERENCES

Bass, A. (2001). It takes one to know one, or whose unconscious is it anyway? *Psychoanalytic Dialogues, 11*, 683–703.

Bergmann, M. (1997). Termination: The Achilles heel of psychoanalytic technique. *Psychoanalytic Psychology, 14*, 163–174.

Bollas, C. (1989). *Forces of destiny*. London: Free Associations.

Cooper, S. (1997). The future of interpretation. *International Journal of Psychoanalysis, 78*, 667–681.

Cooper, S. (2008). Privacy, reverie, and the analyst's ethical imagination. *Psychoanalytic Quarterly, 77*, 1045–1073.

Davies, J. M. (2005). Transformations of desire and despair: Reflections on the termination process from a relational perspective. *Psychoanalytic Dialogues, 15,* 779–805.

Eggars, D. (2000). *A heartbreaking work of staggering genius*. New York: Simon & Schuster.

Ferenczi, S. (1927). The problem of termination of the analysis. In M. Balint (Ed.) & E. Mosbacher (Trans.), *Final contributions to the problems and methods of psycho-analysis* (pp. 77–86). London: Hogarth, 1955.

Freud, S. (1937). Analysis terminable and interminable. *International Journal of Psycho-Analysis, 18*, 373–405.

Hoffman, I. (1998). *Ritual and spontaneity in psychoanalysis: A dialectical-constructivist view*. Hillsdale, NJ: Analytic Press.

Klauber, J. (1977). Analyses that cannot be terminated. *International Journal of Psycho-Analysis, 58*, 473–477.

Levenson, E. (1976). The aesthetics of termination. *Contemporary Psychoanalysis, 12*, 338–341.

Loewald, H. (1960). The therapeutic action of psychoanalysis. *International Journal of Psycho-Analysis, 41*, 16–33.

Marshall, K. (2000). Termination of an "Infinite Conversation": Reflections on the last days of an analysis. *Psychoanalytic Dialogues, 10*, 931–947.

Merleau-Ponty, M. (1964). *The primacy of perception*. Evanston, IL: Northwestern University Press.

Tronick, E. (2003). Of course all relationships are unique: How cocreative processes generate unique mother–infant and patient–therapist relationships and change other relationships. *Psychoanalytic Inquiry*, *23*(3), 473–491.

Winnicott, D. W. (1958). The capacity to be alone. In *The maturational processes and the facilitating environment*. New York: International Universities Press.

Chapter 10

Will you remember me?

Termination and continuity

Sandra Silverman

As life would have it, while in the midst of writing this paper about termination, my 87-year-old father was told that he needed open-heart surgery. The doctors made it clear: If he did not have surgery, death would be imminent. The questions that I am asking in this paper have become the questions that I am living in my day-to-day interactions as my father prepares for surgery. What does it mean to live while knowing we will die? How do we go on in the face of loss of all kinds, loss of those we have loved, loss of those we have been closest to, loss of our health, loss of our former selves, loss of our analysts, loss of our patients, and perhaps most of all, how do we give up the illusion that we can control our lives?

I watch, as my father, a man whose own father died at the age of 58, struggles with the knowledge that he will not live forever. When I was a child, he used to recite Dylan Thomas from time to time. Depending on my mood or my age, I remember thinking he was warding off the darkness of death or he was being dramatic to hold everyone's attention. "Do not go gentle into that good night. Rage, rage against the dying of the light," he would repeat with ferocity in his voice. After he passed the age his father was when he died, my father decided he would live forever. "I know that no one has done it but why can't I be the first?" he would quip with a glint in his eye. And so, the news of surgery and death came to him as quite a shock, even at the age of 87.

How do we live while knowing we will die? And similarly, how do we immerse ourselves in an analytic treatment, whether as analyst or patient, while knowing that it will end, that we are engaging in a deep and intimate relationship and that relationship as we know it will come to a close? These questions are particularly challenging because we find it difficult to sustain a felt awareness of the impermanence of each moment and of life itself (Frommer, 2005). We think about the end of life intellectually, just as we think about the end of treatment intellectually, but accessing our emotional feelings about the finiteness of life, and of the life of an analysis, is remarkably difficult. In this chapter I explore my work with two patients and my relationship with a close friend who was diagnosed with advanced breast cancer. I consider how loss, survival, and what Winnicott (1956) termed "going-on-being" impact the termination of treatment.

Inside the work of analysis a sense of timelessness is essential, but so too is an awareness that the analytic relationship as it has been known comes to an end. Part of what makes an analysis feel more alive is, paradoxically, the knowledge that it will end. Hoffman (1998) likens the avoidance of termination to the denial of time and mortality. But just as it is impossible to fully prepare for death, one's own or someone else's, it is also impossible to fully prepare for termination. The idea that there is a right way to approach termination and a predictable unfolding of the last phase of analytic work crashes into the heart of a relational psychoanalysis that values the intimacy, spontaneity, and uniqueness of each analytic relationship. Both analyst and patient experience a loss when the treatment ends and the acknowledgement of that mutual loss, though felt differently for each member of the dyad, is crucial to ending. The capacity to stay in the experience of termination, to remain connected to one another and to the work in spite of knowing it will end brings the knowledge that we cannot stop time and that we cannot control the future. In my own attempts to think about the complexity of ending analytic treatment, I have turned to the work of Winnicott (1956, 1960, 1965, 1969) because he embraced paradox, could hold contradiction, and did not seek or expect neat, clean resolution. In his concept of going on being, Winnicott invites us to consider the ability not to know and the tolerance of uncertainty as essential to feeling alive (Phillips, 1988).

"Going-on-being" is integral to accepting the uncertainty that is life. It develops early, with the presence of a reliable caretaker and a safe environment for the child "to be able to exist for a time without being either a reactor to an external impingement or an active person with a direction of interest or movement" (Winnicott, 1958, p. 34). A sense of going-on-being is what makes it possible to experience the moment in its fullness and its impermanence as well as to weather the storms inherent in living rather than to live a life of tracking storms in anticipation of their arrival. Phillips (1996) describes the paradox that so much of Winnicott's work is about, "we only need to know, be mindful of, that which we cannot trust depending on" (p. 100). Hence, it is the caretaker's, and later the analyst's, consistency and reliability that make it possible to develop a sense of going-on-being. Without the patient's capacity for going-on-being as well as the patient's sense that the analyst has a capacity for going-on-being, it is difficult if not impossible for a patient to grieve the loss of analysis while experiencing the richness of living beyond it.

The "reliable" caretaker that Winnicott describes as integral to the development of going-on-being becomes reliable in part through the experience of mutual recognition. Building on the ideas of Winnicott, Benjamin (1988) describes mutual recognition as entailing the fundamental paradox that "at the very moment of realizing our own independence, we are dependent upon another to recognize it" (p. 33). Benjamin emphasizes that the other's recognition will only have meaning for us if we have placed the other outside of our omnipotent control, as a separate individual with her own center of subjectivity. According to Winnicott (1969), it is the process of destruction and survival that makes this possible. For Winnicott, destruction is a negation of the other, an insistence that the other does not exist and does not have value, and it is an insistence that the other can be placed under the self's control, only for the self to then discover that the other has survived, is separate, and is beyond omnipotent control. The discovery of the other's survival is the moment when what Benjamin describes as the paradox of recognition comes to life. It is in this moment of mutual recognition that it becomes possible for the self to feel recognized, to feel real and to feel alive. As Benjamin (1988) describes it, "if I fully negate the other he does not exist and if he does not survive he is not there to recognize me" (p. 38). Benjamin applies her work on mutual recognition to maternal subjectivity when she describes the mother as more than an extension of the child's fantasies or a vehicle for the child's growth but also as a separate outside other who the child comes to recognize as existing in her own right. It is the mother's separate and independent self that makes her recognition of the child meaningful. Benjamin (2000) carries this concept into the treatment relationship, emphasizing the subjectivity of the analyst and valuing the tension between both "the need to submerge ourselves in the patient's experience and the importance of providing an experience of otherness" (p. 293).

Our work as analysts is to help our patients not only to live their lives but also to feel alive within them. In Winnicott's view, those individuals who have succeeded in coping with depressed or otherwise fragile mothers* have done no more than that. They have coped. They have existed in a state of reactivity rather than having ever had the experience of being alone in the presence of another (Winnicott, 1958), and what they are awaiting is the right environment to begin to live, to restart their development (Phillips, 1988). In the language of relational analysis, one might say that within those individuals who have had to live in reaction to their "mother's" mood there are selves whose development has been foreclosed, and those selves are waiting in the wings for the opportunity to move out of their dissociated places and into awareness within a relationship where they can continue to grow (Bromberg, 1998, Davies, 2004a). In an analytic relationship, the capacity for going-on-being develops similarly to Davies' (2004b) description of an emergent self, "one who begins to identify with the analyst and with a self

---

* For the purposes of this chapter, I would like to consider Winnicott's "depressed mothers" to include other caretakers as well as social forces that may impinge upon the child's environment and sense of security.

in relation to the analyst and others in her life who have offered something more empathic, more resilient and more alive" (p. 757). Often it is the analyst's recognition of something inside the patient, of a self who is waiting to grow, and it is the patient's recognition of his or her emergent self first held in the analyst's mind (Davies, 2004b) that provides an opportunity for this growth. When there is mutual recognition between analyst and patient, recognition that is inevitably built on the dialectic of destruction and survival (Benjamin, 1988), then the consistency and reliability of the analytic relationship creates a much firmer ground on which going-on-being may be built and on which emergent selves may be discovered.

For patients who experienced profound or traumatic loss and who entered treatment unable to feel their survival of that loss without feeling shame, termination presents particular challenges. These are patients who fear, consciously or unconsciously, that their survival was won only because another's was lost. The difficult decision to end one's treatment and to live beyond the "suspension" (Mitchell, 1993) that analysis provides is an expression of a willingness to take responsibility for one's own life with the intent to live it fully. The shame that once blocked the doorway to feeling and instead opened the door to dissociation may resurface during termination, and it is crucial that both analyst and patient recognize it as a vital part of the termination process. Davies' (2005) work on termination speaks to the importance of many good-byes "between the self-states of patient and analyst, good-byes that emanate from a multitude of developmental epochs and from different centers of developmental trauma, conflict, and meaning making" (p. 783). The emergent self that has developed a sense of going-on-being and the self that has felt shame for surviving and for wanting to live life must both be heard from and interacted with during termination. It is important not only for a patient to have his or her own sense of going-on-being at the end of treatment but for the patient to sense his or her analyst's capacity for going-on-being as well.

The two patients that I discuss in this chapter struggled profoundly with the feeling of survival and with the need to find a reason or a cause for their survival. In our work, they sometimes felt it impossible to find a sense of continuity, of going-on-being. To fully experience the moment meant to them that they would leave themselves open for a crashing storm, an impingement of unmanageable proportion. In different ways, each sought answers for their survival, and the need for those answers interfered with their ability to mourn and to truly live their lives. It was within the analytic relationship that emergent selves carrying a sense of going-on-being came to life. And it was in the move toward termination that their struggles with survival surfaced in unpredictable ways.

In our work as analysts, we carry not only our own histories and experiences but also those of our patients. We sometimes have thoughts of one patient, when working with another, feelings of hope stirred up in one treatment can sometimes feed us in working in another treatment. The wall between our personal lives and our work lives is permeable in our associations, reactions, and musings. In managing various treatment relationships as well as our personal lives, we struggle with our own sense of continuity, with maintaining hope, and with allowing ourselves the care we need to continue to be fully present (Harris & Sinsheimer, 2007). As analysts, we are, in some ways, the thread that binds a quilt, sewing through the various pieces of fabric, each from different times and places and relationships in our lives, both personal and professional.

What follows are three different patches in the quilt, three different relationships, two with patients and one with a close friend. As the edges of each story overlap, they tell of termination, of the ways that living, dying, and surviving are felt in our lives personally, professionally, and internally. I begin with my work with a patient, move to a personal relationship, and then to my work with yet another patient before closing with some reflections on survival, termination, and going-on-being.

THE WIG

Leah came to therapy because she was confused. In the preceding month, at moments that were random and unpredictable, tears began to pour from her eyes for no apparent reason. A likable, engaging, and energetic woman with a hearty laugh, Leah was mystified and unnerved by these storms. She did not like to feel out of control. In our work together we came to recognize the downpour of tears as the emergence of a dissociated part of her self that hungered for closeness and intimacy but dared not take the risk of searching for it. In spite of her many friendships and social activities, Leah had never been in a relationship. She had a few brief affairs with women in college, but in the 6 years since then she had not been involved with anyone. Leah desperately wanted a relationship and, down the road, a child or two. She was a loyal friend and had watched her peers couple but felt persistently like the "have-not," the one who would forever remain unattached.

Leah's need for control became clearer when, in the second year of our work, I became pregnant. Upon my return from a 2-month maternity leave, Leah told me she had to know my "reproductive plans" in order to stay in treatment. She was enraged that I would not provide this information, and she did not understand how I expected her to remain involved in our work when she had to face the uncertainty of the future. She expressed envy and despair that I had a child and a partner, as it was difficult for her to imagine that she would ever have a family of her own. She felt oceans away from the possibility of a real relationship. I suggested to her that she needed to discover what it felt like to be connected to me, to have this relationship before she would be able to have one in the "real" world. She welcomed this idea and seemed relieved by it because it indicated my investment in her. We began a closer look at her need to feel in charge of her life without anyone else impinging on it. As the impinger, I took responsibility for causing disruption in her life and in our work, and I eventually told her that even I did not have the answer to whether or not I would decide to have another child or whether anything else might interfere in the structure of our work together. We began to work more intensely on the nuances of our relationship, what it meant to be close, what it meant to Leah to depend on me, what it meant to be impacted by each other. A year later she began a serious relationship and, for the first time, fell in love.

It was in the fourth year of our work, when Leah was 32 years old, that she had what might be called the ultimate in unexpected, uncontrolled impingements on her life. Leah had experienced pain that prompted her doctor to recommend an abdominal ultrasound. When she went for the sonogram the pain had passed but the procedure showed something small and opaque on the side that she did not experience pain. Surgery was scheduled on the "off chance" of a malignancy. Although Leah realized that there was a risk of ovarian cancer, she had read that it was generally women in their fifties, not their thirties, who developed this type of cancer, and she felt confident that she would be fine. I experienced a strange juxtaposition of emotions at this time in our work. Leah arrived for a session a few weeks prior to her surgery and my concern about her upcoming surgery silently lodged itself in the space between us. "Why do you look so serious?" she asked. I was unsure how to respond. Do I push the point that she may have cancer or do I coast along with her thick and self-protective denial? Clearly, the possibility that she had cancer was so unbearable that she had placed it on a shelf beyond her reach. Who was I to take it down and drop it in front of her? On the other hand, it felt strange to join her in acting as if the surgery was akin to a routine doctor's appointment. I tried to find a middle ground, and asked her what she imagined some of the outcomes of surgery might be. Cancer was not one of them.

I told Leah that I had been doing a bit of my own reading and thought she might want to do the same so that she could ask her doctor any questions she might have about the surgery and the possible outcomes. She began to tear up and said she was amazed that I had taken the time to do this. She returned to the next session with more information and a list of questions for her doctor. She was reassured that ovarian cancer was rare in women her age. "If I do need chemo and my hair falls out then I'd like it to grow back in auburn curls," she said with a mischievous smile. The possibility of cancer was still far from reality but it was now in her range of vision.

Leah called me from the hospital, groggy and stunned after her surgery. "It seems things didn't go quite as planned," she said in a quivering voice. Her life changed rapidly. What was once unthinkable was now good news. The cancer was found early. Her prognosis was good. She would only need a few chemotherapy treatments. Our sessions were now focused on helping her to deal with the surreal experience of having cancer, of finding an oncologist, of informing her friends, family, and work colleagues and then dealing with their responses. She was grateful that her partner, whom she had been with for only 6 months, was so deeply involved and supportive.

It was about 10 days after her first chemotherapy treatment when I went to greet Leah in the waiting room and found her uncharacteristically wearing a scarf tied behind her head like a wide headband. Since our session the day before, Leah had begun losing her hair in clumps. She came into my office and sat across from me silently. Her body was still, but somehow it seemed like she was trembling. She told me that in the hour since leaving her office she had gone to two wig stores but no one could help her. "They were all fashion wigs," she said. "I need a cancer wig." Her voice began to fill with panic, "What am I going to do? Look at this! I am totally unprepared!" She was quiet for a moment and then, with a look of determination, she said, "I have to figure something out right now."

We spoke about how frightened she was, how overwhelmed. She was in unknown territory. There was now no denying that she had cancer. The loss of her hair felt like more evidence of her diagnosis than any other. We also spoke concretely, about what were the next steps that she could take, about bringing her partner with her so that she would not have to face the prospect of buying a wig alone, about calling one of the women's cancer organizations to get recommendations for where she might purchase a wig rather than looking up wig shops in the phone book as she had done today. She acknowledged her fear, her need to seem like she did not need any help.

It was in the last few minutes of the session that I said to Leah, "I've been having a thought. I have a friend who was recently diagnosed with breast cancer and she is also having chemotherapy. She just got a wig and I know she had a good experience buying it. I'd be glad to call her and get the name of the store if you'd like."

Leah brightened. "Would you? I mean, I'm sorry you have a friend with cancer, but would you ask her?" I told Leah I would call and let her know as soon as I reached my friend.

I was aware of feeling relieved that I had something concrete to offer to my patient. But what did that mean? Was I avoiding Leah's anger and despair? Was I unable to bear my own helplessness? And what about my having blurred a boundary in making this offer? While I realized the risks involved, I felt that calling my friend on Leah's behalf was the right thing to do. I could not imagine having this information and not offering it to my patient.

Later that evening I called my friend Kim who was eager to help. She gave me the information about the wig store and the name of the person who helped her. Kim was newly diagnosed with breast cancer and had just had her first chemotherapy treatment. I had not anticipated how pleased she would be to be able to help someone else in the same situation. I called Leah and gave her the information. She thanked me and asked that I thank my friend.

The two women were now linked through me. Periodically, Kim asked how Leah was faring. And from time to time, Leah would ask about Kim, usually in an indirect way. "I hope your friend is doing okay," she might say. She seemed careful not to put me on the spot and never asked in such a way that she needed an answer. She indicated curiosity and what I felt was genuine hope that my friend was okay. We spoke about her concern that I was able to handle having a friend in my personal life with cancer as well as a patient. She did not want to overwhelm me. I was moved by her expression of gratitude for my help and by her willingness to depend on me, something that I knew was difficult for her. And I was impressed by how she had shifted in her approach to having cancer and undergoing chemotherapy. Leah came up with a nickname for her wig, calling it June, and referring to it as "she," making the experience of taking care of and wearing what represented so much loss into a playful, creative experience.

Leah completed three rounds of chemotherapy over the course of 10 weeks. She moved from intense denial to an admirably direct and hopeful approach to her health. A year after completing chemotherapy, Leah said she wanted to "take a break" from treatment. "I know I'll be back," she insisted, "but I want to stop for now." I felt jarred by Leah's wish to stop therapy. As far as I was concerned, it came out of the blue, just like her cancer did and very likely the same way as my pregnancy did for her. It seemed to me that there was now enough space in Leah's psyche for her to begin to deal with her feelings of anger, envy, or resentment that she had cancer and I did not, and, more specifically, that I was able to have a child and her opportunity to become a biological parent, something she had always wanted, was now foreclosed. When I suggested this to Leah she did not disagree but she said she could not go there. She was not aware of feeling angry at this time, and she did not want to start to feel anger toward me. My sense was that she did not want to contaminate her positive feelings toward me with her negative ones. I asked her if she imagined that she would take a break and return without her angry or envious feelings and, if so, where might those feelings have gone. I fought her decision to leave, even temporarily, and spoke of how much we had struggled through together and how meaningful that had been. Why would she want to stop rather than deal with feelings that I know she must be struggling with? Did she not believe we could survive her negative feelings? Leah held firm, saying that she just wanted to leave for awhile, that perhaps she was avoiding negative feelings toward me but she also wanted to focus on living her life, on feeling healthy, on having made it through such a gruesome time.

I finally accepted that this was what she wanted, and we planned a termination. In what was to be our final session, Leah arrived saying she could not go through with it. She had awoken that morning with a memory of being a small child in preschool and of having told her mother that she could go up the two flights to the classroom on her own. She got halfway up, looked down, and realized she could not make it. The steps were familiar but it was scary to climb them alone. Her mother was waiting on the first floor landing and reassured her daughter that she did not have to go alone. She came up and went the rest of the way with her. "I'm that kid again," Leah said. "I thought I could do it by myself but I am just not ready." I let her know that we could change the plan, that she could tell me what would work best for her at this time. This did not have to be an experience of defeat but one of recognizing what she needed. She wanted to continue treatment but at a reduced frequency of once a week. I wanted her to feel that she did not fail but that she made a decision to change her plan to one that would work better for her. We met once weekly for the next year at which point Leah made the decision to terminate. We had worked on her feelings of being a "have-not," but she was rarely willing to do that work directly in the transference. It felt too dangerous to her to tamper with our relationship. She had touched on it, on the reality that I was able to have what she could not, that is, children. But she also said she once felt that she could not have a relationship, that it was something entirely out of her reach. Again, she said that she knew she would return. I felt that I needed to respect her wishes. She did not want to work more deeply at this time, and I believe that I could have let her coast along in a treatment that stayed on the surface but I felt that might damage our chances for deeper work in the future, for maintaining the intensity that had proved so valuable.

It can be difficult to determine when it is more important to continue to question a patient's decision to terminate and when it is time to accept and respect their decision. If we fully recognize that as analysts we are not all knowing, then we must accept that we cannot have a definitive answer on how and when to terminate. Sometimes a patient needs to leave treatment for an unknown period of time and we need to trust their decision and live with the uncertainty of when and if they will come back. While this may be an enactment that we would prefer to work our way out of before the patient terminates, it also may be a way that some patients test out their capacity to find us inside themselves, a way that they discover their ability to trust that we will be there for them when they are ready to return, and that they can assert their own needs and desires without feeling that they will destroy us. Mitchell (1993) emphasizes the importance of analysts realizing that their patients will grow beyond the work that they have done together and that we need to be aware of the risk of placing the patient "forever in a conflict between personal growth and loyalty to the analyst" (p. 230). Like the rest of analytic work, termination is a time of asymmetrical mutuality

(Aron, 1996), a time when we may act as guides because we have traveled similar terrain but not because we can foresee this exact journey or because we know with infinite authority how best to proceed.

In retrospect I feel that much of what was occurring at this time in the treatment was connected to Leah's experience of survival. I did not recognize her feelings of shame in having come through cancer so "smoothly." Leah felt that if she survived then someone else must not have and so she was not entitled to feelings such as envy or anger. I have wondered whether, if I had addressed issues related to shame and survival, she would still have felt the need to leave treatment for a period of time. I will elaborate on this further when I return to my work with Leah.

I would like to segue to a visit to Kim, my friend with breast cancer. As analysts we carry the stories of our patients, the stories of our own histories, and the stories of our personal lives. Those stories and the feelings that accompany them do not sit separately in our minds but are held together, the edge of each story overlapping in our minds and in our bodies, our work informing our personal lives and our personal lives informing our work.

THE VISIT

When I walked into Kim's hospital room, I found her propped up in bed watching a small TV held by a mechanical arm that stretched out from the wall. She looked big-eyed, but that was only because the rest of her was getting smaller. The chemotherapy did not cause her hair to fall out this time, but she had only one treatment since the cancer returned and began to rage inside her like a fire beyond human control. We said our hellos; I hugged her thinning body and felt myself walk into her world, a world of medicines and IV lines, of hope beginning to vanish, of children too young to understand, of a husband searching for miracle cures, of an outside seen through hospital windows and hospital TVs.

"Look at this guy," she said, pointing to the screen. He's some kind of therapist. He goes to people's homes, spends 15 minutes with them and then tells them whether their marriage is going to last."

I was confused and she could see it.

"Can you imagine? After 15 minutes you're told whether your relationship is going to make it or not."

I did not know what to say. Everything felt so surreal. The "therapist" on TV was just one more bizarre presence.

"Could you do that?" she asked.

"Do what?"

"What he's doing, the therapist."

"No," I said. I paused. "I don't think he can do it either."

She was mesmerized by the man on TV. "He does two couples a show. One in the first half and another in the second."

We both watched. The current couple was about to get their verdict. A moment later they were told they were doomed to divorce.

She turned off the TV. We began to talk. Then she looked at me, her head against the pillow, her cheekbones arching across her face, and asked, "Do your patients ever get angry with you?"

I was startled by the question. "Yes," I said.

"Really?" She seemed intrigued by this information. "What do they say?"

I gave her a few examples and then said, "Didn't you ever get mad at any of your therapists?" She rolled her eyes. "God, No."

A nurse came in, took her vital signs, and left.

We began to chat. Small talk. She complained about the doctors; we talked about the kids. Then she was quiet. Staring straight ahead she said, "They're so little, four and five. They're not going to remember me." She swung her big eyes toward me. "Will they?' she asked.

She was speaking to me as if I had the same clairvoyance as the therapist on TV. I could say anything to her, even if I had no right to the words.

"I don't know," I said softly. "They're young but I think they will remember you in some way."

I thought about a patient, a woman who was 4 years old when her mother died, the same age as Kim's daughter. I remembered a pivotal moment in our work when my patient began to feel that her mother was with her, inside her, intangible and inexplicable, but there. For the first time she felt she could hold a sense of her mother and of her self at the same time, one did not destroy the other. I said to Kim, "You're in them. You are inside. You are a part of them forever. And they are going to know that." I paused. "And feel that."

We sat together quietly. She had been crying but now she stopped. There was more small talk. She told me about the specialists, we talked about our friends.

I wondered, in my mind, what she was trying to do when she asked about my patients and their anger. Was she trying to work out her anger? Did she feel that her anger was somehow connected to her illness? Was she angry that no one could really predict the future, make it safe, even the man on TV? What does it mean that she still bothered to try and understand herself now, so close to the end of her life? It mattered to her. She wanted to sort something out. Was she blaming herself? Did she want to know that others felt angry, that they even felt angry with those who tried to help them, with their therapists or their friends?

I'll never know.

Later, I walked out of the hospital feeling dazed. It was only 4:30 but it was already getting dark.

THE MOTHERLESS

It was Sophie who I thought of when Kim asked me if her children would remember her. Sophie began treatment 2 weeks before her 29th birthday. "My mother died when she was 29," Sophie said in our first session. "I was four." The family lore was that Sophie was "lucky" to have been so young when her mother died in a car accident because "it couldn't have affected her much." Early in treatment it became clear to Sophie that her mother's death had a profound impact on her. She realized she had never mourned but instead had lived with grief nesting in her body. Our work was intense from the start. Sophie described frequent feelings of terror, a sense that the world was unsafe and a propensity for relationships with men for whom her love was thin but her fear of abandonment was blindingly thick.

Sophie had a charm, a sweetness, and a razor-sharp wit. She formed long and lasting friendships but she felt profoundly alone. She said she did not know how to live beyond the age of 29, that she was now aware she never imagined growing older and that when she looked to the future it felt endless and lonely. She could not imagine a life in which she would feel vital and a part of the world. She would always be watching from the sidelines. When she described her view of life after 29, I had an image of her living in a box, like her mother. It became clear in our work that, for Sophie, not to retreat inward brought up a fear of her own aggression, a fear that living meant inadvertently destroying. She must have killed her mother. If she did not, then she must have been too insignificant for her mother to want to stay with her. The 4-year-old in Sophie still wondered why else her mother have would left and gone to what everyone told her was "a better place."

Over the course of a 12-year treatment, the loss of Sophie's mother was a loss that flooded the space between us, a loss that felt deep enough to drown us. There were periods of intense and brutal grief, of a longing for the mother she did not know, of anger that her mother had abandoned her, of the recognition that her mother was a part of her and of a wish that a sense of trust could be a feeling rather than a thought. She feared her anger, her power, and her aggression and repeatedly took the position of the victim in relationships with self-centered men. She did not want to see my flaws because they indicated I was human and that meant that I could die, hurt her, or abandon her. Her grief was overpowering for me. I went home thinking about it. When my own children were each 4 years old, I sometimes thought of Sophie while I was with them and of how agonizing the loss of her mother had to have been. I felt a great wish to be the perfect mother to Sophie, to comply with her wishes, and not to fail her, but it was only when I did fail her that we moved through significant and frightening waters and we both discovered that she could survive disappointment, that her aggression was not murderous, and that her life was one that she could truly live.

Throughout our work, Sophie and I periodically talked about the day when we would end treatment. We both acknowledged that, in light of her history, much important work would happen when we said good-bye to one another. After 12 years of working together, we set a termination date for 1 year hence. As the year began, Sophie spoke about what it might be like to end, describing her hopes and her fears, but when the date drew closer she became angry when I brought up the topic of ending. There was always something more pressing, a recent incident to relate, or a story to tell.

"I know I wanted to terminate. I know it was my idea," she said, a few months before our planned final session date. "But I feel like it has to be your way, on your terms and I don't like that. Why can't I just talk about what I need to talk about? I need you to be here for me in that way, not to keep bringing up the fact that we are going to end. "

Sophie said she had fantasies of ultimately ending with a phone call, no build-up, no long talks, just a message to me saying she is done with therapy. It felt like the 4-year-old Sophie was in the room, angry and frustrated and wanting things her way, and wanting me to know what endings have felt like for her. Later in the session she reflected on what she had said and told me she knew we needed to do this but she did not want to. "Why can't we just make a smooth transition into being friends?" she asked, with a mix of humor and sadness.

It was a painful time. Sophie expressed gratitude for the work we had done together, and we both were amazed at the storms we had weathered, the closeness we had found, and the many changes she had made. I felt profoundly sad and thought I was experiencing something akin to a parent allowing her adult child to grow up and into the world. I knew that a part of me did not want to let Sophie go and I told her that, but we both knew that holding her back was the wrong thing to do.

Sophie expressed considerable fear of how she might feel when the treatment ended. She felt certain that she mattered to me now but feared that she would drop out of my mind after she left. Similar to her experience when her mother died, she imagined feeling alone and forgotten, left to fend for herself. As her anxiety about ending and what it would be like afterward increased, we made a plan with the hope that it would make the ending more survivable. Originally the plan was that we would schedule a session for 3 months after our final session date. In that way she would know she could return, check in, and, in her words, she would know that I was still alive and still thought about her. Ultimately, she said 3 months felt too long and so we agreed on a 6-week check-in. We spoke about what it might feel like for each of us after our last session. "I will miss you too," I said to Sophie. "You are a part of me. What we have experienced together has changed and influenced me. It's hard for me to imagine my life without seeing you." Sophie said she knew that now but feared how she would feel later. This was one reason the termination would be important. I hoped she would be able to discover how she could hold me and how I could hold her after our relationship, as we had known it, came to an end.

Three weeks before our termination date, the work took a sudden and intense turn. Sophie could not access any strong feelings about ending. She was now dry-eyed and matter of fact. When I commented on this change she noted it but saw it as a sign of her readiness to terminate. She said she felt ready now and was looking forward to many of the things to come, including having more time and more money. She said she knew she would miss me horribly and she still had fears that I might not think of her but those fears were manageable now.

I began to feel strange and uncomfortable. Why was I still feeling so sad about her leaving when she was indicating she felt ready? I started having thoughts that I was going to die after she left. I recognized these feelings as part of the treatment; but then they began to mushroom. I became preoccupied with my health and with the real possibility that my life would be foreshortened. I felt like Sophie would live her life and mine would stop. What was going on? Was there no way to end without one of us dying? Was she killing me off? Was I abandoning her like her mother did? Did I have an unhealthy need for her to depend on me in order to feel that my life was real and vital? Was I angry with her for leaving and so I pictured doing to her what her mother had done? Perhaps it was her denial of the end that made me feel I would no longer exist.

In our last few sessions Sophie became more present. She spoke about her fears of the initial days and weeks after we would end. I wondered with her whether it was hard to imagine that we could end treatment and we could both survive. She said that what was hardest was to imagine that I would still hold her in my mind. It was, perhaps, a return to her family's way of coping with her mother's death when, in our last session, she said good-bye and walked out the door without deep emotion. She took note of this and said she could do it no other way.

Much as Sophie and I worked to create a less than traumatic termination, aspects of past trauma were being relived as we moved toward saying good-bye. The experience of termination was overwhelming for Sophie and to cope with the flood of feelings she dissociated her youngest self who had been so much a part of our earlier work, the self who feared she was responsible for her mother's death and who did not know how she could go on living without her mother. In Bromberg's (1998) view, when threatened by the reliving of trauma the various self-states within an individual become "unlinked" (p. 12) through dissociation, making it impossible to "feel like one self while being many." Dissociation "does not simply deny the self access to potentially threatening feelings, thoughts and memories; it effectively obliterates, at least temporarily, the existence of that self to whom the trauma could occur and it is in a sense like a 'quasi-death'" (p. 173). Sophie's experience after her mother's death was one in which the impact of the loss of her mother was denied, leaving Sophie without any confirmation of her inner experience. As our termination date drew nearer, she was unable to bear her conflicting feelings of "hope and dread" (Mitchell, 1993), and so those feelings were instead enacted between us. I experienced the fear of being able to survive and she experienced hope for the future.

I received the first phone message from Sophie 2 weeks after our last session. Her voice was soft and sad when she said she missed me, and was finding this harder than she thought. She said that I did not need to return her call. A week later I received another message, this time she asked me to call her. We spoke briefly and agreed that she should come in for a session.

Sophie sat down in my office and said, "I can't find you." She described feeling okay in the first week after we ended but since then she had felt progressively more despair. "I feel like either you have died or you have wiped me out of your mind entirely." In addition to being sad, she was angry. This situation was untenable for her. She wanted to be able to end therapy but she said that the way that we had done it did not work. She wondered whether it would ever be possible to do the work of ending together and she wondered if she needed to see someone else to help her end the work with me. We talked about whether our plan to meet in 6 weeks made things better or worse, that perhaps knowing we would meet kept her in a state where she could not move forward. We both agreed to think about the issues she brought up and to meet again the following week.

When Sophie arrived for our second session, she told me of a dream she had the previous night. In the dream her dog was doing something "bad." Sophie yelled, "no," as she usually does when her dog misbehaves, but then she accidentally killed the dog. She was immediately horrified and full of shame. She desperately wanted to save the dog but she could not. Now she was the one who had misbehaved. "I felt like I was fundamentally bad," she said. Sophie knew the dream was about our work, about terminating and not being able to find me, about the feeling that both of us could not survive.

"It sounds like you can't find me because the 4 year old in you thinks you've killed me and so you don't deserve to find me." I said. "That part of you, the 4 year old part, blames herself for her mother's death and those feelings are all returning now in a way that they couldn't before."

Sophie spoke about her anger, how large and frightening it is for her. She needs me, cares about me, and is furious at me all at the same time. Her ability to tolerate and reflect on all of these feelings feels significant to me. She tells me that she knows she wanted to end treatment but she feels like I left her. I tell Sophie that it feels to me like the period after her mother died is here in a way that it never could be until we ended our work together. She and I craft a new ending, acknowledging that it is an experiment, and that there is no way to know if this will be different. We agree to meet once a week—the treatment prior to our termination was three times a week—for the next 3 months and then to reassess together how to proceed.

We worked during those 3 months with the part of Sophie that had no voice during the time after her mother died. She felt fearful of what kind of person she is and wondered how one is supposed to deal with a loss or a death. She spoke of the denial of grief in her family, a topic we had often visited in the past, and said she felt shame when she missed me, as she must have felt when her mother died. "I think that I somehow believe that to long for someone who is no longer there is selfish." She came into a session saying she had glimmers of me inside of her, glimmers that felt like a comfort, and that she was beginning to feel ready to end. We began to talk about what it means to live in the world with loss and to know it as providing meaning and shape and texture to her life rather than as an indication of her destructiveness. After 3 months, we said good-bye, this time with tears and with hope and with the feeling that we could both go on being.

I still see Sophie from time to time. She comes in for a session, or a few. She leaves me messages about how she is doing. She will always grapple with the issues that arose from her mother's untimely death, but she knows this and sees it as a part of life, a part of survival into the world of the living. I believe it was impossible to evoke the period in Sophie's life that followed her mother's death without an actual termination. In retrospect I wonder if the plan to meet 6 weeks after our last session did not return her even more intensely to the unthinkable time after her mother's death when Sophie quietly, fearfully waited for her to return. While she waited for our 6-week appointment, she felt increasing despair. It became progressively more difficult for her to cope with her fear that I had died or that I had banished her from my mind. When someone suffers such a traumatic loss as Sophie did it is hard to know what kind of termination will genuinely meet her needs and enhance her life. For a while she needed to find me in the outside world in order to find me within herself, to know that we both could live, but with time and sporadic contact that changed. Perhaps it was the failure of our first attempt at ending and the coconstruction of a new termination plan unique to our relationship that made for a more successful termination.

I have had some patients who, after a long treatment, terminate and have little or no contact with me. Perhaps I receive a holiday card or a note letting me know of a new event in their lives such as a child or a marriage. Others, like Sophie, maintain contact in some way. I do not believe that one way of handling termination is superior to another but that it is a matter of finding what fits each particular dyad and of constructing the ending together. If someone needs more and more frequent contact, then I feel it is necessary to revisit the question of termination or possible reentry to treatment, and I feel it is important not to consider a return to treatment as a sign of failure. For Sophie, shaping our termination, and then shaping it again, was crucial to the work of termination.

THE RETURN

Leah returned to treatment after a 5-year "break." In the intervening years, there were sporadic sessions and holiday cards. Once in a while I received a phone message, particularly on the anniversary of her completion of chemotherapy. Leah said she had become increasingly anxious in the past year. There were budget cuts at the special education school where she worked and she felt overwhelmed by her responsibilities. She was preoccupied by a fear that she would make a mistake that would cause a terrible result. Perhaps a child in the school was being abused and she did not recognize it, or possibly worse, perhaps she reported abuse when there was none. We explored her feeling that she was responsible for everyone and everything and that she was doomed to make a terrible mistake. Together we wondered why she felt that she could so easily cause damage or harm. Returning to treatment and having a place to talk about these fears helped her anxiety to move to a more manageable, though still intense, place, fairly rapidly.

It was about 2 months after she returned when, toward the end of a session, Leah said, "I hope your friend is doing okay." I felt touched that she mentioned Kim, but also uncomfortable. Kim had died 3 years earlier. I told her that I appreciated her thoughtfulness. Two weeks later she mentioned Kim again, saying that she sometimes wonders about her. I was unable to come up with a response, a question of exploration, a step into her fantasies about my friend and how she is doing. It felt too strange. "I don't think she is doing well," Leah said to me with concern. I was quiet and she held my gaze. I told her she was right but that I did not know how much she wanted to know about her. Leah insisted that she did want to know and I told her that Kim had died. She said that was what she suspected. I told Leah that my friend's cancer was found at an advanced stage. I felt concern that she would be frightened by hearing that Kim had died and that it would make her more fearful of her own future.

Leah's response was not fear about her own future. She looked horrified. It took her a moment to find words and then she said, in a soft and slow voice, "How can you sit here with me?"

I was confused. The room was silent for a few moments. "You must wish that your friend had lived and I had died instead."

"What do you mean?"

"You can't sit with her and talk with her. She was your friend. You must wish it was the other way around."

I felt stunned. I had not thought about the two of them in this way. My patient was so insistent that I began to wonder if I was simply unaware of having had this thought. I tried to explore Leah's feelings. Why did she feel so certain that I wished my friend had survived "instead" of her? Was there any other way to think about this? What did it mean to her that she lived? Why did she think that she lived?

It was not about who lived, according to Leah, as much as it was about who got the "good cancer." She did not understand why she was fortunate enough to get the "good cancer" when other people got the "bad." "They found my cancer when they weren't even looking for it," she said. She spoke about a colleague whose wife was diagnosed with ovarian cancer and died. She felt similarly about this man as she did about me. How could he stand to work with her, to see her in the office every day? He must be thinking to himself, why is Leah alive and my wife is dead? She felt ashamed that she lived, as if someone had taken life from another and given it to her, as if she had stolen her survival and she would inevitably be caught. It was happening right now. I had caught her.

Leah found it hard to believe that I had not stored feelings of resentment into the pockets of my mind or my heart. In her view, my view must be that she had lived "instead" of my friend. She was attached to the question of why, and with that, she was also attached to the idea that there must be an answer. Because she could not come up with an answer, she thought that perhaps her cancer would return or some other tragedy would strike. Maybe there was a mistake. How could she have gotten off so easily? "Is it possible," I asked, "that some things are random, that there isn't a reason why some people survive and others don't, or why some people get a more deadly cancer than others, that it is not about a trade-off between people?" If she accepted this idea then it meant she had to accept the limits of her own power and of how much any of us could control. We had many sessions that revolved around the question of chance and fate, and around the different ways that each of us thought about survival.

Although we searched for a clear connection between Leah's history and her feelings that she had won her life at the cost of someone else's, we were unable to find one. We looked at her fears of her own anger, envy, and guilt, as they seemed a likely cause for her feelings of undeserved fortune in having survived. We explored her feelings about growing up in what she described as a "social justice" family, a family that was active in the community and taught the children to be mindful of those who are deprived or oppressed. We talked about various family dynamics including a grandmother who was regularly present in her life and who outwardly favored Leah's younger sister, implying that Leah should make sacrifices for her sister. None of these scenarios felt significantly linked to her feeling that she was not fully entitled to a life that could be lived.

In Leah's worldview, I heard echoes of Benjamin's (1988) elaboration of Winnicott (1969). The child of the depressed parent feels that her parent must have sacrificed her own aliveness in order for the child to feel alive, but it is only through the cycle of destruction and survival that the child discovers that it does not have to be "either-or" but can be "both-and" as both parent and child can feel alive together. Although Leah did not describe her mother as having been depressed, somewhere in her history it felt like she had absorbed the fear that her inner world reigned over the outer world. Not only was she unable to have a sense of going-on-being because she had to react to the outside other but she feared her own impact, her own potential for destruction, and had to remain vigilant to ensure that her aliveness did not cause another pain.

I began to think back on Leah's decision to leave treatment years earlier. I remembered feeling that she wanted to leave at a time when she felt the cancer was behind her and she could look forward to a future. While I recognized at the time that she was in a psychic place that might have cleared the way for a range of feelings to arise in the treatment including envy or anger and that those were feelings she feared might damage our relationship, I did not recognize the shame that she may have felt in having survived. I never inquired as deeply as I might have about just what it felt like, not only to have been diagnosed with cancer, but also to have come through it with an excellent prognosis. I was unaware, and perhaps so was she, of how much she was struggling with the feeling of having survived a diagnosis that so quickly destroyed many others. Learning of Kim's death brought these feelings into the treatment.

Leah's anxiety at work, the fear that she would inadvertently cause harm to someone, now made more sense to me as did her refusal to look for a more satisfying work environment. We began to explore more deeply her experience at work as well as the risk she was taking by having returned to smoking cigarettes, ostensibly to deal with work stress. I wondered whether taking care of herself meant to Leah that she would be ignoring the needs of others. At one point I expressed frustration that she would not live her life in a way that would make it more meaningful for her. I told her that I felt she was trying to frustrate those around her, including her partner and me, by making it clear that she was unhappy but acting like it was her lot in life and that she could do nothing about it. She responded with what I felt was genuine surprise that she was negatively impacting others with her lack of self-care.

Leah arrived for her next session and began by saying that she had cleaned and organized her apartment the night before. "When I was done I sat back and thought to myself that everything is in order for when I get cancer again. I couldn't believe I'd had that thought."

"What do you think about that?"

"I'm waiting for it to come back," she said, in a voice weighted with sadness.

"What if it doesn't?"

"I don't know." Then there was a pause before she continued. "In some ways it was easier to be sick. I didn't have to think about the future. I know that sounds strange but it's true. It made sense to me that I was sick. I had to just focus on getting through it. I feel horrible for having these thoughts."

If Leah had cancer again then the shame of survival would not be something she had to bear. We began to work more directly on the experience of cancer itself and on the feeling of having survived. There was a period of mourning for what she had lost, her health, her precancer identity, her hopes of having a child one day. Prior to this time, she had not allowed herself to reflect on what was lost and so she could not mourn. Now she began to think about what it meant to her to take responsibility for her own life, for taking care of herself, for thinking about how she wanted to live even though she could not know what the future might hold.

Leah had just been offered a new job when she heard that the 35-year-old husband of her former neighbor was in the hospital, his cancer having returned. "He has the worst kind of cancer you could possibly get. I had the best," she said when she told me about him and about the visit she made to the hospital. Leah visited regularly during the 4 weeks he was in the hospital. He was not going to live long, Leah said. She felt great compassion for his wife, a young woman who had been her neighbor for several years.

I commented to Leah on how differently she sounded now than she did when she spoke about my friend or about the man at work whose wife died. "I'm not sure what changed," Leah said, "or just when I began to feel differently." She was quiet for a few moments. "I've stopped asking why. Some questions are just unanswerable. I'll never know why my cancer was found so early. Some things are unknown and left to chance. I feel so fortunate and I don't think there is a reason why I had the good fortune," she said.

I felt moved as I listened to her. Something had shifted. In our work Leah and I had spoken about our differing views of her survival and while our focus was on her inner experience of surviving cancer, I did not shy away from letting her know that I had a different perspective when it came to her survival and my friend's death. I directly explored her refusal to take care of herself and the impact that refusal had on those around her, including me. I believe it was as a result of this work that Leah began to "use" me in the Winnicottian sense of the word, to develop an emergent self (Davies, 2004b) and to live within what Benjamin (1995) described as "the sustained tension or rapid movement between the patient's experience of us as inner material and as the recognizing other" (p. 46). At this time, Leah is still in treatment but I would not be surprised if she decides again to take a "break" from treatment and then to return for more work. This seems to be the way in which she is doing the work of analysis.

How do we think about termination when a patient leaves treatment with the intent to return? In a significant sense, treatment never ends. The voices of our analysts remain a part of us for years to come (Bass, 2001), informing our thoughts, our relationships, and our experiences living life and dealing with loss. We hold the paradox of saying good-bye, of ending the analytic relationship as we have known it, and of knowing that in many respects the relationship will never end. Is the patient who terminates with the intent to return denying this reality or doing the work in a different way? Is he or she unable to experience the loss of saying good-bye, or is this "break" a part of the treatment, a period of time during which the patient tests out his or her capacity for going-on-being in part by discovering how the relationship will survive his or her departure and return? Part of grief is chaos, the discombobulating of one's world, as it had been known. Perhaps for Leah, who has come face to face with death, with the loss of the life she thought she would live, and who has grieved much of that loss, a sense of control over just how she lets go of the analytic relationship and just how she returns to it, psychically as well as literally, is a necessary part of our work and will be more fully articulated as this phase of analysis continues.

Much of the movement within any analysis results from the analytic relationship, the reliability of the analyst, the consistency of the work, the enactments lived out, and the intimate moments of vulnerability in both analyst and patient. It is the day-to-day work we do and the immediacy and rawness that we experience together that helps to build and strengthen the reliability of the analytic relationship and what Winnicott described as a sense of going-on-being in our patients. Ultimately, those with an inner sense of continuity are individuals who are able to make use of the failures of their environment and to reflect on those failures, rather than for the failures to define and determine their identities and their lives. For those who have experienced traumatic losses or repeated losses, this is a particularly challenging and central piece of the analytic work.

Going-on-being is essential to the termination of analysis. For those who did not develop or do not have access to the capacity for going-on-being, the development of it is central to analytic work. It is through the process of destruction and survival that the analyst becomes of "use" to the patient and an emergent self with the capacity for going-on-being is discovered. This can occur subtly when the patient reveals to his or her analyst particularly painful or overwhelming parts of his or her inner world and the patient discovers that his or her analyst does not emotionally vanish, or it can occur more blatantly when the patient expresses direct conflict or anger with her analyst. For those patients who experienced particularly traumatic losses, termination will bring up the shame of survival and the sense of going-on-being will be threatened if that shame is not directly addressed so that it is not relived in a way that may become detrimental to the work.

Death is a part of all of our lives, but we keep it cordoned off. We deny it and we turn away from it. The culture we live in is one in which those who are closer to death are avoided. The same is true for termination. Little time is spent on it during analytic training and the literature on the topic is sparse. If in no other way, termination and death are connected because they are repeatedly denied. Facing the fact that we die and that those close to us die also means valuing the experience of being alive. Frommer (2005), writing on mortality, notes that "awareness of one's own mortality can make everything feel both meaningless and extraordinarily meaningful"

(p. 484). The ability to live with this contradiction can enhance the capacity to feel real and vital in one's life.

There is nothing quite like the work of analysis. It is strange in its ways of being personal and professional at the same time and sometimes quite messily so. We engage in deep, rich relationships and call it work. We end those relationships in a process called termination, and we realize that what we do is so much more than work. Our lives and our patient's lives sometimes melt and meld and blend into one another, and one of the things that we learn when we say good-bye is that loss, when held meaningfully, when held in the context of an inner sense of going-on-being, has a way of providing not only pain but comfort.

REFERENCES

Aron, L. (1996). *A meeting of minds: Mutuality in psychoanalysis.* Hillsdale, NJ: Analytic Press.

Bass, A. (2001). It takes one to know one: Or, whose unconscious is it anyway? *Psychoanalytic Dialogues, 11*, 683–703.

Benjamin, J. (1988). *The bonds of love: Psychoanalysis feminism and the problem of domination.* New York: Pantheon.

Benjamin, J. (1995). *Like subjects, love objects.* New Haven, CT: Yale University Press.

Benjamin, J. (2000). Response to commentaries by Mitchell and Butler. *Studies in Gender and Sexuality, 1*(3), 291–308.

Bromberg, P. (1998). *Standing in the spaces: Essays on clinical process, trauma, and dissociation.* Mahwah, NJ: Analytic Press.

Davies, J. M. (2004a). Whose bad objects are we anyway? Repetition and our elusive love affair with evil. *Psychoanalytic Dialogues, 14*(6), 711–732.

Davies, J. M. (2004b). Reply to commentaries. *Psychoanalytic Dialogues, 14*(6), 755–767.

Davies, J. M. (2005). Transformations of desire and despair: Reflections on the termination process. *Psychoanalytic Dialogues, 15*(6), 779–805.

Frommer, M. S. (2005). Living in the liminal spaces of mortality. *Psychoanalytic Dialogues, 15*, 479–498.

Harris, A., & Sinsheimer, K. (2007). The analyst's vulnerability. In F. S. Anderson (Ed.), *Bodies in treatment: The unspoken dimension* (pp. 255–274). Mahwah, NJ: Analytic Press.

Hoffman, I. Z. (1998). *Ritual and spontaneity in the psychoanalytic process: A dialectical-constructivist view.* Hillsdale, NJ: Analytic Press.

Mitchell, S. A. (1993). *Hope and dread in psychoanalysis.* New York: Basic Books.

Phillips, A. (1988). *Winnicott.* Cambridge, MA: Harvard University Press.

Phillips, A. (1996). *Terrors and experts.* Cambridge, MA: Harvard University Press.

Winnicott, D. W. (1958). Primary maternal preoccupation. In *Through pediatrics to psychoanalysis: Collected papers* (pp. 300–305). New York: Basic Books.

Winnicott, D. W. (1958). The capacity to be alone. In *The maturational processes and the facilitating environment: Studies in the theory of emotional development* (pp. 29–36). New York: International Universities Press, 1965.

Winnicott, D. W. (1960). The theory of the parent–child relationship. *International Journal of Psycho-Analysis, 41*, 585–595.

Winnicott, D. W. (1965). *The maturational processes and the facilitating environment: Studies in the theory of the emotional development.* New York: International Universities Press.

Winnicott, D. W. (1969). The use of an object and relating through identification. In *Playing and reality* (pp. 86–94). New York: Basic Books, 1971.

Chapter 11

Maternal resistance

Lynne Layton

Jesse left the office after his last session, and I let myself sob without restraint. We had worked together for more than 9 years, and there had been precious little sobbing until the last few sessions. In fact, the first sobs were Jesse's. The week before we ended, he was saying that he had been here for a long time, 7 years, and I said I thought it was more like 12 (in "material reality," it was 9 years). He burst into tears and said that was really upsetting. I asked why, but all he said was that it was like I was a mother figure. I did not fully understand his answer then, but when, in his final session a few days later, he said that what kept running through his mind was a song lyric that had to do with walking down a path alone, I realized that what had been upsetting was his sudden recognition, fleeting though it may have been, that I had been something of a good mother to him, and that for these long years he had not been alone. He knew well that he was losing something in ending analysis, but it seemed that just for that one moment he was in touch with what he was losing (a precondition, according to Freud, 1917, of mourning). And as he allowed himself to know that, I, too, was able to feel on a deeper level what I was losing.

I hate the word *termination*. It has the ring, to me, of death camp, extermination. Even without the ex-, it feels anything but experience near—the words for which it is often synonymous—"death," "firing," "ending"—pack much more of an emotional and intense punch, and it feels dishonest to cover that intensity and emotion with a Latinate abstraction. Perhaps it even militates against sobbing. I remember that the end of my own analysis bore some similarity to the end of Jesse's. There were a few instances of behavior that signaled dissociation: In my last week of analysis, for example, I did not show up for a lunch date with a colleague who had been one of my first clinical supervisors (not common for me to forget such things). And I had been talking quite a bit in the previous several months about what a dumb thing termination was—to me, it was like a divorce, but from someone with whom you had a wonderful relationship. Were it not for the cost and the time, why would I ever want to stop? But it was only when I brought my analyst a gift that visually displayed what the analysis had meant to me that

I sobbed. And I now realize how important but perhaps infrequent it is that we allow ourselves really to know what we have lost—a safe dependency and the pleasures of a deep intimacy and attachment. I shall argue here that the cultural pathologizing of dependence and undervaluing of attachment frequently get in the way of knowing what we have lost, and thus get in the way of understanding more about the ending of treatment.

Jesse has a good term for the difficulty being in touch with our dependence on and attachment to a caretaking other: He calls it "maternal resistance." Jesse repeatedly enacted "maternal resistance" in his life and in his analysis—that is, resistance to anything that smells like dependence, mothering, nurture, attachment, commitment to an intimate relationship. In what follows, I want to look more closely at "maternal resistance" and its relation to ending analysis. I begin with thoughts stirred by my reading of some of the analytic literature on termination. I then will return to my own clinical experience.

Most analysts who write about termination start by invoking Freud, and I shall do so as well—but not only because of what he wrote about termination. Rather, I want to highlight the deep and seemingly quite unconscious presence of "maternal resistance" in much of his work, including "Analysis Terminable and Interminable" (1937), to which I will return at the end of this essay. Some years ago, I was teaching several Freud papers and began to notice an interesting pattern: Whenever Freud broached the subjects of dependency and attachment (in discussions of infant helplessness and separation anxiety), he would jump quickly to another topic, usually castration anxiety. As many feminist theorists have noted,* Freud's version of autonomy is inextricable from a version of masculinity that relies for its coherence on repudiating and keeping as far from the self as possible states of dependency, emotionality, and whatever else is culturally associated with femininity. Sprengnether (1990) writes specifically about the way that Freud's oedipal theory is conditioned by his failure properly to reckon with the real (versus idealized) pleasures and the real limits of his relation to his mother, and thus, his failure properly to mourn her. Ever since noticing these Freudian slips, I have been alert to the fears of dependency and connection that underlie much psychoanalytic writing, whether the topic is empathy, gender, sexuality, or, in this case, termination. Just as in Freud's papers, these fears are often registered in enactments of doing and undoing, or in disavowal: a writer will bring up the centrality of helpless dependence and of attachment to mother figures only to deny or disavow it in the same paper. Helpless dependence will be aligned with femininity,

---

* See, for example, Benjamin (1988), Chodorow (1978), Dimen (1991), Dinnerstein (1976), Eichenbaum and Orbach (1983), Goldner (1991), Harris (2005), and Layton (1998).

castration anxiety with the more culturally valued masculinity. And some-times helpless dependency is conflated with attachment altogether.*

Such enactments are examples of what I have come to call normative unconscious processes (Layton, 2006), in which we unconsciously collude with discriminatory cultural norms that dichotomize human attributes such as independence and dependency and make one pole representative of an ideal form of masculinity or whatever else is culturally valued and the other pole representative of an ideal form of femininity or whatever is culturally devalued. What we are left with are monstrous versions of dependence and independence, and impoverished versions of masculinity and femininity to which we are encouraged to aspire. In many of Freud's gender papers (1925, 1933), what passes for developmental description is in fact normative prescription that keeps the masculine in the superior posi-tion and denigrates what he refers to as the feminine. As Benjamin (1988) has argued, the split and polarized gender positions leave little possibility for achieving recognition and mutuality.

So it did not surprise me to find, in Bergmann's (1997) historical review of writing on termination, that in 1924, Ferenczi and Rank wrote that an analyst should set a termination date the moment an infantile neurosis becomes a transference neurosis, so as to avoid a repetition that might lead the patient to want to cling to the analyst (p. 163). Many of the quite different historical views on termination have in common a sense that the analysand reaches maturity and thus can successfully terminate when he or she has internalized the analytic function, become securely individuated, thinks for himself or herself, and so forth. Attachment and its attendant affects are generally either ignored or, to a certain extent, pathologized. For example, Freud (1937) opens "Analysis Terminable and Interminable" with the tough-love position that the analyst ought to set a termination date, stick to it, and send the patient to another analyst if more work needs to be done. Novick (1997) writes that, historically, analyses were terminated by the analyst in sadomasochistic ways, and what has been passed down in our analytic training and our practice is a resistance to termination and a bypassing of mourning. This led me to wonder if classical ideas about termination might contain within them the germ of maternal resistance. And, if maternal resistance is present and unanalyzed, if our theories and practices hold to an ideal of auton-omy that rests on the very shaky ground of splitting, do we ever really come to know what we have lost at the end of an analysis?

---

* There is, of course, a tradition in psychoanalysis that countered the devaluation of depen-dency: the British Independents, especially Balint (1969), Fairbairn (1943), and Winnicott (1969). Winnicott, however, had this to say about termination: "But psychoanalysis is no way of life. We all hope that our patients will finish with us and forget us, and that they will find living itself to be the therapy that makes sense" (p. 87).

Given the tendencies to maternal resistance that I found in the literature, it did surprise me to discover that Dorothy Burlingham's analysis with Freud "continued for many years, daily, until close to Freud's death" (Bergmann, 1997, p. 163). Because this practice hardly fits at least some of what Freud said in his paper on termination, one can only speculate about how he understood this ongoing analysis. But it also surprised me because another patient in my practice who was approaching the end of her analysis had a feeling that was quite different from Jesse's about ending. Kyra saw no reason whatsoever to stop seeing me after her analysis ended; Jesse, on the other hand, never even entertained the idea of staying in treatment. For him, an end was an end, as it had been for me in my own analysis. But Kyra made me wonder if my own convictions were born from "maternal resistance," which manifested in my obedience to what—before reading the literature—I considered analytic gospel. Now, as I have become aware that before 1950 candidates were taught little to nothing about termination, that few analytic institutes to this day teach termination, and that there is very little agreement in the literature as to what constitutes a "good" termination (with Levenson, 1976, presenting the gadfly but reasonable position that "it makes no more sense to ask when or how to terminate than to ask when to die," p. 340), I feel a need to take a second look at the disparity between how I felt emotionally about termination and what I thought I "knew" about termination.

JESSE

Jesse's history was nearly barren of loving care. In the early years of the analysis, he spoke of having a desert inside him where nothing grew and where there was little water to make anything grow. Now and then, the desert would get a little water, but what grew would soon die. Sometimes he would talk about feeling like an island with no bridge connecting him to the mainland, a drifting boat with nothing tying him to shore. His father was gone before his birth and gave very little child support and even less personal presence. His mother was way too overwhelmed by her own demons to be able to care properly for him and his siblings. Mother's demons drove her repeatedly to uproot the family—around seven times during Jesse's childhood—always to move to what she hoped would be a better place. But her own internal desert, her great need for help, was stubbornly unacknowledged and thus enacted in the moves and in attention-seeking behavior that, at best, embarrassed Jesse, and, at worst, made him feel he had to suppress his own needs and walk on eggshells around his mother.

I said his history was nearly barren: Jesse's grandparents were the one loving presence in his world, and Jesse was quite special to them among their many grandchildren. Until mother moved him too far away, he spent quite a bit of time with them. But even their loving care and special treatment could not quell Jesse's feelings of having been unwanted from the start. And the constant moves left him with the kind of dialectical trace that always marks trauma: Although he thirsted for connection, as soon as someone tried to bring water to his desert, he felt compelled to act as though the last thing he wanted was water. And this is the kind of thing he referred to as "maternal resistance." Sometimes it came up in a John Wayne kind of way: "A man's gotta do what a man's gotta do." When I went on vacation, he would worry not for himself but for those other patients who had become dependent on me. He seemed to feel it was a moral failure on my part to take more than a 1-week vacation. As for himself, well, he saw the vacations as "opportunities" to go it alone and see how well he could do. Thus, to survive psychically, Jesse had begun at an early age to spurn the need for connection (which he often conflated with helpless dependency), and this spurning became the core of his masculinity, his heterosexuality, and of his identity *tout court*. Indeed, often when Jesse became psychically disorganized in a session, he would suddenly fear he was gay. Freud (1937) might have called this "castration anxiety" and have understood it as bedrock, the male version of "the repudiation of femininity" that analysis sadly cannot resolve. What Jesse repudiated, however, is not femininity but rather the pleasures of intimate connection and the acknowledgment of dependence–interdependence that such connection requires.

Our treatment had been marked throughout by "maternal resistance." It felt "icky" to him to have any reminder that he and I were in a relationship. If he were to tell a dream, for example, and it would be clear both to him and to me that a figure in the dream stood for some part of me, he would recoil. After a tumultuous relationship with a very volatile woman, Jesse met a steady, caring woman whom he "sort of," "sometimes" felt he "might" love. In this relationship, and late in the analysis, he became more aware that periods of feeling warm and close would inevitably be interrupted by detachment. He did not know for sure whether this was a problem of his or whether this just was not the right relationship, but he was beginning to suspect it was him. Toward the end of the analysis, he surprised me by bringing his girlfriend to a session to meet me. After she left and we talked about it, I told him that it had made me feel a bit like he was bringing the girlfriend home to meet the family. He became quite annoyed and lashed out, "You're not my family."

"Maternal resistance"—I hear in the term what I understand to be the multiple faces of resistance: resistance as a defense against a feared repetition, as Stolorow (2007) has described it, and resistance to giving up the painful part of an old object tie because of loyalty to and love for the old object. Some of what transpired in the last year of treatment, once a termination date had been set, supports Loewald's (1988) argument that sometimes the transference neurosis only comes to "full bloom" under the pressure of the decision whether to terminate or not. For it was really only in the last 6 months of the treatment that Jesse got so fed up with the "never enough" acrobatics he had to perform for his mother that he began to set self-protective limits with her. And when he did so, he finally and deeply understood that his mother was not likely ever to be able to see his point of view, so desperately did she need to defend herself against any criticism. Maternal resistance involved, for him, a defense against giving up a fantasy that mother might yet be what he needed her to be. A third face of resistance, then, which Freud (1937) speaks about in his termination essay, is resistance to bearing what you know to be a painful truth. Jesse held fast to the fantasy that mother may yet love him as he wished to be loved. As a result of this disavowal, his desert stayed dry and any attempts by another to water it were, for years, rebuffed.

Just about 1 year before the analysis ended, and just after termination had been raised as a possibility (because of time and money pressures), Jesse reported that he and his girlfriend had gone skiing with a group of friends; everyone else had been skiing their whole lives, but it was Jesse's first time. He was petrified. Jesse rarely tried new things, so frightened was he of looking "lame." But something made him try. When he talked about it in his next session, his focus was on the many conflicted feelings he felt: shame, excitement, and final triumph. Then he spoke of the envy he felt when he saw little kids confidently whizzing by. And this led to a great deal of anger at his parents for offering no encouragement for any activities and providing next to no opportunities. It was only at the end of the session that he mentioned, in passing, that his girlfriend had stayed by his side the whole day, encouraging him, teaching him, and cheering him on.

Now we are in the last 3 weeks of treatment, and it is the session before I leave for a 1-week vacation. We still have 2 weeks left after I return. Jesse wonders if there is any data out there on whether or not you get closer to your partner after you end therapy, whether you use therapy to keep from being close to your partner. He talks about how he needs to express his thoughts and vulnerabilities to someone, so he imagines he will distribute the need among various people. I say, "But it's still a loss." And Jesse replies, "This is always the hard part for me—what I'm losing. Stability. Consistency." But he then notes that a couple of his former girlfriends were consistent and stable. He appreciates that about his current girlfriend. And then he says, "It's kind of like a maternal role that you play." "Maternal," I say. And he goes on: "Or a professor or a mentor." I point out how it seems to get a little more distant with each word. But he goes on to talk about how this has been his version of going to school, where he has gotten an education on how to live life better. I feel again that he comes close to talking about whatever the something more than stability and consistency, what the word "maternal" means for him. While I am sure that he authentically appreciates the education, I think that he is unable to stay with "maternal" because he fears becoming disorganized if he talks about how he feels about me, if he talks about what the attachment feels like rather than about what I supply. Is attachment perhaps what Freud really meant by "repudiation of femininity"?

There are, of course, at least two levels of attachment. One allows us to feel safe enough to go out and explore the world, but Western culture tends to disavow the fact that attachment and dependency on another under-lie this autonomous capacity. Another, in which the boundaries between "self" and "other" are not very clear, is more primal and perhaps even more disavowed. Butler (2004) well articulates the connections between loss, mourning, and identity that exist at this level of attachment:

> Freud reminded us that when we lose someone, we do not always know what it is *in* that person that has been lost. So when one loses, one is also faced with something enigmatic: something is hiding in the loss, something is lost within the recesses of loss.
>
> When we lose certain people, or when we are dispossessed from a place, or a community, we may simply feel that we are undergoing some-thing temporary, that mourning will be over and some restoration of prior order will be achieved. But maybe when we undergo what we do, something about who we are is revealed, something that delineates the ties we have to others, that shows us that these ties constitute what we are, ties or bonds that compose us. It is not as if an "I" exists independently over here and then simply loses a "you" over there, especially if the attachment to "you" is part of what composes who "I" am. (pp. 21–22)

Both levels of attachment, when made conscious, threaten a version of autonomy built on the repudiation of dependency and interdependence.

In the session before my vacation, Jesse hears from a sibling that his mother has shown no interest in what, for the sibling, is a major life event. He is overwhelmed with the feeling that his mother will never show interest in anything he does or is. When I return from vacation, with 2 weeks now to the ending, he begins by saying he does not know how to position his mother. And he links losing her with losing me. He then talks about how much harder it would be if I were moving to the west coast; it is comforting to know I am close by, watching over him. He refers to this as maternal but then immediately begins to tell the story of how he left his mother at age 17, a story that has always made him wonder who really left whom. It seems that now this story is not one about his growing autonomy and readiness to leave; it sounds more like mother made the first move to leave and that he felt prematurely abandoned. I am struck by the fact that the moment of leaving mother occurred in the same month in which we were ending. Did the choice of date signal an unconscious enactment that stirred up the boundary confusion between him, his mother, and me? (See Salberg, 2009, who suggests that all terminations entail mutual unconscious enactments.)

At some point, Jesse says, "I've been here 7 years, right?" I say I think it has been longer, more like 12 years. He begins to cry. "That's upsetting. I don't know why." He talks about why he came to therapy in the first place and why he increased the frequency. And then he says, "It *is* like you're a mom. I'll have to call you mommy." I perhaps should have remained silent, but I decide on an interpretation: I recall the early image of being repelled by his father and not being able to pass through a barrier and move toward either his father or his then girlfriend. I tell him I have felt that part of what we have been looking at these last months is precisely "maternal resistance." I say he had to not need his mom, but that he has also had a hard time experiencing me as maternal, or perhaps it is more accurate to say a hard time acknowledging it. He says it is interesting but he does not really see it. And then I remind him of how annoyed he got with me when I said he had brought his girlfriend to meet the family. "I did? I have a strong feeling about family and yet I keep myself aloof from being with them. But it's kind of weird. You've been there more for me than my family." I say that he had to not need his mother because her own needs made it very difficult for her to attend to his. He says, "But I did need her, and you pay a high price for acting like you don't." Note how his very phrasing reveals the push and pull of repetition and resistance, the personal pronoun owning the pain in the first clause, the habitual retreat (from pain) to the general "you" in the second.

The last week of treatment began where the week before had left off, his upset about how long he had been in treatment. It was not terribly common for Jesse to sustain the connection between sessions over a weekend; he often claimed that by the time he reached the top of my stairs at the end of a session, the session was gone from memory (not quite the case, but the need to assert it is yet another piece of "maternal resistance"). He talks about how few people there are whom he has known as long. (I correct my error in deference to material reality, but it does not matter one whit to Jesse's psychic reality.) He repeats that it has been like going to school and learning how to live life better. "This has been," he says, "like my diary— the others have seen a segment or segments but I've been through so much in these years." And then he begins to tell a story that resonates with the one he had told when he first brought up termination, the report of a skiing trip, this time one he had gone on over the past weekend. He talks about how much fun he had, and he parallels what happened there with what he has gotten from analysis: He is amazed that what he learned last time he had skied, a year ago, was in his body and he could just do it. He describes each slope he tried, how he advanced from easy to harder and harder, how he enjoyed just being able to look around, how he would fall but get up. He emphasized his patience with himself (his superego can be quite harsh and punishing at times). "It's so important," he says. He did again think about how his parents had given him no opportunities and he began to get angry. But it was checked by the excitement of trying something new. He saw little kids whiz by and saw one go down the biggest slope. He did not have the urge to put out his pole and trip them like last time—he was just intently focused on himself. His girlfriend is astounded by his skill, and he wonders if he in fact has a natural talent for it. He does not feel bad even when a friend he is skiing with shows off his prowess. He feels there are many new things he could try. He feels confident. On the way home he got a speeding ticket and his favorite team lost their game; he did not let it bring him down. Just as he had done in the session, he used a positive experience to bring himself out of a darker place. "I thought about the skiing and I came right up. It was amazing. I like to know where the dark stuff comes from; I don't want to just use cognitive tricks all day, but it was amazing." His disdain for and refusal to use "cognitive tricks" had also been a marker of "maternal resistance" in this treatment. He could only respond to tough love, not patient caretaking of the self, the kind of self-care he seemed to have achieved during skiing and on the ride home. I note that being gentle and patient with yourself is not exactly cognitive; it is a capacity he is beginning to have. He agrees. "Being gentle with yourself—it's huge. I had no idea how important it is. So many things that happened while skiing I could have beat myself up about." Then I note the parallel to here—the skills are in your body. (See Davies, 2005, who says that what happens in treatment is the achievement of new implicit relational procedures that live in the body.) He agrees.

And so we come to the last session. He comes in and calls it the "last roundup," which reminds me of the lonely cowboy part of him. He begins with his concern about feeling detached from his girlfriend. Having thought awhile now about maternal resistance, and in response to a part of the previous session where he had spoken about a couple in his building taking up all the space, I suggest that his difficulty committing has something to do with a fear that if he commits, there will be no space for him to be a person, as there is no space for him to be a person with his mother. He agrees, and, with 15 minutes to go, he begins to talk about "here." "I didn't want to wait until the end." He begins to cry. He mentions a song going through his head, a song about walking down a path alone—that is how he feels. He is out there hanging all alone in Massachusetts. I ask, "And this is an anchor?" "Yes. And a place of safety. Even where it is it feels sequestered but also like you're watching over me." The song, the last roundup: I realize that even if he wanted to, he would never be able to ask for anything beyond our ending besides silent watching, so I decide to ask if he would want to maintain some kind of contact, or if he has thought about it. Uh-oh, it is getting what he calls "touchy-feely." "Oops," I say. He says he knows I am here and he can come back for a tune-up (note to self, car analogy, how much more boy can we get today?). He feels I have been so stable, what he did not have. I then say that he can come in, call to talk over something that's hard, or call or come to tell me good things. He gets upset and cries—his mother never wants to hear good things, never praises. "Well," I say, "I'd like to praise you, even if it might be touchy-feely." And I start to cry as I tell him how I see him and what it has been like to know him and work with him. Surprisingly, he begins to talk about his gratitude and his fantasy of what it would have been like for him if I had been his mother, the stable, steady hand. His image is of himself as a child coming down the steps from school and I'm mom and the door is always open. He talks about how much he has changed, how much better he is in relationships; he feels his work here has made other people's lives with him much easier. He is grateful to me and to himself for putting in the work and for facing hard things. I push the touchy-feely and say that he is probably taking a part of me with him; he is not alone. He says an unconvincing yes. And then it is time to say good-bye. I say good-bye with the feeling that, at least for that moment, we both know what we have lost, a particular kind of attachment, a relationship of great depth, where whatever safe or unsafe feelings come up can be talked about, where it is possible that one will be hurt or inflict hurt, but where one knows there is a commitment to work the hurt through, where one experiences the pleasures of attachment (Benjamin, 1988). And I felt I had lost someone I loved and a part of who I am, a feeling I could feel fully in that moment.

As I look back at my verbal response, I realize that when I suggest to Jesse that he will take a part of me with him, I, too, perhaps perform the normative unconscious work (Layton, 2006) of denying that this is a unique bond. Note how I focus there on internalization rather than attachment (Benjamin, 1988)—his unconvincing "yes" calls me out. Gerson (1996) made the case that resistance in analysis is mutually constructed, and I think that here, as elsewhere in the vignettes I present, we can see my difficulty acknowledging what I am for Jesse and what I feel for him. As I suggested in my opening vignette about my own analysis, I had practiced my own form of maternal resistance. I recall rarely feeling any anxiety about my analyst's comings and goings, and yet, on the couple of occasions when I ran into her unexpectedly I nearly fainted. As an analyst, I generally experience little conscious resistance to being a nurturing and caretaking presence (except during certain moments of impasse), but it is something quite different to acknowledge my own attachment and dependence. I wonder about the effects this difficulty has on the course and ending of analyses. Despite the fact that both Jesse and I found ourselves subject to an unconscious drift toward a culturally normative maternal resistance, I do think Jesse left analysis knowing a little more about what you need to have such that flowers might bloom in a desert.

Jesse's story suggests how maternal resistance lurks as a specter that haunts what we in the West experience as our autonomy. Jesse was in many ways quite successful at deploying a defensive version of autonomy, but he was nonetheless subject to the dominant cultural tendency to define autonomy, indeed masculinity, as a state in which you do not need anyone. For identities built on this defense, maternal resistance is a constant companion, and dependence, maternal care, and intimate connection are a threat to identity. The developmental prescription that one must get away from an engulfing mother, a staple of so much prefeminist literature on male gender development, well captures the way cultural norms of masculinity become lived psychic states. This literature never acknowledges how great the cost is, to self and other, of getting away; too often the cost of not acknowledging attachment is the perpetuation of a lonely and omnipotent version of autonomy. There is no way to know what you have lost if you constantly need to defend against letting another in, against recognizing the ways in which we are mutually interdependent. And when we do not allow ourselves to know what we have lost, we continue to legitimize the definition of autonomy that rests on maternal resistance.

CHRIS

In some cases, the resistance to acknowledging our own dependence and attachment to the patient, a resistance that marks the practice of therapy, produces maternal resistance in the patient. Chris ended his treatment with an out of character attack on me and on therapy. He had been in once-weekly treatment for about 5 years, and he had even more hatred of his "weak, unmanly" dependent feelings than Jesse. Chris had been doing some very important therapy work in which, for the first time, he felt less subject to what his wife and others thought about him and more secure about what he was thinking and doing. Unlike his more typical defensive escapes into a withdrawn and withholding isolation, he was feeling both separate and connected. And just when he was fruitfully working on this, he came to my office at the wrong time and I was not there. In the next session, he was apologetic about getting the time wrong, and he reported dreams and associations that suggested he was feeling ignored and that he was angry about being asked to pay for something he did not get. He insisted he had no hurt or angry feelings about the missed session. But in the next session he reported that he did not want to introspect and come up with "yet another problem." And then, two sessions after that, he came in very annoyed and angry, reported that he had to leave early, and told me that he has been dreading coming the past few times and does not know what he is getting from therapy. After awhile, he admitted to being angry and told me that the feeling he has is "Leave Me Alone." But while he did wonder if he might be afraid to find out why he had become such a solitary man, he insisted he wanted to end the treatment. I suggested he come three more times (the sessions left in the month) and that we try to understand more about his sudden desire to leave.

In the next session, he said several critical things about therapy, and said them in a very snotty tone: "I'm sick of picking at scabs" and the like. I was quite perplexed about the hostility. I imagined it stemmed from the rejection of the missed session, but he truly did not think it had anything to do with that. Then I wondered if his anger had to do with his (characteristic) difficulty asking for what he wants. The mood lightened and immediately softened. He said he imagined that if he were to say he wanted to stop and that he was feeling good, I would feel rejected and I would say, "Are you kidding? You're not ready." So he went on the offense (and, parenthetically, did become rejecting). He found this moment quite important and, as soon as these feelings were in the room, he began to talk more about how good he had been feeling lately. He expressed gratitude about therapy and talked about what he might want to focus on if he were at some point to return to therapy. The last two sessions were full of feeling; he reported a dream about being in his old house but now the house had a lot more rooms that he had never been in before; he expressed pride in what he had accomplished in therapy, particularly his new sense of comfort in his own skin; again, he expressed gratitude.

What to make of this? I was sure the anger had come from feelings around the missed session; the dreams and associations seemed to confirm it. But in the end I was convinced by the feeling in the room that what had happened was that he was ready to end treatment and he thought that if he did not end angrily, I would not let him leave. So in the final moments of treatment, an inability to ask for what he wanted and an assumption that I would cling to him was translated into a scene of maternal resistance: "Leave me alone." Maybe he had unconsciously staged the scene by coming at the wrong time and giving himself good cause to feel rejected, angry, and left on his own. But perhaps he was not so off the mark in thinking that a therapist would have a hard time letting a patient end. For we also resist loss and resist acknowledging our dependency on our patients. In this case, I in fact did think there was more work to be done. But because of how it all went, I did not argue with Chris, and perhaps that allowed him to let down some maternal resistance and to come to know something of what he was losing.

KYRA

For an alternative view on knowing what is lost and how it affects the ending of treatment, I return to Kyra. When Kyra first told me she was thinking of ending analysis, I found myself making a lot of unconscious "slips" that likely betrayed my sense of rejection. For various reasons, we had been doing analysis by phone for a few months before she brought this up. In the 2 weeks after she brought it up, I think I dropped the phone three times during our sessions, which I had never done before. And in one session, I walked with the phone into another room, which introduced static on the line. She said nothing about it then, but she dreamed that next night of encountering static on the phone while talking with someone in her life with whom communication had historically been quite difficult. Busted. And for just the kind of thing Chris had feared, my own discomfort dealing with someone who expressed a wish to leave. With Jesse, too, I had found myself doing things that suggested I was hurt or mad or in some way reacting badly to the threat of loss. For example, I suddenly instituted a policy of charging for missed sessions even when given 24 hours' notice. He was furious, and his fury made me look again at what I was doing; I acknowledged to him that it was unfair. But perhaps I missed an opportunity to challenge maternal resistance when I did not acknowledge that I had instituted the policy as an unconscious reaction to painful loss. Again, it is moments such as these that make me conscious of my own tendencies to deny my dependence on my patients (Hirsch, 2008) and to deny the depth of my attachment.

As I mentioned above, Kyra, whose characteristic style is to bypass loss, wanted to end her analysis but did not want to stop coming altogether. In what follows, I want to try to tease out the difference between her tendency to bypass loss, which does have something to do with maternal resistance, and her wish to be in therapy for life, which I think poses a challenge to maternal resistance.

Kyra finds little to no relief in therapy—she is committed to honesty but hates bringing things up that she feels reflect some kind of badness in her; she also hates coming upon unconscious motivations and slips, because she thinks she ought to have been conscious of them. As best as we can tell, what happens to her is that when something painful comes up, she pushes it away. Sometimes she does this simply because whatever it is that comes up is too painful, but often there is an intermediate step: She thinks she ought to have been able to avoid what's caused her pain, and this leads to brutal self-recrimination. But the need to avoid painful thoughts also has something to do with a conscious and unconscious conviction that it will not help to turn to another for soothing. Yet, Kyra comes regularly to treatment and is open and affectively present. We are trying to understand more about why therapy offers so little relief.

Although therapy is not comfortable for her, she feels that she will always have "blind spots" and that therapy has and can continue to help her see what she may be blocking out before those blocked out things result in enactments that cause her greater suffering. Therapy is, of course, not the only route to growth, but there are few other cultural spaces that even acknowledge unconscious processes let alone make space for their emergence. Our analytic literature suggests that, ideally, a treatment is at an end when a patient can do analysis for herself. But perhaps this ideal reflects the cultural form of maternal resistance: If we believe in the unconscious, we must acknowledge that no one can really do that for themselves. Schafer (2002) writes that depressive anxiety and a false depressive position arise to avoid the "burdens of maturity" that termination demands. But if the "burdens of maturity" include the capacity not to need another to know oneself, perhaps that burden is in fact too much to bear. Although Freud (1937) begins his termination essay on a note of tough love, later in the essay he acknowledges that the need for another to help us know ourselves is ongoing throughout life and has little to do with maturity. Writing that both patient and analyst should go back into analysis every 5 years or so, Freud says: "This is as much as to say that not only the patient's analysis but that of the analyst himself is a task which is never finished" (p. 401).

Freud suggests that there are at least three reasons that one might need to return to analysis: the strength of an instinct could become greater and overwhelm the ego, part of the ego resists cure and cannot bear to look at truths that bring unpleasure, and there are some conflicts that are irreconcilable (more on that later). Kyra's reason for wanting to continue treatment resonates with Freud's second point: she acknowledges that there might always be resistance to looking at painful truths. Part of that resistance manifests in her difficulty turning to another as a soothing and containing object.* But her wish to continue treatment is more than an attempt to bypass loss and pain. I think that making the unconscious conscious is painful for Kyra, but I also think her wish to continue treatment throughout life suggests that there is more to the therapy experience than that for her: I think she experiences in treatment a rarely felt safety to "make mistakes," to have blind spots, without retaliatory recrimination, and, even though I know that she feels embarrassment about bringing her fragmented and conflicting parts to me, I also sense an excitement about having a place to bring them. Thus, I think that Kyra, consciously or unconsciously, is saying something akin to what I had felt at the end of my analysis, something that goes beyond blind spots and self-sabotaging instincts: it's the attachment, stupid. In one of her final sessions, Kyra had a dream that put her in touch with the loss of a language she and her mother had once shared. She and I, too, have developed and shared our own language, and I think her dream signaled an awareness that we could lose that in the shift from several to one session a week.

Before her analysis ended, Kyra excitedly realized that, ironically, her choice to shift into another form of treatment rather than leave put her more in touch with what she was losing than might otherwise have been the

---

* I first wrote "taking in" rather than "turning to," which again reflects the normative unconscious pull to favor "internalization" over attachment; see Benjamin (1988).

case. For, in fashioning this way of ending analysis, she had in fact made it impossible to enact what had been her characteristic style of ending a relationship: to walk away (like John Wayne) and never look back. Toward the end, she came to see that in several areas of her life, relationships that had to change did not, for that reason, have to be discarded. And so Kyra taught me quite a bit about termination—and shook up my relationship to analytic gospel.

CONCLUSION

I argued here that, because Western culture promotes an ideal of autonomy and mature adulthood that has classically been aligned with its ideal version of masculinity, both men and women experience maternal resistance in treatment—that is, both men and women tend to feel "weak" when they become conscious of their dependence on and attachment to a caretaking other, when they become conscious of how fluid and illusory the boundary is between self and other. And the therapist, too, is by no means immune to the collusive pull of these cultural norms.

Maternal resistance, when carried through to the end of treatment, makes it hard to know who or what you have lost, and therefore is an obstacle to mourning. Nonetheless, I have also suggested that cultural norms position women as dependent, so women often live with a paradox, what Freud might have called an irreconcilable conflict: a greater comfort with dependence than men have (because dependence is congruent with the norms of femininity) and a simultaneous awareness that dependence is for lower creatures (because masculinity is held out as the norm for proper human being). The form that dependence, once split off from autonomy, generally takes is a fearsome state. And so long as women continue to be the primary caretakers of children of both sexes—in a culture that values separation over dependence—connection to and separation from women will be highly fraught (Benjamin, 1988; Chodorow, 1978). Yet, my experience suggests that the "relational" female celebrated in much of feminist difference theory *does* have the more permeable boundaries that allow her to attach less fearfully. If second-wave feminist theory of gender development is to be believed, the female psychically constituted by traditional middle-class norms often values relationship above all else, even if this mode of attachment is fraught with hostile dependence (Layton, 1998). As a result of the feminist activism that accompanied second-wave theorizing, cultural norms changed, and younger middle-class women, who have been accepted into the halls of power, seem to have become more conflicted about the primacy of relationship (Layton, 2004a, 2004b). Kyra, who is in fact of that younger generation, can experience the wish to remain in treatment forever without feeling weak, even as she sometimes struggles against acknowledging the depth of the attachment and has difficulty finding relief in it.

Gender is central to maternal resistance in another perhaps more important and certainly less visible way: Cultural norms that split dependence and autonomy, and gender them female and male, respectively, express themselves in our theories as well as our practices. Although Balint, Fairbairn, Winnicott, and other British independents countered the classical disparagement of dependency, much of the analytic writing on termination is still grounded in the sexist discourse that makes dependence and interdependence separate from and secondary to a particular version of autonomy. But if we look carefully at such writing, we find that it often is not able consistently to sustain this false separation of dependence and autonomy. To illustrate, I will conclude by looking at the ways that Loewald, Bergmann, Schafer, and Freud simultaneously collude with and question sexist norms in their important papers on termination.

Loewald's (1988) thesis is that the most important aspect of termination is mourning, which he goes on to describe in terms of a relationship that becomes an internal structure, much like the way the superego develops from the dissolution of the Oedipus complex. He does, however, at a later point in the essay, acknowledge the significance of the real relationship. There he notes that internalization is not only about reconstituting a renounced lost object (pp. 164–165). Indeed, in the case of ending an analysis, he writes, the mourning has a communal aspect. The analyst helps the patient mourn. For Loewald, this is evidence of the "nonmourning elements of internalization" (p. 165), but I think that it is rather evidence of a relationship like no other, a relationship that, again, were it not for time and money, one might be "crazy" to want to give up.

Bergmann (1997) is clearer about the significance of the real relationship. Loewald keeps his interesting aside in the frame of internalization, and Bergmann seems to struggle against his own recognition that there is something "crazy" about ending the analytic relationship. He writes:

> In real life, we encounter three types of termination of human relationships: geographical separation, transformation of a friendly or love relationship into a hostile one, and death. The analysand, however, is supposed to bring about separation under conditions of love and gratitude. All life experience runs against such a termination. (p. 168)

Yet, he addresses this by focusing on fantasy, idealization, and the fact that the analytic relationship makes few demands on the patient in comparison to relationships outside of analysis. He goes on to say that what is mourned is not the analyst but the loss of a part of the self, often an infantile one (p. 169). He speaks of the analyst's need to foster "the necessary ego strength for termination" (p. 171). And yet, just after this paragraph, with reference to what he has learned from former patients who return when confronted with a terminal illness, he says, "...these returning analysands have convinced me with particular force that the analyst remains the libidinal object often of last resort" (p. 171).

The back and forth movement strikes me as having more than a pinch of maternal resistance. Where in these descriptions are the elements that create the love of which Bergmann speaks? What about recognition, understanding, empathy, and the willingness to bear the patient's pain and even his or her assaults, the willingness to work through relational impasses, the willingness to make oneself vulnerable to the patient?—all of which, in one way or another, have been traditionally aligned with norms of femininity. The denial or downplaying of these aspects of the real relationship makes these theories of termination ring somewhat hollow to me.

Schafer (2007) presents what I consider one of the more compelling cases for the need to terminate as well as compelling criteria for termination. He writes that we all live with what he calls tragic knots, "a recognizably fateful situation that is insufficiently under (our) control" (p. 1152). In these situations, "each course of action will involve suffering, impairment, or loss for the self, of the self, or in the lives of loved others" (p. 1152). Schafer endorses what he believes to be Freud's final understanding of a reality principle inclusive of both the pain and joy of living: "the ego's ideal relation to reality is one in which it recognizes and accepts the emotional costs of attachment to that which will be lost and the affirmation of values held dear whatever the risk" (p. 1164). And so he turns to the crucial question that determines readiness for termination: has the analysand reached "the inclusiveness that manifests a stronger, more reliable, even if inconstant adherence to the reality principle? This is the inclusiveness that takes in the inevitability of existentially based tragic knots in life after analysis. It also takes in a readiness to reflect on conflictual intrapsychic and interpersonal responses to these knots and their consequences" (p. 1167). Schafer does not minimize the loss of the analytic relationship:

> And to top it off, termination of an effective, meaningful analysis may itself be regarded as a grand knot, for it requires, at one and the same time, voluntary participation in losing and mourning one of the most special relationships one has ever had and yet accepting, even if not fully—never fully—the idea that it is unrealistic and might be counterproductive to defer termination or try to block it. A sense of falseness will hang over analyses that are unduly prolonged. (p. 1167)

This last statement is certainly true, particularly if either analyst, patient, or both fall prey to the fantasy that all conflicts will be resolved at the end of an analysis, or if idealization of the analyst has not been analyzed (idealization and good-enough attachment are not the same thing—good-enough attachment requires recognition of the analyst's fallibility). But what of Kyra's recognition that it always takes more than one to understand what is going on in oneself? Is it *necessarily* "unrealistic" or "immature" to want to stay in analytic treatment?

Finally, we come to Freud (1937), who, as so often, sheds much light on the source of even his own contradictions. Freud's late work, "Analysis Terminable and Interminable," is truly a remarkable essay. For the most part, it is remarkable in its depth and in its humility about what analysis can accomplish. But its ending is remarkable for being just the kind of non sequitur that I drew attention to in the opening of this essay, Freud's tendency simultaneously to acknowledge and then enact or disavow maternal resistance. As I said earlier, Freud argues in this essay that the task of analysis, for both patient and analyst, is likely to be interminable, never finished. In the final section of the essay, Freud gives what seems to be a third reason for this: irreconcilable conflict. Two such conflicts are proposed as examples. The first has to do with resistance to bisexuality, and Freud suggests that it is the death instinct (not homophobia) that makes so many people unable to experience sexual desire for both sexes. The paper then ends with the second irreconcilable conflict, which Freud calls analytic bedrock and defines as the "repudiation of femininity" common to both sexes. He elaborates: bedrock in men is the refusal to adopt a passive attitude in relation to other men, in short, castration anxiety; in women it is the wish for a penis. My fantasy is that Freud is in fact talking about "maternal resistance," and that what is being repudiated in both sexes are feelings of dependence and mutual interdependence. Because they are defined in opposition to autonomy, such feelings are experienced not as safe, secure, and pleasurable, but as dangerous, helpless, and weak. My fantasy is that, were autonomy and dependence not split, we would discover much healthier versions of each (Layton, 1998). Then we could have a different conversation about termination, and about so many other things. For example, we could look more honestly at our lifelong dependency on another to help us know ourselves.

Maternal resistance is a particular version of bypassing mourning that is embedded in cultural norms as well as in individual psyches. It is manifest not only in the long psychoanalytic history of not attending to termination, but also and primarily in defining mourning and termination in terms that have to do with being an autonomous mature adult. A patient of mine once reported that a psychiatrist–psychoanalyst supervisor told her that if she was serious about her career, she would switch to a training analyst and get going already. She and I were both rather horrified to realize that, for this prominent analyst, her attachment to her therapist of 5 years meant nothing. Fraught with the wish to avoid loss altogether as Kyra's challenge to orthodoxy may be, we might want to think twice before pathologizing it as immature. Most of us are terrified of acknowledging our need for others, particularly in a culture that defines dependence in opposition to autonomy. Too often the feared state of helpless dependency is conflated with attachment; in repudiating the former, one loses the capacity to experience the pleasures of the latter. Because maternal resistance haunts our experiences of autonomy in the West, it is very hard to know what you have lost at the end of an analysis, a prerequisite of mourning.

I am not arguing for or against terminating analysis; rather, I am arguing for a greater recognition of the significance of attachment and the real relationship to the process of analysis and the process of ending, or not ending, treatment. At the end of the termination essay, Freud notes that Ferenczi (1927) felt that the overcoming of "bedrock" was necessary to a successful analysis. If bedrock is "the repudiation of femininity," I suppose I am saying the same. A successful treatment, I would argue, should produce a version of autonomy that is not in split opposition to dependency: it should produce an agency based in connection, a relational autonomy. What we have lost when we end treatment will differ for different people, but perhaps we can only truly be in touch with what we have lost if we have attained some capacity for relational autonomy. And when we are truly in touch with what we have lost, we might, as I did and do, at least wonder why on earth anyone would want to end.

REFERENCES

Balint, M. (1969). *The basic fault*. London: Tavistock
Benjamin, J. (1988). *The bonds of love*. New York: Pantheon.
Bergmann, M. S. (1997). Termination: The Achilles heel of psychoanalytic technique. *Psychoanalytic Psychology*, 14, 163–174.
Butler, J. (2004). Violence, mourning, politics. In *Precarious life* (pp. 19–49). London: Verso.
Chodorow, N. (1978). *The reproduction of mothering*. Berkeley: University of California Press.
Davies, J. M. (2005). Transformations of desire and despair: Reflections on the termination process from a relational perspective. *Psychoanalytic Dialogues*, 15, 779–805.
Dimen, M. (1991). Deconstructing difference: Gender, splitting, and transitional space. *Psychoanalytic Dialogues*, 1, 335–352.
Dinnerstein, D. (1976). *The mermaid and the Minotaur*. New York: Harper & Row.
Eichenbaum, L., & Orbach, S. (1999/1983). *What do women want? Exploding the myth of dependency*. New York: Berkley.
Fairbairn, W. R. D. (1943). The repression and return of bad objects. In *Psychoanalytic studies of the personality* (pp. 59–81). London: Routledge & Kegan Paul, 1952.
Ferenczi, S. (1927/1955). The problem of the termination of the analysis. In M. Balint (Ed.), *Final contributions to the problems and methods of psycho-analysis* (pp. 77–86). London: Hogarth.

Freud, S. (1917). Mourning and melancholia. In J. Strachey (Ed. & Trans.), *The standard edition of the complete psychological works of Sigmund Freud* (Vol. 14, pp. 239–258). London: Hogarth.

Freud, S. (1925). Some psychical consequences of the anatomical distinction between the sexes. In J. Strachey (Ed. & Trans.), *The standard edition of the complete psychological works of Sigmund Freud* (Vol. 21, pp. 243–258). London: Hogarth.

Freud, S. (1933). Femininity. In J. Strachey (Ed. & Trans.), *The standard edition of the complete psychological works of Sigmund Freud* (Vol. 22, pp. 112–135). London: Hogarth.

Freud, S. (1937). Analysis terminable and interminable. *International Journal of Psycho-Analysis*, *18*, 373–405.

Gerson, S. (1996). Neutrality, resistance, and self-disclosure in an intersubjective psychoanalysis. *Psychoanalytic Dialogues*, *6*, 623–645.

Goldner, V. (1991). Toward a critical relational theory of gender. *Psychoanalytic Dialogues*, *1*, 249–272.

Harris, A. (2005). *Gender as soft assembly*. Hillsdale, NJ: Analytic Press.

Hirsch, I. (2008). *Coasting in the countertransference: Conflicts of self-interest between analyst and patient*. New York: Analytic Press.

Layton, L. (1998). *Who's that girl? Who's that boy? Clinical practice meets postmodern gender theory*. Hillsdale, NJ: Analytic Press.

Layton, L. (2004a). Working nine to nine: The new women of prime time. *Studies in Gender and Sexuality*, *5*(3), 351–369.

Layton, L. (2004b). Relational no more: Defensive autonomy in middle-class women. In J. A. Winer & J. W. Anderson (Eds.), *The annual of psychoanalysis* (Vol. 32): *Psychoanalysis and women* (pp. 29–57). Hillsdale, NJ: Analytic Press.

Layton, L. (2006). Racial identities, racial enactments, and normative unconscious processes. *Psychoanalytic Quarterly*, *75*(1), 237–269.

Levenson, E. (1976). The aesthetics of termination. *Contemporary Psychoanalysis*, *12*, 338–341.

Loewald, H. (1988). Termination analyzable and unanalyzable. *Psychoanalytic Study of the Child*, *43*, 155–166.

Novick, J. (1997). Termination conceivable and inconceivable. *Psychoanalytic Psychology*, *14*, 145–162.

Salberg, J. (2009). Leaning into termination. *Psychoanalytic Dialogues, 19*(6), 703–722.

Schafer, R. (2002). Experiencing termination: Authentic and false depressive positions. *Psychoanalytic Psychology*, *19*, 235–253.

Schafer, R. (2007). The reality principle, tragic knots, and the analytic process. *Journal of the American Psychoanalytic Association*, *55*(4), 1151–1168.

Sprengnether, M. (1990). *The spectral mother*. Ithaca: Cornell University Press.

Stolorow, R. D. (2007). *Trauma and human existence: Autobiographical, psychoanalytic, and philosophical reflections*. New York: Analytic Press.

Winnicott, D. W. (1969). The use of an object and relating through identifications. In *Playing and reality* (pp. 86–94). London: Tavistock, 1971.

Part III

Musings on the multiple meanings of ending

Chapter 12

Afterwardness and termination

Bruce Reis

Termination. The word sounds so...final. But what ends? Or, we may ask, in ending, how does an analysis go on past its end? Is the termination of a psychoanalysis like the termination of a life—perhaps in some ways it is. But then it surely is not that either, as both analyst and analysand very much continue to live and breathe, and even analyze their dreams and fantasies. They just no longer do that together. So is the termination of an analysis more than about the termination of a relationship? Analyst and patient no longer formally meet to exchange their mutual insights and reactions. They do not physically meet at least. But does that mean that they are no longer in a psychical relation to each other? And is not my patient always, in some very important ways including psychically, forever my patient, even after the termination of our analysis? If I were to encounter my former patient in a restaurant, at the theater, or walking down the street with his family, do I not continue to have particular responsibilities and limitations toward him; as well as strong feelings of love or frustration past the time that we have discontinued our meeting? At what point do we believe that countertransference ends? Or transference?

As analysts, we think of psychoanalysis as a discrete process of steps, and treatment as organized around "issues." This is what is done in the initial consultation. Now the patient is working on transferential issues relating to her mother. Dissociated material is being symbolized, losses are being mourned, and we know what the resolution of these issues is supposed to look like. The patient starts a new relationship. She gets married! At long last he stops working so hard, realizing that the approval he always sought is not likely to come from slaving at the law firm. Eventually we are in the termination phase and I can open my responses more fully. And then with a nod, a handshake, or a hug, we are done. It is all very schematic, very procedural, like a process that we already know the outcome of. Termination seems complete because it is the end of a story that we wove on the first day of our meeting with the patient, and saw through to its expectable conclusion. There is great comfort in telling this story time and time again, as a repetition compulsion that insists on the analyst's control and understanding.

Stopping an analysis is a peculiar notion, lodged in a unidirectional schema of time where after one "stops" the analysis is over. In this notion there is an "after" to the analysis, as well as a before that precedes this ending. Yet psychically we cannot abide the cleanliness of this determination, as we know that our feelings toward patient or analyst continue past this "stopping." Until now it has only been possible to regard these feelings as failures of the analysis or of the analyst. But we may say, with some degree of confidence, that a psychoanalysis never stops at its end and never ends at its stopping.

How would the story read if it were told differently? It would be changed if we broke the linear, sequential narrative of complaint, treatment phases (that is, enactment), and resolution. So many of our case studies read this way, like little novellas, or moral plays. It is such an implicit form for the consideration of a treatment that a patient's ending analysis on his or her own, or dying in the middle of the analysis is referred to as an abrupt termination, because it flies in the face of what we agreed should be the proper ending to the story. This idea of termination is so ingrained, so agreed upon, that it is even hard, very hard, to think about the subject of termination in any other way. And when we do try to think about it in other ways, a great deal of what we count on as expectable is upended and our own magical thinking about psychoanalysis, as well as our being situated in a real and unpredictable world is revealed.

In a heartbreakingly beautiful report of a patient's dying, Marshall (2008) describes the utter shock of losing a 10-year analytic relationship to an unexpected traffic accident. In this case, the termination was, very literally, like the termination of a life. But that did not mean that the relationship ended with the death of the patient. Marshall finds in Freud assurance of the permanence of loving attachments, and she writes:

> My lost patient seems still present in my office as I look at a plant or pick up my water glass and recall her pithy comments about these incidental objects. I notice a letter from her among the papers on my desk, her neat handwriting poking out of the pile. She is still here, communicating with me. She is all over the place. Her words and mind seem to have touched everything in my work space. (p. 226)

Marshall lays bare her struggle around her attachment to and her detaching from her patient, and how she has to fight against coming to some rational closure, rather than allowing irresolution. In facing the existential contingency of a life, Marshall rejects the "silent fictions" (p. 232) she finds arising from her self, the stories that seek to explain and understand what happened.

Marshall's use of Freud to describe the experience of the permanence of loving attachments in the context of their loss opens us to a truth that is too easily obscured by common assumptions we apply to ourselves and to our worlds. Our assumption is that time flows in a unilinear direction and takes the form of a single stream of experience. Freud's (1917) conception of the problem of loss and mourning was, ingeniously, to realize that we keep the lost object alive. By the survivor's introjecting or identifying with the lost object, that object lives on, after its loss. Freud was flirting with a nonlinear temporality, beginning to dislodge our feeling that time and memory are ordered through a clear sense of before and after. Marshall (2008) writes that her patient was "gone but not yet gone" (p. 222), refusing to think of this as a denial of reality, and instead describing for us the experience of a "dual reality" where time does not march in a horizontal line of succession, but where past and present coexist.

TERMINATION AND AFTERWARDNESS

The death of a patient or of an analyst is not the way analyses generally end. More often, good-byes are said, after a period of review and continued work. The patient may transition from couch to chair to signal to all involved that something is ending. Finally, analyst and patient go their separate ways and the analysis is considered concluded. But how, as I asked earlier, does an analysis go on beyond its ending? And in what ways is this ending not an ending?

In taking up the topic of the memory of childhood sexualized experiences, Freud proposed that a system of *delay* occurs, between the original experience which is not coded as sexual, and the later, retrospective attribution of sexual meaning to that experience. The subsequent attribution of this meaning, Freud proposed, opened up the experience as fully sexual or sexualized. Freud (1896) wrote in a letter to Fliess that "Our psychical mechanism has come into being by a process of stratification: the material presence in the form of memory-tracing being subject from time to time to a re-arrangement in accordance with fresh circumstances—to a re-transcription" (p. 223) Laplanche (1998) critically extended the Freudian notion of delay into one of "afterwardness" wherein a nonlinear form of temporality disrupts the notion of causality that extends from the past to the present. For Laplanche, temporal vectors of past and present coexist in the moments in which the individual attempts the translation and transcription of earlier experience. In a manner of speaking, Laplanche is asserting that a trauma only becomes a trauma later on, after meaning is attributed to the event, and so the experience is at the time not fully an experience of something traumatic, and the boundaries of that experience do not confine themselves to the past. Similarly, we might say that an analysis is continually reworked through time and memory, and that its narratives and conclusions remain open to rearrangement, in this manner of afterwardness, past the formal end of the analysis. Earlier (Reis, 2006) I wrote:

> Who has had an analysis and not continued it after the official good-bye of termination? New experience calls forth memory, and memory itself changes shape....A ray of sun, a moment in conversation, or nothing apparent at all will immediately reopen the analysis, even in the context of its finality. It used to be said that much of the most important work of an analysis was done during the termination phase, but perhaps that was too hasty. Perhaps much of the most important work of an analysis is done after termination occurs, through a deferred action, an après coup, a *nachträglichkeit*. We would be foolish to think that the therapeutic effect of an analysis stops at its termination and does not continue its work years past the formal ending of analyst and patient's meeting. (p. 601)

To access memory is to change that memory. This understanding is based on current conceptions of memory, its storage, and its retrieval. Rather than think of memory as having been set, these ideas of memory and its transformations recognize that memory is a mutable and ever-changing process (e.g., Schacter, 2004). Memory is never complete. In the laboratory Freeman (1999) demonstrated that when young rabbits are first exposed to a new smell, such as carrots, a pattern of neural activation is established. He later introduced those same rabbits to a second smell, turnips for instance, and found a different pattern of neural activation to have been established in response to that smell. But, Freeman found that the neural activation pattern in response to carrots was changed by the introduction of the neural activation pattern responsive to turnips; and when a third smell was introduced with its own pattern of activation, the two previous patterns were altered. Daniel Stern (2004) noted that Freeman's experiment demonstrated that

> The past is always being permanently revised, both as a neural pattern and as an experience of recall. Or to put it more strongly, the present can change the past. Of course it does not change it from a historical perspective, but it is changed functionally and experientially, and that is where we live. (p. 201)

Because we are so accustomed to thinking about the past as the personal property of an individual, we may be closed to thinking of memory in such ways. But what if the past was not conceived as merely a dead repository of events, or as an archive passively awaiting the present that will recover it? What if the accessing of memory constantly changed memory? Could we then not say that a memory is not finished, or might never be finished? And if memory can never be "fixed," because it is always changing in these ways, then is the analysis or its work ever really finished at termination? When I ask my patient about a detail of an experience, or how something felt, or why he never understood something in a particular way, I am becoming a part of that memory. Memories and histories are not isolated in consciousness but are part of an intersubjective field that shapes and creates experience as it is discovered. They are fluid and context dependent rather than events already stored in one's head.

Bonovitz (2007) writes of the "inevitable incompleteness" of termination as a "finality juxtaposed with incompleteness." I agree with his position, and I would add that this incompleteness progresses after the analysis toward an unreachable ending in this process of après coup. Thus, years after an analysis, memory may be cued by affect, or affect by memory and reworking continues in the present context of a past moment. I very much think that this is how people really operate—that they do not completely address all of their issues in the here and now of the treatment and then are done with them—they revisit these issues as they come up months or years after the treatment ends. Thus, to use Bonovitz's felicitous phrase, the finality of treatment is interspersed with the inevitable experience of the incompleteness of a terminable analysis.

Perhaps it is something that was denied in the treatment, that now one realizes is actually the case about oneself; or alternately, perhaps one insisted on a perspective that he or she felt the analyst could not abide, and later gleaned the truth of that perspective. These are examples of analysis reopened, of a conversation continued, and developed, past its formal ending. For those of us who have treated patients in a second analysis, it is clear that they continue to dialogue with their former analysts while sitting with us. For those of us who have undertaken our own second analyses, it is clear that idiomatic themes and dynamics will repeat, now having been partly shaped by their engagement with the first analyst.

TERMINATION AND THE ANALYST'S VULNERABILITIES

Some analysts are very good at getting to the aggressive parts of a patient's personality. They are known in analytic communities for the importance they place on addressing these issues in the treatments they conduct, and often patients are referred to them for just this reason. Yet at the same time as these analysts are helping their patients transferentially work through archaic aggression, they are likely not helping them work on issues of intimacy. Every analyst is limited in professional and personal ways. The analyst who works so well with aggression may not work as well or give as much analytic "air time" to matters of intimacy; and the analyst who works so well with trauma and traumatized patients may not accord an important enough place for the role of the patient's aggression. It seems obvious to state that the fiction of a completed analysis is based on the presupposition of a generic analyst who works equally well with, and can afford the patient an experience of working through the entire range of psychological issues that are likely to come up or need to be addressed in the analysis. Such an analyst would have a very full practice, and was this not the case when psychoanalysis enjoyed its heyday in a postwar America that believed in science and the scientific conduct of an analysis that would reveal to knowing, and thus to cure, the buried complexes of an infantile past.

What termination makes plain is the analyst's failed omnipotence and narcissism. There is no resolution as the term implies, no final determination. Issues are worked on, as much as they can be worked on, with this analyst, at this time, and termination is more of the end of this process, though I just argued that it is not even that. We live our lives according to the perspectives of our time. At a point in a life, one is only able to consider psychological issues from a particular vantage, yet at another point in time new developmental or life considerations lead to other evaluations. Because analysis is limited in time—it generally does not go on for decades—it will necessarily yield situated perspectives. There will be no final determinations.

Maybe what we mean by termination is really self referential to the analyst—that this is the termination of the patient's treatment with *me*, although both the patient and I know that it is not an ending at all. To think in terms of finality and cure is to think in terms of end states that psychoanalysis cannot approach—the resolution of all transferences that leaves a patient with a warm sense of gratitude and completion. I am suggesting here that this warm sense of gratitude and completion is itself the pat ending that gives lie to the method.

It is more likely that the mere mention of termination is enough to incite in analyst and patient a set of new iatrogenic anxieties that will not be soothed by the process that initiated them. Frankiel (2007) observed,

> Once termination is mentioned seriously and patients begin to press in earnest for gratification of one or more unconscious or preconscious transference fantasies, the analyst has to face whatever guilty feeling he or she may be prone to; it may be guilt over not having done enough, or done well enough, or whatever else reinforces fantasies of incompleteness and inferiority in doing ones' work. (p. 286)

But perhaps the analyst's guilty feelings about the work done are not limited to fantasy; and in addition to the press for gratification from the patient, there is also the analyst's inevitable coming to terms with both fantasy anxiety as well as actual limitation.

However, the analyst's terminology around termination would leave one thinking that resolution is still a possibility. We still hear talk of completed analyses, many years after it has been widely accepted that there is no such completion. Analysts have a very hard time accepting the reality of this situation, given their multiple investments in the patient, and their own theoretical and even personal goals for any analysis (Cooper, 1997). The truth is, however, that patients leave analysis constantly, and without the formal endings we would like to apply to their treatments. They leave to take work in another city. They leave because they are furious at us. They leave because they can no longer afford, or no longer value the work. Or they leave and come back, as so many patients do. In these situations our step-wise methods fail to do justice to the fluid, staccato, and even chaotic nature of our patients' lives, and our own lives, too. These are situations in which our own omnipotence and narcissism as analysts are challenged, situations in which we must confront a helplessness on the part of the analyst that is infrequently discussed in the literature. Consequently, we have no way of adequately conceptualizing these situations within the schematic, step-wise narrative of termination that continues to prevail. In an article on the subject of sudden endings, Sapountzis (2007) deeply laments the abrupt ending of a child analysis, once again illustrating the narcissistic investment of the analyst, and the analyst's impotence:

> The violent ending left no room for further exploration of these thoughts and obliterated my efforts to establish contact, to understand. It was a denial, a violent dismissal of all that had transpired between me and Patrick. But for me, this was more than a denial. It was an assault on everything I believed and had tried to do, and made a mockery of my efforts, of what I valued and sought to become in my work. Worst, it rekindled countless times when I felt that the only option I had when faced with the fragility of my own parents who, just like Patrick's, could be not only irrational and overpowering, but also completely overwhelmed by their own inadequacies and defeats, was to deny my embarrassment, to numb my mind and soften my objections. (p. 307)

Sapountzis's remarkable candor provides a window into the vulnerability of the person of the analyst behind the employed method, and of the extraordinary vulnerabilities engendered in doing analytic work that could end at any moment.

THE FATE OF THE ANALYTIC OBJECT

One aspect of termination that receives very little attention from analysts is the question of what happens to the relationship with the analyst after the termination of the treatment. Bergmann (1988), having questioned the classical assumption of the resolution of transference in the termination of a psychoanalysis, wrote that the analyst remains important for the patient after the end of the analysis. Because Bergmann felt that the analyst inevitably became "the first reliable object" for the patient, the importance of the internalization and identification with this object precluded any consideration of transference resolution.

Object relations approaches have stressed the internalization of the analyst as a new object in the patient's psychic world. The analogy is to something like the implantation of a pace maker, that while not fixing the original problem, can by its presence serve to continue to right matters when they would otherwise have gone wrong. The level of the pace maker must be adjusted to allow the individual their own autonomy, that is to say, a reasonable degree of continued dependence, that permits them to continue their life, but now with additional degrees of freedom.

Mitchell (1997), having rejected the notion of the generic analyst as well as the myth of the completed analysis as the resolution of all transferences, asked the same question of what happens to the analytic relationship post termination. "What is the fate of the analytic object?" asked Mitchell, and his answer was surprisingly similar to the object relations answer. He concluded that "termination must result in important internalizations of and identifications with the analyst as an internal object. But if the patient's autonomy is to be preserved, these identifications must allow and nourish personal freedom and creativity rather than binding the patient through unconscious loyalties" (p. 26).

It is curious that Mitchell never developed this idea past its embeddedness in the language of internalized objects and identifications, but his focus was on the development of thought around the issue of autonomy and not termination *per se*. Staying within the language of object relations we find an intriguing observation by Winnicott (1971) that may be as applicable to the termination of an analysis as to the relinquishment of a cherished object. If Mitchell asked, "What is the fate of the analytic object," Winnicott asked, "What is the fate of the transitional object?" Winnicott's answer is fascinatingly without recourse to the language of object relations, indeed Winnicott expressly rejects these ideas for a much subtler one. The fate of the transitional object

> is to be gradually allowed to be decathected, so that in the course of years it becomes not so much forgotten as relegated to limbo. By this I mean that in health the transitional object does not "go inside" nor does the feeling about it necessarily undergo repression. It is not forgotten and it is not mourned. It loses meaning, and this is because the transitional phenomena have become diffused, have become spread out over the whole intermediate territory between "inner psychic reality"

and "the external world as perceived by two persons in common," that is to say, over the whole cultural field. (p. 5)

Winnicott offers a fate for the transitional object that is similar to the fate of the analytic relationship posttermination.* Its fate is not conclusive, neither is it experienced as lost or put out of the mind. By referring to a limbo, Winnicott is expressing a form of ending that is outside of the dichotomous distinction of completion or incompletion. Instead he suggests a creative "diffusion," something not done or undone, but something instead spread out over the whole intermediate territory. Most interestingly, Winnicott does not claim that the transitional object is internalized in some way; it does not, he says in his inimitable style, "go inside." Winnicott wrote little of psychic agencies or structures of the mind, preferring instead to focus on movements in relationships that make aliveness sustainable (Dodi Goldman, personal communication). The transitional object then is not implanted as an alien object that becomes part of the individual. Winnicott breaks from analytic thinking of the day that emphasized the internalization or identification with the analyst—the benefit to the patient of his becoming like his or her analyst (usually meaning taking in the analyst's presumed goodness), or replicating in himself his analyst's analyzing function.

Mourning is not indicated in Winnicott's conception of the fate of the transitional object, as ending does not mean a grim finality. Termination can be thought in Winnicott's terms as opportunity for the patient, by relegating the analyst to limbo, to discover his or her own inventiveness. The analyst has hopefully been helpful and has been able to play with the patient analytically. He has been used, so as to be of use, and now is left when the doing is done. Limbo then is the fate of a relationship that spreads out over the whole cultural field, neither lost, nor present in any recognizable sense other than in the creative apperception of continuing experience.

The fate of the transitional object is that it simply loses its meaning as its cathected power is spread out between our inner psychic reality and the world in which we live. As the experience of illusion with the analyst extends from consulting room to broadening areas of life, the individual can now engage more in a creative exchange with the world. To my mind this is a very beautiful way to describe the ongoing posttermination relationship with the analyst, or with the patient. In my own experience, when a patient has left treatment I continue to think of them, sometimes continuously, and sometimes the memory of them comes in a flash. Patients do not so much feel lost to me as they feel somewhere between the experience we had together and their subsequent lives in the world. To the degree that

---

* My comparison of the fate of the transitional object to the process of termination has been informed by conversation with Dodi Goldman who was kind enough to share his expertise of Winnicott's oeuvre with me.

a patient feels implanted in me (or me in them, I would argue) that is an indication that termination has not followed the course of "health" that Winnicott proposed.

REFERENCES

Bergmann, M. S. (1988). On the fate of the intrapsychic image of the psychoanalyst after termination. *Psychoanalytic Study of the Child, 43*, 137–153.
Bonovitz, C. (2007). Termination never ends: The inevitable incompleteness of psychoanalysis. *Contemporary Psychoanalysis, 43*, 229–246.
Cooper, S. H. (1997). Interpretation and the psychic future. *International Journal of Psychoanalysis, 78*, 667–681.
Frankiel, R. (2007). The long good-bye: Omnipotence, pathological mourning and the patient who cannot terminate. In B. Willock, L. Bohm, & R. Curtis (Eds.), *On death and endings* (pp. 281–292). London: Routledge.
Freeman, W. (1999). *How brains make up their minds*. London: Weidenfeld and Nicholson.
Freud, S. (1896). Letter 52, 6 December 1896. In J. Strachey (Ed. & Trans.), *The standard edition of the complete psychological works of Sigmund Freud* (Vol. 1, p. 223). London: Hogarth.
Freud, S. (1917). Mourning and melancholia. In J. Strachey (Ed. & Trans.), *The standard edition of the complete psychological works of Sigmund Freud* (Vol. 14, pp. 237–258). London: Hogarth.
Laplanche, J. (1998). *Essays on otherness* (J. Fletcher, Ed.). New York: Routledge.
Marshall, K. (2008). Treating mourning: Knowing loss. *Contemporary Psychoanalysis, 44*(2), 219–233.
Mitchell, S. A. (1997). *Influence and autonomy in psychoanalysis*. Hillsdale, NJ: Analytic Press.
Reis, B. (2006). Time passes: Commentary on paper by Jody Messler Davies. *Psychoanalytic Dialogues, 16*(5), 599–602.
Sapountzis, I. (2007). On sudden endings and self-imposed silences. In B. Willock, L. Bohm, & R. Curtis (Eds.), *On death and endings* (pp. 303–318). London: Routledge.
Schacter, D. L. (2004). When memory sins. In J. T. Cacioppo & G. C. Berntson (Eds.), *Essays in social neuroscience* (pp. 93–105). Cambridge, MA: MIT Press.
Stern, D. (2004). *The present moment in psychotherapy and everyday life*. New York: Norton & Company.
Winnicott, D. W. (1971). Transitional objects and transitional phenomena. In *Playing and reality* (pp. 1–25). New York: Routledge.

Chapter 13

Termination in psychoanalysis

It's about time

Neil J. Skolnick

Termination, the end or ending of a psychoanalytic treatment, presents the analyst and the patient with challenges both unique to the occasion and emblematic of the entire treatment endeavor. Issues analyzed and reanalyzed throughout the therapy rear their heads as if to give one more dying gasp before crossing over the line into postanalysis space and time. Enactments of multiple self and other configurations (Davies, 2005), both internal and external, once again take center stage, also preparing for their flying solo following the final session. At the same time, the very real here and now inevitability of separation casts its effects on the two players as they struggle to reconcile the closeness they achieved with the ultimate end of that very same closeness. Similar to a loss, but not quite the same, how do both analyst and patient maintain an internal connection while losing the other?

The concept of termination appeared in the psychoanalytic lexicon following Joan Riviere's translation of Freud's (1937) paper, *Die Undliche und Die Unendliche Analyse*, as "Analysis Terminable and Interminable." Actually, the etymological understanding of the word *termination* to indicate the end of a psychoanalytic treatment is somewhat puzzling. As pointed out by others (Schlesinger, 2005), Riviere's translation was a curious one because there are no roots to the word *termination* in the German language. Others (Leupold-Lowenthal, 1988) suggested alternate translations such as finite and infinite which capture the greater richness of the original German.

Interestingly, Freud's intent in writing the paper did not have much to do with the process of ending an analysis. He was primarily concerned with spelling out the criteria for a successful ending of treatment. These criteria provided a bookend to his earlier considerations of the specific criteria for analyzability. Using the structural hallmarks of id and ego, he pronounced those patients who suffered from a traumatic event as being the only candidates to achieve successful analyses. He states that the most successful endings occur in patients in whom there was a genuine trauma. Furthermore, he pronounced those patients with excessive libido or alteration in the ego unable to achieve a viable conclusion to their analytic work.

So we see that Freud was not particularly concerned with the process of ending a treatment in the very article which, through a slip of translation, gave us the name to the process of ending a treatment. The term he used to refer to the end of treatment, *Undliche*, was not translated aptly into English to capture the richness of the process that occurs at the end of a psychoanalytic therapy. Nevertheless, the word *termination* stuck and has been used widely to refer both to the end of a psychoanalysis and the process of ending a psychoanalysis.

This paper will examine aspects of termination from a relational model. I maintain that a relational model applied to the end of an analysis captures more of the fluidity and texture than traditional models. It sits squarely in a two-person psychology so that it wrestles with the end of a mutual relationship that has focused on the analyst's process, the patient's process, and the interaction of the two. The loss of the analytic relationship, by relational definition, includes the struggles, both internally and externally of both the analyst and the patient as they prepare to, and ultimately do, separate. More traditional models focus primarily on the patient's loss of the analyst. Like the analytic work, the drama of termination is cocreated and lived by both the treater and treated in intrapsychic as well as interpersonal space.

What happens when the patient exits the scene for the last time? Is it necessarily the last time? Is mourning the most apt metaphor with which to consider the process of termination? What changes occur in both the therapist and the analysand after the treatment is over? What remains of the analytic connection and the unique configuration of two people that has been profound, intense, and hopefully mutagenic? Why are some terminations easier or harder for the analyst to endure than others? What constitutes a bad termination?

Of the many ironies we come to live with as psychoanalysts is that the intimate, genuine, authentic relationship we strive to create with our patients comes to an end. Especially in relatively successful treatments, but by no means limited to them, we come to know an enormous amount about the makeup of our patients, their strivings, their fears, their cherished successes and their humiliating failures, and their secrets, loves, and hatreds. And yet, the relationship ends relatively abruptly, and the person ventures back into his or her world, and then we know nothing. Even though we can spend weeks, months, and even years preparing our patients for the end of treatment, when it arrives, the patient evaporates into the world, and we are left clueless about the continuing sagas of their lives. Like a death, we mourn them and they mourn us, but unlike a death, both parties undergo a mourning process, an impossibility with actual death, when mourning is limited to the person remaining alive. The nature, depth, and length of mourning can be influenced by the nature, quality and affective tone of the relationship. Our affective responses toward our patients can achieve a full palate. At one time or another with all our patients and at different times with the same patient, we can fall in love, have sexual feelings, struggle with enormous rage or hate, admire, envy, be disgusted or proud, become frustrated or in awe, to name just a few of the possibilities. Then we have to say goodbye. Again, our responses to the therapy ending can be as varied and complex as our feelings evoked toward the patients during the therapy. I have found my feelings ranging from painful sadness and loss to apathetic indifference to good riddance! At times, particularly when experiencing sadness at the impending loss, I have felt it helpful to share some of my reactions with the patient. But I have no doubt it is also helpful for me as well. It is important to keep in mind that the processing of the end of therapy, like the therapy itself, needs to be focused on the patient's needs, not our own, to avoid, as Fairbairn (1958) cautioned, exploitation of the patient in the service of our own needs. But I do maintain that some modicum of authentic expression of our struggle with separation at the finalizing of a therapy can be enormously helpful in normalizing the patient's struggle with these difficult feelings.

In any event, we more often than not are clueless to each other's lives once the relationship is severed. What becomes of the patient becomes, in our mind, a mixture of hope and fear for their future life. We work in a field with only a precious few indications of our efficacy. And these become even less following the departure of our patients. What becomes remembered, forgotten, or distorted? How does the patient fare? How do we fare in their memory? Most of the time, we simply do not know. Like a death, the rest is silence. We need to be aware of our complex reactions to termination, continually monitoring our own as well as our patient's experience. We sometimes have a rarified glimpse into a patient's experience following termination, usually through reports by a third party. As I noted, occasionally, people return to treatment at some future date. We are then accorded a privileged opportunity to observe what has transpired since treatment ended. Has the change "stuck" or has the patient reverted to obsolete, less satisfying organizations of their psyche, ones that were neither adaptive nor beneficial to the cohesiveness and continuity of their self?

Just as the patient goes through a process of internalizing the ways of being with the analyst, so does the analyst go through a similar process. The multiple ways in which the analyst and patient relate to one another are internalized and referred to at the onset of separation. If the analyst has been woven into the patient's ways of being, so has the patient's being been similarly woven into the analyst. As Bass (2001) notes, "...neither is the same again for having met the other in the way they did, and the trajectory of both lives will not be quite the same for the encounter" (p. 783). We do, as the analysis spins out its narrative develop a set of intimate experiences that are unique to each patient–analyst dyad. Sometimes loving, sometimes not so loving, each patient can evoke within us just about any constellation of feelings that ultimately constitute extraordinarily intimate, authentic, and meaningful relationships. Relationships whose self and other intersubjective patterns become an integral part of our selves.

The reactions of therapists to the loss of their patient at termination are also a multifaceted, multidetermined event. How does one begin to cast the end of a therapy that has endured months, years, even decades? My question for the purposes of this paper is not to tease apart the multiplicities of endings, but to provide questions about the fate of each of our heroes as they return to life without the other.

ON BEYOND DEATH

The verb *to terminate*, taken out of the context of psychoanalysis is typically associated with sinister motives and connotations: to be separated from a job, for example, or end a pregnancy, or, of course, worse, to be rendered dead. Similarly, the process of termination in psychoanalysis has been likened to a death. In its most classical sense, the death referred to is the death of the possibility of gratifying infantile wishes by one's parents in life, and in analysis by the transference figure of the analyst. Theoretically, to end neurotic hope would serve to free libidinal energy to be utilized for more adaptive purposes by the ego, with new and better objects. In the homeostatic balance of the psyche, the end of neurotic hope and dread would be replaced by a more realistic hope and dread. But first a mourning process would need to take place in order to release one's energy from neurotic aims with old objects and redirect it toward new, more satisfactory aims with new objects. The work of mourning has been described well by Freud (1917) in "Mourning and Melancholia," and the work of mourning has traditionally been considered to be the work of termination. The predominant issues evoked during the analysis, particularly those of the transference neurosis, would be relived and reworked through one last time before the analyst and patient separate for a final time.

At some point during the history of analytic practice the convention changed. Although termination was still thought to represent a type of loss or death, it no longer was limited to the death of childhood wishes, but instead started to take on the meaning of the death of the analyst or the relationship with the analyst, both real and fantasized. Concepts of termination evolved, along with changes in the field of psychoanalysis, to derive less meaning rooted in drive psychology, and more of a meaning rooted in object relations. No longer did the end of an analysis evoke the relinquishing of drives, as much as it did the relinquishing of relationship. Our primary need for relationship (Fairbairn, 1952), unmoored from its role in bringing about libidinal gratification, now became the focus of a treatment termination. Relational theory posits that the most influential ingredient in the bringing about of change is to be found in the analytic relationship (Fairbairn, 1958; Skolnick, 2006). It naturally follows that the relationship should take its rightful place at the center of the termination process.

Even in its simplest form, the mourning of relationship during termination involves several different and overlapping mourning processes. First, the wished-for relationship with the analyst as a replacement for earlier unsatisfactory relationship templates needs to be relinquished. Closely related is the need to mourn the different fantasies of the analyst, fantasies rooted largely in the patient's previous object relationships. But also to be mourned is the real relationship with the real analyst, the person who sits with his or her patient hour after hour, week after week, year after year and attempts, from a continuous and benevolent vantage point, to help him untangle the strands of meaning in his life.

The picture has become even more complicated. From a relational perspective that is deconstructed out of the limitations of traditional transference and countertransference models, the analytic relationship becomes an ever shifting, mutually contributed to and more often than not, cocreated series of interactions occurring between patient and analyst. As emphasized by both Bromberg (1998) and Davies (2005), the interactions among a multiplicity of both patient and analyst selves and self states construct an endless array of old and new relationship configurations. Davies notes that when viewed from the vantage point of multiplicity, what is both renewed and relinquished during a termination process is not a singular patient–analyst configuration, but an array of self–other configurations that have come to the fore during the period of the analytic endeavor. During the termination period, it is hoped that older, less beneficial ways of being will rear their heads and take their seat in the background while newer configurations of self and other will be reinforced in the foreground.

Also, as concepts of self have become increasingly contextualized, contemporary relational psychoanalysts have worked more and more from the vantage point of intersubjectivity, the interplay between the subjectivities of the analyst and the patient (Stolorow & Atwood, 1992). Ogden (1994) considers the unique interplay between each analyst–patient dyad an entity in itself, which he refers to as the analytic third. It is within the context of the third in which the therapeutic narrative is lived and created. This entity, the third, now also needs to be mourned at the end of psychoanalysis. More on this will be presented later.

We see then that the focus of termination changed from drives to objects, to multiplicities, to intersubjectivities. What has stayed constant throughout this perspective shift is emphasis on the end of an analysis being likened to a death. As long as the end of psychoanalysis meant the end of therapy with a particular analyst, it made sense to liken it to a death or loss. The finality of the treatment was considered necessary for the patient to face the relinquishing of either drive or object wishes. Analysts of many theoretical colors were advised to not leave an open door available. It is over when it is over, the clock has run out. Period. An open door would short circuit the finality of the old ways of being and leave open the hope for neurotic solutions to be realized. Anything less than a permanent separation with one's analyst at the end of treatment would both promote and signal incomplete work, or acting out.

But as with other shibboleths of classical theory, clinical experience has forced a reconsideration of the termination process so that it could no longer be contained solely within a death and mourning model. Irwin Hoffman (1998) takes issue with the tendency to equate death with termination. Death, he states, places a limit on any "chance to revise the meaning of our experience by reinterpreting earlier experiences in light of later ones" (p. 246). This is not necessarily the case with termination, especially when one's analyst is available for possible future contact. In this paper, I would like to further challenge the traditional linking of termination with death and mourning. Although like a death in important ways, there are dimensions of the termination experience that can only be explored through other models, including other models of time.

Priel (1997), drawing from advances in mother–infant research, has noted the close association of the concept and experience of time and early mother–infant configurations. Freud rooted the infant's growing understanding of time in the gap between stimulation and gratification—that is, in the workings of a solitary isolated mind. Priel states, however, that

> a different perspective on the sense and concept of time can be envisioned, not as pertaining to an isolated perceiving mind, but as a mutually construed organizational principle characteristic of mother–infant interactional patterns.... The sense of time can be better understood as the unfolding of basic meanings related to identity and differentiation, continuity and change, in the context of infant caregiver interactional patterns. (p. 435)

Bollas (1989), also writing from a perspective that contextualizes the psychological conception of time, invokes Winnicott and makes a distinction between somatic time and object time. Somatic time is routed in a timelessness, provided by the subject mother who, by accommodating to the infant's cycle of needs protects the child from the ultimate demands of time. As the mother gradually fails the infant's omnipotent desires and becomes an object for the child, so too does she teach the child about object time, whereby the child gradually construes a realistic sense of time during the gap between the mother's absence and presence.

I think of somatic time and object time as remaining in our psychological senses of time dialectically and in tension with each other. Termination, then, reckons with both senses of time. That we need to end a psychoanalysis evokes issues of real, object time, clock-ticking time. A death–loss model of termination deals with the realities of object time, the clock running out of ticks.

When we leave our door open for future contact, we are evoking issues of maternal somatic time, which also continues to exist in the internal world of the adult. In this case, time does not become limited to the length of the episode of therapy. Instead, the possibility existing for future contact with a nondead analyst can ease the stresses of the running out of object time. Like the workings of an hourglass, once the sand runs out, the hourglass can be flipped over, restarting the flow of time.

Gradually, throughout my career, I started responding to the end of the treatment more as a moment in somatic time by leaving open the possibility of future therapeutic contact. I did not neglect object time, in that the therapy would end and a termination date would be set and honored with a termination process. But not to overstate the obvious, unless one of the treatment pair has died, no one has actually died in real time, and that is a fact of the termination as well. This reality places an obvious but important limit on the death/mourning/grieving model of termination. To end a period of analytic work with the offer of an open door in the future takes the termination out of the realm of the finite. The message given is no longer, "You must now learn to accept the limitations of our relationship because it is permanently finished. You will be able to have continued contact with me as I exist in your internal world, but you must relinquish all other wishes for it to be otherwise." It has become rather, "Our relationship is over for the time being and we will be separating. Yes, the therapy and termination process has involved the loss of pieces of yourself and pieces of us, but it has also provided new ways and possibilities of being— new ways of being that have been obtained partially through our relationship. The relationship is over for now, but do know that I am available for your use in the future."

This change in message pertaining to termination parallels a basic sea change that has come about in the shift to a relational psychoanalysis. A one-person model asks the analysand to relinquish any attachments to the analyst rooted in the solipsism of one's closed internal world. The analyst's role has been essentially to evoke the past connections in the internal world, elucidate them, and render them vestigial. The clock starts ticking from the moment the analysis begins. There will be a fixed amount of energy rearranged in a linear, fixed amount of time. There is plenty of time to explore, contemplate, act out, enact, and identify with the analyst, but time is of the essence! It is over when it is over, and hopefully the analysand will hit the road moving forward by giving up old ways of being and with new more reality pegged ways of being firmly entrenched within the psyche to assure durability over time. The analysand must accept the limits of time, make those changes, relinquish hurtful, self-destructive connections, mourn their loss, and move on.

As opposed to a closed system, energic model of psychoanalysis, which asks the patient to go back in time in order to move forward, a two-person relational model, even though not eschewing the past, invites the patient to connect in the present time in order to create an altered narrative, and then move forward. The new narrative does not assume a fixed amount of energy or linear directionality. The treatment dyad is freer to move back and forward in time. Both older and newer ways of being and connecting are tried on, accepted, or discarded. As I stated elsewhere (Skolnick, 2006), the hope is that the patient has, in the therapy, interacted with a good object in the form of the analyst and then carried the interactions into their lives following termination. The relinquish-or-not sensibility of an older one person model is replaced by a relinquish-and-not tension of a newer relational model of treatment. It is assumed that the older maladaptive ways of being will not evaporate, but they will continue to live in tension with the newer ways of being. In that the older self states and self–other interactions are not necessarily given up, but rather added to, there is less emphasis on mourning a "dead" subjectively created analyst. The analyst, as new object, is allowed to survive. In that he or she survives, the analyst is available to interact with the patient at some time in the future. Future contacts are not mourned, as they are in a classical model, but are welcomed as a possibility in a relational model.

TIME AFTER TIME: A CLINICAL EXAMPLE

M, a bright, articulate, and affable man in his thirties, was having a hard time wading through his ambivalence about getting married. He was in a relationship with a woman whom he loved and wanted to marry but remained inexplicitly stuck and unable to actually tie the knot. Our work together was extremely helpful in elucidating the source of his paralysis and enabled him to move ahead and, with lessened conflict, marry. His paralyzing conflicts had reliably surfaced at various times throughout his life, typically during periods of rites of passage. When confronted with transitions to new life stages, the primary issue evoked was one of separation from his alcoholic mother whom he wished to protect and cure. He had become her self-proclaimed caretaker from a very young age. His father, though well meaning, had in essence abandoned his wife by virtue of his high-powered job and frequent travel. He was rarely home to monitor her serious alcohol abuse, a task that fell largely into M's lap. In the world, M functioned as a well-integrated person, probably by virtue of his two considerably older brothers who raised him. But to his mother he was press ganged into part object functioning. As he put it, he was a penis for her, virile, protective, and a fount of strength. When approaching new episodes in life, episodes signaling increased autonomy and growth, his internalized abandoned and fragile mother would languish, if not die. I was for him a father who stuck around, protecting him from the burdens of caring for his mother and allowing him the freedom to leave her as he progressed into life.

The termination process proceeded well. He was psychologically sophisticated and was able to revisit many corners of our work together. We traveled back and forth, reliving moments of our relationship including the good and idealized, as well as episodes of anger, competition, and disappointment. But when the actual time came to say goodbye, as he was about to leave the room he informed me that he would be back to see me again when it was time to have children, referring to the next developmental bridge-crossing he was likely to face. Sure enough, several years later, he contacted me for therapy because he and his wife were contemplating having children and he once again felt terrifically stuck. His issues were similar; his having a child would represent a further separation from and abandonment of his mother.

Therapy with M took place at a time in my career when I worked from a heightened conviction in a more traditional ego-psychological model of termination, one that likened it more exclusively to a death. Furthermore, death being final, my model of termination also included in it the supposition that a "proper" termination was one in which all childhood wishes were abandoned, the ego was strengthened, the superego was made more flexible, and the work was complete. Should further treatment be required, it indicated that the first treatment, including the termination work, had been incomplete. From the moment M informed me, upon leaving, that he would see me again, I had doubted the efficacy of the first treatment. Had I failed to conduct a complete therapy? Had I missed some powerful dependency issues that needed further analysis? Had I not indeed been mourned (or mourn) like in a "proper" termination process so that the patient or I was hanging on to ungratified wishes for need fulfillment?

During the second period of work with M, we went over much of the same territory as we had in the first. I was not hearing new issues and wondered what I was missing. The issues surrounding separation from his dysfunctional family resurfaced. The strengthening of his self and lessening of his experience of guilt and shame were also revisited. I was not surprised then when, after a much shorter stay in therapy, he announced that he wanted to end treatment. He told me he felt he was indeed ready to start a family. About a year later, I received a birth announcement, followed by several more over the course of time. I now happily receive a Christmas picture every year of his of burgeoning family, all of whom appear, at least in the picture, to be thriving.

My patient was wiser than I was. When M informed me at the end of our first course of work that he would be back, my fear of an incomplete analysis was born in theory; he, by contrast, knew what he needed in actuality. Today I no longer hold solely to a death model of termination. My relational sensibilities inform my approach to ending therapy. Termination is like a death, and can awaken issues of death and permanent loss, but it is not a death, either an actual one or of primitive drives and wishes. I prefer to regard it as one of many iterations of separation accompanied by a loss. It may or may not be a final separation. I always leave my door open at the end of treatment in the event that the patient might want to return at some future time for additional work. With many I emphasize that we all, being more human than not, can run into difficulty at any time in life, and that returning need not be considered a failure or defeat. In my experience, patients have returned for a number of reasons; some for another round of treatment to pick up where they left off. Some develop difficulties in reaction to a real-life trauma or difficulty. Some come for a session or two, frequently referring to such a return as a "tune-up." Some, like M, returned to be able to transition to another stage of life. To regard termination as a death would preclude allowing a patient to return. But aside from a real death, neither of us has actually died for the other, externally or internally.

I have since worked with a number of patients who have come, left, and returned during the course of a therapy that spanned many years. Some might consider such treatments unsuccessful, or in Freud's word, interminable. As such, it might be posited that the internal economy of character structures remain unbalanced, or insufficiently treated. I prefer to regard such therapies as existing outside of a conventional time structure that we arbitrarily cast around a treatment. As such, it is not that each segment of therapy is incomplete, but our temporal definition of a course of therapy needs to be expanded. Rather than limiting therapy to a specific period of time, might it be that the "perfect storm" that propels someone into treatment at any particular time involves a confluence of factors that includes a temporal context? The question we often ask—"why now?"—can be expanded into "why now, and then?"

CONSOLIDATION

On more than one occasion, I noticed that a period away from treatment after termination has served to consolidate the gains of therapy for some patients. These patients appear to have shifted significantly in their psychological development during the period away from treatment. Integrations are made, self-regulation has expanded, and reality testing exists more consistently. Their relationships can be seen to have provided more satisfaction reflecting both growth and expansion of character adaptations. Potentials for changing, hinted at but never realized during the therapy *per se*, blossom and flourish when the patient is away from the therapeutic arena.

If we posit (Skolnick, 2006) that identifying with the analytic processes of the analyst in a therapeutic relationship is a powerful force contributing to therapeutic change, it would suggest that when identificatory processes are interfered with, change is harder to come by. A consistent factor in each of the cases where consolidation occurred after termination has been the presence of powerful annihilation fantasies and enormous destructive ideation. These forces seemed to derail adaptive processes and identifications in the presence of the analyst. Distance from the analyst appears to be the only way such identifications can occur safely. In the analyst's presence, the level of rage, envy, and other equally destructive forces does not allow internalizing interactions or the consolidation of these internalizations within one's own self–other object representations. A similar type of phenomena can be encountered in some patients who report a greater degree of closeness and ease with the therapeutic interaction during phone sessions. These patients have noted to me repeatedly that the distance provided by phone contact increases a feeling of safety and reduces anxiety. My sense is that non-phone, in-person sessions can rouse too many destructive forces that interfere with therapeutic internalizations.

Paul, a middle-aged man with considerable difficulties in life left a more than 10-year treatment following the death of his mother. Paul led an exceptionally limited existence. Although talented at his craft, he obtained only very limited professional success. His immersion in his work was sporadic and with tentative engagement. He might spend several months focused and determined to achieve, followed by lengthy down times of little or no involvement, often sticking to a reverse sleep–wake cycle. He lived alone and rarely ventured out from what we came to call his cave, his safe retreat from the dangers and insults of the world at large. He was hampered by an unfortunate combination of perfectionistic rigidity, a severely compromised self-esteem, and massive paranoid projections, so that the simplest of tasks, such as going to the store and buying a shirt, became fraught with fear, overly obsessive planning, and paranoia.

Paul suffered from enormous annihilation fantasies that dominated the transference and provided the most consistent and pervasive coloring to our relationship. In his mind I was perpetually attempting to destroy him, belittle him, and abscond with his achievements. Whether I was affirming an accomplishment, being empathic for a difficult set of affects, or merely being supportive, he experienced me as demeaning or more typically, attempting to destroy him. He remained secretive with me and refused to reveal many of the details of his ongoing experience, again feeling that my destructive desires rendered him vulnerable. When his mother died, his inner world threatened to so thoroughly overwhelm him that he made a hasty departure from treatment, claiming that I no longer, if ever, provided help. He left precipitously, against my recommendations and allowing no termination process. To some extent, I was not surprised. Therapy with him had always been less than satisfying for both of us. Although he made some progress, it was anathema for him to let me in on it, and I typically had to glean his victories from indirect, unobtrusive hints he would sparingly throw my way.

He contacted me again approximately 2 years later when he was beset by powerful psychosomatic fears of dying. He had a litany of physical symptoms, all of which had proven negative by the medical consultations he frequently undertook. Yet he felt strongly that he was dying and that all his doctors either had been incompetent or were afraid to tell him the truth. I regarded his psychosomatic ideation as an extreme identification with his dead mother who had suffered a prolonged debilitating decline prior to her death.

Of note for this discussion, however, was that during his 2 years away from treatment, he appeared to have improved considerably. His career had progressed. He was working at it more consistently and with heightened perseverance. He had also been successfully taking control of his mother's estate. She had been a celebrity and left a complicated and extensive legacy in need of organization and legal protection. Paul, who typically could quiver with trepidation at having to talk with a store clerk, was now taking meetings and holding his own with powerful agents and attorneys, demonstrating a sophistication that heretofore I had never witnessed.

It was startling to behold, and equally as puzzling to understand. Had he taken therapeutic processes (i.e., identifications) gathered during treatment into the world where they remained free to flourish and strengthen away from the analyst's perceived destructiveness? Perhaps the analyst's presence during treatment needed to be skirted so that changes could be made in an autonomous space, free from perceived threats by the analyst's expectations or his own projection of annihilation vulnerabilities?* What was truly remarkable was to witness the improvement he had made during time away from treatment as opposed to in it. Although one might claim that treatment had served destructive rather than beneficial purposes, given that the changes observed after termination were in the arenas worked on while in treatment, it would appear to indicate that interruptions were indeed necessary to further experience and consolidate gains aimed for in therapy.

I have observed similar, if not as marked, improvement in other patients who have left and returned to therapy. I have become more sanguine with patients who announce their wish to leave therapy at inopportune times. Some do respond to my offer of an open door and return to continue to do the work at a later time. Of those who return, it is clear to me that many

---

* Although Bion's goal of the analyst freeing himself or herself from desire is a worthwhile and crucial goal, I believe the analyst's expectations are always present in some fashion, even if not explicitly or clearly stated or known consciously by the analyst.

have continued to undertake the work of analysis away from our live inter-action. If I may paraphrase Winnicott in saying that we often strive with our patients to help them achieve autonomy in the presence of another, perhaps for some patients, those harboring excessive anger and rage, auton-omy can only be achieved away from the actual presence of another.

GOOD, GOOD-ENOUGH, AND BAD TERMINATIONS

The end of a psychoanalytic treatment can take many forms, both planned and unplanned. Freud (1937) mused about what actually constitutes the end of a psychoanalysis. He distinguished between the end of a treatment and a proper termination process, the former being a truncated therapy that has not worked through a termination process, *per se*. As we know from our work, the end of therapy can take an infinite number of forms, ranging from setting a planned end date that leaves time to process the ending, to the circumstance in which a patient exits without announcement and disappears without a trace.

When to end an analysis is the subject of much speculation. In its infancy, when analysis as a technique was nascent, its aim was to treat a certain set of neurotic symptoms so the ending was more or less dictated by the ces-sation of symptoms. The analysis of symptoms, through time, gave way to the analysis of character and character dysfunction. Once detached from symptom cessation *per se*, when to end the analytic endeavor entered into a far more nebulous region of uncertainty. Ferenczi (in Davies, 2005) was known to have written, "The proper ending of an analysis is when nei-ther the physician nor the patient puts an end to it, but when it dies of exhaustion, so to speak" (p. 780). Writing much later, Levenson (1978) likened the decision to end a treatment with the aesthetic decision of an artist to declare that his or her work is complete. Overall, I tend to agree with Martin Bergmann (1997), that as a field, psychoanalysis has said little to adequately address this issue.

A discussion of when to end a therapy must include a mentioning of the types of obstacles and pitfalls we run into that interfere with our clinical judgment about when to end a treatment. Extraneous issues to the criteria for terminating abound, such as the inherent conflict of inter-est between ending a therapy and the analyst's maintenance of income, or the reluctance of either party to end a mutually satisfying authentic attachment, just to name a few. Aside from the imperative that the analyst be vigilant about not privileging his or her own needs ahead of those of the patient, my bias is to try not to have a bias about timely endings of treatment. Categorical recommendations frequently fail to recognize the uniqueness of each analytic dyad and likewise the unique circumstances of each termination and when they occur. The time for ending needs to be determined by a mutual exploration by each individual analytic pair. A comprehensive listing of the reasons for ending would take us way beyond the scope of this paper. The point I wish to stress here is that there is no easy set of ending criteria.

Once we decide on ending, however, what makes the ending a good one? What are the qualities that distinguish a "good" termination from ones that go poorly? My contention is that a good termination is one that allows some dedicated period to process the multitude of meanings of the termination for both patient and analyst. The scope of the termination process can cover an extremely broad universe of issues and experiences ranging from the specific ideographic events of the work together to more generic issues of separation and loss. It can be focused on what has been lost and what has been gained in the work, hopes for the future, as well as disappointments in the therapy. Surprises can arise, such as the appearance of completely new issues. Sometimes symptoms can arise, either a recrudescence of older ones or completely new ones. Schafer (2002) describes a defensive organization he calls the false depressive position, a pseudo-mature manner of coping with the stresses and strains of termination. He ascribes this stance to patients, but I believe an analyst needs to be on the watch for a similar defensive movement in him- or herself.

As with when to end an analysis, I recommend that there be no formulaic prescription as to the actual length of time set aside to complete the termination. The length of time can vary from dyad to dyad. I used to go by the rough estimate, supplied by precedent, which dictated about 1 month for each year in treatment. This at times had disastrous consequences. During one instance, the length of a successful treatment translated into such a prolonged and ultimately unproductive termination process, that we mutually decided to truncate the termination and be done with each other already. The needed work had been done early during the termination and it continuing was probably some expression of a lack of willingness for either of us to call it quits and say goodbye. For me personally, a prolonged termination is a signal of some difficulty one or both of us has with ending a productive relationship that has nonetheless run its course and is in need of ending. Likewise, I have found, at times, terminations of a relatively short duration to be profound, deeply authentic, and mutually satisfying. As with the question of when to end a treatment, I have found there to be no categorical clues as to what might be a "correct" timely course to a termination process. We need to enter into each ending with a suspension of preconceived ideas about its proper length. That said, I find that "natural" ending points, such as a vacation or holiday, provide a reasonable, good enough broad-stroke indicator of when to set a termination date, provided some period of time is allotted to work through the termination.

To some extent, the end of the analytic relationship is present through-out the entire treatment,* but in my experience, once a final date is set, the termination process has begun. The content of future sessions will sub-sequently bring another filter, that of separation, always present but not always attended to, into the foreground of the analyst's listening process. Created "meaning" will now contain elements of the treatment ending and what that awakes in both the analyst and the patient.

Sometimes ending dates are forced upon a dyad by circumstances beyond either party's control, such as a business transfer or move. At such times, I would once again recommend that some period of time be spent defining a termination period so that some work be undertaken, even if by phone, and however truncated by time and distance constraints.

I have generally, but by no means exclusively, found that the quality of a termination process corresponds roughly to the quality of the therapy that has preceded it. With patients who have participated in a profound, genuine, and multitextured experience with me, the process of ending the work similarly is as profound, genuine, and multitextured and will reflect the entire range of the distance traveled in the work. Older, less adaptive ways of engaging each other will arise as well as newer, more successful, and expansive ways of being. The actual ending has typically been a mutually experienced bittersweet event in which profound feelings of sadness for the separation were expressed and hopeful expectations for the future were enjoyed. Such a termination usually gives way to a naturally occurring hearty hug before the final goodbye.

But this is not the case for all terminations. Treatments that have felt deficient in one way or another will typically end with less than satisfying termination processes. An ending with a patient who has been difficult to engage affectively will often reflect a similar disengagement. This can be the case regardless of the progress made or distance traveled in the work. Similarly, when the treatment has been unbalanced on some dimension, be it with an excess of anger, grandiosity, dissatisfaction with the analyst, or unanalyzed idealization, the ending will also feel similarly unbalanced. Again, the work may have produced mutually recognized gains but the end-ing can feel dull and flat, often with the nagging sensation that an essential piece has been and still is missing. Often, when such is the case, a mutual hug does not even enter into the range of possibilities for a final contact.

And some terminations can feel devastatingly empty, enraging, or futile. I recall the shock, anger, and hopeless feelings that set in when a patient with whom I had been working intensively for several years disappeared suddenly from therapy. He merely did not show for his next session. My calls and letters went unanswered. He took the end of treatment into his

---

* Entire models of short-term therapy have been developed based on the inevitability of the final separation of therapist and patient. See Davanloo (1992) or Della Selva (1999) for discussions of short-term dynamic psychotherapy.

own omnipotent control, as if there had never been an "us." My best guess about such endings is that the patient, via a projective identification, has communicated to us a nonverbal understanding of an overwhelming and devastatingly futile object relationship they have experienced and is now ensconced in their inner world, a relationship replete with hopelessness and feelings of annihilation.

TERMINATION AND THE END OF COCONSTRUCTION

For an endeavor that leaves no stone unturned in its quest to comprehend and construct meaning in human experience, psychoanalysis has been remarkably silent about the process of termination that continues after the analysis has ended. We rarely, if ever, study posttreatment phenomena and processes, behaviors, and continued construction of meanings after the analyst and patient have separated.

In this paper, I described and illustrated several circumstances whereby I caught a glimpse of the termination process that occurs following the cessation of therapy sessions. I would like to conclude by considering another aspect of the termination, the ending of coconstruction.

The interactions between patient and analyst undergo a seismic shift following the last session in treatment. Although no longer are the two in actual proximity, they remain ensconced in each other as a set of internalized representations. As I noted, hopefully the ways of being of the analyst are internalized sufficiently by the patient to withstand the separation, as each analyst and patient continues in time without the other. Both Freud and Klein emphasized the importance to psychic equilibrium of maintaining internal object ties after a death, usually through identifications. Inasmuch as terminations can resemble a death, at least for the current episode of therapy, it is similarly hoped that the relationship with the analyst will continue in some internalized form.

The internalizations, however, are subjected to the major currents in each person's character and may take on different shadings, meanings, forms, recollections, and affective valence following the last session. Coconstruction of memories, both actual and procedural, in both the analyst and the patient, comes to an end following the final session. What is remembered and maintained becomes subjected to the distortions and vagaries of memory, circumstance, and time. Choices of what and how to remember the other become more and more affected by one-person internal operations.

We might find the diversions and back roads that shape treatment memories growing in disparate ways so that each person maintains recollections that have grown apart from, and gradually become less and less similar from, the other. When reconnecting with a patient after a period in which treatment has been in abeyance, I am struck by the number of times I have the jarring experience of coming across divergent memories. Usually I become aware of this phenomenon when a patient announces, "And I always have remembered what you said…" or "And the most important thing you ever said was…" and then proceeds to recollect a quote of mine that not only am I fairly certain I have never said, but I am also of the firm conviction that those words, or anything similar to them, never would have crossed my lips.

We find that treatment memories are not encoded similarly, stored similarly, or recalled in identical ways. In the context of termination, coconstruction, it would appear to me, is ephemeral. It might exist for the moment during the treatment and contribute to the making of meaning, but does it continue over time? Ogden's third, the mingling of two subjectivities, can be viewed as a relatively brief phenomenon contextualized during the treatment but not after. Like life in the primordial soup, it is the temporary dance created by two separate molecules, creating a higher-order system that rapidly disintegrates unless contact, now internal following termination, is maintained and repetition is allowed. As Hoffman (1995) so very well put it, "Although we cannot change any moment as it was experienced, we can make choices that affect the meaning to us of any particular moment as we think of it in retrospect" (p. 245).

I would add that coconstruction cannot take place in retrospect. It becomes a victim of object time. The end of coconstruction that comes with termination provides but yet another stress for both analyst and analysand as they part. Will the creation of meaning, so alive and vital during the intensity of their contact, be maintained? Will the illusion of their dance together survive the separation? And in what form will it survive? At the moment of departure, this question sits with the analytic pair as they move beyond the precipice into future time, and only time will tell.

REFERENCES

Bass, A. (2001). It takes one to know one: Or, whose unconscious is it anyway? *Psychoanalytic Dialogues, 11*, 683–703.

Bergmann, M. S. (1997). Termination: The Achilles heel of psychoanalytic technique. *Psychoanalytic Psychology, 14*, 163–174.

Bollas, C. (1989). *Forces of destiny*. London: Free Association Books.

Bromberg, P. (1998). *Standing in the spaces*. Hillsdale, NJ: Analytic Press.

Davanloo, H. (1992). *Short-term dynamic psychotherapy*. New York: Aronson.

Davies, J. M. (2005) Transformations of desire and despair: Reflections on the termination process from a relational perspective. *Psychoanalytic Dialogues, 15*, 779–807.

Della Selva, P. M. (1999). *Intensive short-term dynamic psychotherapy: Theory and technique*. London: Karnac.

Fairbairn, W. R. D. (1952). *Psychoanalytic studies of the personality*. London: Routledge and Kegan Paul.

Fairbairn, W. R. D. (1958). On the nature and aims of psycho-analytic treatment. *International Journal of Psychoanalysis, 29*, 374–385.

Freud, S. (1917). Mourning and melancholia. In J. Strachey (Ed. & Trans.), *The standard edition of the complete psychological works of Sigmund Freud* (Vol. 14, pp. 239–258). London: Hogarth.

Freud, S. (1937). Analysis terminable and interminable. In J. Strachey (Ed. & Trans.), *The standard edition of the complete psychological works of Sigmund Freud* (Vol. 23, pp. 211–253). London: Hogarth.

Hoffman, I. Z. (1998). *Ritual and spontaneity in the psychoanalytic process: A dialectical-constructivist view*. Hillsdale, NJ: Analytic Press.

Leupold-Lowenthal, H. (1988). Notes on Sigmund Freud's "Analysis Terminable and Interminable." *International Journal of Psycho-Analysis, 69*, 261–272.

Levenson, E. A. (1978). The aesthetics of termination. *Contemporary Psychoanalysis, 12*, 338–341.

Ogden, T. (1994). *Subjects of analysis*. Northvale, NJ: Jason Aronson.

Priel, B. (1997). Time and self. *Psychoanalytic Dialogues, 7*, 431–451.

Schafer, R. (2002). Experiencing termination: Authentic and false depressive positions. *Psychoanalytic Psychology, 19*, 235–253.

Schlesinger, H. J. (2005). *Endings and beginnings: On terminating psychotherapy and psychoanalysis*. Hillsdale, NJ: Analytic Press.

Skolnick, N. J. (2006). What's a good object to do? *Psychoanalytic Dialogues, 16*, 1–29.

Stolorow, R. D., & Atwood, G. E. (1992). *Contexts of being: The intersubjective foundations of psychological life*. Hillsdale, NJ: Analytic Press.

Chapter 14

Parting ways

Dodi Goldman

> Perhaps the best hope for the psychoanalyst lies not in "theory" at all, but in the old fashioned arts of speaking opportunely and knowing when to stop.
>
> Malcolm Bowie

It obviously makes a difference if one thinks of psychoanalysis as a treatment—a cure for an ailment—or as an experience. Accounts of psychoanalysis as treatment demand plausibility and coherence, not to mention intelligibly formulated criteria for professional efficiency. From the point of view of treatment, psychoanalysis is an elaborate exercise in problem solving expected to adhere to the satisfying narrative structure of a beginning, a middle, and, preferably, a happy end. But to the extent that the purview of psychoanalysis is experience—the place where the singularity of a person's idiosyncratic desire meets the contingencies of life—it is virtually impossible to create a consensual vocabulary for knowing when enough is enough.

Of all aspects of the psychoanalytic process, it is perhaps the ending of a psychoanalysis that brings most vividly into relief the tension between accountability and desire. The language of accountability provides words like "analyzability," "boundaries," "agency," and yes, "termination." But the language of unconscious desire—and the freedom to live with its accidental consequences—is captured by Emerson (1904) when he writes:

> The results of life are uncalculated and uncalculable. The years teach much which the days never know. The persons who compose our company converse, and come and go, and design and execute many things, and somewhat come of it all, but an unlooked-for result. The individual is always mistaken. He designed many things, and drew in other persons as coadjutors, quarreled with some or all, blundered much, and something is done; all are a little advanced, but the individual is always mistaken. It turns out somewhat new and very unlike what he promised himself. (pp. 69–70)

As an experience, psychoanalysis is more often than not, as Emerson suggests, quite unlike what we promise ourselves.

These two currents—treatment and experience—make uneasy bedfellows. When inclined toward psychoanalysis as treatment, the analyst holds in mind a linear trajectory evidenced by alteration of symptoms, enhanced capacities, and developmental achievement. From the outset, the therapist is at the *beginning* of treatment and the patient is somewhere in the *middle*, seeking professional help because his or her own efforts at self-cure have thus far failed. Criteria for *ending*—in the language of whatever theory they might be cast—serve as benchmarks in an instrumental relationship designed for a purpose external to the relationship. No matter how long the treatment takes, the unalterable "not-me" aspect of time—what Kipling calls "the unforgiving minute"—is always, in some way, of the essence. Although the constricting repetitions—the unconscious limiting of potential life stories—that bring people to analysis carry the *appearance* of time having stopped, the person also knows very well otherwise. To not monitor movement in time, to seductively ablate awareness of living in passing time, is felt as doing the patient a disservice.

When inclined toward psychoanalysis as experience, on the other hand, the analyst participates in the patient's engagement with the kaleidoscope of unconscious life without necessarily concerning himself or herself with purpose, direction, or time. Or to state this in more nuanced terms, the sense of time in play is less a linear trajectory moving *toward* something as it is the recognition that ends are recursively consonant with origins. Furthermore, endings, like beginnings, can be delinked from chronological implications and instead be understood as "states of mind" in which one feels that one is either leaving a familiar situation or facing a new one. From this point of view, analysis is a potentially infinite series of beginnings and endings (Schlesinger, 2005). Are there not many moments in the course of an analysis when the patient, on the brink of entering uncharted territory, suddenly experiences the analyst as an unsafe stranger? For the analyst concerned with safeguarding analysis as experience, the question is not "What is the model best suited to explain and facilitate a 'successful termination,'" but, rather, "How are the multiple beginnings and endings experienced by patient and analyst alike?" Undue emphasis on prescribed theories of mourning, growth, loss, or developmental achievements runs the risk of silencing some aspect of the patient's internal world. As Adam Phillips (1994) notes, "for the psychoanalyst...the most misleading theories are the ones he cannot do without" (p. 153).

A particular analyst's inclination—his or her sensibility regarding these currents—will inevitably tilt how the ending of a treatment is negotiated. The point is that it is inadequate to think of the timing of ending analysis as simply a matter of the patient's pace—what Freud once referred to as the "length" of an analysand's "stride." Instead, the analyst's preference will also have significant bearing on the how and the when of ending. It can be useful to note how, at any given moment, a particular patient's use of analysis may be in concord, collude, or collide with an analyst's inclination. And to be clear, both the patient's use and the analyst's inclination can, and often do, shift over time. Whether formulated or not, patient and analyst alike continuously feel each other out both transferentially and in actuality: Is it safe to stay? Is it time to go? What is the rush? When will it end? Idiosyncratic rhythms of engagement—seeking contact and safeguarding solitude—certainly play their part in the dance over time. A patient communicating, whether in words or not, "When will this treatment start working?" may prompt the analyst to communicate "Can't you let the experience be?" Similarly, a patient's apparent obliviousness to change might prompt the same analyst to communicate "We don't have all the time in the world!" Concordant and complementary identifications (Racker, 1968) and dissociated self-states (Bromberg, 1998) play out in unpredictable ways. There are, as Paul Simon put it, 50 ways to leave (or not leave) your lover.

This is not to say that people necessarily know what they really want. Central to Freud's original project was to draw attention to how people are, in Emerson's sense, "always mistaken." Freud was, therefore, equally suspicious of patients stopping—be it chains of associations or commitments to battle their neuroses—as he was about their continuing treatment indefinitely. Stopping and not stopping are each readily viewed as "resistance." Ludwig Wittgenstein (1968) seemed particularly struck by this aspect of psychoanalysis when he remarked that Freud's

> procedure of free association and so on is queer, because Freud never shows how we know where to stop-where is the right solution. Sometimes he says that the right solution, or the right analysis, is the one which satisfies the patient. Sometimes he says that the doctor knows what the right solution or analysis of the dream is, whereas the patient doesn't: the doctor can say that the patient is wrong. The reason why he calls one sort of analysis the right one does not seem to be a matter of evidence. (pp. 376–377)

Perhaps what Wittgenstein found "queer" about psychoanalysis was the paradox that Freud's method of free association—which by its very nature has no end point—was employed as a treatment designed to come to a satisfactory conclusion. Essential to Freud's vision of unconscious life are what Malcolm Bowie (1993) refers to as "unstoppable transformational processes" (p. 127) that "prevents meaning from reaching fullness, completion, closure, consummation" (p. 98). Freud ironically presumed that speaking as truthfully as possible with no end in sight would necessarily bring self-deception into plain view. But how does one ever find the "right solution" if self-deception is vital to psychic survival? And how—given the unstoppability of the signifying process described by Bowie—can either analyst or patient possibly "know" with conviction when an analysis should come to an end?

The "evidence" that Wittgenstein failed to notice were the signs Freud claimed to observe through the overcoming of resistances. The *obstacle* to finding the "right solution" and arriving at a satisfactory conclusion, in other words, was generally understood to reflect the patient's stubborn self-protective obstructionism. More specifically, the reason held responsible for the fact that analyses are not self-terminating was that the patient had an unrealistic grasp of the satisfactions to be expected from love and life. Describing termination as the "Achilles heel" of psychoanalysis, Martin Bergmann (1997) notes that "for many analysands, transference love is the best love relationship that life has offered. Understandably, they are reluctant to give it up... In real life, only death and hostility bring a libidinal relationship to an end. The kind of termination psychoanalysis demands is without precedent" (p. 163).

As long as the analytic bond was thought of primarily as a "libidinal relationship," the ending of treatment could only be envisioned in terms of the patient "overcoming" unrealistic childish wishes. Ferenczi would even suggest that the battle waged against these wishes was usually won, if at all, by sheer attrition. "The proper ending of an analysis," writes Ferenczi (1955),

> is when neither the physician nor the patient put an end to it, but when it *dies of exhaustion*...a truly cured patient frees himself from analysis slowly but surely; so long as he wishes to come to analysis he should continue to do so....The patient finally becomes convinced that he is continuing analysis *only because he is treating it as a new but still a fantasy source of gratification*, which in terms of reality yields him nothing. (p. 85, italics added)

It is worth considering, however, what happens to our understanding of ending an analysis when we view it from a lens other than one of misplaced libidinal gratification. What avenues of understanding open up if the question of ending is not seen as a matter of the patient's inadequacy in relinquishing forbidden desire or accepting reality? After all, Freud's hermeneutic of suspicion—the state of mind that aims to expose that which we conceal from ourselves—is only part of what constitutes the psychoanalytic enterprise. No less potent than the desire to conceal is the human urge to communicate. People do not only want to hide, they also seek other people to know, to be known by, and to know themselves. Even though it may be a joy to be hidden, Winnicott (1963) notes, it is also disaster not to be found. One interesting trend in psychoanalytic theorizing is the increasing emphasis on how the analyst becomes, as Emerson put it, a "coadjutor, quarreled with...blundered much," as part of the patient's project to be recognized. And in the midst of the conversing, the quarreling, and the blundering—as the patient clamors to be heard—there is no escaping that the analyst, and not only the patient, is also always in some way mistaken.

Put differently, just as the language of "libidinal gratification" is inadequate to describe why people come together, "termination" is an inappropriate term to describe what happens when a relationship ends. Obviously, people part, in anger or sorrow, disgust, or relief; people stop doing things together, working, living in the same city, or sleeping in the same bed. People may never see each other again or even consciously think about each other. But one can never know or control how the departed, forgotten, exiled, abandoned, or lost other might return unbidden as one's own mood or to haunt one's dreams. Echoes of objects reverberate in ways not readily predictable. And these echoes—their role in pain, suffering, witnessing, and self-transformation—bear significantly upon how endings are experienced.

Freud (1926) asks, "When does separation from an object produce anxiety, when does it produce mourning, and when does it produce, it may be, only pain?" (p. 169). As is often the case, the question Freud asks is more interesting—in the sense of opening possibilities—than the answer he provides. What is striking about the choices Freud offers—anxiety, mourning, and pain—is that despite his general view of reality as inherently frustrating, actual separation from an object is viewed as a loss with significant consequences. Even mourning, which, from Freud's point of view, "occurs under the influence of reality testing" and categorically demands of the bereaved a "detachment of libido," involves a greater degree of continuity of relationship than Freud acknowledges. Attachments, it turns out, are far less interchangeable than Freud's theory of libido would suggest.

But even more telling than the range of emotional choices Freud highlights is his intriguing proposal that some forms of separation might involve "only pain." "Pain" is an affective state Freud sidelined after his first speculative musings in the "Project for a Scientific Psychology" (Pontalis, 1977). In that early work, the primary distinction Freud draws is not between pleasure and unpleasure (which are on a single tension continuum) but between pleasure–unpleasure on the one hand and pain on the other. The experience of pain is independent of the experience of unsatisfied desire. Pain—which involves a traumatic break in the stimulus barrier—is of an entirely different order than frustration or thwarted desire. What generates the earliest experiences of pain is the newborn's experience of helplessness when separated from mother. Helplessness—and the traumatic pain that accompanies it—is, Freud tells us, the primordial condition of the human species. As an affective state, pain is not the result of a fantasized danger; it is a reaction appropriate to an actual loss. The primitive psyche cannot think about, transform, or elaborate pain. By introducing the distinction between anxiety, mourning, and "only pain," Freud was revisiting his earlier notion that there are certain traumatizing experiences that cannot be psychically elaborated.

Bion (1970), picking up this aspect of Freud's thinking, provides his own compelling version. "Patients," he writes, "experience pain but not suffering.... The intensity of the patient's pain contributes to his fear of suffering pain...Pain is inflicted or accepted but is not suffered except in the view of the analyst or other observer" (p. 19). Mental pain, Bion suggests, emerges when the person lacks a capacity to suffer. Suffering, which is associated with the capacity for containment and psychic elaboration of painful emotions, is suitable for description in words. Pain— a "nameless dread"—resists elaboration and is thereby devoid of any meaning. But if psychoanalysis teaches us anything, it is that pain can be transformed by applying words to wounds. But for words to carry a transformative potential, it is not enough that they simply be spoken; they need also to be heard.

For Winnicott, too, there is a meaningful difference between pain and suffering. Suffering, for Winnicott as for Bion, is a developmental achievement associated with a relatively healthy relationship to the difficulties inherent in life. "Probably the greatest suffering in the human world," writes Winnicott (1988), "is the suffering of normal or healthy or mature persons. This is not generally recognized. It is a false guide to observe manifest perplexity, misery, and pain in a mental hospital. Nevertheless it is usual for degree of suffering to be assessed in this superficial way" (p. 80).

Christian upbringing probably drew both Bion and Winnicott to the word "suffering" to capture the profundity of love, loss, lack, and life. (Psychoanalytic theory offers a rich vocabulary to explain transformations of excitement, but is rendered silent when it comes to describing what makes an experience poignant.) It may also be the case that Bion and Winnicott were reaching for a language to express an intriguing potential overlap between religious and psychoanalytic experiences. As Masud Khan (1981) observed,

> It is my inference from what I know of the history of religions, especially the three monotheistic ones, that it is precisely this need in the human individual for his or her psychic pain to be witnessed silently and unobtrusively by *the other* that led to the creation of the omnipresence of God in human lives. Over the past two centuries and more, with the increasing disappearance of God as the witnessing *other* from man's privacy with himself, the experience of psychic pain has changed from tolerated and accepted suffering to its pathological substitutes, and the need has rapidly increased for psycho-therapeutic interventions to alleviate these pathological masochistic states. (p. 414)

Putting aside Khan's assertion that the "disappearance of God" gives rise to increased masochism and need for psychotherapy, it is potentially instructive to ponder what he refers to as this need in the individual to have psychic pain "recognized silently and unobtrusively by the other." It is precisely the basic human need to have pain transformed by an Other that links—despite meaningful differences—Winnicott's "holding" with Bion's "containment." Winnicott's mother safeguards the infant's spontaneous rhythms—the infant's experience of aliveness—in part by insulating him from premature awareness of the painful "not-me" aspects of the passage of time (Goldman, in press; Ogden, 2004). For Bion, mother does the unconscious psychological work of dreaming the infant's unbearable pain and making it available in a form that can be made use of in dreaming his or her own experience. For each of them, the mother is reliably available *not only as an object of desire* but as an *animating presence*. We are, both Winnicott and Bion suggest, vitally enmeshed in relatedness with an Other *prior* to the time we can mentally represent them in our minds. The vestiges of this early sensorimotor environmental set-up (distinct from what is traditionally thought of as "libidinally cathected" or "object related") becomes the rudiment of our later well-being.

Christopher Bollas (1987) coins the term "transformational object" to capture an aspect of embedded relatedness implied by Winnicott and Bion. Bollas describes the transformational object as

> experientially identified by the infant with processes that alter self experience. It is an identification...where the first object is "known" not so much by putting it into an object representation, but as a recurrent experience of being—a more existential as opposed to representational knowing. As the mother helps to integrate the infant's being... the rhythms of this process...inform the nature of the "object" relation rather than the qualities of the object as object. (p. 14)

Beginning before mother is mentally represented as an Other, the transformational object relation emerges not from desire but from a perceptual identification of the object with its function as transformer of the rhythms of self-experience.

This form of early relating, Bollas suggests, "lives on in certain forms of object seeking in adult life." People search for transformational objects not to possess them so much as "to surrender to them as a medium that alters the self" (p. 14). The patient's use of the analyst as a transformational object, Bollas (1992) believes, is aimed less at gaining understanding than to free "the instinct to elaborate oneself" (p. 70). But, if this is to happen— and it is a big "if"—the analyst has to be available in a way that allows the patient to discover his or her own inventiveness. It is a catastrophe, Bollas implies, to be trapped in someone else's preconceptions—including the analyst's theory of successful endings.

To state all this in terms of the question at hand: If, as Freud suggests, pain is a primordial condition of the human species beyond the pleasure–unpleasure principle; and if, as Winnicott and Bion suggest, relationships are essential to transform pain into suffering and suffering is a way of describing what makes living meaningful; and, as Khan and the evidence of major religions suggest, having one's pain transformed by an unobtrusive Other is a fundamental human need; and, as Bollas claims, there is a life-long search for transformational objects; why, it must be asked, should an analytic relationship ever be expected to come to an end? Not, what obstacle in the patient is obstructing termination, but rather, how does each analytic couple wish to negotiate this basic human situation over time?

And to take this one step farther: Why must psychoanalysis only be about pain and suffering? There is, after all, an inherent pleasure, of the kind that accompanies exercising one's faculties and competencies—stretching one's psychic muscles so to speak—that is often a part of the analytic experience. Why might we tend to disparage an individual for simply finding pleasure in psychoanalysis? And what do we do when it becomes an addictive pleasure?

Addiction, it has been said, is what happens when we can never get enough of what we do not really want. And if psychoanalysis teaches us anything, it is that we often do not know what we really want. Bergmann (1997), discussing an early paper on termination by Ferenczi and Rank, noted that "in keeping with Freud's idea that during psychoanalysis the infantile neurosis is transformed into a transference neurosis, they advocated the analyst set termination date the moment this transference occurs. They believed that only then could a repetition of *clinging* to the early object be avoided" (p. 164).

Clinging—the dread of a patient never leaving because of an "addiction" to psychoanalysis—was sympathetically and usefully explored by the Hungarian analyst Imre Hermann. The natural instinctive urge to cling to mother, says Hermann, eventually becomes a source of shame. "We come to the conclusion," writes Hermann (1976),

> That...the human child is torn from his mother's body prematurely perhaps, among other things, as the consequence of an egotistical act on the part of the primal father. The urge to cling, therefore, continues to exist, reflecting a yearning for the primal state in which mother and child constitute an undivided dual unit. The fulfillment of that yearning is thwarted by a trauma, in actual fact by a series of traumata, repeated over and over again. (p. 7)

Hermann—an unacknowledged ancestor of attachment theory—describes a psychic conflict between the urge to cling to, and the reactive tendency to be free of, mother. These conflicting tendencies support two contrary fantasies: the fantasy of the lost unity and the fantasy of total independence. The instinct to cling inevitably remains unsatisfied because any real object will merely be an insufficient substitute for the sought after primal object. Human attachments, Hermann implies, are immersed in a sphere of nostalgia, inconsolability, and reactive detachment (Van Haute & Geyskens, 2007).

At first glance, Hermann appears to offer an instinctual twist on the traumatic pain of helplessness described by Freud. But there is a distinction that makes all the difference: for Freud, helplessness is understood in terms of the basic experiences of hunger and thirst. Attachment—the remedy for helplessness—is akin to an emergency measure to manage the tension of needs. (Klein will add to this a fear of the death instinct.) But for Hermann, clinging is an innate tendency adaptationally designed to manage a universal insecurity he calls *Haltlosigkeit*—a lack of hold or being without foothold (Van Haute & Geyskens, 2007). The primal catastrophe, according to Hermann, is not a question of hunger or innate destructiveness but the traumatic separation from mother to whom we cling so as to feel grounded. Hermann introduces us to the idea that clinging might profitably be thought of as a grasping for groundedness. Is it not common, while entertaining the idea of ending important relationships, to experience sensations of "losing support," "feeling unmoored," "dropped," or "being on shaky ground?"

Hermann's view of "the yearning to cling" as "thwarted by trauma" implies that the negotiation of this adaptational tendency is a fundamentally relational event. We are, in other words, all vulnerable to the shame of having the need for supportive grounding dismissed. Perhaps that is why mutual shame is a common emotional current running between analyst and patient when ending is contemplated. The patient may be wondering if the analyst can still love him or her despite the ways he or she has not changed. And the analyst might feel a need to cling to the patient so as to avoid the recognition of his or her own limitations. Referring to this as "the blood and guts" of therapy, Peggy Crastnopol writes:

> The clinging of the patient seems to be about the need for reassurance that "staying the same" in some ways, even on termination, is acceptable to the analyst. The patient keeps wanting to discover whether the analyst can value him *notwithstanding* his or her remaining imperfection. On the analyst's side, clinging to the patient often comes from a residual "sticky devotedness" to the patient and their shared process. To this we'd have to add the analyst's wish to convince himself that he really can cure the hardest things about the patient, and to avert feelings of failure at what still remains of the patient's neurosis. (Personal correspondence, March 12, 2009)

Another angle of vision from which to consider this matter of clinging and ending—the way we are poised between inconsolability and detachment —is a potentially terrifying element at the core of Winnicott's vision. "I think we must take it for granted," Winnicott (in Rodman, 1987) wrote privately to Money Kyrle,

> that emotionally there is no contribution from the individual to the environment or from the environment to the individual. The individual only communicates with a self-created world and the people in the environment only communicate with the individual in so far as they can create him or her. *Nevertheless, in health, there is the illusion of contact and it is this which provides the high spots of human life.* (p. 43, italics added)

Contact, the sustaining nutrient of relationship that constitutes the "high spots of human life," is, Winnicott suggests, a certain kind of illusion. (Hermann might say that neurosis is a pathology of contact.) Or, to turn the matter around, it is the capacity for illusion—the "blood and vital juices of our minds" as Wordsworth (1974) once said—that allows an experience of contact. It is not a far stretch to suggest that what we call psychopathologies—the irksome maladies that bring people to psychoanalysis as a treatment—have as their common denominator an approach to the outside world that is insufficiently supported by illusion. "Panic seized her. Blood seemed to pour from her shoes," writes Virginia Woolf (1941), "This is death, death, death...when illusion fails" (p. 125). Illusion—the root of all symbolism that allows a thing to be itself *and* something else at the same time—Marion Milner (1969) reminds us, "is needed for restoring broken links, bridges, to the outer world, as well as forming the first bridges. As necessary for healthy living as night dreams seem to be—and as playing is" (p. 416).

Milner's plea is not for illusion as a substitute for reality but, rather, as a formative and restorative bridge to reality. Whether cast in the language of "ego mastery," "renunciation of omnipotence," "having the reality principle supplant (and protect) the pleasure principle," "achieving the depressive position," or "developing a mature capacity for mourning," psychoanalysis suggests that the healthy individual needs to tolerate a not-me reality beyond magical control. Some form of loss, in other words, is believed to structure the psyche's relationship to external reality. The question is, How does the acceptance of loss become something other than an empty lifeless accommodation? How does a person navigate between the "thingness" of the world and his or her own subjectivity so that brute reality may be gradually brought to life with meaning? Psychoanalysis, it might be said, takes place in the space where reality—or at least the effort to speak as truthfully as possible about reality—meets up with the vital illusory "juices" of our minds.

As Emily Dickinson (1960) wrote,

> Tell all the Truth but tell it slant—
> Success in Circuit lies
> Too bright for our infirm Delight
> The Truth's superb surprise
> As Lightening to the Children eased
> With explanation kind
> The Truth must dazzle gradually
> Or every man be blind— (p. 506)

What if the problem of knowing when to end is not simply about learning to accept reality—Freud's bleak pursuit of an illusion-free existence—but, rather, about being better able to employ creative illusion such that one is not blind to, or blinded by, the truth. As Bruce Reis has suggested,

> it is the disillusionment accompanying termination, it's (tolerably) failed treatment goals, and/or the inability to ever provide "enough" which helps to create subjective meaning....Because psychoanalysis takes place in between timelessness and temporality, and in between reality and unreality, the dissolution of a treatment could also be thought of as the gift of reality that accompanies loss, a further structuring of the inside occurring as a result of what happens (in illusion) on the outside. (Personal communication, March 14, 2009)

For Reis, tolerable disillusionment—including disillusionment with psycho-analysis itself—helps create the "gift" of finding meaning in reality. Or, to state this in its active form: It is misleading to think it helpful for the analyst to insist on the externality of external things. The patient does not come to simply accept reality but to make use of disillusionment.

The capacity to "make use of disillusionment" in ending, however, does not reside solely within the patient. It is also a relational moment, a shared construction allowing for simultaneous union and separateness held in mind by both parties without either needing to dissociate the experience (Bromberg, 1998). It is an expression of what is containable within the context of the relationship at any given time. Put another way, within potential space we do not ask the question: "Whose reality is it?" (Modell, 1989). The patient's reality is not experienced by the analyst as something to be "penetrated" or "overcome" or "demystified" or "decoded." The analyst's reality is not experienced by the patient as an "intrusion" or "impinge-ment" or "confrontation." If the patient is relating to the analyst only as a self-object in Kohut's sense, or only as representing an external world with which one is lacking a true relationship, it is unlikely he or she will be able to make use of the analyst's construction of reality. If the analyst, on the other hand, is relating to the patient only as a "distorter" or "resister" of reality, or as only representing an inner world with which one is lacking a true relationship, then it is unlikely he or she will be able to make use of the patient's construction of reality. Just as the hallmark of a "good" analytic hour is not quite knowing for sure which of the participants made the interpretation, it is probably a feature of a "good-enough" ending to not know whose decision it "really" was.

Making use of disillusionment can also be understood as a way of retaining contact so as to mitigate what Winnicott calls "essential aloneness." "At the start," Winnicott (1988) notes,

> is an essential aloneness. At the same time this aloneness can only take place under maximum conditions of dependence. Throughout the life of the individual there continues *a fundamental unalterable and inherent aloneness, along with which goes unawareness of the conditions that are essential to the state of aloneness.* (p. 132, italics added)

Whatever else stopping treatment means—no matter how well or how badly it ends—it is liable to reintroduce us to our essential aloneness made bearable, Winnicott suggests, only through "conditions" about which we are not aware. Winnicott (1958) tells us a great deal about how the "capacity to be alone" comes about—having its roots in an early experience of being alone in the presence of an other—but he tells us little about what that capacity actually entails except to intriguingly inform us that

> When alone in the sense that I am using the term, and only when alone, the infant is able to do the equivalent of what in an adult would be called relaxing. The infant is able to become unintegrated, to flounder, to be in a state in which there is no orientation, to be able to exist for a time without being either a reactor to an external impingement or an active person with a direction of interest or movement. (p. 34)

It is worth pondering what bearing this capacity to be alone, in Winnicott's sense, might have on endings. Winnicott draws our attention not to an end state so much as to a freedom to drift about—"to flounder, to be in a state in which there is no orientations"—without needing any prematurely built-up coherent version of a self. (Winnicott is the first analyst to propose that, in addition to a desiring subject, there is a nonsensical subject.) What makes the pulses of drifting and gelling—transitioning from state to state without needing to immediately make sense—life-enhancing as opposed to alarming is the tether of connection to an Other of which we need not, indeed cannot, be aware. Coherence—including coherent explanations of endings—might suggest too vigilant a need for self-holding, a precipitate foreclosure of the nonpurposive resting state essential for creative reaching out to take place. "Free association that reveals a coherent theme," Winnicott (1971) writes elsewhere, "is already affected by anxiety, and the cohesion of ideas is a defense organization" (pp. 55–56).

One way to think about what it means to relax—or what might make stopping possible—is in terms of how the individual no longer feels the vigilant need to make sense. It is a mistaken notion worth dispelling that psychoanalysis helps a person make sense of his or her life. At best, it contributes to the lesser, but still quite valuable feat, of making sense of the ways people need and try to make sense of their lives.

Knowing something about how we try to make sense of our lives also means an awareness of what Bollas (1992) calls "the oddity of possessing one's own mind" (p. 239). Situating the origins of this awareness in the oedipal dilemma, Bollas describes the child's discovery of the complexity of his or her own mind, which includes the advent of the notion of point of view. The child wakes up to the realization that he or she is one mind among many and, to complicate matters even more, he or she is of many minds! For Bollas, the oedipal moment announces the presence of perspective and the discovery of the multiplicity of points of view. "Most people," writes Bollas (1992), "find consciousness of this aspect of the human condition—the complexity born of having a mind to oneself—simply too hard to bear" (p. 242).

In a speculative leap that bears on the question of ending, Bollas suggests that to find relief from "the ordinary unbearableness of this complexity," people often take flight—they "regress"—into the collusive consolation of couples, families, and groups. It is as if joining the "madness" of others is preferable to being left alone with one's own "madness." "We call this regression 'marriage' or 'partnership,'" writes Bollas, "in which the person becomes part of a mutually interdependent couple that evokes and sustains the bodies of the mother and the father, the warmth of the pre-Oedipal vision of life, before the solitary recognition of subjectivity grips the child" (p. 242).

Might Bollas' vision be one way of understanding the clinical observation that married or socially active individuals often find it easier to end treatment than those more isolated and alone? Could it be that seemingly unattached people are actually individuals who found other people's madness more disturbing than their own? And might a form of "regression"—in Bollas' sense—be a useful way of understanding why some endings—including certain psychoanalyses or marriages—stubbornly stall?

While negotiating endings, each analytic dyad takes measure of their madness. And it is not necessarily the patient who is the most "mad." Sanity—whatever else it entails—includes some acceptance of the enigma of the rhythm of relationship, the natural course of living experiences

together. To be sane one also needs to be able to take some comfort in completion—an arc with a beginning, a middle, and an end—no matter how
incomplete. But we are poor indeed, as Winnicott once remarked, if we are
only sane. Like all languages, psychoanalysis seeks freedom of expression
but also needs punctuation. Is this particular moment—when one person
pauses—a comma, a period, or an exclamation point? How do analyst and
patient alike feel when treatment benchmarks that seemed fitting at the outset later lose their luster? Or when the experience of psychoanalysis outlives
its usefulness? Not only: How is the treatment progressing? But also: How
are the analyst and patient currently treating each other? Are analyst and
patient collaborating, colluding, or colliding?

Truth be told, although analysts anticipate patients ending treatment in
a way consistent with the way they generally experience relationships—
perhaps a definition of a "good treatment" is one that ends differently than
would have been expected—it is not easy to gauge how "well" or how
"badly" a psychoanalysis really ends. There are even unusual cases where
the beginning does not simply foreshadow the end but actually is the end.

This was vividly brought home to me by a young man, engaged to be
married, who came for a consultation. He was experiencing "odd, disorienting, sensations" that his fiancée kept reassuring him were "nothing but
wedding jitters." He accepted that he had wedding jitters but was convinced
that something else was also going on. "I'm nervous about the wedding,"
he says, "It's a big step and I'm scared, but this isn't that!" "Well, if these
aren't the jitters," I ask him, "what *do* they feel like?" "A blunt pain," he
replies, "it is just a blunt pain." This blunt pain—he had no other word
to say how he was feeling—troubled his days, disturbed his nights, and,
tellingly, "interrupted his dreams." He confides in me how much he loves
his fiancée, how he knows he will need to adjust to her "quirks," yet how
hopeful he is about their future together. "That's why this pain makes no
sense at all."

"I see how hard you are trying to make sense of it," I say. "With the wedding coming up, I imagine it might even feel somewhat urgent."

"Odd that you should say that," he replies. "It does feel urgent because of
the wedding, but at the same time I have the odd feeling that this has been
with me my whole life."

At this point in our conversation, the young man surprises himself: "I
can't believe I'm thinking about this right now. But I'm remembering a
specific moment—I must have been in second grade—I was in school, at
my desk, and suddenly, out of the blue, I had this acute realization that
nobody—not the teacher, or my mother, or my father, or my sister—can
ever really know what's inside my head. And I can never really know what
is inside theirs!" At the time, he found the realization both "exhilarating"
and "terrifying." And he remembers how it preoccupied him for quite a
while and put him into a mood similar to the one he has been in lately.

"You figured out that you are all alone with a mind of your own," I comment. "I did," he replies, "and I will remain alone even though I love my fiancée to death and she loves me too." We talk about this a bit more and as the session approaches its end I am acutely aware that I do not know if I will see this likeable young man ever again. From the point of view of psychoanalysis as treatment—the "work" felt as if it had just begun. But, from the point of view of psychoanalysis as an experience, this man seems—there is no way to know for sure—to have found what he had not even known he was looking for. He had taken a risk, used our time together, and, as in all forms of playing, could be rid of something after getting what he wanted from it. "I guess I don't need to see you again," he remarks. As he utters these words, I surprise myself by replying, "'*Guess*' feels to me like *just* the right word." He smiles. And so we part ways. What happens next is anybody's guess.

REFERENCES

Bergmann, M. (1997). Termination: The Achilles heel of psychoanalytic technique. *Psychoanalytic Psychology, 14,* 163–174.

Bion, W. (1970). *Attention and interpretation.* London: Maresfield Library.

Bollas, C. (1987). *The shadow of the object: Psychoanalysis of the Unthought Known.* New York: Columbia University Press.

Bollas, C. (1992). *Being a character: Psychoanalysis and self experience.* New York: Hill & Wang.

Bowie, M. (1993). *Psychoanalysis and the future of theory.* Oxford and Cambridge, MA: Blackwell.

Bromberg, P. (1998). *Standing in the spaces: Essays on clinical process, trauma and dissociation.* Hillsdale, NJ: Analytic Press.

Dickinson, E. (1960). *The complete poems of Emily Dickinson* (T. Johnson, Ed.). New York: Little, Brown.

Emerson, R. W. (1904). *The complete works of Ralph Waldo Emerson.* Boston & New York: Houghton, Mifflin.

Ferenczi, S. (1955). The problem of termination of the analysis. In M. Balint (Ed.), *Final contributions to the problems and methods of psycho-analysis* (pp. 77–86). London: Hogarth.

Freud, S. (1926). Inhibitions, symptoms, and anxiety. In J. Strachey (Ed. & Trans.), *The standard edition of the complete psychological works of Sigmund Freud* (Vol. 20, pp. 77–174). London: Hogarth.

Goldman, D. (in press). Vital sparks and the form of things unknown. *New Library of Psychoanalysis.*

Hermann, I. (1976). Clinging—Going-in-search—A contrasting pair of instincts and their relation to sadism and masochism. *Psychoanalytic Quarterly, 45,* 5–36.

Khan, M. R. (1981). From masochism to psychic pain. *Contemporary Psychoanalysis, 17,* 413–421.

Milner, M. (1969). *The hands of the living God.* London: Hogarth.

Modell, A. (1989). The psychoanalytic setting as a container of multiple levels of reality: A perspective on the theory of psychoanalytic treatment. *Psychoanalytic Inquiry, 9*, 67–87.

Ogden, T. (2004). On holding and containing, being and dreaming. *International Journal of Psychoanalysis, 85*, 1349–1364.

Phillips, A. (1994). *On flirtation*. Cambridge, MA: Harvard University Press.

Pontalis, J. -B. (1977). *Frontiers in psychoanalysis: Between the dream and psychic pain*. New York: International Universities Press.

Racker, H. (1968). *Transference and countertransference*. New York: International Universities Press.

Rodman, R. F. (1987). *The spontaneous gesture: Selected letters of D. W. Winnicott*. Cambridge, MA: Harvard University Press.

Schlesinger, H. J. (2005). *Endings and beginnings: On terminating psychotherapy and psychoanalysis*. Hillsdale, NJ: Analytic Press.

Van Haute, P., & Geyskens, T. (2007). *From death instinct to attachment theory*. New York: Other Press.

Winnicott, D. W. (1958). The capacity to be alone. In *The maturational processes and the facilitating environment* (pp. 29–36). London: Hogarth.

Winnicott, D. W. (1963). Communicating and not communicating leading to a study of certain opposites. In *The maturational processes and the facilitating environment* (pp. 179–192). London: Hogarth.

Winnicott, D. W. (1971). *Playing and reality*. London: Routledge.

Winnicott, D. W. (1988). *Human nature*. New York: Schocken Books.

Wittgenstein, L., & Rhees, R. (1968). Conversations on Freud. *Psychoanalytic Review, 55*, 376–386.

Woolf, V. (1941). *Between the acts*. Harmondsworth, UK: Penguin.

Wordsworth, W. (1974). *The prose works of William Wordsworth* (W. J. B. Owen & J. Worthington Smyser, Eds.). London: Oxford University Press.

Chapter 15

Relational analyses

Are they more difficult to terminate?

Stefanie Solow Glennon

In our increasingly relational world of psychoanalysis, I find myself troubled regarding the degree to which the intimacy and power of the relationship between patient and analyst can elongate the length of the treatment or even make termination unthinkable. If a patient has done a substantial piece of analytic work and is quite ready for the termination phase but feels reluctant to leave the relationship with the analyst because the relationship feels so good, is so meaningful, is one of love and caring, and because he or she feels so close to the analyst, whom he or she now knows quite intimately (given the openness and lack of anonymity with which most of us carry on our analytic work), then we have a problem. I am suggesting that the dilemma of finding the line to walk such that the relationship can sustain optimal therapeutic action, but at the same time be a relationship that one can willingly leave, is a difficult task. Some analysts allow the relationship with the patient to cross over into friendship and they socialize outside the analytic space and thereby avoid the dilemma. They can terminate the treatment but sustain the loving relationship. Is that where we are all headed as an alternative to interminable analyses? I worry about the impact of a complete loss of asymmetry on what was an analytic/therapeutic relationship. I also still believe that the ability to terminate, to go through a separation or mourning, and to not only survive, but do fine, is an important therapeutic goal. Yet what aspects of the relationship have to be sacrificed in order to make leaving less abortive. I do not think it is just a question of there being more work to be done if the patient is unwilling to leave, although that certainly could be the case in some instances. But I think there is now a reality factor at work that has to be taken into consideration, the reality that few people would willingly terminate an intense relationship that is loving, supportive, mutual, and meaningful even if more therapeutic work is not deemed necessary. It can feel like a crazy thing to do without the press of death. I have no answers to the dilemma, but certainly would welcome dialogue regarding this conundrum that I see looming in our relational psychoanalytic work.

The above thoughts were initially jotted down for myself following a particularly difficult session with a patient around the issue of termination.

It occurred to me as I listened to her chasten me for even thinking about an ending of her analysis, that her reasoning made sense. It made sense in terms of the intensity and mutuality of our long relationship. What she said was, "Why would I even consider that? I have had enough losses in my life. Why would I *choose* to say goodbye to you? Why would I *choose* to sever a relationship that is so dear to me, so special and like none I've ever had before? It feels so unnatural. In life outside this office the only time a relationship like this would end would be due to death." In response to my saying something about the benefits of separating and discovering that she could be just fine without me, she said, "I know I can do that but I don't want to. It seems crazy to me. I can afford to come here, I have the time and the money and I can't even imagine not seeing you anymore." She's not in the field and is likely correct that our paths would not cross. She refused to hear of it and proceeded to go on with our work as she has done for the last 21 years. I stopped bringing it up.

In presenting this case, I do not want to tempt readers into supervisory thoughts, which I have no doubt would be helpful, but rather I think the issue she raises is universal enough to be thought about apart from whatever have been for her the particular meanings involved in separation. Therefore, the clinical material that follows is devoid for the most part of psychodynamic history and transference–countertransference issues that have arisen and been worked on throughout our time together. I understand that more in-depth explication of what the underlying issues have been might very well shed more light on the specifics of why termination might be so difficult for this woman and what in our relationship and in the countertransference might be contributing to that difficulty. But in spite of that awareness, I still am convinced that she is on to something, that there is an issue that has solely to do with the fact of the intensity and vividness of our real relationship, or what she refers to as "the friendship part" that has added to whatever underlying reasons there might be in her reluctance to leave me. I must say though that in my judgment those issues have been adequately worked through between us, and that what remains has mainly to do with what she has verbalized about not wanting to say goodbye forever to someone whom she now cares so deeply about and whom she knows cares so deeply about her. This is the issue I am underlining in this paper and want to focus upon. I also intend to ask the patient for permission to publish the paper and, if very personal psychodynamic material were included, I am certain she would not grant that permission. So this is my compromise, at the same time knowing that it might understandably frustrate some of my readers.

Julia is a 67-year-old woman with whom I began working three times a week in 1988. At that time she had just ended a 17-year-long relationship with a married man who was always holding out the possibility that he would leave his wife to be with her. She had finally and painfully given up on him and was facing a serious depression. Her defining statement at the time (which is now part of our litany) was "I have to find my own light." The light of her life was now out with the love of her life. She had been married for 7 years and divorced, but that relationship never reached the deep part of her that was touched and nourished by the relationship that had just ended.

When we began, Julia, though not a lawyer, was working for a law firm, was living in a one-bedroom apartment where she had been for many years, and had little hope that she could lead a truly fulfilling independent existence. For example, she had never gone to a movie by herself, no less a restaurant or theater.

During the course of our work she went into business with a partner and became highly successful. She purchased and furnished an apartment in Manhattan and a lovely weekend home (she has shown me pictures) outside of the city. She has bought expensive artwork that she adores and has become quite knowledgeable about. She has returned to the piano which she had not played for decades though she had been an accomplished classical pianist as a child and young adult and had been accepted to Juilliard after high school but could not attend because her parents could not afford the expense. She now studies and plays regularly and has purchased two Steinways—one for each home.

She serves on several boards, one in New York City and two others in the small town where her second home is located and, since recently retiring, has taken on more responsibility and leadership roles in these organizations.

For some years she has been actively engaged in planning and speaking at cultural events in the small town outside the city, where she has her second home, and has become quite a celebrity there. She is an active member of that community, has numbers of close friends, a full social life, and oftentimes complains about how busy she is even though now retired from her business—from which she continues to get financial support. In addition, along the way she lost 35 pounds, cut and colored her hair, changed her wardrobe, and is very attractive. Most importantly, she now for the most part is pleased with the way she looks, which is highly significant given her previous self-perception as being a "wallflower" and totally unattractive to men. She has had several relationships over the years, but not one that has sustained. At one time she actively got involved in Internet dating, but was not successful at meeting an appropriate man.

She has done a good deal of travel alone and with female friends. And recall this is a woman who at the beginning of our work had never done anything of a social nature by herself.

I have gone into such detail about the positive changes Julia has made in her life because I wanted to limn what she has been able to accomplish over the last 21 years and emphasize my view that she does not have a problem with dependency or autonomy—the main problem put forth in the literature regarding why patients do not want to leave their analysts. The shape of her life is part of the reason why termination thoughts have arisen in me.

I am concerned that what has been described might give the impression that our relationship over the years has been only positive and easygoing. On the contrary, I can clearly remember, I think in perhaps the sixth year of our work, walking down the hallway from my office to the elevator (she was my last patient of the night) thinking, "Oh my god, this work is tough." She had really put me through what she has since called one of our "World War III's."

The battles would arise around issues of what she considered to be my not understanding. For example, how could I unilaterally raise her fee (this was when she was now making at least three times my income from the business she had started in the third or fourth year of our work)? It was the unilateral nature of the decision that got to her. When she wants to pay me more money, she will do it. I held to my guns, and she did finally accept the increase.

Another time I suggested that she consider joining a group that I was running. How could I be so insensitive? How could I not know that she had enough lifelong pain stemming from the birth of her younger, beautiful sister (an Elizabeth Taylor look-alike) that she would certainly not want to have any analytic siblings. She never did join the group.

Or the time when my first grandson was born 13 years ago and I offered to show her a picture of him when I came back from visiting him in California and she knew where I had been. She raved at me. Again I should have known that she would worry that he would take me away from her—another sibling of sorts. Near irrational and coupled with sometimes vicious sarcasm that almost leveled me. She always sprang back and it was almost like dealing with two different people. At the time I did not have the concept of differing self-states, but that was certainly what was occurring.

So, in addition to myriad loving, supportive, and positive aspects, our relationship has been forged out of a great deal of what Michael Eigen (1992) refers to as "coming through." In the last few years when another world war threatens to erupt, she is able to step back and engage me in her attempt to understand herself and what is going on between us that is threatening to trigger her rage—what she euphemistically calls "being annoyed." At times her complaints about me have been justified, and when I have apologized and agree with her perceptions and sense of reality, it always has had the effect of softening the space between us. I now know that she has been as distressed by the shifts in her as I have been in being the attacked object. But through all of the harangues, our connection sustained and kept growing and deepening even though there were times when I worried she would leave in a rage and never return.

Julia now clearly "has her own light," is extremely creative and success-ful in her life, and is capable of thinking through whatever it is that is interpersonally problematic for her either with her children (she adopted her sister's grown children a few years after her sister's death from cancer at age 44), or with members of the various boards on which she serves, and I sincerely feel that she is fully capable of doing without me. For the most part she does think through these issues and frequently acts on them and then brings them in to me *after* she has done her own work.

When I again raised the termination issue with her and met her resistance by pointing out to her that she will carry me inside of her and that the work we have done together will always be available to her, she acknowledged that she could see the truth in what I said but still said "I don't want to stop seeing you or not have you in my life. It feels like an inhuman, arbitrary, prescribed, insane choice." I then stopped bringing it up for another long piece of time. I do not feel comfortable making a unilateral decision to set a termination date, which has been so prevalent in the history of psychoanalysis (Orgel, 2000), even though I sometimes feel guilty about taking her money, about perhaps depriving her of the separation and necessary mourning process that might be standing in the way of her finding an intimate relationship outside my office.

The one thing this patient has not been able to establish in her life is a love relationship with a man. Issues around intimacy have been worked through to a considerable degree. In the beginning of our work, she would come in with a list of things she wanted to talk about and would adhere to that control and was rigid in her presentations and way of being. It also became clear to both of us that she was terrified of letting another man in, of having another intimate sexual relationship. She and I now share exceptional closeness. She is open, easy, spontaneous, frequently delightful, and I am confident that with the right man she would be capable of achieving the kind of relationship she now yearns for. However she is in her late sixties, is a highly accomplished, cultured, and now wealthy woman who would not be able to love someone who was not able to share her life and her values. And most men of the appropriate age are either married or not suitable. So there is a reality factor at work here.

Although, as stated above, I sincerely believe Julia would be able to have the kind of relationship she wants if someone were available, I still cannot help worrying that her attachment to me might in some way be making that more difficult.

Raising what I see as an as yet unanswered and difficult issue in psychoanalysis, I went to the literature to see what others have said. I started with Irwin Hoffman (1998) and the chapter in his book entitled "Constructing Good Enough Endings in Psychoanalysis." Whereas Hoffman covers in great detail the myriad aspects of termination from the patient's and as well as the analyst's points of view and makes an invaluable contribution to the subject, he does not address the specific issue I am raising. It is not addressed by Jody Davies (2005) in her extraordinary paper on the termination process. Edgar Levenson (1976), Orgel (2000), Christopher Bonovitz

(2007), and others do not address it. (See: Ferenczi, 1927; Firestein, 1994; Novick, 1997; Schafer, 2002; Schlesinger, 2005.)

I then thought of Ralph Greenson, remembering a quote of his that I read when in graduate school, in which he boldly stated that without the existence of what he called the "real relationship" between the person of the analyst and the person of the patient, there is a "copiousness of insight and a paucity of change." Because he was stressing the importance of this real relationship and not just focusing on the transference relationship, I was hoping I would find something about the difficulty in giving up a "real relationship" and how that variable might affect a patient's reluctance to terminate. But unfortunately Greenson (1971, 1972) does not address the issue.

However, somewhat incidentally, I was amazed at how prescient Greenson was in terms of the relational turn in psychoanalysis. One of his quotes, written in 1971, could have come right out of Irwin Singer's seminal and at the time thought to be iconoclastic article "The Fiction of the Anonymous Analyst" (1977), written in opposition to classical Freudian anonymity. Greenson stated:

> It is important to keep in mind that our patients know us really far less than we know them. Their beliefs and judgments are based on much less evidence than is available to us. Yet, everything we do or say, or don't do or say, from the décor of our office, the magazines in the waiting room, the way we open the door, greet the patient, make interpretations, keep silent, and end the hour, reveals something about our real self, and not only our professional self. (p. 91)

It is likely that Greenson did not experience the difficulty, the conundrum that I am facing with Julia, because what he meant by being a real person with his patients did not include being as open and self-disclosing, responsive to questioning, focusing on and talking about enactments, and so forth, as is frequently done today in our relational way of working.

In an attempt to flesh out for myself what Julia might be missing in terms of the mourning process involved in separating from me and our work, I turned to Loewald (1962), who stresses what he considers to be the crucial importance of going through a termination phase of analysis:

> The relinquishment of external objects and their internalization involves a process of separation, of loss and restitution in many ways similar to mourning.... The internalizations by which the patient's character structure became established in earlier years have been partially undone in the analytic process and have been replaced by relationships with an external object—the analyst standing for various objects at different times.... The pressure of the impending separation helps to accelerate this renewed internalization, although the process of internalization

will continue and come to relative completion only after termination of the analysis. (pp. 259–260)

Loewald definitely considers a termination phase to be crucial to optimal development of internal structures (i.e., strengthening of the ego)—something I certainly would not want to deprive my patient of. But he addresses only the transference relationship and the overcoming of the transference neurosis. He does not address the impact or even the existence of a "real relationship" between patient and analysts. But what is certainly clear is his conviction that ending an analysis is a psychically invaluable aspect of analytic work.

Edgar Levenson (1976), whom I greatly admire and respect, finally says that ending an analysis is an aesthetic decision and that each analysis will end in its own way. Quoting Masud Khan (1965), he says we are "the servants of the patient's process." He then continues,

> I would say that it makes no more sense to ask when or how to terminate than to ask when to die. It is a natural event in the course of therapy…. Every conceivable permutation and combination of position about the meaning of termination is represented in the psychoanalytic literature and one can find scriptures to one's purpose without any great difficult. (p. 341)

Whereas Levenson does focus on the real relationship, he does not address difficulties in leaving because of the power of that relationship. He also does not emphasize the importance of the mourning aspect of termination and the psychic benefits of the hoped for resultant internalizations.

I was well into the writing of this chapter when I came across Martin Bergmann's article (1997) entitled "Termination: The Achilles Heel of Psychoanalytic Technique." In the abstract of this paper he states, "In real life, only death and hostility bring a libidinal relationship to an end. The kind of termination psychoanalysis demands is without precedent" (p. 163). And I sighed with relief and felt affirmed. At least he was acknowledging the problem. After doing a fairly extensive review of what others have said about termination, Bergmann ends his paper as follows:

> In spite of the large literature on termination, no paradigm of termination has been made part of the professional equipment of the psychoanalytic practitioner. In this absence, the psychoanalyst is under the pressure of his superego to terminate treatment, often prematurely, to escape the inner accusation that he exploits the analysand for libidinal or financial purposes. At the same time, he is under the opposite pressure, based on the idealization of psychoanalysis, that more would have been achieved had he or she been more experienced or knowledgeable.

Though there are general signs that the analysand has entered the termination phase, *the termination moment is still a matter of art rather than science*. (p. 172, italics added)

In effect, he comes to the same conclusion as did Levenson 30 years ago, but with considerably more angst about that decision, more like my own. What he does not address though, like Greenson, is the degree to which the libidinal relationship, by dint of being "real" and not just transferential, is even harder to let go. I am suggesting that the glue or stickiness of the libido is firmer, more difficult to break loose from if the analyst allows himself or herself to be a real person, known well beyond the transference and therefore more susceptible to being healthfully loved and missed as a unique individual.

Undoubtedly Julia's and my real relationship was intensified and made more specific due to the death of my husband in 1998 and my current husband's traumatic brain injury resulting from a bicycle accident in May of 2006. My deceased husband was a character actor and Julia had recognized him in my waiting room several times. She had seen him on Broadway, on TV, and in the movies and put it together that he was my husband. I confirmed that. Subsequently, she went to see him in any production in the city that he was in. When he died there was an announcement of a memorial for him in the *New York Times*, which she attended, where she saw both my children and grandchildren, heard his friends and colleagues speak of him, and thereby got a very detailed look into my personal life. On occasion after his death she would ask how I was doing but did not press for more information than I offered.

When I remarried 5 years later, she knew of that, and even saw my new husband when he too waited for me in the waiting room. I introduced them one evening when she was coming out of the elevator in the lobby of my office building at the same time that I was greeting my husband who was waiting for me downstairs. I had not known that she had stayed on in the bathroom in my office and so left a few minutes before she.

When my husband's accident occurred, I had to cancel my appointments with her at the last minute and it would have felt unnatural not to tell her what had happened. During his long convalescence, she would on occasion check in with me and sincerely wanted to know how I was doing. This time short answers did not suffice. In addition, over the years I have become much more open with numbers of patients about what is going on for me internally. It has felt as if the real relationship sometimes requires information that can hopefully be kept orthogonal to the analytic relationship. I am very diligent in pursuing my patients' reactions to whatever it is they hear from me. Whether or not I have been able to catch all that is in the space between us, having to do with me and my situation, I certainly cannot know.

In addition to what in my personal life impacted upon our analytic relationship, Julia at one time had surgery for a life-threatening condition and I visited her in the hospital.

Regarding the delicate balance between asymmetry and mutuality in the analytic dyad, Hoffman (1998) has this to say: "...finding an optimal balance between asymmetry and mutuality can sometimes be difficult, and overcorrections of the classical asymmetrical atmosphere can sometimes be harmful, leading to endings that repeat earlier traumas more than they realize potentials for new experience" (p. 272). And this caveat comes from someone who is so sensitively attuned to the need in analysis for spontaneity and the meeting of two unique individuals forging new experience from the old. It is a very difficult line to find and the issue is one with which I am currently grappling in my work with Julia and others.

For Freud (1937) and others (Orgel, 2000), the problem of seemingly interminable analyses was mainly one of the patient and analyst arriving at an impasse where no further progress is being made. It is Freud's idea to unilaterally set a termination date in an attempt to force issues to the fore. When the time comes, he admonishes that the termination plan must be adhered to or the patient will lose respect for the authority of the analyst. His view is that the looming termination will facilitate further analytic work and thereby undo the impasse. He also focuses on the problem of patients leaving precipitously, but he does not address the issue I am raising.

Again, I am faced with the question of have I gone too far in the direction of mutuality with this patient, making myself just too difficult to leave. Thankfully this has not been a problem to this extent with other patients who have been able to leave after having voiced similar thoughts about the strangeness of the decision. One woman after 9 years struggled with similar feelings, expressed almost in the same words as Julia, but she was able to leave. However, she is in the field and we have run into one another on occasion. She even attended a presentation of mine at her analytic institute which initiated some e-mailing between us and very connected contact at the end of the evening. She, of course, knew when she terminated that it was likely we would meet at professional gathering, which, as I have stated, is not the case with Julia.

Confounding the issue is the fact that Julia has arguably achieved more from her analysis and made more life changes than anyone I have worked with. In addition to the life changes described previously, she is no longer depressed, no longer uncomfortable and awkward in the world, and, for the most part, is okay with who she is as well as being okay with who I am. It is difficult, therefore, to say that perhaps I should have done it otherwise. What might have been lost if I had? Certainly, I am hypothesizing that termination might have been easier for her—and for me. (I am not suggesting that I do not struggle with the thought of "losing" her, what my life would be like without having her in it—the other side of the coin of being known.)

And she might very well have gained from the mourning experience attendant upon termination, but at what price?

These questions inevitably resulted in my remembering my own termination from my analyst of 10 years. She is an interpersonal analyst trained at the William Alanson White Institute, but one whose first analysis was with a Freudian and her second an Interpersonalist. I had the same experience, having had a 6-year-long analysis through the New York Psychoanalytic Institute clinic, five times a week, which I found for the most part frustrating and unhelpful. My analyst was in training at the time and was right out of central casting for the stereotypic anonymous, silent, enigmatic Freudian. I finally left after staying too long and was referred to my second analyst by a trusted supervisor.

From the beginning, she felt right, and with hindsight it seems that, at least for me, she struck a good balance between being a real person in the room but at the same time being distant enough not to smudge or dilute the emergence of transference material. Although I sometimes wished she were more supportive and loving, I would often feel more whole when I would bang up against her difference, her separateness, which actually felt like boundary building, a defining activity of my own subjectivity. I would have an image of two wheels with different ridges and cut-outs banging up against each other and in so doing, each edge got stronger and more defined. Where does one end and the other begin? The opposite of merger, which is exactly what I needed given my mother's narcissism. But it is also the character of this very bounded, clear cut, yet emotionally present woman. We were a good match, at least from my vantage point. I knew very little about her personally, but I knew a great deal about her personality and how she felt about things, including me, most of the time. I knew when she was pleased or when she was angered, and usually she could tell me why. She got me, she understood, and I knew I was in the presence of someone, an other, who was alike and yet her own person. I knew she would never let me go over a line and that her boundaries would be so clear that I would know easily where and who she was at any given moment. We argued, we sometimes fought, but I never felt in danger of destroying either her or what we had. Those disagreements were self-defining and boundary reinforcing for me. It was not a question of power or winning, but rather a meeting of minds including difference. Interestingly, numbers of my patients over the years have commented on my having clear boundaries, usually said with relief.

I left this analyst feeling buoyant, hopeful, and internally stable. I sent her a gift of two beautiful but different vases crafted by a gifted potter and received a thank you note from her telling me that they both sat on her mantle-piece in her home. The most moving part of the note was her saying, "thank you for knowing."

And I did know, and I could leave and did not experience the feelings expressed by some of my patients, especially Julia. Now of course I knew that I would run into her at professional gatherings. (I actually have seen her very few times—twice in a restaurant we coincidentally both frequent and love and her comment when last we met there was "it is a special place to both of us." But I have not seen her in years.)

I am not proposing that my analyst was perfect in navigating the difficult divide between nurturance and distance, but perhaps she was better than I—at least how I have been with Julia. I really do not know. I think that Julia's love of me is more than my love of my analyst or at least is more personal and intimate—whatever that means in the context of an analytic relationship that certainly still is asymmetrical. I also think that a case could be made that Julia has derived more from her analysis than I from mine.

A fundamental question then is to what extent is love (and what form of love) mutative, constituting a corrective, generative experience, and to what extent does it prohibit leaving and transferring that loving capacity, that intimacy, onto someone with whom one can spend more than several hours a week.

Also, since plunging into this chapter, I find myself questioning the need for mourning via termination and its presumed universal efficacy. Hoffman (1998) again in his wisdom has this to say: "...it would be contrived and unnecessarily wrenching for the patient to try to terminate his or her analysis in any formal or decisive say. In general, it would be rigidly objectivistic to insist that deliberately planning and constructing an ending for analysis is desirable for everybody" (p. 256).

In speaking with a friend/colleague while engaged in thinking about and writing this chapter, I heard from him that he questions whether or not termination need be thought of as a mourning. Perhaps placing it in that category, as has been done by so many theorists (Loewald, Klein, Schaefer, et al.) is inaccurate. After all, even patients who are not in the field know that if something in their lives arises of a difficult nature, they can come back. To that extent it is *not* like death with its finality of loss and requisite mourning. This analyst told me that at least with one patient who had difficulty leaving permanently, they arrange for a once yearly "checkup" or check-in," not unlike a yearly exam with a medical doctor. And that has worked quite well with his patient.

Is my colleague's patient being deprived of the experience of letting go even further (i.e., not seeing his analyst at all unless some problem he needs help with arises), which would still be different from what we usually mean by mourning? Certainly a once-a-year meeting takes the edge off what we have been equating with a death and mourning. If all our patients know that they can see us if they are in need, does that not make termination different, of a different color or hue than that which is designed to produce mourning? The argument I previously made to myself is that all of us have to at one time or another face great loss either of a loved one or the loss attendant upon our own aging and declining health. But who is to say that having had the experience with the loss of an analyst, one is more prepared or more practiced at handling loss if that experience is gone through with the analyst.

As stated previously, I am aware of Loewald and others' idea of internal structures or the ego being strengthened by the further internalization of the analyst through the ability to have mourned his or her loss, and perhaps that is a good enough argument for termination even if it is not analogous to mourning a death. For patients who have persistent issues around dependency and a fear of autonomy, discovering that they are capable of facing life on their own would certainly be a crucial experience. Perhaps we are once again at the point of saying that the termination process must be different for different people and that one of the determinants—aside from the success of the analysis—is the degree to which someone would benefit or unnecessarily suffer from permanent separation from the analyst. As Levenson (1976) said in his usual off-beat, poetic, and imagistic way, "Psychoanalysts, like mushrooms, flourish best in the dark" (p. 342).

Quite surprisingly, in the last few weeks there has been some movement, at least indirectly, toward Julia's leaving our work. What follows are two sessions 1 week apart that I was able to take notes on because they were telephone sessions. (Since her retirement we have been meeting twice a week instead of three times due to the fact that she has been spending more time at her home in the country. She comes into the office for one session and we conduct the second on the phone. This could be considered a kind of weaning, although she would argue against that interpretation.)

On December 11, 2008, in the course of an in-person session, I had recommended a book to her (I cannot now remember in what context), saying that it had been given to me by a patient. "I gave it to you!" she said, and then I vaguely remembered that was so. How I could have forgotten has worried me about the state of my decreasing memory ever since. But she said nothing more, and I, having had a tooth extraction that morning and in some pain with an ice pack on my swollen face, was relieved that she seemed to accept my confusion, my belief that of course she was correct and my subsequent apology. I did not as I would have under usual circumstances explore her reaction to my attributing her gift to someone else.

She started the subsequent phone session by saying something about having worked through something by herself that she considered very meaningful, and of which she was proud. These were her thoughts; my responses are in parentheses.

> Why can't she remember this? And then I thought, it's because you're too busy and that you're being so busy is having an effect on me. I also thought to myself, that's who she is and that's all. Somehow you and

she have crossed over this fine line and you can't just look at her as your therapist. At another time I would have gotten so annoyed, I would have gone bonkers if that had happened, but this time I said to myself don't look at her that way. That's who she is and it has nothing to do with you or with anything about you. It just has to do with who she is. Because our relationship has changed so much. Well honey, I said talking to myself, that's what you wanted and that's what you got." (I think that's terrific.) You do? (Yeah.) I still think you're too busy. It's odd that I came to this way of thinking. (Odd?) Yes, the other way of thinking would have been it doesn't really matter how far beyond therapist/patient this has gone, you still have a right to resent that, to resent her forgetting you were the one who gave her the book and what it meant to go out and buy it because I knew she would enjoy it, because I had so much enjoyed it. After all you pay for your therapy. However, the relationship has gone where it's gone and that's how I have wanted it to go. (Why would it have been better to think that way?) There was a time if this had happened I would have gotten very, very upset. Remember the weeks and weeks of harangue over the Halcyon Days present I gave you and you never opened it to look at the inscription, which was the reason I gave it to you! (I laughed and of course remembered and said I hadn't even known at the time that those little porceline *objects d'arte* opened—a reference to her being so much more knowledgeable about those things than I. Why didn't you tell me all of this on Monday when you were in the office?) I would have talked about it if your face hadn't been all blown up. I'm happy I went to a better place without you. Nothing was lost. If I want to feel a little sorry for you with an ice pack on your face, that's okay. (I agree you're now capable of doing that kind of work by yourself, which is not to say that I wasn't disappointed in myself for forgetting that you had given me the book. I'm truly sorry about that. Maybe I *am* too busy.)

At the end of this session I thought to myself that we might very well be getting closer to some kind of ending.

On the following Monday, in the office, she spoke about thinking quite seriously of following her dream of living for 6 months in London and traveling around Europe. She had casually mentioned this before but without any plans. She spoke about getting older, that she can afford it, feels up to it physically and now has a few friends who live there and could facilitate a life there.

I listened to her plans and did not say what was on my mind about our work together and this move seeming to represent at least some sort of separation. However, when next we spoke on the phone I did raise the issue and spoke of it as perhaps an indirect way of terminating the analysis. What she said was,

I don't think this has any implications for you and me. I really don't think this has any meaning other than I would ask myself well, so would I write to Stefanie, would I call, what would I do. It's over a year away, so I have time to think about that. It never occurred to me that we couldn't start right back up. It never occurred to me. What I did worry about was what would I do if I got sick? What kinds of precautionary tests would I take before I left. I would miss you but it never occurred to me that I would be leaving you yet. It's like when you go away for seven weeks in the summer (I said that it's never been seven, usually five, once or twice six. I don't know why I needed to clarify that.) "Is it a coward's way of at least seeing how I do? *No*, it's like an adventure that I'll come back from and resume seeing you. At this moment I can't imagine that not happening. Do you think that it indicates that I'm leaving the nest? (Yes I do. I think it indicates that you *can* leave the nest.) There are other things I'm leaving that could be dangerous, that I could really lose by leaving. (She was referring to boards she is on and one that she chairs.) I could really lose them. Would that stop me? No. So I worry far more about the implication of these things. I don't think anything about our relationship would change. Would it be the beginning of the end? I don't think so. I'm going on a sabbatical. (It sounds very exciting.) It does, it does sound exciting. It could be very exciting and a chance to see parts of Europe I've never seen before.

The likelihood is that Julia is in fact on her way toward ending our analytic relationship and this is the way she has had to do it. Not unlike Manny, Irwin Hoffman's 84-year-old patient (discussed in the chapter of his book, "Constructing Good-Enough Endings in Psychoanalysis") who went off to Florida for several months, also on a "sabbatical," in lieu of leaving treatment. But we will have to see.

As an interesting aside, Levenson (1976), in his article "The Aesthetics of Termination," states "It has been said that, in retrospect, a therapist could find in the first dream of the patient the entire enfolded story of the analysis. It might be interesting to do a study in which therapists try to predict the nature and style of termination of a specific patient from the first dream" (p. 341).

I vaguely remembered Julia's first dream as being the two of us playful and equal. Fortunately, I was able to locate the dream dated 4/7/88. (She began the treatment on 4/5/88.) I was able to do that, because, with the exception of intake notes, the only notes that I take down verbatim during sessions (before the advent of telephone sessions) are dreams. I have them all filed in "dream boxes." Here is the dream:

We were out in the hall of this hotel (My office at the time was in a residential hotel) and we were both dressed in slacks. There was a column from floor to ceiling and we were sitting on the floor at right angles of the column, laughing and it was silly. You were saying something about it being nice to have somebody in therapy who does something....Oh yes, that's just wonderful. We were having a good old time....She wears pants all the time, her leg over the chair....Or maybe it's that I feel I can work with you. (There were a few words in my speedwriting that I could not decipher, but what I have transcribed is accurate.)

Perhaps what the dream is saying is that what she has been yearning for is fun, is mutuality, is equality of a relationship in a way of being that is not formal, is not prescribed, is spontaneous and perhaps at times even silly—in great contrast to how she had presented herself to the world as always in control and conventional. If so, we certainly are much closer to that ideal and perhaps one reason why she can now conceive of leaving for 6 months, even if it is a year away.

I find it intriguing to think that a first dream in analysis might be a fore-shadowing of what the patient unconsciously "knows" has to be achieved in his or her treatment. Perhaps I will go back to those dream boxes and look into other first dreams.

In my reading of the analytic literature on termination, it is clear that there is no clarity. There is uncertainty about what constitutes readiness for ter-mination, who should make the decision to end the analysis, whether or not it should be mutual, whether or not there should be alterations in how the analyst works or in the frame during the termination phase, and whether or not termination is even a goal toward which to strive. Some analysts make a strong case for the ameliorative aspects of patients going through a mourning in the presence of the mourned object—the analyst. (This is a position I still take, but with the awareness that it may not be beneficial or at least attain-able for every patient.) It is thought that crucial, developmental psychic gains can be lost if the patient does not have this experience. Some analysts with some patients come to the conclusion that the pain of loss is not worth what-ever psychic gains are theoretically possible. The only explanation offered leading to patients' not wanting to leave is the one of pathological depen-dence or lack of autonomy. I have not yet encountered, with the exception of Bergmann's speaking of transference love, a discussion of a nonsymptomatic, nonpathologized reluctance to leave based on the intensity and profundity of the new, real relationship with the analyst.

The significant issue of the inseparability of the transference relationship from the "real relationship" (Hoffman, 1983, 1998) is one with which I fully concur. How could it be otherwise when transference is always present, to some degree, in a relationship between two human beings? However, what I am suggesting in this chapter is that over and above the analytic relationship that, as stated above, always includes inextricable elements of the transfer-ence and the real relationship, there can be something that Julia calls "the friendship part" that has grown over the years and does feel, for both of us, somehow, to some extent, separate from the analytic relationship. And that is the variable that has made termination so inconceivable to her.

What I presented certainly answers none of the questions posed but I hope addresses a perplexing new facet of the termination problem that is worth thinking about. Because this issue has come up in my practice, I have spoken to a number of relational colleagues, who, not surprisingly, have told me of long-term patients who have struggled, or are still struggling, with a similar difficulty in terminating. A few others have attempted friendships with their own analysts after termination and have been disillusioned by how the attempted "friendship" diluted, in one case damaged, the ongoing therapeutic benefits of the internalized analytic relationship. (What might be lost of a good-enough analysis if the analytic couple attempts to convert the relationship into a friendship outside of the office, outside of the asymmetry of psychoanalysis, is a topic for another paper. But what I have learned certainly does reinforce my reluctance to give in to that pull.)

It is interesting that Julia has never lobbied for a friendship outside of my office. Very early in our work, after answering her question about the possibility of a postanalytic friendship by explaining that it was not how I saw the work, she accepted my position and then said, "Why would I let myself care about you when I know I will have to leave someday?" But she did let herself care and now does not want to leave. Might there not have been some unconscious prescience at work here as well?

At this point, I still am unclear as to how Julia's analysis will end, if it does, and even how I understand what all the issues have been for her around leaving me. I am also more *uncertain* as to what would be best for her than when I started this chapter. But I am sure that one variable in her reluctance to leave has been the reality factor of her feeling it to be weird, inhuman, and inauthentic to make a decision to terminate our relationship because *I* think it might produce some further psychic gains. Such a directive and dogmatic stance would be contrary to the mutuality of our relationship and the value she has gleaned from authenticity, trusting her feelings, allowing for the deepening of relationships and not aborting them out of some dictate that does not come from her heart.

It is curious to me that the patient who so pointedly activated my concern about some relational analyses being interminable should have begun termination stirrings while I was writing this chapter. Are we speaking of unconscious communication or the coincidence that she needed 21 years to get to this point? If the latter, then perhaps once again what her case illustrates is that every patient has to leave according to his or her own timetable.

If she begins to separate from me by going off to London for 6 months, we will still have a chance to set a date and deal with termination or mourning issues upon her return. But the question of leaving having been existentially more difficult for her because of the way in which I have worked with her (i.e., the degree of openness and self-disclosure) and not a linger-ing inadequately worked psychodynamic, is still an important one that has not been addressed in the current relational literature on termination.

In light of the degree to which I have worried about Julia and what I may have done or may not have done optimally, I am heartened by these words of Irwin Hoffman (1998) which appear in the last paragraph of his remarkable book:

> How life goes for the patient in the long run depends on many factors outside of the analyst's control, including the patient's own resource-fulness and the ever-present factor of luck. The ultimate challenge is to absorb the uncertainty of what fate will bring, along with the certainty that in the end it will always bring death, and despite those realities, to choose to celebrate and care for our lives and the lives of others with commitment, with passion, and with the wisest judgment we can muster. (p. 273)

ADDENDUM

As stated previously, because of the inclusion of verbatim session material and insufficient disguise (in the service of wanting to present the case as veridically as possible), I asked the patient for her permission to publish. After she granted permission, I asked if she would like to comment on what she had read. What follows is her response.

Stefanie Glennon has asked me to comment on her paper on termination.

I should begin by saying that, I found her words affirming and buoying and was delighted, though not surprised, by her candid and thoughtful approach to the subject. The scope and clarity of her presentation appealed to my "usually" logical mind and allowed me to view the conundrum posed with some objectivity. I even wondered if by writing and sharing this material with me now, she was indirectly speaking to that penchant for logic, perhaps hop-ing it might nudge me toward the "termination door." When I mentioned that to her she responded that, while she could understand that thought could occur to me, it had never crossed her mind.

It was especially thought-provoking for me to read her comment that, following our initial conversation on the subject, I had surprisingly never pur-sued the possibility of a posttherapy friendship between us. And, while that has come in and out of my mind numerous times, I've not wanted until now to focus on, or share, my reasons for that inaction.

First, I've never been able to find a valid argument to dispute her position that, were we to have such a relationship, she could not revert to being my therapist should a life circumstance arise that would again make me seek that option.

Also, part of me has feared that if, for some reason, a posttherapy relationship proved less meaningful than the one we currently share, it might somehow diminish the authenticity of the latter for me, and perhaps even compromise the entire process in my mind. I think this point is not as irrational as it might initially sound. Clearly the potent therapeutic relationship we have, coupled with our very strong personal connection creates a particular intensity that would be hard, if not impossible, to duplicate if one of these two elements no longer existed.

As the last point on this issue, we already have a deep mutually caring friendship apart from our therapeutic bond. That it developed within—perhaps in spite of, or even in part, because of—the therapeutic structure in which it is rooted, is something those more knowledgeable than I would find it useful to consider.

There is a second issue Stefanie Glennon raises which I'll try to address. It's her concern that the closeness of our personal connection, combined with my age and circumstance, makes me less likely to assertively pursue the male love relationship I've longed for. I think I understand what she means, and if I were 50 instead of 67 I might look at it differently than I do now. When you start therapy in middle age the timetable for achieving psychological health doesn't always track favorably with the aging process. I may be, and hope I am, now fully ready to have and enjoy such a relationship, but at 67 the chances of actually finding one are probably pretty slim and I can't really see how terminating my relationship with Stefanie Glennon is going to change that reality.

On a personal note, it is quite true that intimacy has been a pivotal issue for me. Nevertheless, I am absolutely certain that even for those without that issue, there are few relationships in each of our lifetimes that really touch our core. As the patient in this chapter I'm convinced that the important ingredient in the therapeutic experience is authenticity. It is also the most important thing about this chapter and about my relationship with Stefanie Glennon. It is authenticity above all that I have used to measure her as a therapist, the genuineness of my own changing and, ultimately, the value of the therapeutic process to me. I also understand the courage it took for her to travel down this sometimes rocky "relationship road" with me, to navigate it successfully for us both, and to bring the issues it's presented for her to her peers. It is that authenticity that I cherish most about her and the reason I have gleaned so much from therapy.

REFERENCES

Bergmann, M. S. (1997). Termination: The Achilles heel of psychoanalytic technique. *Psychoanalytic Psychology, 14*, 163–174.
Bonovitz, C. (2007). Termination never ends: The inevitable incompleteness of psychoanalysis. *Contemporary Psychoanalysis, 43*, 229–246.
Davies, J. M. (2005). Transformations of desire and despair: Reflections on the termination process from a relational perspective. *Psychoanalytic Dialogues, 15*(6), 779–805.
Eigen, M. (1992). *Coming through the whirlwind.* New York: Chiron.
Ferenczi, S. (1927). The problem of the termination of the psychoanalysis. In M. Balint (Ed.), *Final contributions to the problems and methods of psycho-analysis* (pp. 77–86). New York: Brunner/Mazel, 1980.
Firestein, S. K. (1974). Termination of psychoanalysis of adults: A review of the literature. *Journal of the American Psychoanalytic Association, 22*(4), 873–894.
Freud, S. (1937). Analysis terminable and interminable. In J. Strachey (Ed. & Trans.), *The standard edition of the complete psychological works of Sigmund Freud* (Vol. 23, pp. 209–253). London: Hogarth, 1964.
Greenson, R. R. (1971). The "real" relationship between the patient and the psychoanalyst. In M. Kanzer (Ed.), *The unconscious today* (pp. 213–232). New York: International Universities Press.
Greenson, R. R. (1972). Beyond transference and interpretation. *International Journal of Psychoanalysis, 53*(2), 213–217.
Hoffman, I. Z. (1983). The patient as interpreter of the analyst's experience. *Contemporary Psychoanalysis, 19*, 389–422.
Hoffman, I. Z. (1998). *Ritual and spontaneity in the psychoanalytic process: A dialectical-constructivist view.* Hillsdale: Analytic Press.
Khan, M. (1969). Introduction to Marion Milner's *The Hands of the Living God.* New York: International University Press.
Levenson, E. A. (1976). The aesthetics of termination. *Contemporary Psychoanalysis, 12*, 338–341.
Loewald, H. (1962). Internalization, separation, mourning, and the superego. In *Papers on psychoanalysis* (pp. 257–276). New Haven, CT: Yale University Press.
Novick, J. (1997). Termination conceivable and inconceivable. *Psychoanalytic Psychology, 14*, 145–162.
Orgel, S. (2000). Letting go: Some thoughts about termination. *Journal of the American Psychoanalytic Association, 48*, 719–738.
Schafer, R. (2002). Experiencing termination: Authentic and false depressive positions. *Psychoanalytic Psychology, 19*, 235–253.
Schlesinger, H. J. (2005). *Endings and beginnings: On terminating psychotherapy and psychoanalysis.* Hillsdale, NJ: Analytic Press.
Singer, E. (1977). The fiction of analytic anonymity. In K. A. Frank (Ed.), *The human dimension in psychoanalytic practice* (pp. 181–192). New York: Grune & Stratton.

Chapter 16

"It ain't over till it's over"

Infinite conversations, imperfect
endings, and the elusive
nature of termination*

Anthony Bass

The shadow of its final session is cast across each analysis from its first hour to its elusive end. It is not uncommon for prospective patients to refer to the end of analysis before they really begin, during the first few (consultation) sessions, raising questions about how long analytic work is likely to take. Such questions are often among the first of many that the analyst cannot really answer, except to say that it depends (on how useful the work continues to be, or how far the patient and analyst are able to go), because he or she knows from experience that no two analytic destinations are alike. Each analytic dyad will forge a unique winding path to an unpredictable end.

The internal experience of time in analysis is highly elastic as the process unfolds, reflecting the shifting subjectivities of the two participants. In actuality, some analytic work is relatively contained, lasting just a year or two, while other analyses continue to be fruitful for a decade or more. From first session to last, some patients struggle with the question of how their analytic work might end, imagining and working through many provisional endings before finding that they can say good-bye. The issue of ending comes up in myriad contexts and guises, directly and implicitly, as patients dream, imagine, associate to, and think about the end of analysis. Separation, individuation, autonomy, loss, agency, dependency, and intimacy are just a few of the many central themes that may be represented and worked through as patient and analyst consider together how they might bring their work to a close.

Direct references to the end of analysis may arise when the work is going well, life has improved, and the patient wonders about what, if any, further changes he or she may need the analyst's help to accomplish. Or, they might arise when life's circumstances or priorities change, making paying for analytic sessions, or scheduling them, more challenging. References to ending analysis commonly arise, as well, when the work is proving frustrating,

---

* An earlier version of this chapter originally appeared in *Psychoanalytic Dialogues*, 19(6), 2009, 744–759.

unhelpful, or has reached an impasse, when the patient, or analyst, wonders if the work has outlived its usefulness or feels that it is downright counterproductive.

Even though exploring both the potentials and the limits of analysis are part of the daily fare of psychoanalytic work, endings themselves occur far less frequently. Psychoanalysis is a process that commonly extends over many years, and because ending analysis involves bringing a therapeutic process to a close, and ending what has become a personal relationship as well, managing the ending presents unusual challenges to both participants. Exploring the patient's thoughts and feelings about the analyst, including the dependencies that develop as well as the limits of the relationship, is, of course, a central dimension of the analytic process. Such explorations contribute to the special kind of depth, resonance, and intimacy that characterize psychoanalytic relations, even as they eventually lend themselves to the creation of a unique kind of psychoanalytic ending.

SOME PATIENTS' REFLECTIONS ON ENDING ANALYSIS

References to the end of analysis occur at all phases of analytic work, as a virtually quotidian part of analytic life. For most patients, feelings, reflections, images, and dreams related to separation, loss, and the ending of the analytic relationship in particular recur many times over the course of analysis. Most often, such images and associations alternate between background and foreground, embodying many forms of experience that will be explored in depth before analysis is brought to an end. Here are some brief examples of reflections about the end of analysis made by several of my patients at different phases of their analytic work.

Jane: Till death do us part

Jane has been in analysis for 13 years. She expressed concern when she entered analysis that she not be like an aunt of hers, who had been in analysis all her adult life, the subject of many critical family discussions about the perils of interminable analysis. Though from time to time she had raised the possibility of completing her analysis, she recently commented that she knew that she would not have been able to make some important changes in her life without the work that we continued to do. "What if I had stopped analysis at one of those times I had imagined ending?" she sometimes wondered. "If I had," she added, "I would have missed out on the benefits that I have gained from the work we had done since." She was glad that she had continued. "I realized after I left yesterday," she said, "that I had had the thought that one of us would die first. That one of us would have to deal with losing the other. That is the way our therapy will end. Because I just don't see that I would want to stop talking to you if I don't have to." I wondered about the image of our continuing "till death do us part." Reflecting on the idea of our being together for life led us to a renewed, more sharpened discussion of how the feeling that we would be with each other forever reassured her in some ways while it also, perhaps, served to inhibit her being able to imagine or actualize certain kinds of possibilities and freedoms that being on her own might provide.

John: Needing analysis versus wanting analysis

John has been in a second analysis for 4 years, and recent career changes have put pressure on our ability to schedule sessions after the summer break. In addition, the problems for which he had sought his second analysis had been substantially ameliorated over the course of these 4 years, as new work directions and a new relationship had become solidified, and he had begun to raise the question of stopping analysis as we approach our usual August hiatus. Other concerns, however, had recently interrupted our consideration of what it would be like to bring our work to a close. John started, "I realize that we never got back to the question of what we would do about next year. It is weird to think about ending. (Therapist: How does it feel weird?) "Well, it is a relationship. It is not like taking a yoga class, where when your schedule changes, you might come to the conclusion that you will end the class, or take a different one, even if you like your yoga teacher perfectly well. You have gotten a lot out of it, you are feeling a lot better, and now it is time for one reason or another to move on. In analysis, it is a relationship, albeit one with parameters, and it is harder to separate the relationship from what it is that I am getting out of it. So the idea of just stopping it, especially when I am still getting a lot out of the conversations, is a whole different thing. It is not so much a question as to whether I need it anymore. I don't actually think I need it, *per se*. Certainly not in the sense that I did when I first came here, when there was no question about it. But I am not sure that I don't want it. Wanting it but not needing it makes it a more complicated question for me. I know that I have come a long way. And the problems that I came here to deal with—well, they are substantially gone. It is just, well: How do you end a relationship when you are continuing to get something useful from it?" The distinction between wanting and needing that John began to explore in the context of considering leaving analysis turned out to be relevant to a number of other questions with which he was struggling, and became one of the central themes of our conversations over the course of the next final 5 months of our work.

Tom: "I won't miss our conversations but I will miss you"

I had seen Tom for 12 years of therapy, with a hiatus of almost 2 years in the middle when he had been pursuing a project that had taken him to a different city. The project completed, he returned to analysis, as he suggested he would when he left. We had talked about whether it might be time for us to finish our work many times over the past couple of years, as his life had felt so much fuller than it ever had before. Each time we considered ending our sessions, new feelings and thoughts about aspects of his work, or his experience of himself, or about analysis, or about how he saw our relationship arose, and talking about these things led us into something new, or into familiar territory that we talked about in a new way.

Four months prior to this session, he broached the topic in a different way, saying that he felt that we had gone as far as we could—for now. Or, at least, we had gone as far as he wanted to, even though he could imagine carrying on our conversations forever. I could imagine it too, and we both shared some thoughts about what we might continue to talk about if he wanted to continue. But I also recognized how much he had accomplished, and appreciated his sense that it was time to bring our work to a close. It was evident to me that his life was rich, fulfilling, and interesting, and I was confident that it would continue to be without me. I enjoyed my work with Tom, felt a sense of loss in anticipating the end of our relationship after all these years, but believed that our circuitous path had finally brought us to the work of ending analysis. We agreed that it would be useful to set a date some months down the road to have our last session, so that we could talk about what would come up in anticipation of the actual end of our long conversation.

At our last session, he said he barely recognized the person he was when we started. At the same time, he knows it is him. We reminisced about the changes in his life, both external (the facts of his life, his work, his relationship), and in the ways that he experiences himself. We remembered some different phases of the therapy. He mentioned the "I hate myself" parts, doing things in his life that were entirely "not me." Remunerative things he could do well, but which felt so inauthentic that he would find at times that he literally could not breathe. He has been breathing easier these past couple of years.

He said it will be strange not to see me, and I ask if he will miss our conversations. "No. I won't miss the conversations. I will miss you. The person you are. It is not easy to find someone intelligent, thoughtful, caring. I have more people like that in my life than I used to, but not so many that it is easy to give one up. The conversations, for a long time now, have really been the occasion for meeting with you. I think I had tired of the conversations themselves some time ago, I don't know that I have said anything so new in a while. But just talking the way we do has been reassuring. And I would not have wanted to talk to anyone else. It is not the conversation, not in the sense of the content of what we are talking about or the words that I say. It is just the fact of talking to you that it is hard to give up."

(One year after writing the preceding final session note, Tom called to reenter therapy, having encountered difficulties in his life that he felt would benefit from further work. We spent another year working together, on a once-a-week basis, before we again felt ready to part ways.)

Emily: "When I am here...when I am not here"

Emily has been thinking about whether to stop analytic sessions with me after 2 years. She had two previous analyses, the last one a very helpful experience that she had to stop after 2 years because of a work opportunity that had required geographical relocation. She is concerned about whether she can afford the sessions at this point, given several important family financial commitments she has had to take on in the past year. Yet her finances are not the only consideration suggesting the idea of stopping therapy. There are many sessions in which she feels that we are staying on the surface of things, and she wonders whether the progress she is making is sufficient to warrant the investment. In fact, her ambivalence about continuing our work has been evident since our first ambivalent sessions, in which she was not entirely sure that I was the right therapist for her. Over the course of these 2 years, her sense of me and the value of the therapy for her has oscillated between a secure sense of the value of the work and a feeling that the work is going to have to end, sooner or later, so why get more deeply into it?

"I just don't know," she says. "There is a part of me that is curious about what it would be like to stop, what would happen. How I would be and what I would do, on my own. Some of the things that I am doing now feel like they are directly related to seeing you, but I am not altogether sure that I would keep them up. I can't be sure what is being internalized as long as I am seeing you. But there is also a way that I am curious about what would happen if we continue. What we would get to? And what would I miss out on if I stop? When I am not here, I imagine coming in and telling you, this is it, I am really stopping—maybe not today, but let's say, at the end of the month. But then when I get here, it feels hard to say that to you."

"What makes it hard to say?" I ask. "Is it hard to say to me because you feel it is something that I won't want to hear, that I will have a hard time letting you go, or because saying it when you are here makes it real for you?" (My question is informed by my thinking about whether her ongoing questions about continuing or stopping therapy represent in part an enactment of some complex issues related to dependency, her mother's and her own, and consequent conflicts about separation that have constituted one of the recurring themes of our work.)

"Well, it is a very strange thing," she says. "How do you end a personal relationship when it is going well? There is no other situation in which I would do that. As you know, I do end relationships when they are not going so well. And I know that I do that sometimes even when the other person doesn't know that I am not getting what I need. But that is not the case here. I know I question this situation at times, when I come in and say I thought that you missed something, or when the work seems superficial. But usually, when I am able to bring up those kinds of feelings with you, the work seems to get deeper and we have our best sessions. I have been finding our sessions, for the most part, useful. On the one hand this is a business relationship, in a way, and I have come to the point where I am not sure that I can really afford it, responsibly. You once said that you didn't think, looking back on my life, that I would regret money spent on analysis. But given my parents' case, I don't see how I can be sure that I won't run out of money some day.

"Still, it is not the same as cutting back a day on a housekeeper, or another service provider. When I come here to tell you that I am going to stop, once we are talking I don't really want to say that because I find that I am liking talking to you, even if I am talking to you about stopping. Even when I am talking about whether to stop coming, at least the talking seems real, and so it feels like it has the potential to lead to something that could be helpful to me. When I am here talking to you, I can sort of ease into the myth for the moment that these sessions are just an ongoing part of my life, with no thought to the fact that one day they will end. When I am not here, it doesn't feel quite that way. When I am not here, and thinking about stopping therapy, I am in a quite different state of mind than the one I am usually in when I am here. It would be easier to end the analysis when I am not here, like by calling and leaving you a message that I won't be coming back. I have thought about doing that once or twice. I don't think that I could actually do that, though."

HOW FAR IS FAR ENOUGH?

Despite general agreement as to the importance of the final phase of psychoanalysis, the way that analytic work is brought to a close has been both undertheorized and problematic in practice. Mitchell (1997) noted that there is less useful literature on the termination of analysis than on any other major feature of the work" (p. 26). In most training programs for analysts, far greater emphasis is placed on studying technical considerations related to beginning analysis than ending it. A relative imbalance of emphasis between beginning and ending analysis is perhaps understandable, given that training in the fundamentals of analytic technique typically begins with the focus on engaging patients in analysis and getting started, and that the analytic process, once engaged, typically lasts as long as or longer than training itself.

But in my own training, and in several analytic training programs at which I have taught, courses on termination have been entirely absent from the curriculum. The degree to which emphasis on beginning analysis so completely overshadows concern with ending is perplexing, perhaps analogous to training for pilots that teaches its students how to take off while neglecting the equally important skill of bringing the plane in for a safe landing. In the case of analysis, "landing" requires the collaborative work of pilot and copilot, analyst and patient. And though ending analysis, like beginning it, is a decision that ultimately rests with the patient, it is, like other aspects of analytic work, a collaborative process characterized by complex forms of interpersonal and intersubjective exploration, consideration, and negotiation (Pizer, 1998).

How, and under what conditions, a psychoanalytic process might best be brought to an end is a problem that has plagued psychoanalytic theorists, clinicians, and their patients from the earliest days of psychoanalysis. When is the work of analysis done? How do a patient and analyst know when their psychoanalytic exploration has gone far enough? Patient and analyst do not discover a "royal road" to the end of analysis. Rather, patient and analyst come together and forge a trail through the thickets of their work to a juncture at which they find that their paths can finally once again diverge. No two analytic endings are alike, and there are no psychoanalytic global positioning satellites to announce that a final destination has been reached. Levenson (1976), commenting on what he called the "aesthetics of termination," suggested that

> one might expect that a patient would terminate more or less in the configural style in which he operates. One would hope that the improvement would be evident in that the configuration would be markedly extended and modulated.... I would say that it makes no more sense when to terminate than to ask when to die. It is a natural event in the course of therapy. (p. 341)

While analysts struggle (with each patient anew) with how best to end analytic work throughout their professional lives, much of the writing about termination has been done by analysts relatively late in their careers (Ferenczi, 1927; Freud, 1937), when they have acquired sufficient experience in facing analytic endings to recognize their special challenges. The long time line of psychoanalytic work means that it takes a psychoanalyst many years to gain wide experience (with a large number of patients) in bringing psychoanalytic work to its conclusion, in resuming work with patients who return for further analysis, and in working with patients in second and third analyses. Each of these kinds of experiences has much to teach an analyst about psychoanalytic endings, and so about psychoanalysis itself. It is the rare analyst who actually brings a case of analysis to completion during his training years. It is not uncommon for analysts to continue to work with patients they began with in training many years into their practice. And although much of what analysts learn about doing analysis comes through the direct experience of their own personal analysis, the majority of analysts will not have experienced an end to their own personal analysis by the time they finish training. Many continue their own analytic work until deep into their careers, when they must first come to personal terms with the complexities and contradictions of finishing analysis. Even when analysts do finish their own analysis, they often continue to interact with their analyst in a variety of ways, both personal and professional. And it is not unusual for analysts to return for further analysis periodically during the course of their careers, as doing analytic work places special demands on the analyst that require further work from time to time. Thus, it is often many years into their postgraduate practices before analysts have gained enough experience completing analytic work to feel confident that they can help a patient through to a satisfactory ending, capable of exploring in depth the intense and often contradictory feelings (for analyst and patient alike) that most often accompany the final stages of psychoanalytic work.

Consequently, even quite experienced analysts ordinarily have less experience dealing with the termination of analysis than other features of psychoanalytic technique. Balint (1950) commented that very little data were available on analysis carried through to completion, observing that he (and most analysts, he believed) came to an end of analytic work with a patient once, or perhaps twice, a year. Balint's observation about the relative rarity of analytic terminations is consistent with our experience some 60 years following his report. Having practiced as a full-time psychoanalyst for more than 25 years now, I have participated in many first sessions and last sessions. Yet, of course, the number of last sessions that I have participated in pales in comparison with the thousands of analytic sessions that I have conducted, and the process of bringing analytic work to a satisfactory close remains one of the greatest personal challenges that I face as an analyst.

TERMINABLE AND INTERMINABLE

Termination is the term psychoanalysts have adopted in their professional discourse to refer to the process of shepherding the work through its final phase to a satisfactory end. I, along with many contemporary analysts, find the word unwieldy and problematic, a particularly poor signifier for the process to which it refers. With its connotations of finality, confinement, bringing something to a stop that extends no further, the forced end of employment, or death, the term seems especially ill-suited to the ambiguity and rich complex affective experience of bringing psychoanalytic relations to their elusive and hard won end. Endings are often ambiguous and provisional, punctuated with an ellipsis rather than a full stop. As Mitchell (1993) put it,

> The technical term termination suggests sober finality, so difficult to grasp in a relationship not interrupted by death or growing estrangement. The king's instructions to the White Rabbit in *Alice in Wonderland* have always captured for me the feeling of abruptness and arbitrariness of termination. "Begin at the beginning and go on till you come to the end: then stop." (p. 229)

But when have we reached the end?

The use of the word *termination* may have been better suited for its original purpose (Freud, 1937) of exploring the theoretical question of whether psychoanalysis can ever be said to be complete, or truly self-limiting. Does psychoanalysis constitute a process with a natural end point at which a patient and analyst can say that their work is finally complete? Or does it inevitably lead to an imperfect compromise, a multidetermined, complex choice to step out of a relationship that could just as well continue to be fruitful—that could, in fact, be a dialogue with no intrinsic end, limited only by the limits of life itself?

Writings addressing the issue of termination were few and far between in the first decades of psychoanalysis. Freud (1937) first addressed the issue in a substantive way late in his career when he explored the question of whether there is such a thing as a natural and complete end to an analysis, or whether it is possible to conduct an analysis toward such an end. Is analysis terminable or interminable, the title of his paper asked. The conflation of a theoretical point of finality, a platonic ideal of what psychoanalysis might hope to accomplish at its best according to any given psychoanalytic perspective, with how any analyst and patient manage to find their way to their own uniquely cocreated last session is, in my view, an error of category. The former concerns an epistemological question of what kinds of knowledge and experience psychoanalysis generates; the latter constitutes the way any two people, patient and analyst, fulfill their potential in the special kind of relationship that psychoanalysis provides.

Mitchell (1993) suggested that terms like *completed analysis* and *natural termination* may have had some meaning in the early decades of analysis, when the process generally lasted several months and was expected to reach certain prescribed dynamic issues. "In today's analytic world, with its plethora of theories and its staggering proliferation of different ways of thinking about mind, these terms have little real meaning" (p. 229). The weight of an idealized, contrived image of what an imaginary completed analysis might look like can contribute to the strain that both patient and analyst feel in working their way toward an ending that best reflects their own goals.

WHEN DO THE MEANS JUSTIFY THE ENDS?

In what ways do different theoretical orientations influence how analysts view the final phases of analytic work? Analysts of different theoretical persuasions are guided by different beliefs about how psychoanalysis should be conducted and what an analyst strives to accomplish. The analytic values and ideals held by each analyst dictate how an analytic process takes shape, how its participants construe the fulfillment of its potential, and so how they envision its end point. Each ending is experienced relative to what the analyst and patient regard as possible or desirable to achieve. An analysis organized around the traditional medical model of curing a mental disorder, restoring the strength of a compromised ego, and resolving the pathologies of mental functioning will generate a process with a different set of implicit outcome criteria from one organized around contemporary analytic models emphasizing enhanced capacities for personal growth, development, and an enriched personal fulfillment in living.

Ferenczi (1927), close to the end of his life, in taking on the problem of termination for the first time, noted the difference between what he believed to be possible and what he had in fact experienced in his daily practice of clinical psychoanalysis:

> I have brought all these observations to your notice today in support of my conviction that analysis is not an endless practice, but one which can be brought to a natural end with sufficient skill and patience on the analyst's part. If I am asked whether I can point to many such completed analysis, my answer must be no. (p. 86)

Ferenczi, the pioneer of a two-person, intersubjective perspective that initiated the development of a relational psychoanalysis, recognized that one crucial wild card in analysis, the analyzability of the patient, rested not simply in the mind of the patient, but in the hand of the analyst. "I am firmly convinced that when we have learned sufficiently from our errors and mistakes, when we have gradually learned to take into account the weak points in our personality, the number of fully analyzed cases will increase" (p. 86).

Similarly, Balint (1950), writing on his view of what constitutes a proper ending for psychoanalytic work, noted that "taking all those of my cases which went beyond the trial period, I could observe the end phase as described in this paper roughly in two cases out of ten. A very poor proportion indeed" (p. 196). Like Ferenczi, he suggested that the fault, the insufficiency of analytic endings, rested squarely on the analysts' own shoulders: "...I remain convinced...that in every case in which we have failed to achieve a proper termination, I think I know what went wrong, although I must admit that once the mistake was made...it was hardly possible to remedy the situation" (p. 197).

Bergmann (1997), on the other hand, saw the problem of termination as more fundamental than the mistakes or personal insufficiencies of any given patient or analyst. Referring to a fundamental paradox at the heart of the problem of termination, he noted that psychoanalysis is the only significant relationship that terminates abruptly:

> In real life we encounter three types of termination of human relationships: geographical separation, transformation of a friendly or love relationship into a hostile one, and death. The analysand, however is supposed to bring about separation under conditions of love and gratitude.... Under these conditions, an analysis is exceptionally difficult to end, for patient and analyst alike.... All life experience runs against such a termination.... Psychoanalysis makes demands on internalization that are not asked for in any other human relationship. (p. 168)

Glover (1955), too, noted the gap between expectations and realities within classical analysis when he observed that

> opportunities for watching a classical analysis coming to a classical termination are much less frequent than is generally supposed.... The great majority of cases end for external reasons, when a symptomatic improvement occurs, or when the patient defeats the analyst in an Oedipal struggle expressed in premature termination. (p. 140)

These latter perspectives suggest that the gaps between the analytic endings envisioned and those that are actually discovered in analytic work reside in the inherent limitations of psychoanalysis itself rather than in the mistakes and failures of either patient or analyst or in the limitations of the particular theories that guide their work.

ENDING ANALYSIS IS EASIER SAID THAN DONE

Analysts, like patients, often feel on more solid footing in the beginning of an analysis than at the end. The special demands of ending a rich and rewarding relationship apply to patient and analyst alike. We begin analysis with hope, a sense that we can help a patient to heal and to grow. We end analysis celebrating the changes that have occurred and anticipating the loss of a relationship that has deepened through the work. At the same time, we must come to terms with the limits of the process, and those we have faced in ourselves (whether patient or analyst). In the absence of reliable and reassuring guidelines, most analytic patients and their analysts eventually recognize that they have carried their work as far as they can, or as far as they are prepared to go at that time. This point may come relatively quickly in cases in which symptom relief persuades the patient that he has gotten what he needed. But many analysts feel in cases of relatively quick symptom relief in analysis of short duration (work lasting less than a couple of years) that the work has never truly become analysis. The patient has not actually become an analytic patient. The realization of an end point in a fruitful analysis often takes many years to accomplish, and even after a decade or even two of intense analytic work, endings may remain elusive, with patients feeling that the benefits of continuing analysis outweigh the costs.

Ideally, when psychoanalysis is brought to an end, analyst and patient devote a substantial amount of time (usually a matter of at least some months) to the exploration of the feelings associated with the impending separation. Even then, most analyses end for the patient not with a sense of finality, but rather with recognition of both the loss of the analyst and the continuation of a process that has become internalized (which often includes an ongoing internal dialogue with the analyst), and the possibility of resuming the process at a later point. In fact, a feeling of reliable finality, of certainty that the time is right for ending analysis, rarely characterizes a decision to end analytic work. A patient ending analysis often does so with an experience of ambivalence and loss, which often includes a consideration of the work left undone, at least for the present. It is not uncommon for analysts and patients to schedule follow-up or checking-in sessions at some interval after a last session and to explore, as part of the late stages of analytic work, the possibility of returning for further work if the patient chooses to do so. Analytic practices typically include patients who have returned for further work with their analyst, and others who have terminated analyses with other analysts and are seeking a new experience.

WHY END ANALYSIS?

Psychoanalytic work is defined in part by the presence and management of a frame (setting of fees, times, ground rules, etc.) that explicitly differentiates it from other relationships, both personal and professional, defines its limits, marks its boundaries, and so implicitly suggests its temporality. The end of each session, emphasizing the boundary between analytic and other forms of relationship, coming as it does right on schedule, whether at a good moment to stop talking or not (and often it is not a good moment at all), serves as a synechdoche for the entire process, linking it to limits, endings, and so to the ultimate end of sessions. The monthly bill is an intermittent reminder that as a hybrid personal/professional/business relationship, the analytic relationship differs in important ways from other relationships that both partners hope to nurture and sustain as long as they live.

Unlike other relationships that, when all goes well, may last a lifetime, or which evolve and transform themselves in response to relatively predetermined developmental milestones (as when a child leaves home for college or a student graduates and his or her relationship to his or her mentor changes to that of colleague), analysts and patients engage in a relationship that is intended to be time limited, however indeterminate that time may be. When the work of analysis is done, by whatever definition of its goals the dyad constructs, and however that definition evolves during the course of an analysis, the patient is meant to leave the analyst and live his or her life more fully and freely than would have been possible otherwise. And part of that freedom is associated with the working through of the separation process. Framed by the inevitability of ending, patient and analyst construct an ending according to their own (conscious and unconscious) specifications and timetable, toward which they move in a nonlinear but nonetheless inexorable path toward the day they will say goodbye.

The psychoanalyst holds this in mind as part of an internal frame (Bass, 2007a; Parsons, 2007) or frame of reference that plays a central role in keeping analytic work moving forward at the same time that it can encompass the experience of timelessness that is required in order to inhabit the unconscious. Along similar lines, Lear (2004), making a developmental analogy, suggested that we

> think of parents who manifest their love for their child by facilitating the process by which the child grows up and becomes more independent. The eventual letting go was always there as part of the relationship. In this sense, the end was always in sight. Part of facilitating the analysis must be facilitating the analysis through to the very end. Analysis is a relationship with a termination and it is only by keeping that in mind that the analyst can really answer the question of what does and does not facilitate the analysis. (p. 58)

Though extrinsic factors such as relocation, changes in work, childbirth, and child care responsibilities or other scheduling or financial constraints (though we tend to think of many of these as extrinsic factors, the changes that they reflect are often brought about in part through the analysis itself) often contribute to the decision to end an analysis, the nature of psychoanalytic work, including its careful attention to the patient's sense of agency, responsibility, and the role unconscious factors play in shaping choices in life, ensures that such factors will not be taken lightly or at face value. Both patient and analyst will take as much responsibility as they can for the decision to end the work, and to experience and process as much as possible about its end. Living through the experience of ending analysis brings psychological challenges and rewards that cannot be anticipated in advance, and which, for many patients, contribute in important ways to the special kinds of personal growth experience that analysis provides.

Hoffman (1998) put it this way:

> To bring analysis to an end can mean owning one's own experience more completely and taking a greater responsibility for its construction. For that to happen, one must come to terms with the impact of one's own and other's limitations, with the givens of one's experience, with the hand one has been dealt. For many people, that developmental achievement cannot be a prerequisite for termination, because the termination itself is necessary for it to occur. (p. 259)

Similarly, Mitchell (1993) observed that "one of the startling realizations upon leaving analysis is the sense that one is now fully responsible for one's life. The suspension that analysis provides—useful, necessary, enriching, is now over" (p. 229).

ANALYTIC TERMINATION AS A MOVING TARGET

Patient and analyst meet for the first time as strangers but quickly begin to develop a unique kind of relationship that is integral to therapeutic change. And so a patient's desire and resolve to bring analytic work to a close is typically more complicated than his or her motivation to begin it. The end of analysis is perhaps more in sight at the beginning of an analysis, before the process is fully engaged, than at any time prior to its end. As analytic work unfolds, symptoms recede, new possibilities for living emerge, the process of analysis develops a life of its own, and the relationship with the analyst becomes meaningful in its own right. Analysis has become an enriching part of the patient's life, with ongoing benefits that go far beyond any original expectations of what analysis might bring, making a decision to end the relationship a far more problematic challenge than could have been anticipated the day the patient met the analyst/stranger. In many analyses, the patient has become capable, through his or her analytic work, of a far richer experience of meaning making and personal relating than was possible before the analysis. Thus, in ending their work, both participants will find that they are giving up something that they have discovered with each other along the way, and could not have anticipated when they began.

Ferenczi (1927) suggested that "a truly cured patient frees himself from analysis slowly but surely; he should continue to come to analysis as long as he wishes to do so" (p. 85). But with one foot still firmly planted in the

classical perspective on transference, fantasy and the fool's gold of gratification, he went on to say that

> the patient finally becomes convinced that he is continuing analysis
> only because he is treating it as a new but still fantasy source of grati-
> fication, which in terms of reality, yields him nothing. When he has
> slowly overcome his mourning over this discovery, he inevitably looks
> around for other, more real sources of gratification. The renunciation
> of analysis is thus the final winding up of the infantile situation of frus-
> tration that lay at the basis of symptom formation. (p. 85)

This latter perspective, central to traditional theorizing about termination, fails to take into account the developments in psychoanalytic theorizing that Ferenczi himself initiated and inspired. As psychoanalytic theory,
at least in some lines of its multifarious development, has evolved over time,
from an emphasis on transference, to countertransference, to a transfer-
ence/countertransference field, to intersubjectivity to relational theory, the
idea that the gratifications of analysis are simply illusory appears increasingly illusory in its own right. In my view, far from the idea that the patient
is able to terminate the process when he or she realizes the absence of real
sources of gratification in the analytic relationship, the patient must mourn,
in choosing to end analysis, the loss of many real gratifications, satisfactions, and sustaining personal meanings that the relationship with his or
her analyst provides. The last phase of analytic work often involves coming
to terms with the recognition that termination means he or she is choosing
to give up a relationship that continues to be valuable, in the service of the
benefits that can be gained in moving on.

Experiencing and working through the sense of loss (not simply of an illusion but of the relationship) that ending analytic work entails is not a linear
process, but one that is revisited many times over the course of an analysis.
As a result, the end of analytic work frequently appears as a moving target. Patient and analyst are likely to have struggled with the dread, desire,
doubt, and ambivalence, toward the inevitability of ending the relationship
many times over the course of their relationship, before an actual ending
can be successfully negotiated. As we have seen, unlike many other modes
of symptom-focused psychotherapy in which endings naturally follow a significant amelioration of the presenting problems, coming to terms with the
wide range of feelings and states of mind associated with leaving the analyst
and analysis behind is an important part of the process of analysis, and one
whose psychological benefits and challenges are uniquely psychoanalytic.

Increasing awareness and acknowledgment among analysts of the ways
in which psychoanalytic work is a highly mutual endeavor, mutually
enriching and facilitative of the growth of both participants, as has been
especially emphasized in relational theory, have highlighted the ways in

which ending psychoanalytic work poses special personal challenges for the analyst. Analyst and patient each celebrate the achievements of analysis, even as they mourn its loss.

When Freud was a relatively inexperienced analyst, comparing psychoanalysis to a game of chess (1912), he observed that beginnings and endings were far less complex than the middle phase of analysis, and that as such they lent themselves to more systematic technical formulation, unlike the infinitely more varied middle phase. The oft-cited metaphor suggested that there were fewer pieces in play in the early and late stages of analysis, and so there was a less complex field of experience to navigate. This perspective was, I believe, directly related to the state of transference theory as it existed at the time. As transference was interpreted, its power diminished over time, preparing the way for the termination that Ferenczi referred to when the patient realized that his or her gratifications in analysis were embedded in illusions of transference. As the transference was increasingly resolved through interpretation, the field of analysis grew simpler, bringing analyst and patient closer to the inevitable end. In contemporary psychoanalytic practice, unlike a game of chess, it may be closer to the truth to say that there are an increasing number of pieces on the board as the process of psychoanalysis progresses. The patient gains access to more of himself or herself as the work unfolds, his or her experience of his or her analyst made that much richer as a result. Thus, far from growing simpler over time, analytic experience grows increasingly complex, complicating the patient's experience of himself or herself, the analyst, and of his or her desire to end the analytic process.

The decision to end analytic work bears less resemblance to a chess game coming to its inevitable end as piece after piece is removed from the board than to the decision made by a pair of longstanding chess partners to end their triweekly meetings over a chessboard. Each of them has enjoyed the games, their collaboration, their struggles with one another, the challenges that have brought them to a capacity for deeper playing, increased depth, elegance of play, and creativity, as well as the stimulation and satisfaction of conversation that has evolved and the relationship that has progressed as a result. The players' evolving relationship with each other, their grasp and appreciation of one another's way of playing, and the depth of their play become intertwined. Each will mourn the loss of the play and the relationship that developed over the course of it when their collaboration over the board ends.

ONE ANALYSIS, MANY ENDINGS

Each analytic couple will eventually construct an ending for their work, one of many different potential endings that they will have faced along the way. The exploration of a variety of imagined endings, or trial endings, is an important aspect of the ongoing work of analysis. Each analytic couple will explore a variety of endings in fantasy before actually ending an analysis. The way that a patient and analyst are able to imaginatively explore the ways in which their relationship may come to an end plays an important role in the development of the analytic work and prepares the way for a good enough ending when it actually occurs.

Endings, though present in the minds of both patient and analyst from the beginning, are held outside of awareness for long periods of time, during which time a sense of timelessness and infinite possibility prevails. During such periods, and in states of mind that alternate with a sense of the limits of analysis, analyst and patient may share a sense that they can go on talking forever. The sense of limits and the sense of timelessness alternate, moving in and out of focus, throughout psychoanalytic work, and are fundamental to the analytic experience. The management of these shifting states of mind regarding ending and endlessness pose special challenges and opportunities for patient and analyst alike. Ferenczi (1927), in one of the earliest psychoanalytic papers addressing the complexity of endings, highlighted this very paradox of timelessness as a fundamental feature of psychoanalysis, noting that the completion of an analysis is possible only if, so to speak, unlimited time is at one's disposal. "I agree," he said "with those who think that the more unlimited it is, the greater are the chances of quick success. By this I mean not so much the physical time at the patient's disposal, as his determination to persist for so long as may be necessary, irrespective of how long this may turn out to be" (p. 82).

But of course, the question of just what any patient and analyst construe as "as long as necessary" is a profoundly subjective and intersubjective matter, which the analytic process is likely to take as a central consideration for long periods of time. For many analyst–patient dyads, the process through which they come to a decision to end the work of analysis, and to say good-bye, is the most difficult, perplexing part of their relationship, a development that is made possible only by the analytic work. In that sense, good psychoanalytic work makes possible its own obsolescence, as it enables the patient to internalize a sense of going-on-being that makes leaving the analyst possible.

Yet approaching the end of analytic work tests and may strain the very relationship that has made the contemplation of its end possible. Such strains are especially important to work through in a careful, constructive way, because the experience of ending analytic work plays a central role in determining the ultimate fate of its therapeutic effect over time and contributes significantly to shaping the way the patient and analyst hold the work that they have done in mind, retrospectively. Although it may overstate the case to say that "all's well that ends well," successful analytic work prepares the way for a constructive and collaborative end, which makes it possible for the patient to hold the analyst in mind as a positive presence throughout his life.

STARTING OVER BUT NEVER FROM SCRATCH

In working with patients who have had prior analytic experiences that have ended badly, I have seen that it can take much new analytic work for a patient to separate the wheat from the chaff, and recognize that prior work that ended unsatisfactorily, was not all bad. Therapeutic work that ends poorly may leave the patient with a sense that the work did more harm than good, and the damage incurred by poorly worked through analytic endings often becomes the occasion for the patient seeking out a new analysis to help with its frankly traumatic effects.

When the work in analysis is completed, life may generate new growth, possibilities, and obstacles, and so patients frequently return to their analyst for more work, and to new analysts when emerging life goals and challenges seem better explored in a new relationship. For many patients, it is only when they decide to seek analysis with a new analyst that they begin to recognize ways that they had felt thwarted in getting to new places with their previous analyst. The fundamentally intersubjective nature of analysis is especially evident when patients begin second or third analyses with anxiety about "starting from scratch," telling their whole story again, only to find that once they begin with a different analyst, the process bears little resemblance to what had taken place before.

ZENO'S PARADOX

Ending in analysis may seem for long periods of time to have an asymptotic quality, a real-life demonstration of Zeno's paradox, in which the distance to the final seems to narrow by half, and half again, never reaching its final destination, until one day, surrendering to the limits of life and the work, patient and analyst do find a way to say good-bye.

Given that ending analysis is woven into the fabric of the work, and that trial endings often precede actual ones, how do patients and analysts discern the difference between the ordinary workaday references to the possibility and necessity of reaching the end of the analytic work and the recognition, negotiation, and ultimate accomplishment of the actual end? I do not believe that they do, except in retrospect. As the baseball great and philosopher Yogi Berra averred, "It ain't over till it's over," and in the case of psychoanalysis, as we have seen, it is not necessarily over even then, judging by the number of patients who return to their analysts for further posttermination work, and to other analysts for a second analysis that often includes reworking aspects of the first analysis that did not appear to be accessible for further exploration there. In psychoanalysis, working in the realm of unconscious experience means that apparent endings frequently make way for new beginnings, initiated by coming face to face with what turned out to be, in retrospect, an illusory end. When an analyst is too certain that thoughts of ending analysis suggest that an actual end is near, he or she may have abandoned, for the moment, the psychoanalytic process and may miss opportunities for the analysis to open up to new possibilities.

Self-state perspectives in contemporary relational theory (Bromberg 1998; Davies 2005) highlighted some of the complexities of discerning end points in analysis, as they emphasized the ways in which different parts of the patient may express themselves at different times and in different ways (including through enactment) on the matter of their readiness to end analysis. Davies (2005), in particular, highlighted that many of the problems, challenges, and opportunities of termination are embedded in the fact that different patient–analyst pairings, represented by an array of different self-states of both analyst and patient, are implicated in the termination process. The process, as Davies describes, requires a series of partings among the variety of self–other configurations that emerged over the course of the work:

> The termination, seen from such a vantage point, is not, then, just a long good-bye. Termination so conceived involves a multitude of good-byes—yes, many, many good-byes—between the self-states of patient and analyst, good-byes that emanate from a multitude of developmental epochs and from different centers of developmental traumas, conflict and meaning making. From my own perspective, each good-bye deserves its own attention; each one is different; each one holds the potential not only for growth emergence and liberation but also grief, despair and narcissistic collapse. Termination is not a unitary and linear process, but one that is contradictory and complex, containing many often irreconcilable, experiences of the same separation and ending. (p. 788)

From Davies's perspective, the analyst must listen to the full range of voices that have a stake in the analysis. Sometimes different voices can speak for themselves, while at other times they speak through an enacted dimension, and sometimes, to the peril of the patient and the analysis, they are silenced altogether when an analyst is too quick to recognize one voice within the patient to the shaming exclusion of all the others.

A patient of mine expressed apprehension about such a possibility when she expressed the idea for the first time in a long analysis that she might want to think about finishing analysis, and added that there was a part of her that worried that I would take that wish as the whole story, and proceed with termination before she was really ready. She worried that the end of her analysis would somehow be thrust upon her, taken out of her own hands if I were too ready to accede to the wish of one part of her, and that such willingness on my part would reflect my own, perhaps unconscious, wish to end the analysis.

Of course, a patient may not have access to alternative voices at the time that he or she brings up his or her wish to end the analysis, and when his or her analyst (in the throes of an enactment or expressing his or her own countertransference conflicts) is too quick to accede to the patient's wish, moving ahead with insufficient exploration toward setting a date for termination, parts of the patient may be frozen out altogether, sometimes leading to a treacherous, shame-filled retraumatization.

Schafer (2005), speaking of his first analysis (in an interview recorded and archived on the Web site of the online journal, *The Candidate*), referred to the embittering experience as "short, inadequate, and entirely inappropriate." Asked by the interviewer what had happened to leave him feeling so bitter about his analysis, he said, "I acted out in proposing that I end the analysis. My analyst, who had crammed me into his schedule, too readily agreed." Similarly, a subject in Tessman's (2003) study of what patients (all of whom were analysts in training when they were in the analyses under consideration) take from their analysis, commented about the ending of his: "Afterward I wondered, why did he push termination once he thought my associations meant I had it in mind?" (p. 246).

Many of us have known the experience, from both sides of the proverbial couch, of the analyst holding on too tightly to a patient who feels ready to leave, and equally, too eager to take the patient's expressed wish to leave the treatment at face value. The analyst's response to any patient's references and stated desire or intention to leaving analysis requires a delicate negotiation between the Scylla of overly quick compliance and the Charybdis of overly harsh and stubborn resistance to the idea of ending. The latter problem often takes the form of the analyst interpreting the patient's wish to finish analysis as resistance, or suggesting that the patient's plan to terminate the process is merely an enactment of the very problem that the patient needs continued analysis to work through. Such arguments can be compelling to the patient, exploiting his or her anxiety and vulnerability in the service of the analyst's own dependency needs or grandiosity. The perspective that Davies articulates, that the analyst must gain access to not just one voice, but to all the voices that speak for the patient sheds a special light on the importance of giving a process of ending its full due, and the necessity to provide room for the sense of timelessness that it will take for various parts of the patient to find their respective voices and participate fully in the decision to end analysis.

SALLY: POSSIBLE ENDINGS AND NEW BEGINNINGS

In the case of Sally, which follows, we encountered a possible end point 3 years into our work, a second analysis. In this case, the sense of an imminent end, or at least the beginning of the end, soon receded and made way for a new phase of work, involving the working through of a number of issues that would prepare the way for a successful experience of termination phase 2 years later.

Sally, a 34-year-old physician several years into her second analysis, began her session by reflecting on the fact that she had recently made some important changes in her life. We had begun our work just a few years after she completed what she regarded as a successful first analysis, undertaken to help her sort out some difficulties encountered during her professional training, and in her relationship with her boyfriend, whom she began dating shortly before beginning her analysis. That work ended after 5 years with a strong sense of accomplishment and gratitude toward her analyst, for whom she felt affection, respect, and appreciation. The work had been very helpful, and she finished it with a sense of a job well done, not anticipating the need to go back for further analysis.

She got my name from her first analyst about a year after relocating to New York City, when she found that the strains of the move, some physical symptoms of uncertain origin but probably stress related, and some strains in her relationship seemed to be bringing up some "unfinished business." In phone consultation with her analyst, they decided that working with a man this time might provide a useful complement to the work that they already accomplished, especially given some of her concerns about her relationships with men. As is often the case when patients seek second analyses, and contrary to her expectation, Sally did not have so much a sense of picking up where she left off when she came to consult with me as a sense of surprise at how different it felt to talk to someone else. She noted how differently I often responded to what she said, and the different ways that she came to see herself in her new psychoanalytic context. Fresh work was done, and new memories and different perspectives on her history emerged; much of the work she had done in her first analysis seemed to be reworked in the context of a new relationship, contextualized by a different set of feelings, different affects befitting an alternate transference–countertransference field of analytic exploration that seemed to shed a different light on much of what she had already discovered about herself and her way of relating to the important people in her life. While continuing to think of her first analysis in very positive ways, with evident love and gratitude toward her analyst, she wondered at times how things would have unfolded if she had seen me first. Analytic work, she was realizing, now that she had a point of comparison, seemed so strongly shaped by the person of the analyst. "There is a part of me that wishes I had seen you first, like it would have saved me a lot of time," she said. "But I wonder if I could have done this work with you if not for my time with Beth." I responded: "I think you are talking about realizing that you have needed both a mother and a father," to her immediate assent. In very real ways, she had neither, having had a mother who was deeply, and ultimately suicidally depressed, and a father who had abandoned the family when she was just a child.

Now, having explored considerable new ground in her personal history that she was often surprised to note had not come up in her first analysis ("it was not that I had not known this before, I am not saying anything that I didn't know in some way; it is just that I didn't think of it there"), having made significant and satisfying changes in her professional life, including acquiring further training in a new medical specialty, and most recently, having initiated and unilaterally effected a major change in her relationship, she wondered if it might be time to consider ending our work together.

"I think," she said, "that I probably came to analysis to find a way to end my relationship with John. I couldn't have said that that is what I meant to do at the time we started. Consciously, I thought I was coming here, in part, to work on the relationship, to make it work. I knew that there were certain strains having to do with ways that we were so different, that we wanted some different things for our lives, but wouldn't say that I knew that I wanted to end it. I think I would have said that I couldn't manage without him. In retrospect, though, I think that I had a sense that I did need to end that relationship eventually; that it couldn't go on forever." It occurred to me here that she might have been thinking about, or at least unconsciously referencing her relationship with me as well.

"For one thing, I was coming to feel, even though it took me a long time to be able to say it out loud, that ultimately we would inhibit each other's growth rather than support it. I think that once we get over the shock of the relationship ending the way it did, as precipitously as it did, in a way, we will both feel liberated. I know John doesn't feel that way now. He is pretty devastated. But on our own, we will be able to develop in ways that we could not do with each other. I think we were actually somehow restricting each other from developing in some ways. And now that I have been able to make that change, I am not sure what else I would be trying to do here.

"You know, I know that I could continue to be in analysis for—well, forever. I like coming here; there are always things that it is helpful to think about with you...but I suppose I can't keep coming here forever. Can I? I don't know if I really want to stop coming. It actually scares me to bring this up. And I don't want you to just agree with it. But the thought occurred to me and I didn't want to hold it back."

Her raising the prospect of ending our work did not take me by surprise. For the past 2 weeks I had sensed that it was in the air. I felt that I had heard, between the lines of what she was talking about, the possibility that she was beginning to think about beginning a termination process, but that whatever communication that was taking place about it seemed to me to be implicit, inchoate, and came to me as an intuition, a feeling more subliminal than something that I could put my finger on, or locate directly in what I was hearing. And so I had decided to wait until I could link the feeling more clearly to what she was saying before sharing my sense of it with her.

The sense of our moving toward a consideration of ending grew over the next few sessions; I was beginning to hear the footsteps approaching an end point much more clearly. References to ending seemed more palpably in the air, and I could hear them with greater clarity in the derivatives of her associations to the end of her relationship with John.

She had not known she had needed to end it, she said, but she had recently come to recognize that it was time to stop. Her further development required that she move on from a relationship that she believed, increasingly, had inhibited some aspects of her personal growth. Could the same be said of our relationship in analysis? Did she feel that we would both feel liberated after we had been able to end our work together? Would I too feel a sense of liberation once we had been able to accomplish our end, though it is not what I felt now as I imagined not seeing Sally any more, any more than it was what John was apparently feeling, according to Sally's account of his resistance to the end of their relationship?

It had been 2 weeks (six sessions) since I first consciously anticipated this conversation, having had the thought on at least two separate moments during sessions that the idea of considering an endpoint of our work was on the tip of her tongue. It is not unusual for me, working with a patient that I know very well, to notice when I find myself anticipating themes, and even specific associations, completing her sentences in my mind. It is of special note, arousing of a special kind of curiosity, when I find myself completing my patient's sentences, incorrectly. Sometimes at such moments I say something like, "you know, I thought you were going to say something else there. I guess it must have been what I was thinking, more than what you were. I wonder why I was thinking that." Such moments often lead to interesting developments in the analytic process, including the revelation that what I thought she was going to say was actually something that she had thought but did not say. Or had not thought, but now hearing it stimulated curiosity about where the thought had been, because it seemed to flow so naturally from what she had been thinking just before. But typically in such circumstances I have a clearer idea about where my thought had derived from in our prior experience together, and so have more to say about the discrepancy between my expectation and what I have heard than I could now muster.

What had I noticed so far? Sally would begin a session by saying something like, "I have been giving some thought to..." and then she would take a breath, pause, perhaps just a beat or two longer than she might typically.

Maybe it was the breath, or the barely pregnant pause, or the subtly heavy tone of her voice, that led me to expect that what she was giving thought to was, in fact, that we were approaching the end of our work, though she would finish her sentence in a way that steered the conversation clear of any thought she might be having about ending.

Or could I have been responding to a sense, not yet formulated in my mind clearly enough for me to raise in its own right, that few new thoughts or feelings had been emerging in recent sessions? Was I wondering if she was herself aware of some staleness or diminishment of vitality along these lines, as indeed she had begun to recognize about her relationship with John some months ago? Or was it my own sense that she had actually achieved her goals in analysis and we were in a kind of stalled state that we had not been able to identify as such because we were both finding it difficult to recognize that we were much closer to the end of our work than our beginning?

In each of these moments, though, after the second or two pause, I was surprised that she would finish the sentence, not with the thought about ending that I was expecting, but with something else that she had been thinking about, an elaboration of a familiar theme. What could this mean, I wondered? Had I detected something that Sally was not quite aware of yet in herself? Or was it something in myself I was able to see first in her, projecting onto her some countertransference withdrawal or resistance of my own to something that was now emerging between us? Or had I subliminally detected something that Sally herself was conscious of, that was on her mind but she was not yet ready to say?

As I have written about elsewhere (2001, p. 685), it is often difficult in the highly specialized form of relationship that is psychoanalysis in which, as Freud (1912) put it, "the analyst must bend his own unconscious like a receptive organ to the transmitting unconscious of the patient" (pp. 115–116) to know just whose unconscious is receiving and whose is submitting at any given moment. Was it I who was thinking that we might be reaching the end of our work? Or, was I, subliminally, registering a shift in her that might signal the beginning of what might turn out to be a final phase of our work together?

Whatever the source of its reverberations in the distant thunder of recent sessions, I felt relieved to have the idea of her ending now a part of the conscious flow of analytic material and work. I expressed interest and curiosity about the thought. Had it just arisen? No, she thought that she had mentioned it before (around the time that I first thought it myself). There had been a dream, right around the time that she thought that she had mentioned. Had she not told me the dream? "No, I don't recall hearing a dream recently," I said. No, she realizes now with surprise, she had not mentioned it. She had gone so far as to say that she had made an important breakthrough in her work, being able to end her relationship with John, and to see herself and what she wanted in life differently, but had not said the rest of it. That maybe this was as far as she could go, or as far as we could go. As she spoke about her feelings that we might be approaching an end, we both felt more engaged. Something new was happening between us.

"Are there ways that we are holding each other back?" I wondered aloud. "It is true that we will not meet in analysis forever, but is there something about how you are feeling in your new single state, being at the beginning of a new phase of your life, that makes it feel like maybe this would be the right time to stop? Are there ways that it might feel like coming here for analysis with me might actually be inhibiting you at this point, holding you back the way you felt that your relationship with John might have been holding you back at a certain point?"

"That is possible," she said. "I hadn't thought of it before, but I wonder if seeing you three times a week for therapy meets enough of my need for contact with a man who will actually listen to me that it undercuts my motivation to go after what I want out there." We were off, for the moment, in a new direction, exploring dimensions of her experience of herself and of me, the ways that our talking together helped her to grow in some ways, while inhibiting her development in others. Over time, we were able to identify a number of different feelings and sources of identification and counteridentification that appeared relevant to her recent conflicts about continuing analysis. She identified ways that she had experienced both of us as the dependent, depressed mother whom she had to find a way to leave, even if it meant struggling with the guilt of leaving a woman who could not manage without her. She recognized ways in which her unconscious identification with her abandoning father, whom she had consciously resented for sacrificing her for his own freedom and happiness, provided her with some internal resources to pursue her own desires, while at the same time making it difficult to trust that she could rely on anyone, or for that matter, be reliable for another. We were able to do much more work on these and other dimensions of her psychic life as a function of what we came to understand about the preceding brush with termination. But for the moment, thoughts of termination, noted, registered, acknowledged, now on the record, a part of our conversation that we would return to again and again before saying our final good-bye, had receded into the background. This work proved to be very helpful, preparing the way for a gradual, emotional, but less intensely conflictual ending of our sessions nearly 2 years later.

Because mindfulness of its limits frames the ebb and flow of the currents toward termination for patient and analyst, how do they determine their approach to a true end? In my view, the patient and analyst eventually reach a point when the patient is living his or her life, unhampered by major obstacles to fulfillment, and feels as though there is little reason to meet except for the value and satisfactions of the analytic relationship. At such a point, both patient and analyst may begin to feel that there is less and less to differentiate the analysis from any other important relationships in their lives, and it becomes increasingly difficult to sustain within the frame of analytic work.

Yet analyst and analysand, having come to recognize the limits of their conscious awareness and the ultimate uncertainty at the heart of the psychoanalytic process must live with the tension generated in the encounter between the inherent limits that eventually will herald the end of analysis, and the recognition of new possibilities that beckon the pair into new byways of analytic exploration. Because we can never be certain when ending analysis forecloses promising avenues of new growth, or when continuing analysis constitutes a collusion between patient and analyst in eluding the difficult but ultimately generative ending of analysis, I find it preferable to hold the notion of termination lightly, trying as best I can throughout an analysis to facilitate the exploration of its very boundaries. As illustrated in the case of Sally, it is a fact of psychoanalytic life that while working toward a presumed termination of analysis, new developments arise that take patient and analyst into surprising and rewarding realms of experience. Yet as we explore each new dimension of analytic life that opens up before us, we inexorably move closer to the day that we will truly say good-bye.

REFERENCES

Aron, L. (1992). Interpretation as expression of the analyst's subjectivity. *Psychoanalytic Dialogues, 2*, 475–507.

Balint, M. (1950). On the termination of analysis. *International Journal of Psycho-Analysis, 31*, 196–199.

Bass, A. (2001). It takes one to know one; Or, whose unconscious is it anyway? *Psychoanalytic Dialogues, 11*, 683–702.

Bass, A. (2007a). When the frame doesn't fit the picture. *Psychoanalytic Dialogues, 17*(1), 1–28.

Bass, A. (2007b). Framing further considerations: Reply to commentaries by Philip Bromberg and Glen Gabbard. *Psychoanalytic Dialogues, 17*(6), 931–943.

Bergmann, M. S. (1997). Termination: The Achilles heel of psychoanalytic technique. *Psychoanalytic Psychology, 14*, 163–174.

Bromberg, P. M. (1998). *Standing in the spaces: Essays on clinical process, trauma and dissociation*. Hillsdale, NJ: Analytic Press.

Davies, J. M. (2005). Transformations of desire and despair: Reflections on the termination process from a relational perspective. *Psychoanalytic Dialogues, 15*, 779–805.

Ferenczi, S. (1927). The problem of the termination of the analysis. In *Final contributions to the problems and methods of psychoanalysis* (pp. 77–86). London: Bruner/Mazel, 1955.

Freud, S. (1912). Recommendations to physicians practicing psychoanalysis. In J. Strachey (Ed. & Trans.), *The standard edition of the complete psychological works of Sigmund Freud* (Vol. 12, pp. 109–120). London: Hogarth.

Freud, S. (1913). On beginning the treatment. In J. Strachey (Ed. & Trans.), *The standard edition of the complete psychological works of Sigmund Freud* (Vol. 12, pp. 121–144). London: Hogarth.

Freud, S. (1937). Analysis terminable and interminable. In J. Strachey (Ed. & Trans.), *The standard edition of the complete psychological works of Sigmund Freud* (Vol. 23, pp. 211–253). London: Hogarth.

Glover, E. (1955). *The technique of psychoanalysis.* New York: International Universities Press.

Hoffman, I. Z. (1998). *Ritual and spontaneity in the psychoanalytic process: A dialectical-constructivist view.* Hillsdale, NJ: Analytic Press.

Lear, J. (2004). *Therapeutic action: An earnest plea for irony.* New York: Other Press.

Levenson, E. A. (1976). The aesthetics of termination. *Contemporary Psychoanalysis, 12,* 1–29.

Mitchell, S. A. (1993). *Hope and dread in psychoanalysis.* New York: Basic Books.

Mitchell, S. A. (1997). *Influence and autonomy in psychoanalysis.* Hillsdale, NJ: Analytic Press.

Parsons, M. (2007). Raiding the inarticulate: The internal analytic setting and listening beyond countertransference. *International Journal of Psychoanalysis, 88,* 1441–1456.

Pizer, S. A. (1998). *Building bridges: The negotiation of paradox in psychoanalysis.* Hillsdale, NJ: Analytic Press.

Schafer, R. (2005). I was a psychoanalytic candidate (1954–1959). Videotaped Interview: *The Candidate: Perspective from an evolving psychoanalytic community.* Available at: http://www.thecandidatejournal.org/#video.

Symington, N. (1983). The analyst's act of freedom as agent of therapeutic change. *International Review of Psycho-Analysis, 10,* 283–291.

Tessman, L. (2003). *The analyst's analyst within.* Hillsdale, NJ: Analytic Press.

Index

Burlingham, D., 26, 194
Butler, J., 197
Buxbaum, E., 10–11, 14

C

Caretakers, 169
Case-by-case approach to endings, 19–20
Cassidy, J., 71
Castration; *See* Bedrock issues
Cavell, M., 75
Chasseguet-Smirgel, J., 26
Chess metaphor, 292
Chodorow, N., 192, 205
Classical psychoanalysis; *See also* Freud, S.
    attachment perspective versus, 71
    Klein on limitations of, 10
    relational approach versus, 84, 91, 227–228
Clinging, 248–250
Clinical Diary of Sandor Ferenczi, The (DuPont, ed.), 6
Clinicians; *See* Analysts/clinicians/ therapists
Coconstruction of endings, 18, 19–20, 69–70, 235–236, 238–240, 292–294
Cognitive Analytic Therapy (CAT), 74, 78
Coherence, 252–253
Coltart, N., 139
"Coming through," 260
Completed analysis, definition problems, 7
Conflict
    Brennerian model, 29–30
    equilibrium establishment, 34
Construction of reality, analyst's, 251–252
Container/contained concept, 42–43
Cooper, S., 9, 90, 145–164, 219
Countertransference, 20, 109–128
    forms of engagement during termination, 145–164
    interminability as pathological feature, 43
    relational perspectives, 91
    theorizing separation and loss, 65–69
Craige, H., 19

Crastnopol, P., 249
Criteria, termination readiness, 11–12, 16
Cultural norms, 192–193; *See also* Mother/maternal role, maternal resistance
Cure by analysis, questions concerning, 51–52
Cyclical development model, 48

D

Date, termination, 10, 97, 229, 235, 236–237, 261, 265, 280, 296
    patient reactions, 122, 124, 126, 127, 145, 179, 180, 181
    setting in advance, 3, 26, 31, 47, 193, 248
Davanloo, H., 237
Davies, J. M., 9, 20, 83–103, 110, 123, 135, 139, 149, 150, 169–170, 186, 199, 223, 227, 235, 261, 295
Deactivating attachment style, 67, 70
Death, 18, 19, 47, 63; *See also* Going-on-being
    evolution of termination concepts, 226
    existential aspects, 18
    of patient, 214–215
    theorizing separation and loss, 66–67
Death anxiety, attachment perspective, 78–79
Death instinct/death wish; *See* Eros/ Thanatos
Death model of termination, 230, 231; *See also* Mourning
Defense structure, indicators of termination readiness, 12
Defenses, 31
    systems describing, 42
Defining termination, 223–239
    classical theory, 227–229
    coconstruction, end of, 238–240
    goals: good, good-enough, and bad terminations, 235–238
    relational approach, 224–229
    somatic time and object time, 228–230
    terminology, 223–224
Della Selva, P., 78, 237